Photographing San Francisco

Digital Field Guide

Photographing San Francisco

Digital Field Guide

Bruce Sawle

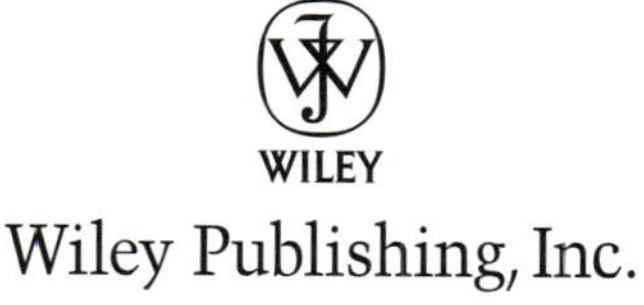

Wiley Publishing, Inc.

Photographing San Francisco Digital Field Guide

Published by
Wiley Publishing, Inc.
10475 Crosspoint Boulevard
Indianapolis, IN 46256
www.wiley.com

Published simultaneously in Canada

ISBN: 978-0-470-58684-6

Manufactured in the United States of America

10 9 8 7 6 5 4 3 2 1

For general information on our other products and services or to obtain technical support, please contact our Customer Care Department within the U.S. at (877) 762-2974, outside the U.S. at (317) 572-3993 or fax (317) 572-4002.

Wiley also publishes its books in a variety of electronic formats. Some content that appears in print may not be available in electronic books.

Library of Congress Control Number: 2010920662

About the Author

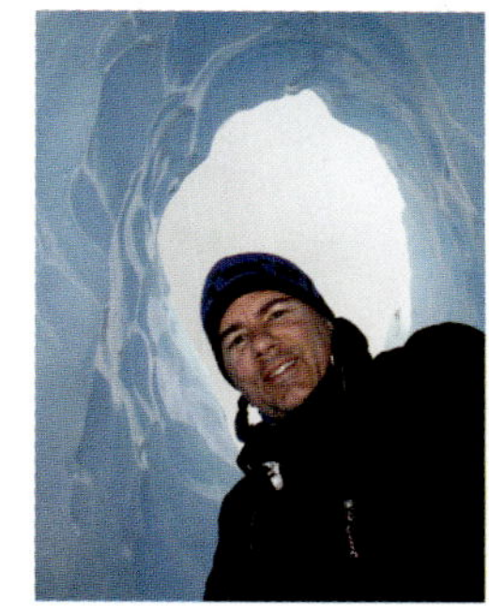

Bruce Sawle is a self-taught San Francisco–based photographer who is passionate about creating beautiful, timeless photographs. He believes in capturing the essence, whether he is photographing landscapes, cityscapes, or people. Bruce's Dare to be Fun philosophy on photography enables him to capture everyday moments in the most extraordinary way. His goal is to produce pieces of art that can be cherished by people forever. He loves capturing images that are timeless and celebrate the heart and soul of the moment.

Credits

Senior Acquisitions Editor
Stephanie McComb

Project Editor
Jama Carter

Technical Editor
Mike Hagen

Copy Editor
Beth Taylor

Editorial Director
Robyn Siesky

Business Manager
Amy Knies

Senior Marketing Manager
Sandy Smith

Vice President and Executive Group Publisher
Richard Swadley

Vice President and Executive Publisher
Barry Pruett

Project Coordinator
Patrick Redmond

Graphics and Production Specialists
Ana Carrillo
Jennifer Mayberry
Jill A. Proll
Ronald Terry

Quality Control Technician
John Greenough

Proofreading and Indexing
Penny Stuart
Potomac Indexing, LLC

To my gorgeous wife, Jennifer — the greatest gift
I have been given and with whom I will forever be in love —
and the three greatest gifts she has given me:
our two beautiful daughters Raya and Jordyn and my son Hayden.
This book is for my family, my inspiration, and the reason
I fell in love with photography. And an extra special dedication
to Raya who I love more than life itself; her almond-shaped brown eyes
and innocence have inspired me to capture beauty as it is.

Acknowledgments

I would like to acknowledge Chris Hurtt, Bryan Peterson, and Perfect Picture School of Photography for the inspiration of making me into the photographer I am today. These two photographers, whom I look up to, have given me the instruction and motivation I needed to take my passion to the next level. I would also like to thank my mother for all the years of support. A special thanks to my father who has been there for me and my family for the past eight years; without his support, guidance, and love I would not be who I am today.

Contents

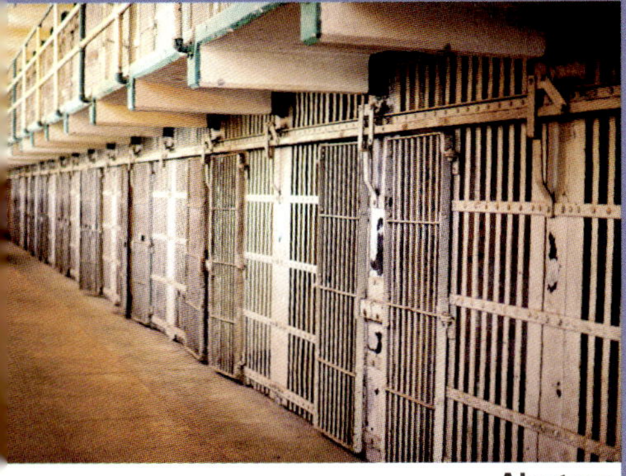
Alcatraz

California Academy of Sciences

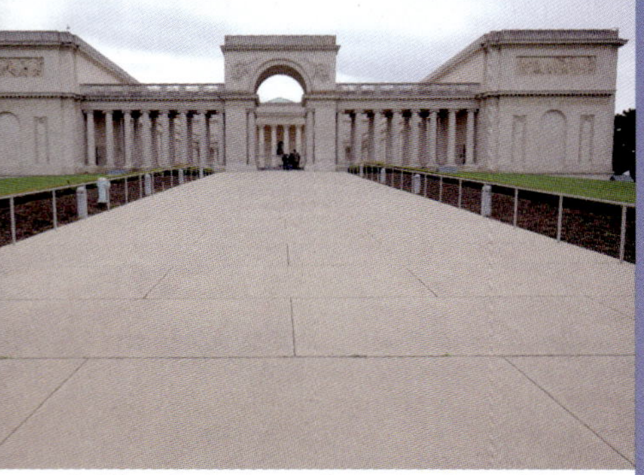
California Palace of the Legion of Honor

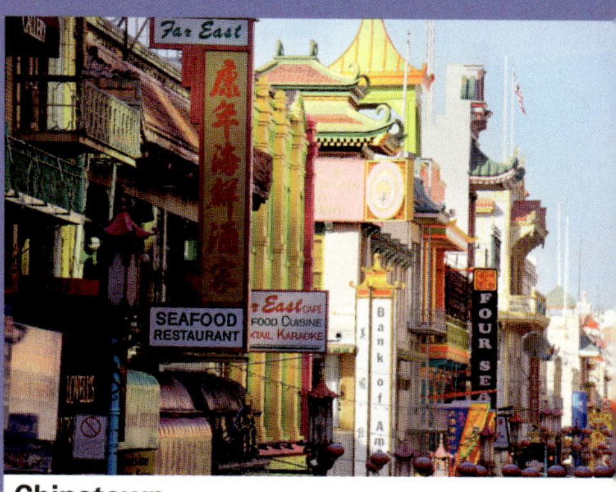

Chinatown

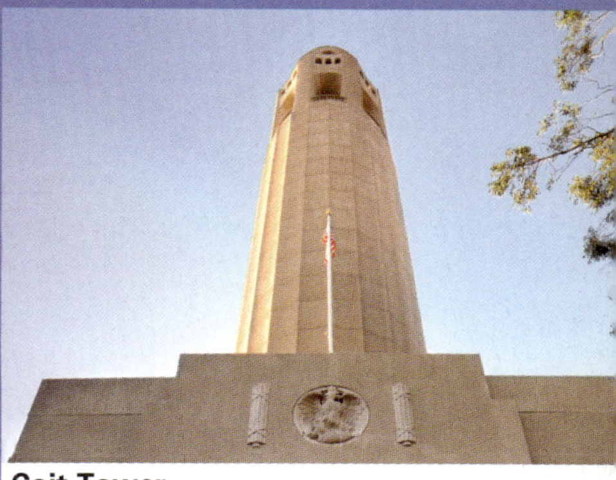
Coit Tower

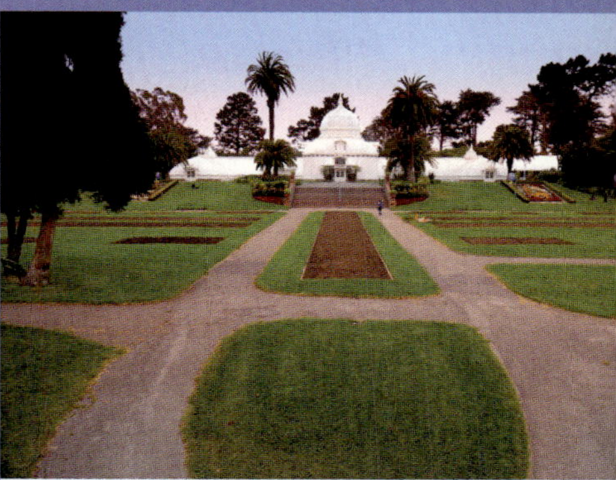
Conservatory of Flowers

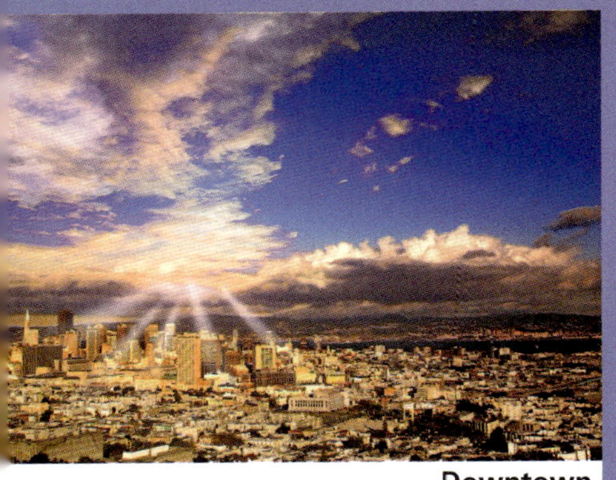
Downtown

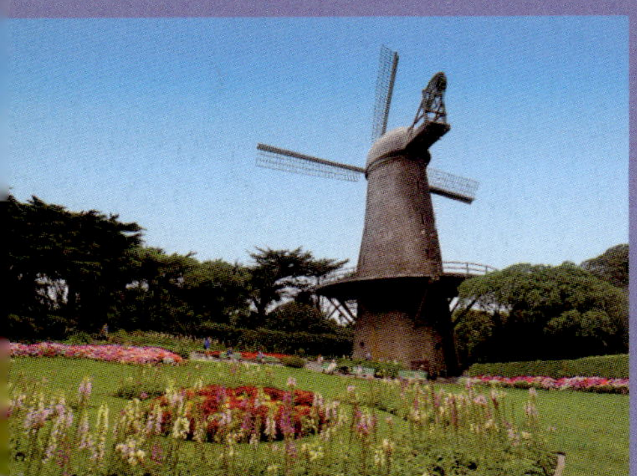
Dutch Windmill

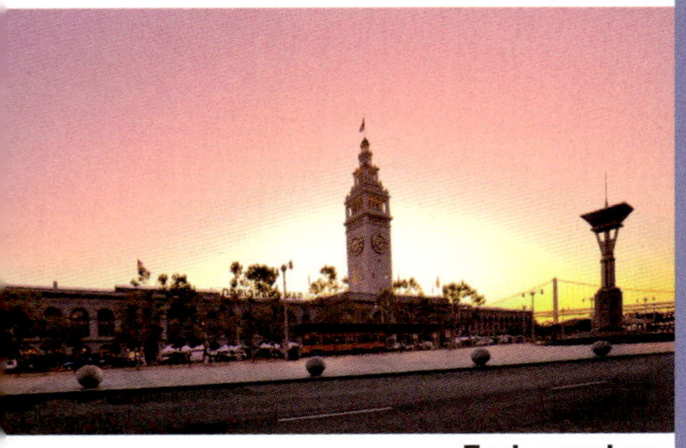
Embarcadero

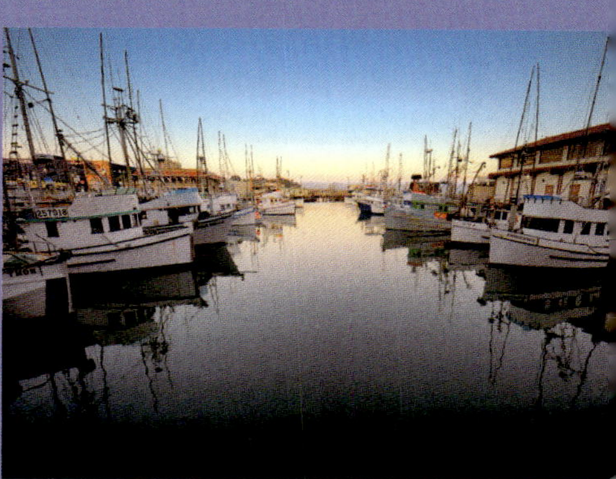

Fisherman's Wharf

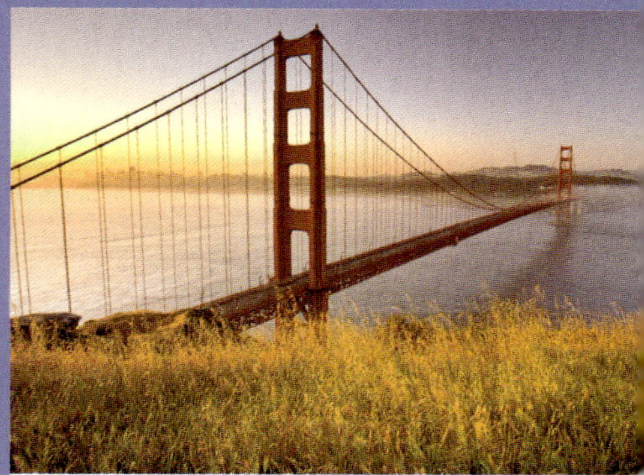

Golden Gate Bridge

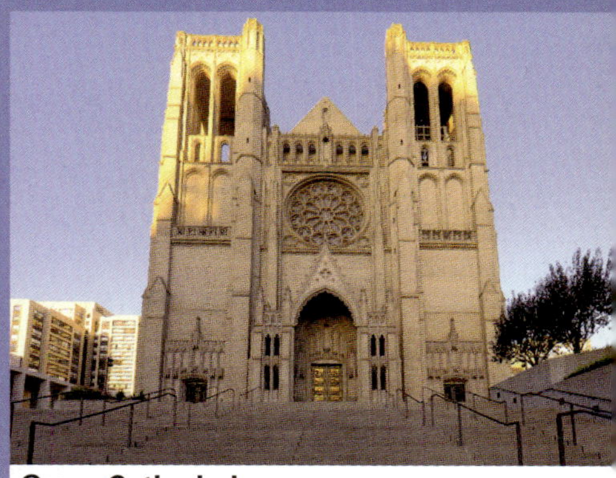

Grace Cathedral

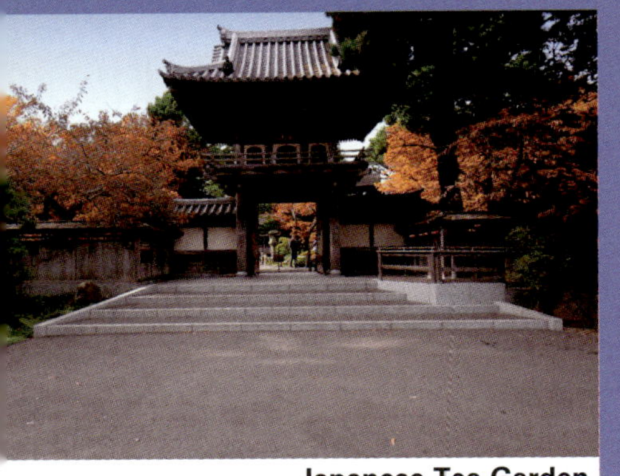
Japanese Tea Garden

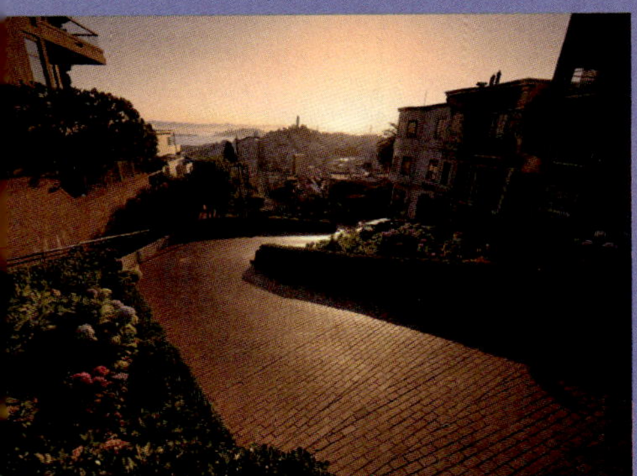
Lombard Street

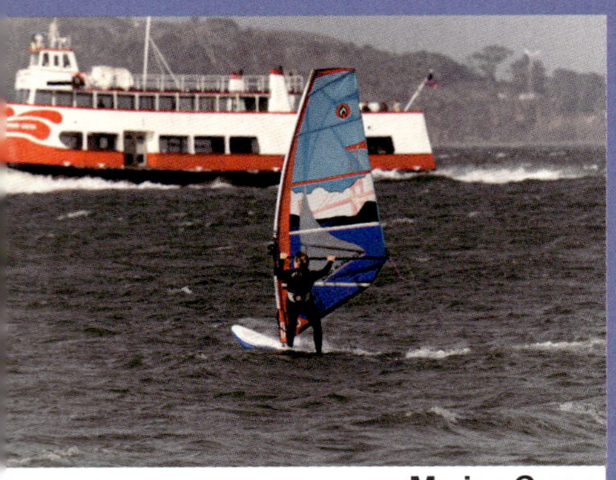
Marina Green

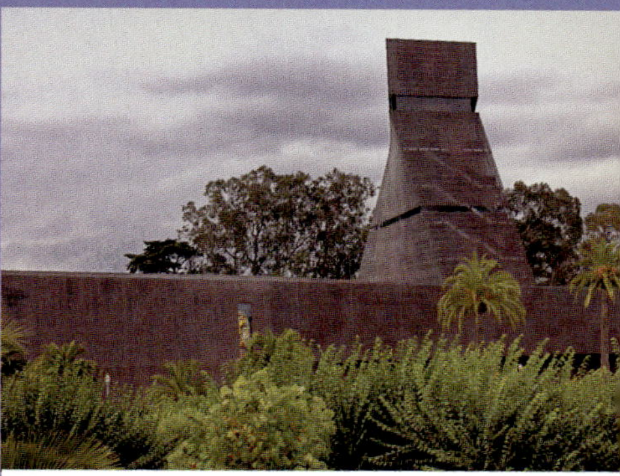

M.H. de Young Museum

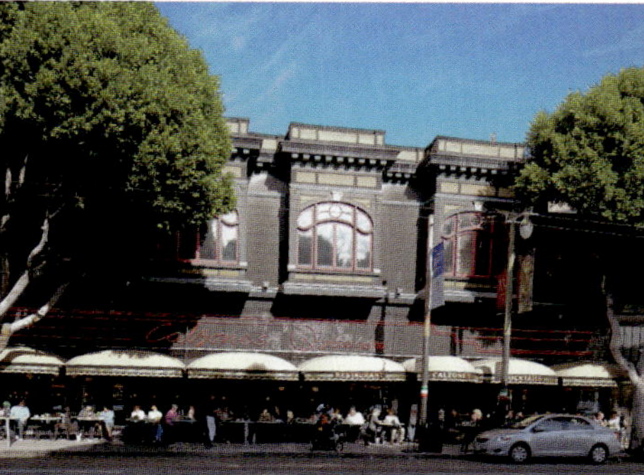

North Beach

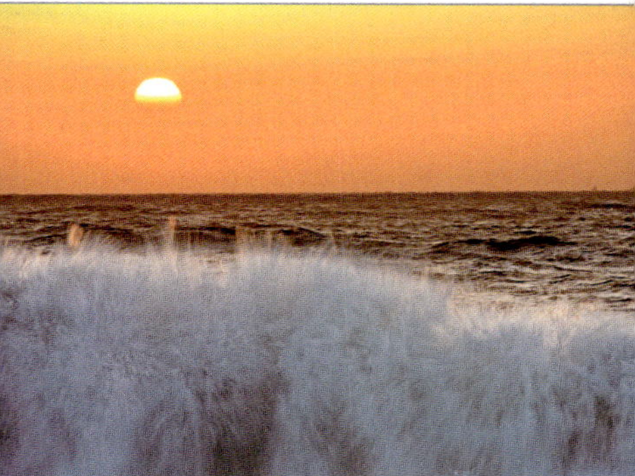

Ocean Beach

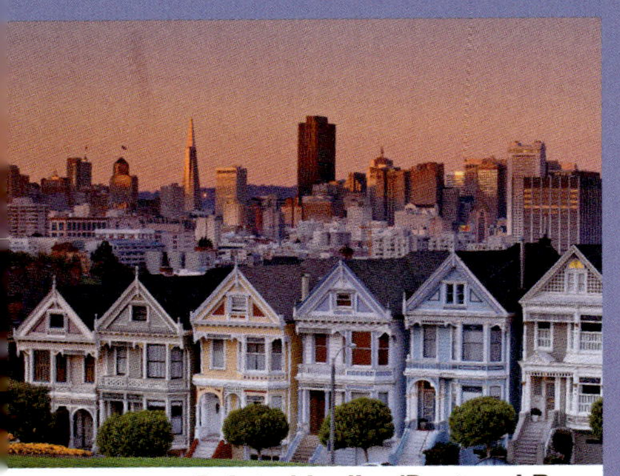
Painted Ladies/Postcard Row

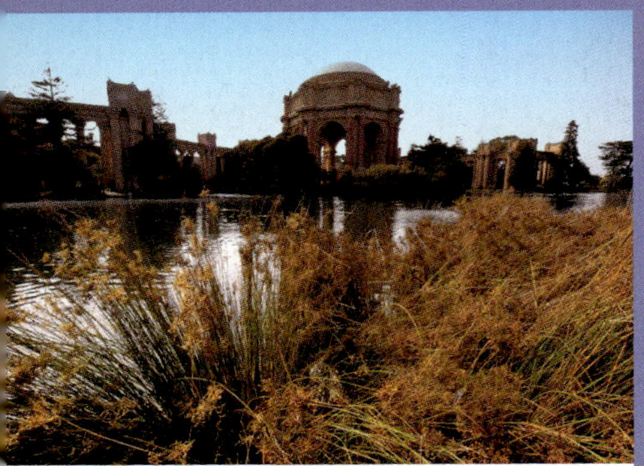
Palace of Fine Arts

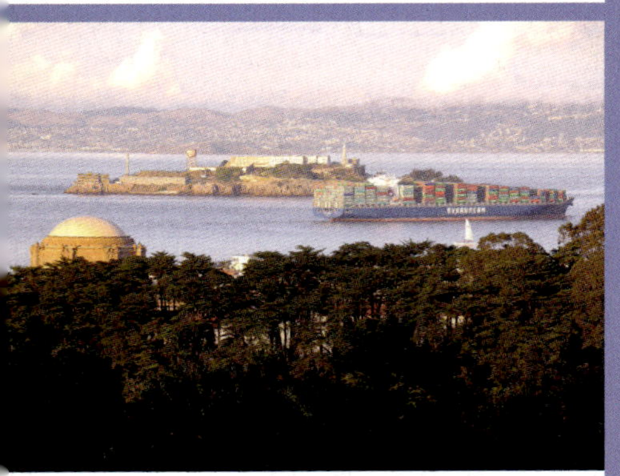
Presidio of San Francisco

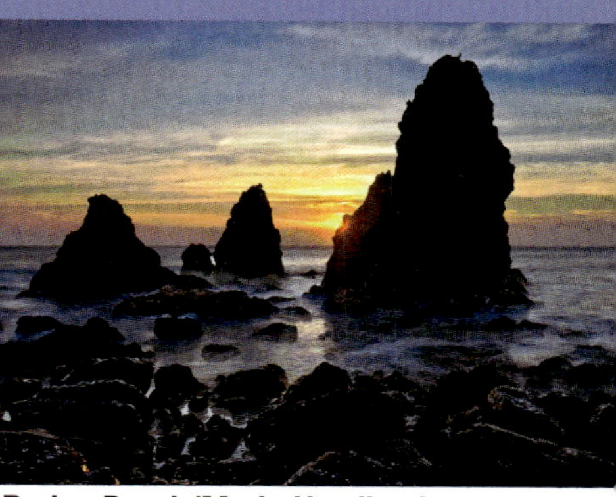

Rodeo Beach/Marin Headlands

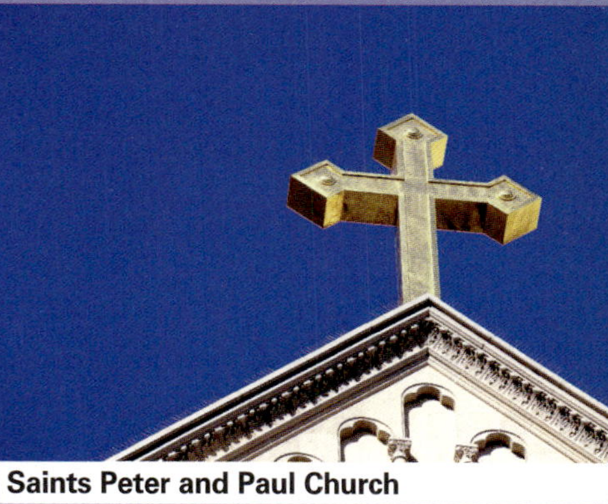

Saints Peter and Paul Church

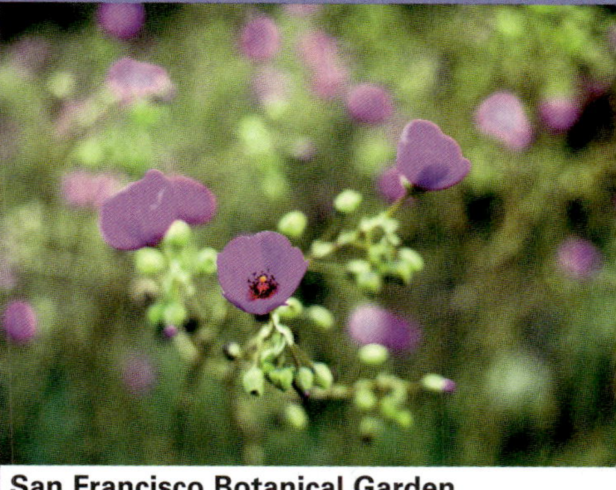

San Francisco Botanical Garden

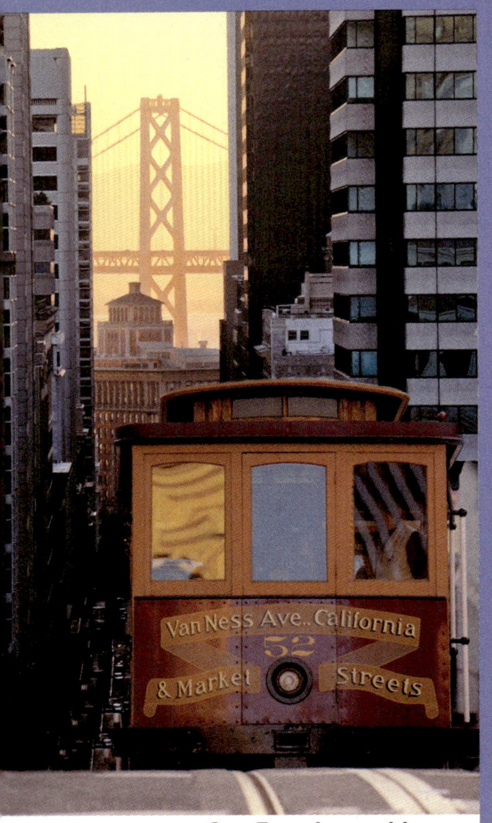

San Francisco cable cars

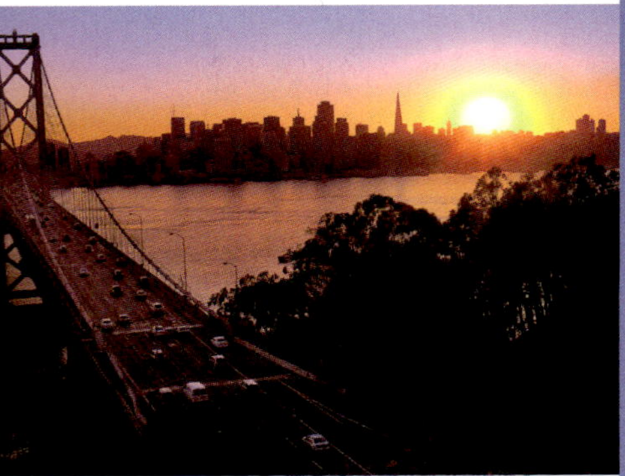
San Francisco-Oakland Bay Bridge

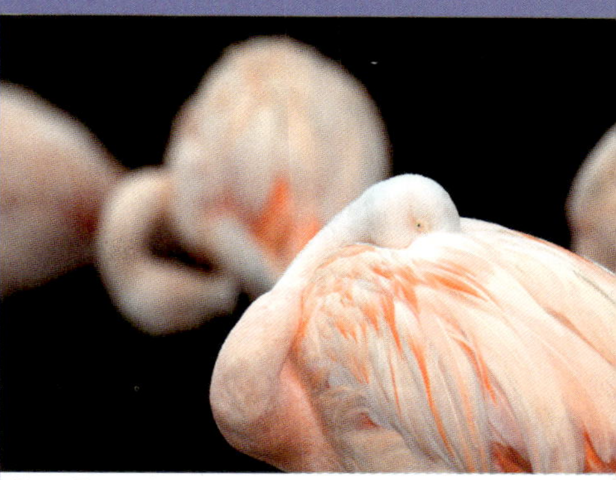

San Francisco Zoo

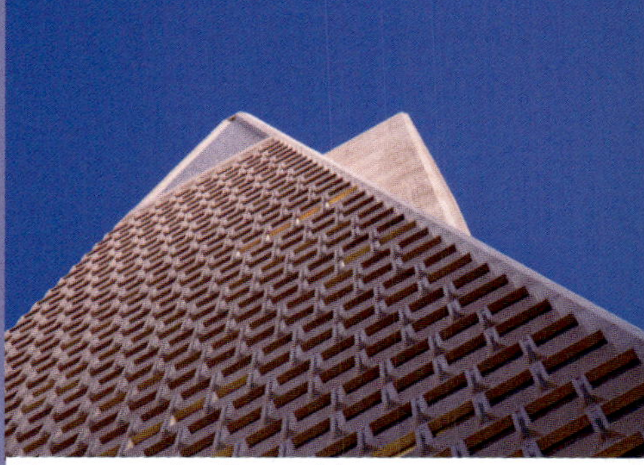

Transamerica Pyramid

Introduction

At one time or another, most of us have probably looked at and admired photos in books, magazines, postcards, and on the Internet, and wondered what a wonderful idea, what a great capture, what a beautiful scene. Photography, like many other arts, is unique to each individual. What makes each representation special is the ability for a photographer to capture and create something that has not yet been done before. For travel photography, this is a bit of a challenge because most popular landmarks have been photographed every which way. What inspires me and makes me want to go back and keep photographing these same landmarks over and over again is that one day I will capture the perfect picture. Living in San Francisco for the better part of 40 years, I live, breathe, and speak San Franciscan. The intent of this book is to help you capture and create wonderful pictures of the city by the bay and what I refer to as home.

Photographing San Francisco Digital Field Guide is a guide written to help all levels of photographers. From the beginner who has just bought his first dSLR to the advanced amateur who wants to take her travel photography to the next level. With the help of this book, I hope to help you discover the beauty of San Francisco, its hidden treasures, and its most-loved sights in this memorable photographic expedition. What I want to share with you throughout the 28 chapters in this book are new perspectives of the city with spectacular imagery of its most popular and celebrated landmarks including the Golden Gate Bridge, Transamerica Pyramid, and Alcatraz as well as lesser-known but equally beautiful sites such as the Dutch windmill and Saints Peter and Paul Church. With the hundreds of amazing and breathtaking photos of San Francisco, this book's main purpose is to guide you to the best vantage points for each landmark, give you a sense of the best time of day to shoot, the best settings to use, and how to work around the weather. The ability to see the potential for a strong and powerful photo is instrumental in capturing unique and beautiful photos. The single most important factor is to help you create a postcard image of each and every landmark. I want you to see, to create, and to aspire to capture what you envision, not just what you see.

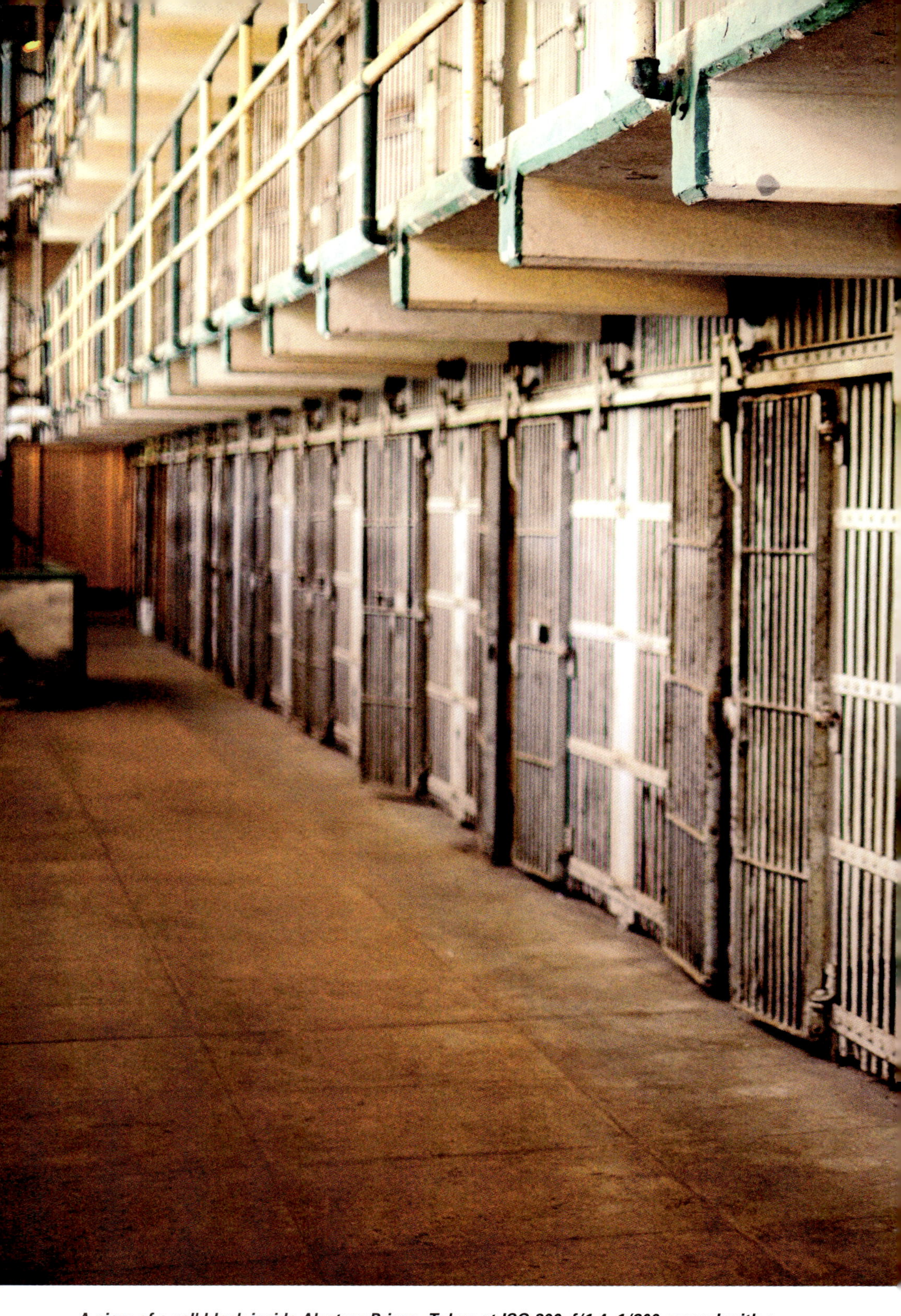

A view of a cell block inside Alcatraz Prison. Taken at ISO 800, f/1.4, 1/200 second with a 50mm lens.

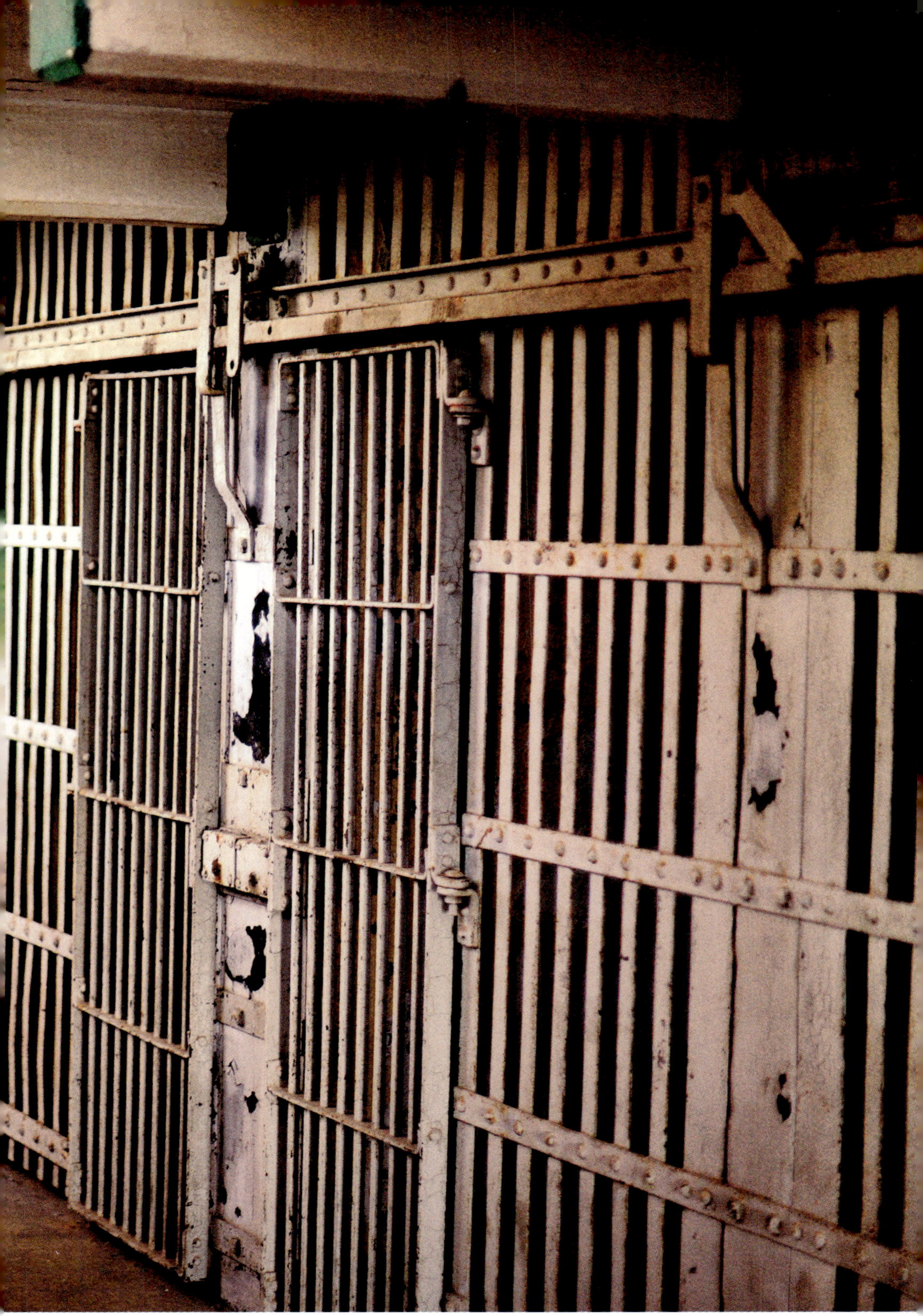

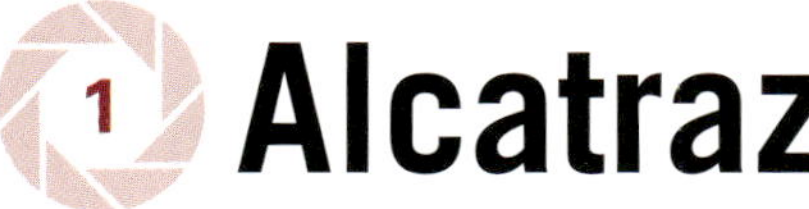

1 Alcatraz

Why It's Worth a Photograph

Alcatraz Island is one of Golden Gate National Recreation Area's most popular destinations, offering a close-up look at a historic and arguably the most famous federal prison. Often referred to as The Rock, the island is located in the San Francisco Bay, 1.5 miles offshore from San Francisco, California. The small island served as a lighthouse, a military fortification, a military prison, and a federal prison until 1963. In 1972, Alcatraz became a national recreation area. Today, the island is an historic site operated by the National Park Service as part of the Golden Gate National Recreation Area and is open to tours. Visitors can reach the island by ferry ride from Pier 33, near Fisherman's Wharf in San Francisco. The island of Alcatraz is one of the marvels that San Francisco has to offer photographers. On any given day, you can go from crystal blue skies surrounded by sea green water and intense warm sunlight to layers of fog surrounding this infamous mysterious island.

Where Can I Get the Best Shot?

Besides Alcatraz Island, there are three mainland locations that will offer you a different perspective when photographing Alcatraz. The first is at Hyde Street and Lombard Street, the second is St. Francis Yacht Club, and the third is Treasure Island.

Hyde Street and Lombard Street

Hyde Street at Lombard Street (see A on the map) provides a great vantage point to photograph Alcatraz. The elevation of the hill creates a clear shot straight down onto Alcatraz and the San Francisco Bay (see figure 1.1). The sweeping views and warm afternoon or late morning light give wonderful front lighting on the prison island creating deep blacks and saturated colors. A long lens of 300-400mm is a must.

St. Francis Yacht Club

St. Francis Yacht Club provides the best overall vantage point for photographing Alcatraz. The proximity to the island and the low angle from the bay enable you to create wonderfully detailed photos of the prison (see figure 1.2). A long lens of 100-300mm is a must. The ideal time is late in the day, one hour before sunset when the sun is low and casting a warm, soft light across the bay. This light is void of harsh shadows, making it an ideal time to capture detailed images of Alcatraz.

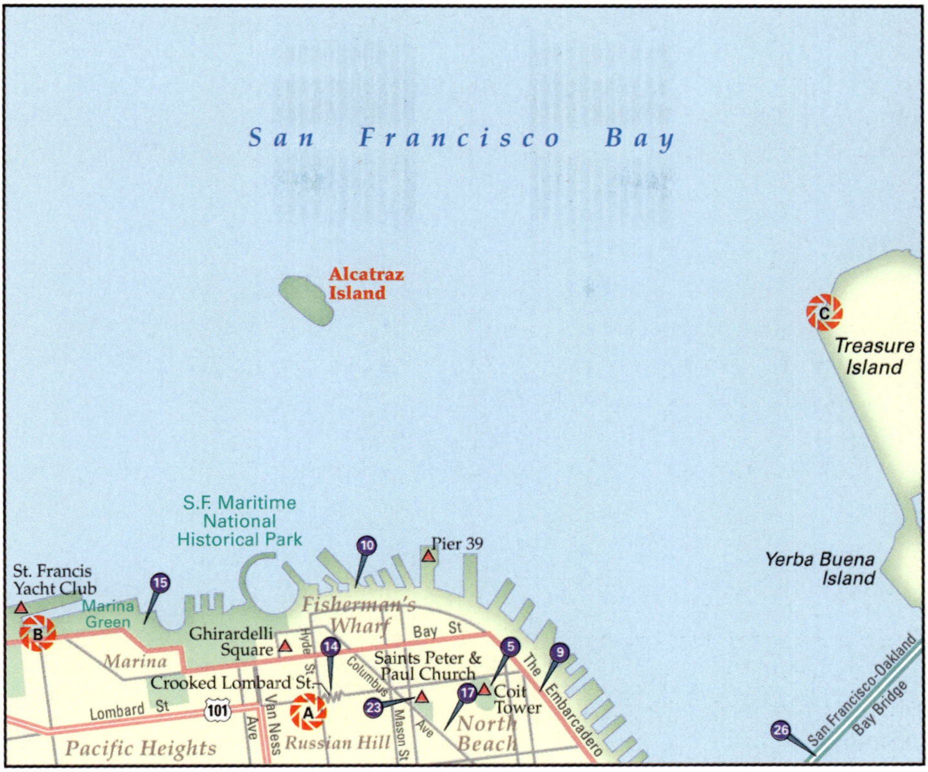

San Francisco Bay
Alcatraz Island
Treasure Island
Yerba Buena Island
S.F. Maritime National Historical Park
Pier 39
St. Francis Yacht Club
Marina Green
Fisherman's Wharf
Bay St
Ghirardelli Square
Hyde St
Columbus Ave
Saints Peter & Paul Church
Coit Tower
The Embarcadero
Marina
Crooked Lombard St.
Lombard St
101
Van Ness Ave
Mason St
North Beach
Russian Hill
Pacific Heights
San Francisco-Oakland Bay Bridge

The best locations from which to photograph Alcatraz: (A) Hyde Street and Lombard Street, (B) St. Francis Yacht Club, (C) Treasure Island. Other photo ops: (5) Coit Tower, (9) Embarcadero, (10) Fisherman's Wharf, (14) Lombard Street, (15) Marina Green, (17) North Beach, (23) Saints Peter and Paul Church, (26) San Francisco-Oakland Bay Bridge.

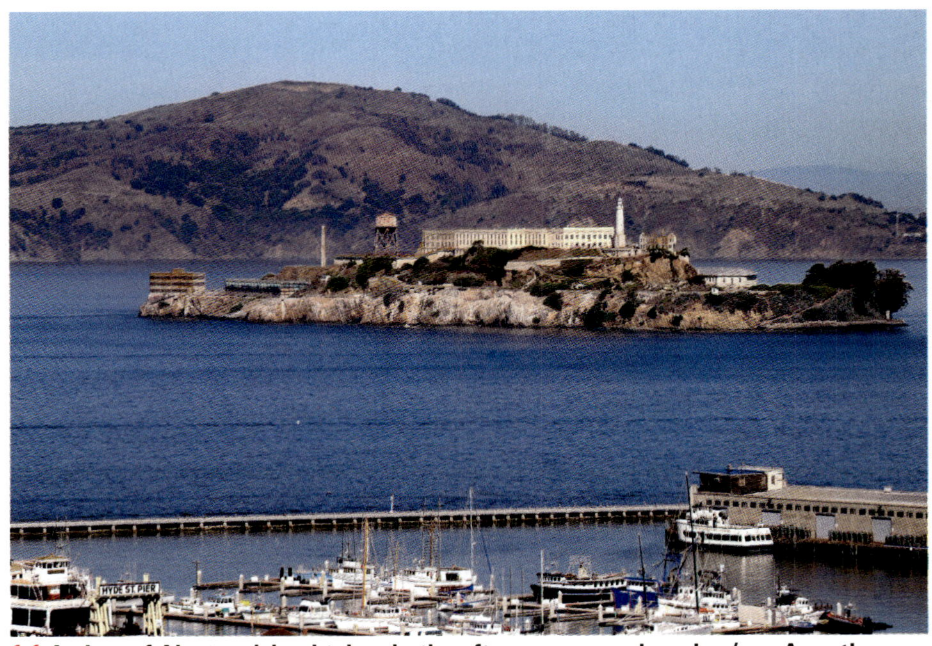

1.1 A view of Alcatraz Island taken in the afternoon on a clear day (see A on the map). Taken at ISO 100, f/8, 1/500 second with a 300mm lens.

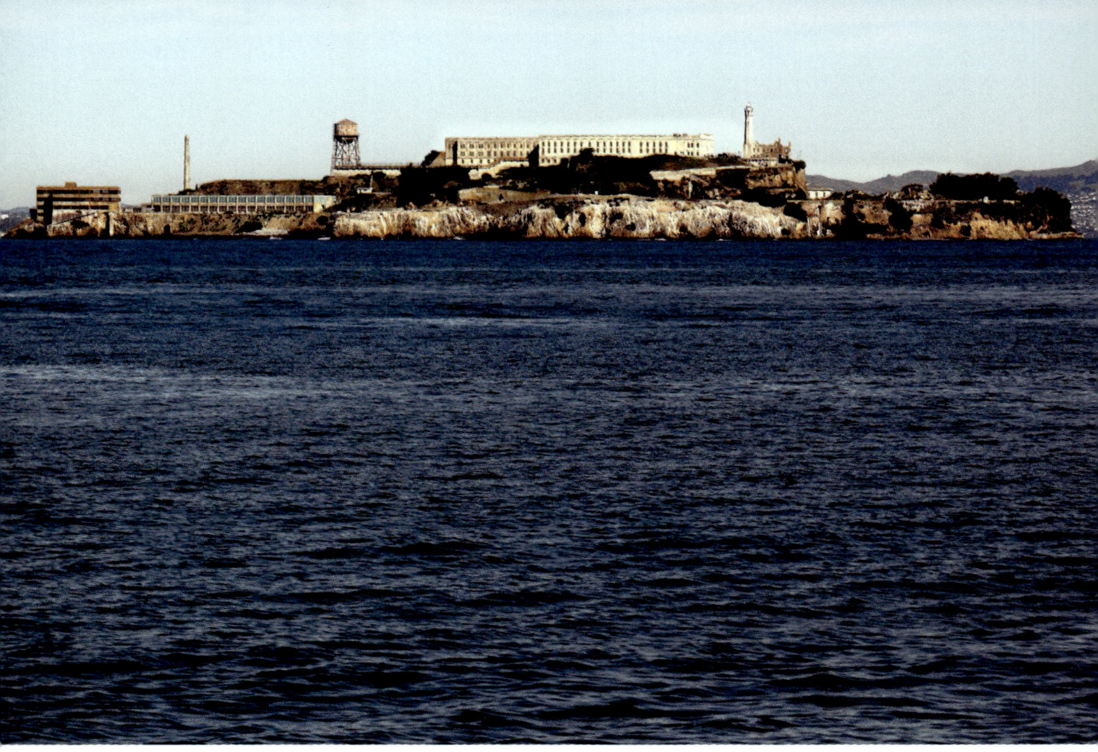

1.2 A view of Alcatraz Island taken from the St. Francis Yacht Club on a clear fall afternoon (see B on the map). Taken at ISO 200, f/9, 1/800 second with a 120-300mm lens.

Treasure Island

Treasure Island offers a different perspective when photographing Alcatraz. My favorite time to shoot from this location is 30 minutes before sunset. The light is almost below the city skyline casting this soft, diffused, warm orange light across the bay (see figure 1.3). This light is so soft that it creates the mystical warm light with soft subtle detail and black shadows.

How Can I Get the Best Shot?

Light is the key to capturing the best photograph of Alcatraz. The late afternoon or early morning light is warm, low, soft light, which is void of harsh shadows. A tripod is highly recommended when shooting with your long lens. Nothing is worse than having to delete a series of photos because of camera shake. When visiting the island, a wide-angle lens, fast prime lens, and flash give you the most flexibility; the prison quarters are tight and not well lit.

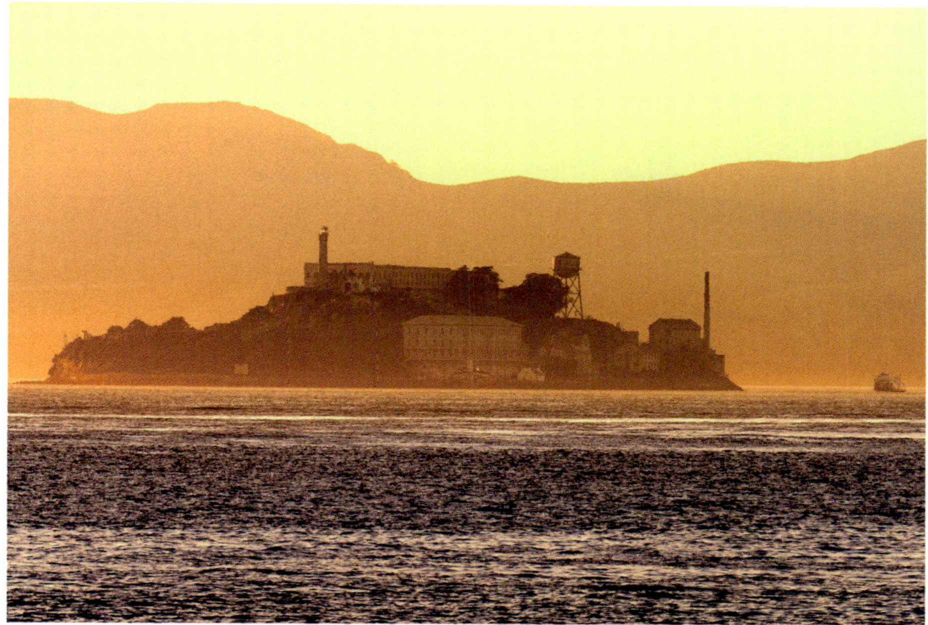

1.3 **A view of Alcatraz Island taken from Treasure Island on a sunny fall evening (see C on the map). Taken at ISO 200, f/8, 1/400 second with a 300mm lens.**

Equipment

You need a long lens and tripod for photographing Alcatraz from a distance. If you visit the island, a wide lens, fast prime lens, and flash are my equipment of choice.

Lenses

The three best lenses to use when photographing Alcatraz are an ultrawide lens for those tight quarters inside the prison, a long zoom lens for capturing the island from a distance, and finally a fast prime lens to allow you to isolate a subject and shoot inside the prison.

- **Ultrawide zoom lens in the 14-24mm range.** The ultrawide lens gives you the ability to create a unique perspective and allows you to capture more of the space due to the wider angle of view.
- **A zoom lens somewhere in the 100-300mm range.** This focal range gives you the ability to isolate Alcatraz from San Francisco.
- **A fast prime lens.** A fast prime is a great lens for shooting inside. The large aperture and shallow depth of field allow this lens to gather a lot of light so it can isolate things a normal lens cannot.

Extras

A tripod is useful when shooting Alcatraz with a long lens. A tripod helps stabilize the camera and lens and ensures that camera shake will not affect the photo.

Camera settings

Setting up your camera comes down to time of day, amount of light, and composition. When shooting with a long lens from a distance, mount your camera on a tripod and set the aperture from f/8 to f/11 to maximize your image quality. When shooting inside and using a fast prime or wide lens with only available light, set your aperture from f/1.4 to f/2 to gather more light. You may need to bump up your ISO to create a fast enough shutter speed to hand hold your camera. Try to create a shutter speed equal to your longest focal length. For a 14-24mm lens, you want at least 1/24 second. If you brought an off-camera flash, don't point it directly in front. Use the walls to direct light by angling the flash to bounce off walls behind and to the side of you to create interesting light patterns.

- **Exposure mode.** For outside shots, use Aperture Priority mode. For inside with or without a flash, use Manual mode and adjust your settings until you get the exposure you want. Use your shutter speed and aperture to create a certain mood. When shooting in a prison, dark and moody photos are always a treat.
- **White balance.** The Automatic White Balance (AWB) setting works best for shooting inside the prison. When shooting Alcatraz from outside, set your white balance to AWB for a standard look or to Shade or Cloudy for a warmer look. White balance can also be adjusted in post-processing.
- **ISO.** Bump up your ISO when you're shooting inside the prison.

Exposure

Protect your highlights when shooting Alcatraz with a long lens. I usually dial in –1/3 exposure compensation to protect against blowing out the sky. When shooting inside with or without a flash, be careful to not underexpose your subject to the point where you introduce dark shadows void of detail. Look at your histogram on the back of your camera to determine whether you need to add some plus or minus exposure compensation.

Ideal time to shoot

The ideal time to shoot is in the late morning or late in the day when the sun is low. The low sun helps accentuate the sky and makes for some dramatic lighting.

Using a Histogram

The histogram is a handy tool we photographers can use to help judge exposure. The histogram is a graph that represents the maximum range of light values your camera can capture. In the middle of the histogram are the midrange values that represent middle colors like grays, light browns, and greens. The histogram's left to right directions are related to the darkness and lightness of the image, while the up and down directions of the histogram (valleys and peaks) have to do with color information. The left (dark) to right (light) directions are very important for your image making. If the image is too dark (underexposed), the histogram will favor the left side by clipping off the light values on the left, and if it's too light (overexposed), the histogram will show clipping on the right.

Working around the weather

Knowing the weather is important, because you don't want to be outside shooting in the rain. My recommendation is the late spring and fall. The sunrises and sunsets are spectacular for creating wonderful soft, warm, and colorful hues and long shadows. Coincidently, these are the months where there is the least amount of fog.

Getting creative

If you decide to visit the island, there are many opportunities to try low light and ultrawide-angle shooting. Shooting inside and outside can be a lot of fun if you use the available light to your advantage. Creating a mood to convey a sense of place is the most challenging part of shooting at Alcatraz. When using a fast prime lens or an ultrawide lens, shooting with available light can create moody photos with unique angles and artistic qualities. Inside the prison I bumped up the ISO to give me a faster shutter speed and to create a little grainy noise to give the photo that authentic feel (see figure 1.4). Outside I used an ultrawide lens to capture this wonderful old staircase built into the granite rock surrounded by overgrown ivy (see figure 1.5).

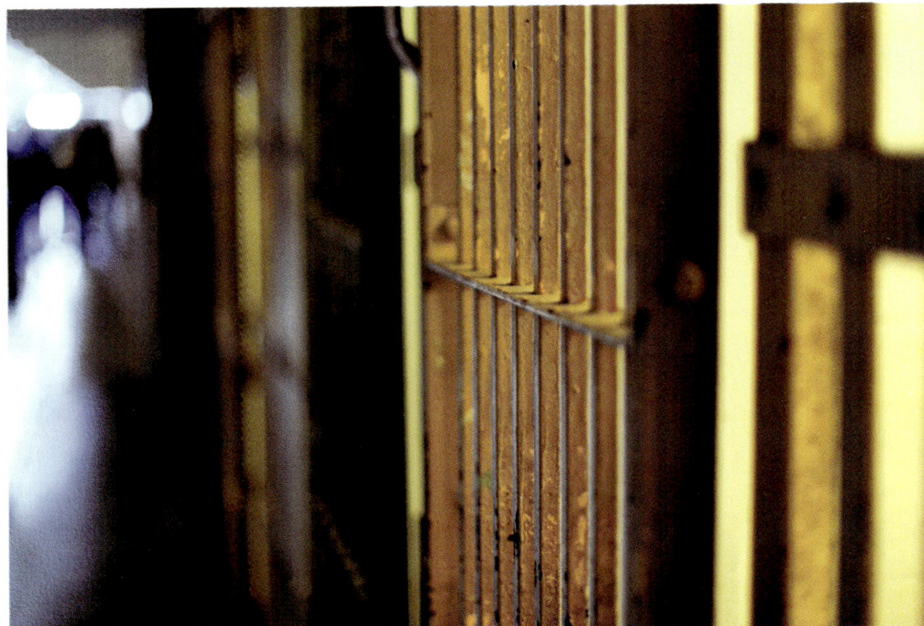

1.4 A view of the prison's cells. Taken at ISO 1250, f/1.4, 1/100 second with a 50mm lens.

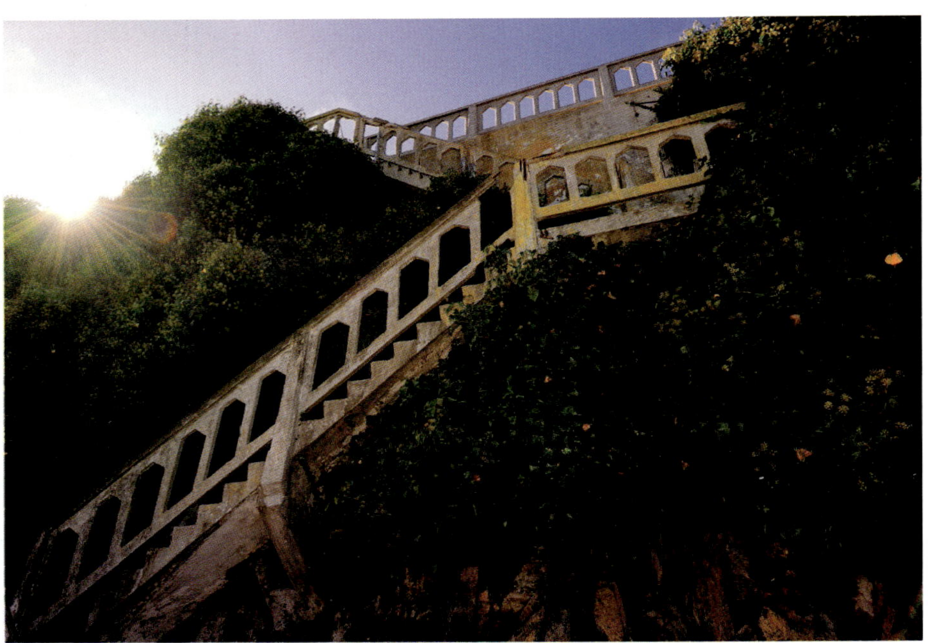

1.5 A view of the prison stairs taken on a sunny fall morning. Taken at ISO 100, f/8, 1/320 second with a 14-24mm lens.

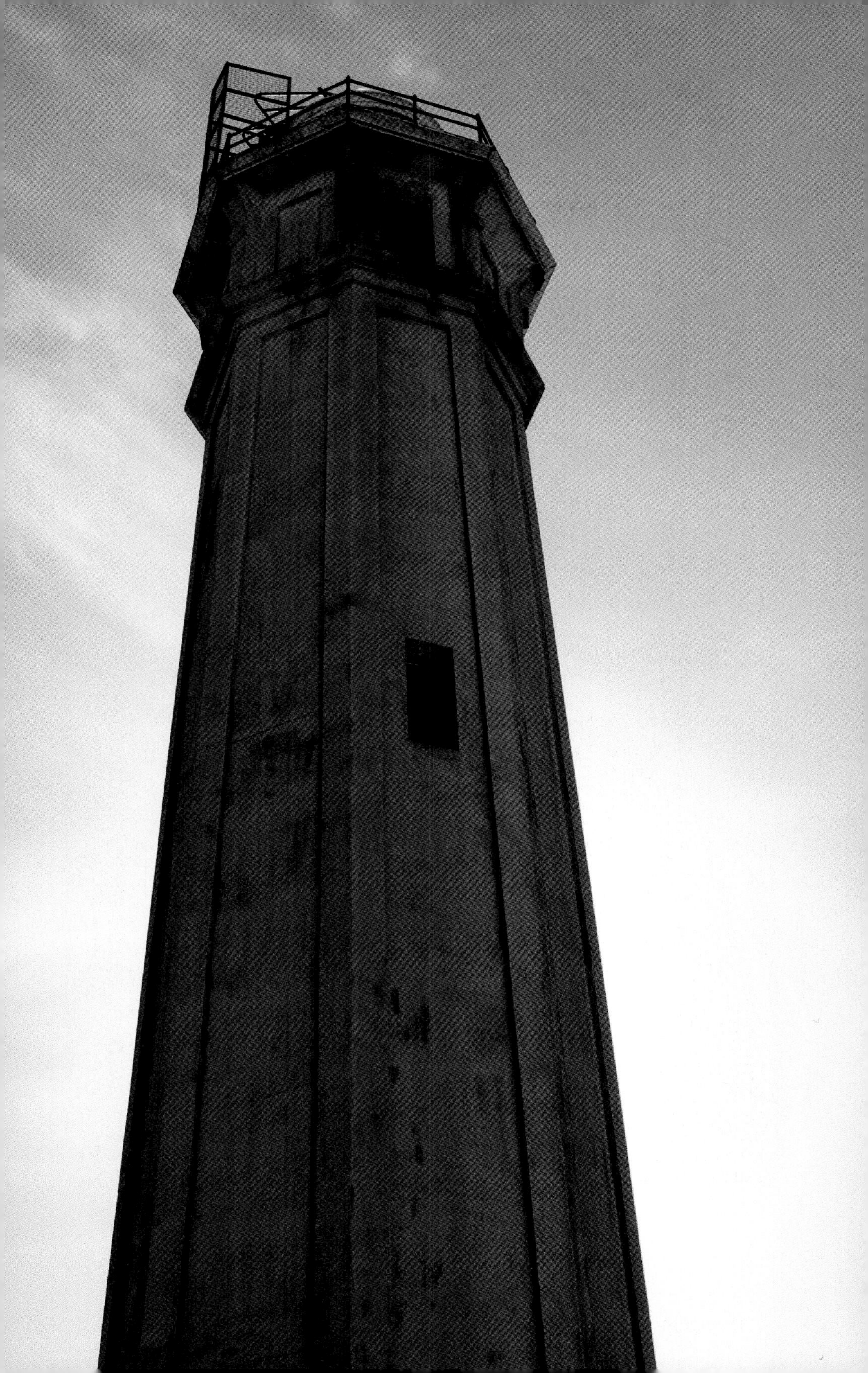

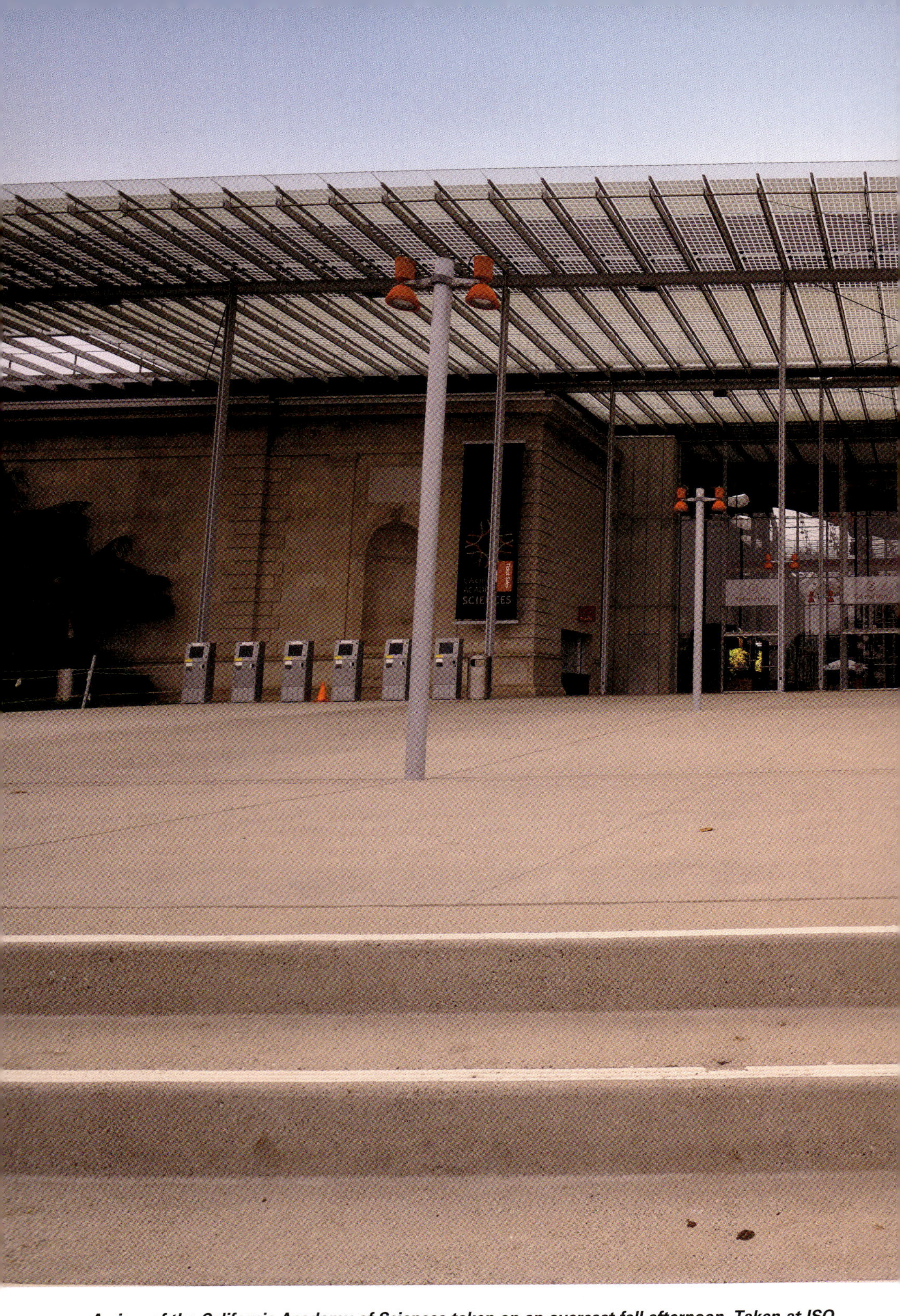

A view of the California Academy of Sciences taken on an overcast fall afternoon. Taken at ISO 400, f/18, 1/13 second, with a 14-24mm lens.

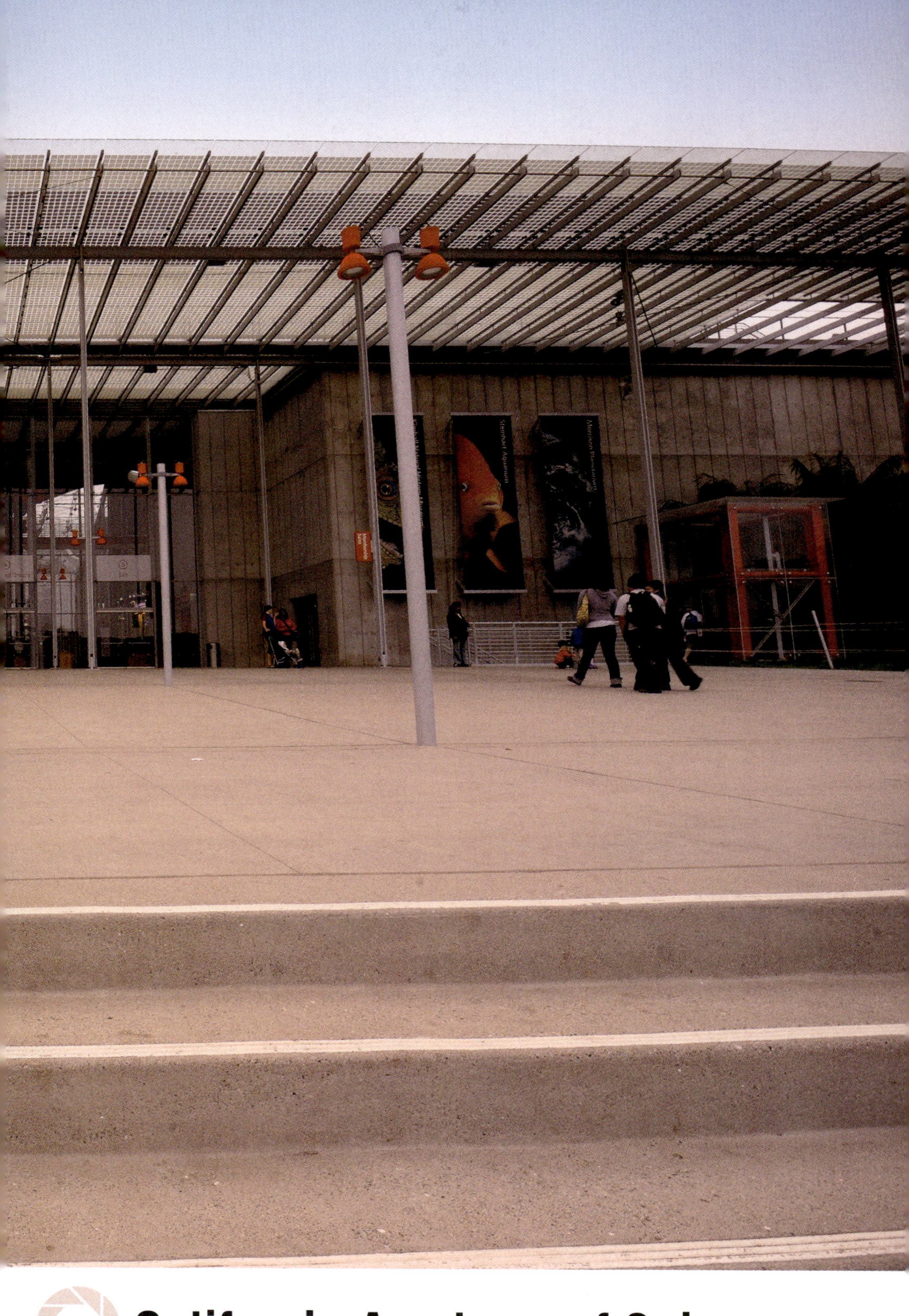

2 California Academy of Sciences

Why It's Worth a Photograph

The California Academy of Sciences is one of the largest museums of natural history in the world. Founded in 1853, the Academy's first official museum opened in 1874. Completely rebuilt in 2008, it is now one of the newest museums in the United States. Located in Golden Gate Park in San Francisco, the Academy is the only place in the world with an aquarium, a planetarium, a history museum, and a rainforest all under one roof. The building that houses these exhibits is a stunning architectural achievement with hundreds of incredibly unique exhibits and thousands of live animals. The Academy redefines what it means to be a science museum: a single building that demonstrates the mutual dependence of earth, ocean, and space. The building is not only physically impressive, but it is considered to be one of the greenest museums in the world, with a 2½-acre living roof comprised of a living tapestry of native plant species, an expansive solar canopy, an extensive water reclamation system, and walls insulated with recycled blue jeans. Everywhere you look inside and out are hundreds of subjects to photograph. Whether you choose to photograph the incredible architecture or the wonderful exhibits, you will walk away with photographs of one of the most unique museums in the world.

Where Can I Get the Best Shot?

You can find many wonderful things to photograph at the California Academy of Sciences (see A on the map), from the ultramodern and eco-friendly architecture (see figure 2.1) to the wonderful exhibits that reside inside the building. Spend a couple hours walking around this wonderful building and you encounter exhibits that transport you to other areas of this planet as well as the universe. One of my favorite exhibits to photograph is the four-story Rainforest, where each level represents a different rainforest around the world, including Borneo, Madagascar, Costa Rica, and the Amazon (see figure 2.2). When shooting through glass, a flash is useless as you will create massive glare that will all but ruin your photo. For the shot in figure 2.3, I used the reflection created by the top of the water to create a cool visual effect.

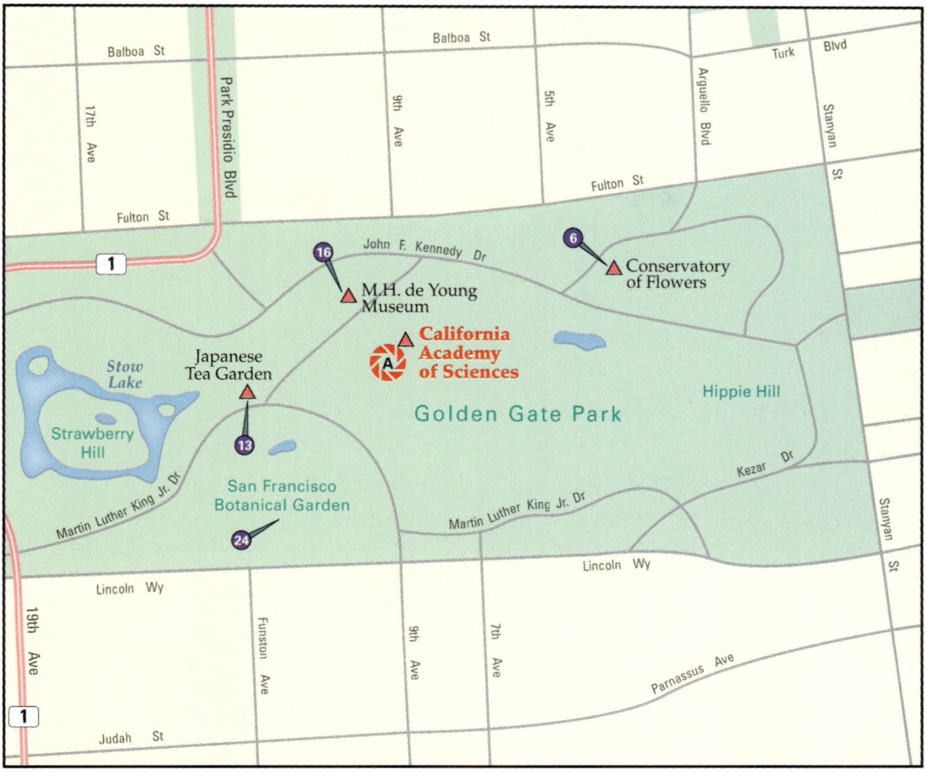

The best location from which to photograph the California Academy of Sciences: (A) inside the museum. Other photo ops: (6) Conservatory of Flowers, (13) Japanese Tea Garden, (16) M.H. de Young Museum, (24) San Francisco Botanical Garden.

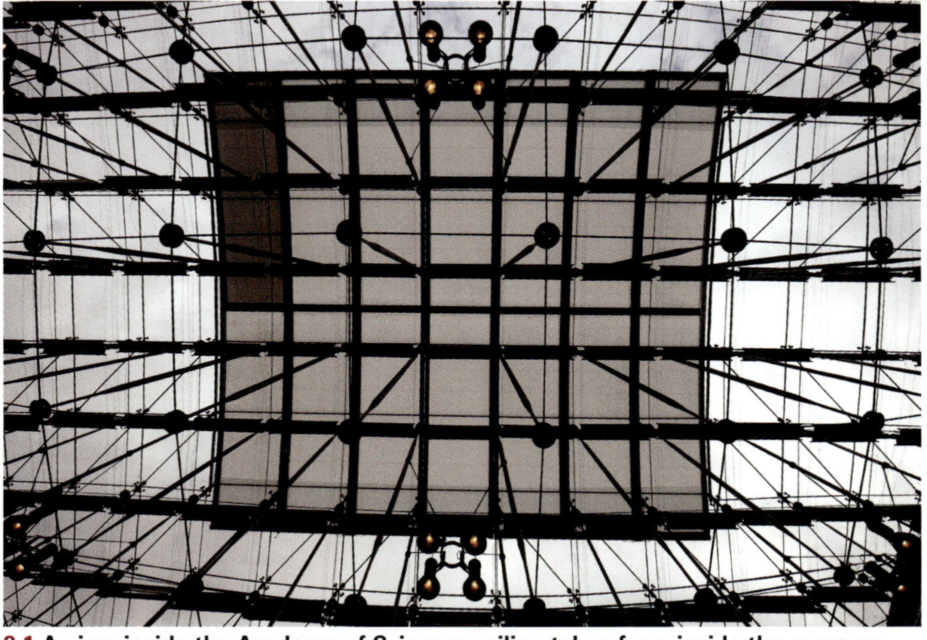

2.1 A view inside the Academy of Sciences ceiling taken from inside the museum (see A on the map). Taken at ISO 500, f/6.6, 1/1000 second, -1 exposure compensation, with a 14-24mm lens.

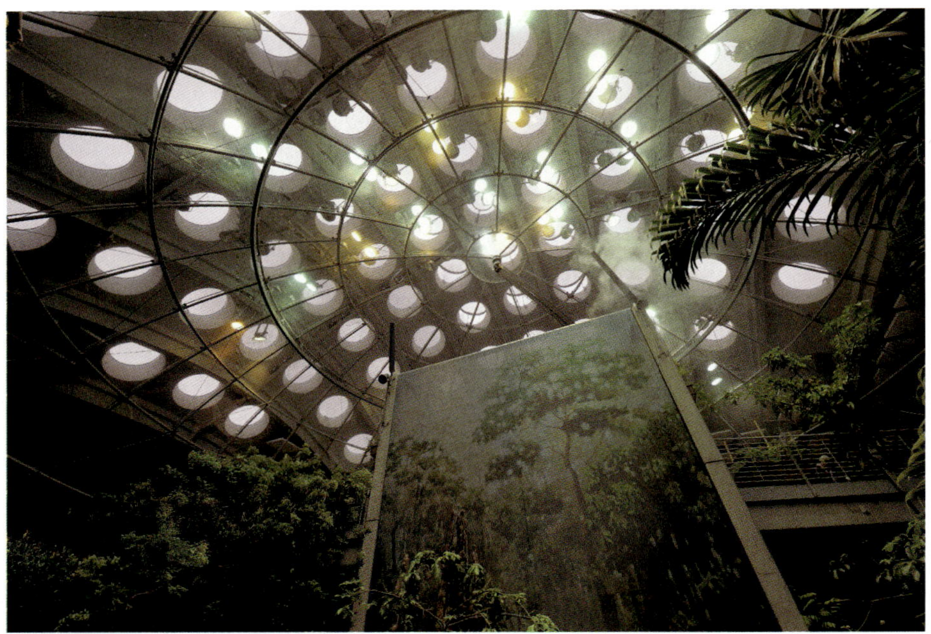

2.2 A view of the tropical rainforest. Taken at ISO 500, f/22, 1/13 second, 1/3 exposure compensation, with a 14-24mm lens.

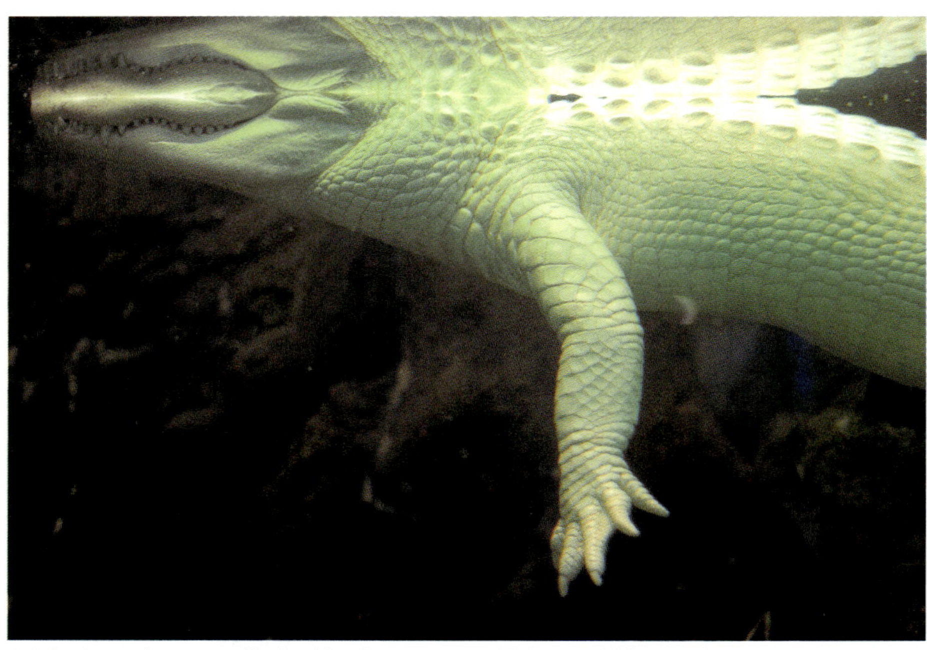

2.3 A view of a crocodile inside the museum. Taken at ISO 800, f/1.4, 1/60 second, 1/3 exposure compensation, with a 50mm lens.

How Can I Get the Best Shot?

Unlike many of the other locations in this book, time of day is less important than the weather. A trip to the California Academy of Sciences can be done at any time of year at any time of day. Most of your photos are from inside the building, so plan your trip during the operating hours of the museum. Bring a wide-to-medium-length lens and don't even bother with a tripod because they are not allowed. Expect to use higher ISO and larger apertures.

Equipment

An ultrawide, standard zoom, fast prime, and flash are the four pieces of equipment that are critical for capturing images at the Academy.

Lenses

The best lenses to use when photographing the California Academy of Sciences are an ultrawide lens for those tight quarters inside the museum and for exterior shots, a standard zoom lens for capturing your interior shots, and finally a fast prime lens to allow you to isolate a subject and shoot in extremely dark conditions.

The best focal ranges for capturing photos inside and out of the Academy are:

- **Ultrawide zoom lens in the 14-24mm range.** An ultrawide lens gives you the ability to create a unique perspective. This type of lens comes in handy for creating an ultrawide perspective of the interior of the building and exterior architecture.
- **A standard zoom lens in the 24-100mm range.** This can give you much more versatility when traveling. This lens is the jack-of-all-trades and is best used for street shooting and inside buildings. This lens is great, especially if you have one with image stabilization because this can come in handy in the darker areas of the museum.
- **A fast prime lens.** A fast prime is a great lens for shooting inside. The large aperture and shallow depth of field allow this lens to gather a lot of light so it can isolate things a normal lens cannot.

Extras

A flash can come in handy in many areas of the building where glass will not interfere with the shot.

Camera settings

Setting up your camera for photographing indoors can be much different than setting up for outdoors. When shooting indoors without a tripod, you must use a higher ISO value and a larger aperture to create a shutter speed fast enough to prevent camera shake. A good rule of thumb is if you have a 24mm lens, then you need at least 1/24 second shutter speed to prevent camera shake from degrading your image. Not everyone is the same. I can hand hold a 24mm lens at 1/13 second, so it varies for each person. Image stabilization can also help you shoot at much slower shutter speeds than normal. My recommendation is to keep your shutter speed the equivalent or greater than your focal length. Set your camera to Auto White Balance and bump up your ISO. Use your camera meter and shoot primarily in Aperture Priority mode as this will make shooting in low light much easier.

- **Exposure mode.** Inside I use Aperture Priority mode and let my camera choose the shutter speed. I set my aperture to the largest aperture, which in this case was f/2.8 and f/1.4 for the two lenses I had. I then adjusted my ISO so that I achieved a shutter speed that I was comfortable handholding. I dialed in minus exposure compensation to compensate for the harsh lighting that was causing overexposure on many of my photos.
- **White balance.** White balance I never touch as I find the Auto White Balance of all modern day cameras to be pretty good.
- **ISO.** In this case adjust your ISO to a range that gives you a fast enough shutter speed. In my case most of my photos from inside the Academy were at ISO 500 or greater.

Exposure

Metering can be tough inside. I shoot in Aperture Priority and add a +1/3 exposure compensation to help combat the noise from the higher ISO and to expose for the shadows.

Ideal time to shoot

The California Academy of Sciences is open during normal business hours, so shooting in the wee morning or late evening isn't going to happen unless you know someone. Plan your trip when the museum is open. If you get there early or stay late, this would be the best time to photograph the exterior as the sun is not directly above casting harsh light on the building.

Working around the weather

Weather is the least important. If I am going to spend a few hours inside a museum, I would rather the weather be poor. If possible, plan your trip on one of those dreary, foggy afternoons.

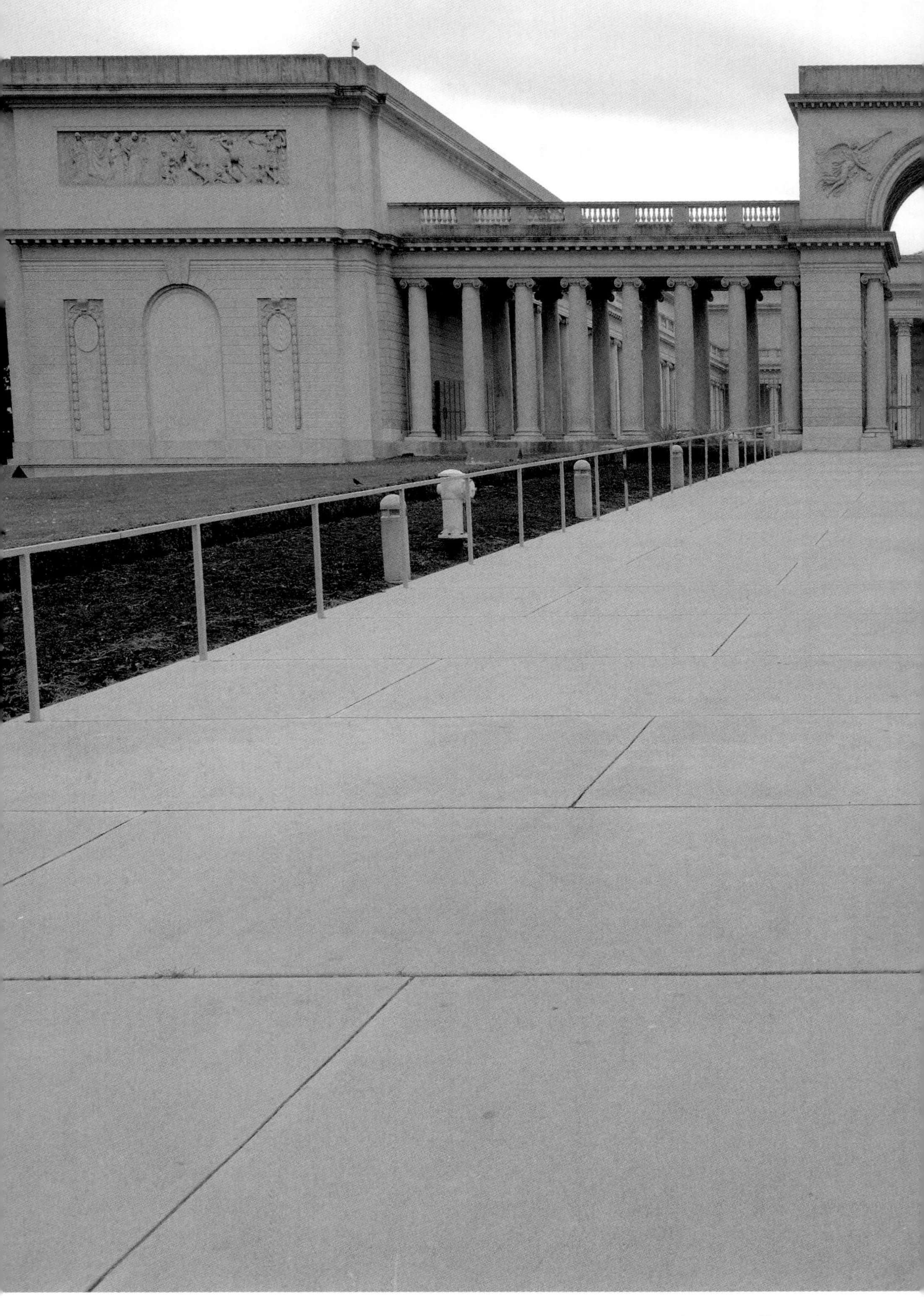

The California Palace of the Legion of Honor on a clear autumn afternoon. Taken at ISO 100, f/11, 1/125 second with a 14-24mm lens.

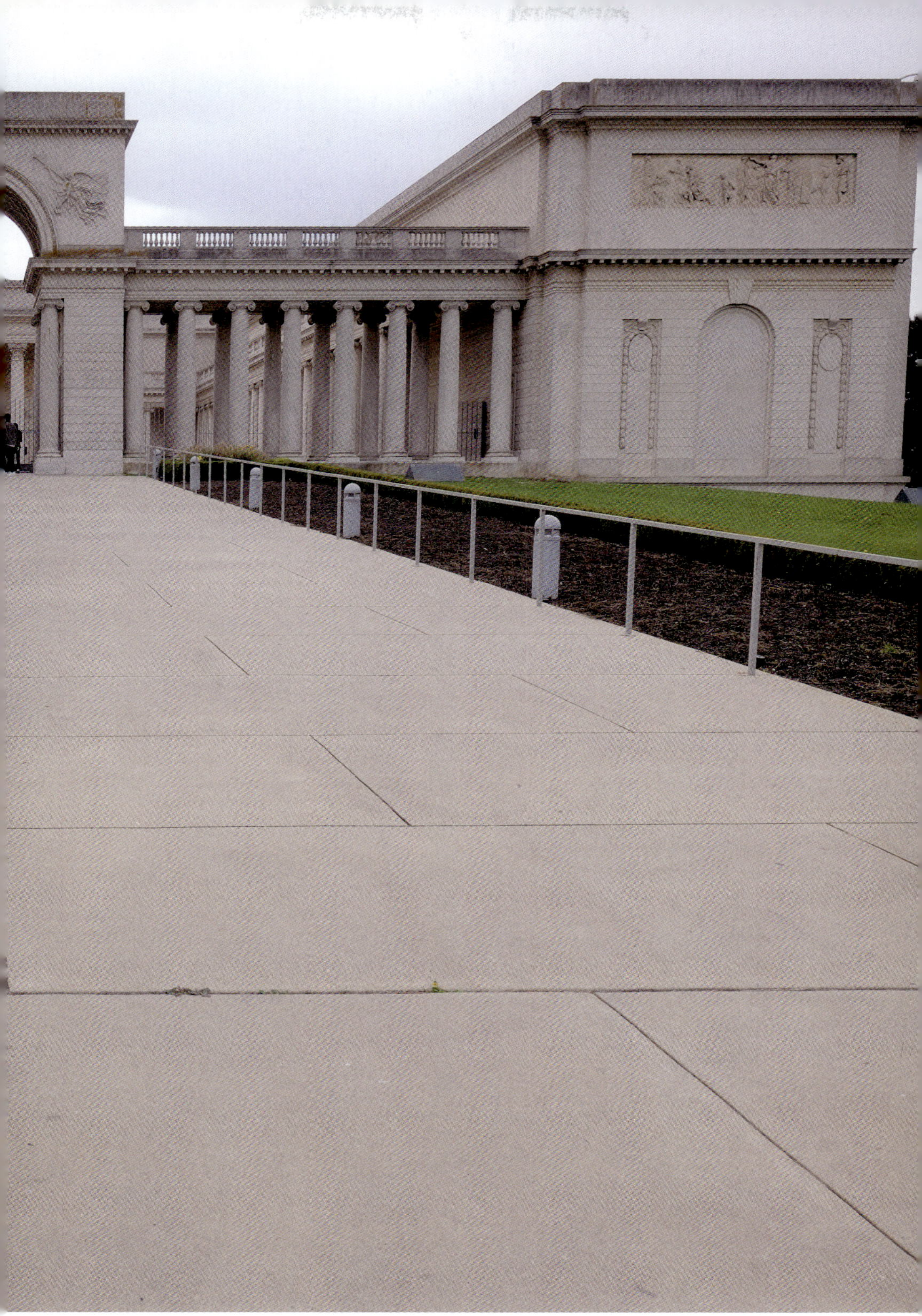

3 California Palace of the Legion of Honor

Why It's Worth a Photograph

The California Palace of the Legion of Honor, San Francisco's most beautiful museum, displays an impressive collection of 4,000 years of ancient and European art. The beautiful Beaux-Arts museum is a three-quarter scale adaptation of the eighteenth century Palais de Legion d'Honneur in Paris. Built to honor the California soldiers who died in France during World War I, the museum is located inside Lincoln Park in San Francisco. The museum is perched atop the cliffs of Lands End; this location overlooks the Pacific Ocean and San Francisco. The wonderful architecture combined with the scenic views makes this an ideal place for you to photograph.

Where Can I Get the Best Shot?

Lincoln Park offers a wonderful opportunity to photograph this beautiful museum (see A on the map).

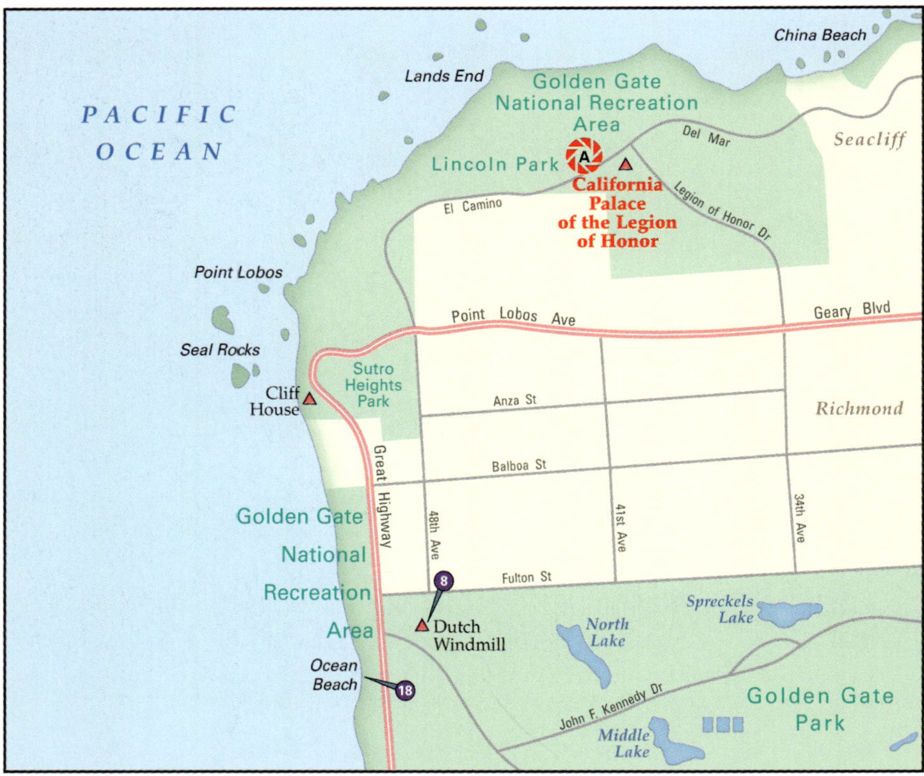

The best location from which to photograph the California Palace of the Legion of Honor: (A) Lincoln Park. Other photo ops: (8) Dutch Windmill, (18) Ocean Beach.

Lincoln Park

The architecture here is absolutely stunning and combined with the right light and time of day you can really create some wonderful photos (see figure 3.1). Be sure to bring a wide and a medium telephoto lens as the exterior of the museum has many great places to capture beautiful detailing on the stone and wonderful arches (see figure 3.2).

The columns of the museum make a wonderful abstract photo when shot with a long lens and small aperture (see figure 3.3). Spend the afternoon visiting the museum, enjoying the exhibits, taking in the breathtaking views, and admiring the wonderful French-inspired architecture. The Legion of Honor is truly a wonderful place to visit and photograph.

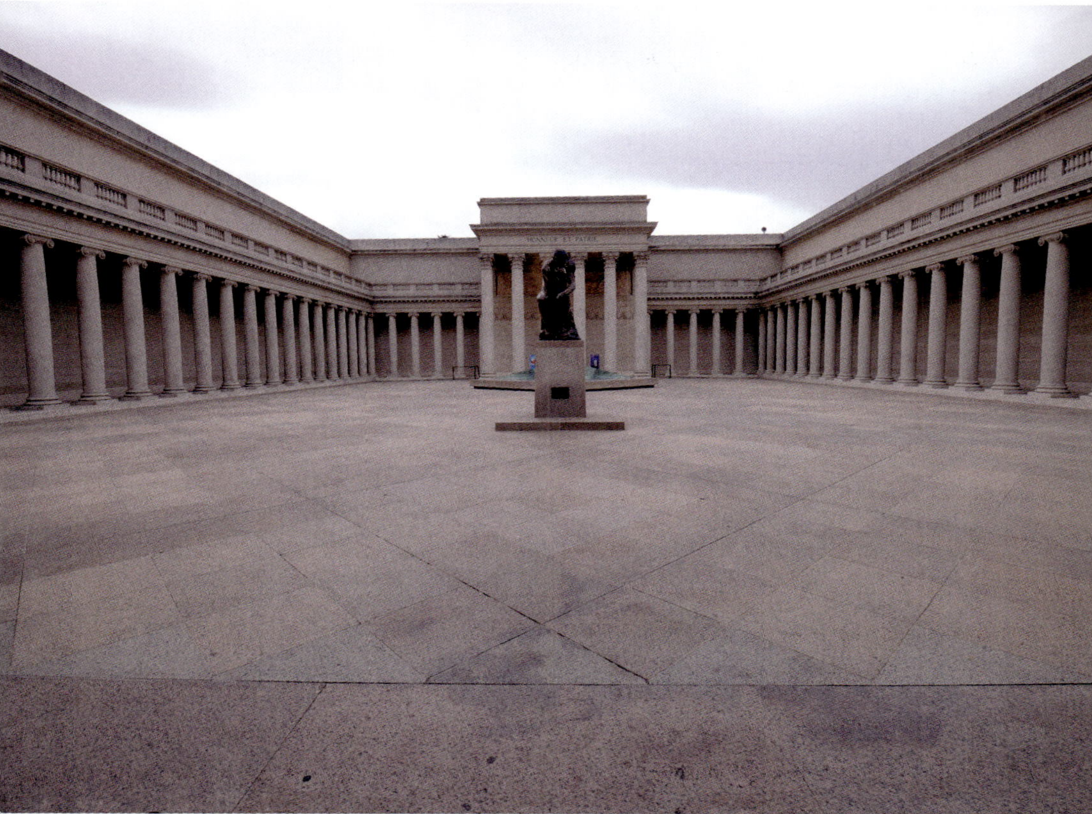

3.1 A view of the California Palace of the Legion of Honor on a clear autumn afternoon (see A on the map). Taken at ISO 100, f/11, 1/100 second with a 14-24mm lens.

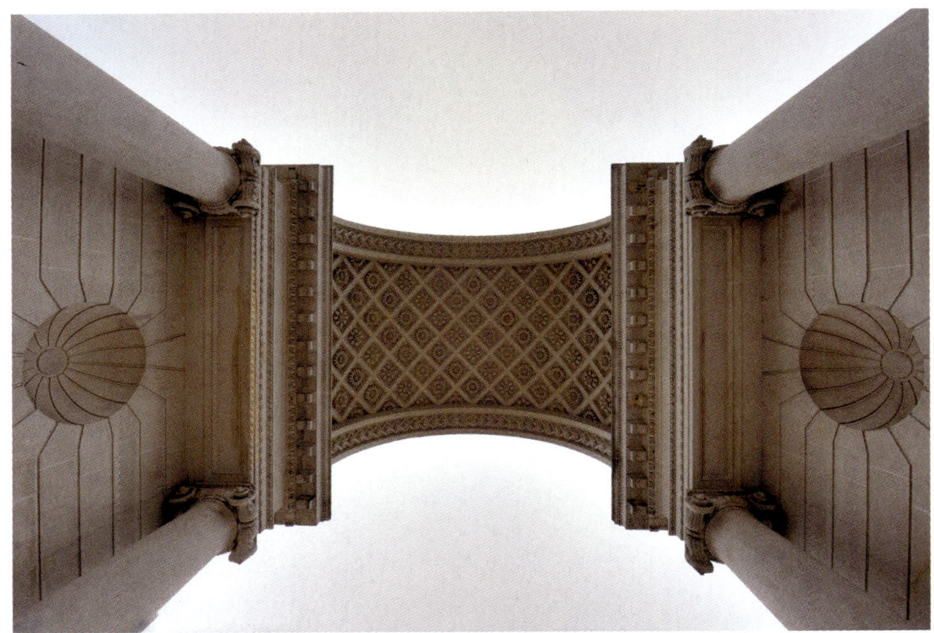

3.2 A view of the California Palace of the Legion of Honor arches on a clear autumn afternoon. Taken at ISO 100, f/8, 1/100 second with a 14-24mm lens.

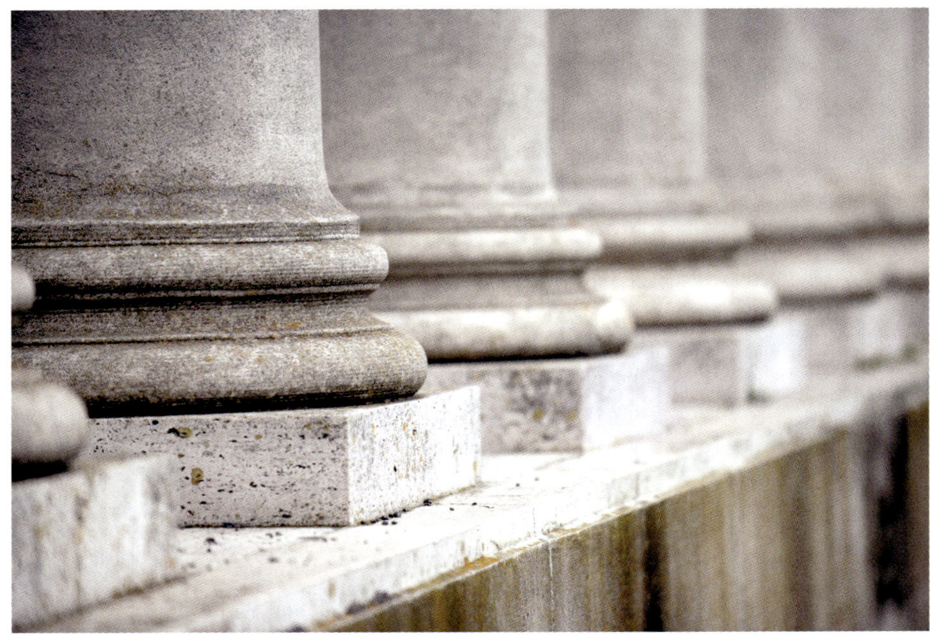

3.3 A view of the California Palace of the Legion of Honor columns on a clear autumn afternoon. Taken at ISO 100, f/2.8, 1/500 second with a 70-200mm lens.

How Can I Get the Best Shot?

Plan your trip to the Legion of Honor late in the day when the sky is clear and the sun is going down, and the warm hues are in the sky. Let this warm, colorful low light enhance your photos by creating wonderful long, soft shadows and turning the usually cold white stone a warm tone. Use a tripod because doing so can help you steady the camera on those San Francisco days when the wind is blowing off the ocean.

Equipment

A tripod, ultrawide-angle lens, and a medium telephoto lens are the three pieces of equipment you should consider bringing to the Legion of Honor.

Lenses

Ultrawide and medium telephoto lenses are the two that can help capture the essence of the Legion of Honor. The wide lens creates the wonderful wide perspective while the longer lens allows you to isolate detail.

- **Ultrawide-angle lens in the 14-24mm range.** The ultrawide lens gives you the ability to frame the Legion of Honor from one end to the other. It allows you a much more creative aspect because more things can be included in the final photograph. When using an ultrawide-angle lens, you must be wary about including elements on the outer edge of the frame that you may not want.
- **A medium telephoto lens 70-200mm range.** This lens allows you the ability to isolate a particular subject such as the pillars, or gives you the extra reach when shooting subjects that are too far off for a standard zoom lens.

Filters

A colored graduated density filter such as cranberry is a great tool to help create special effects in the sky. A cranberry graduated density filter allows you to expose the sky and ground properly and adds a wonderful reddish hue to the sky.

Camera settings

Set your camera to Aperture Priority mode. Dial in f/8 or f/11 for maximum detail. On your longer zooms, your aperture may vary from f/2.8 to f/5.6. I chose these larger apertures to create a smaller depth of field.

- **Exposure mode.** I set my camera in Aperture Priority mode and let my camera choose the shutter speed. I dial in a plus or minus exposure composition depending on the overall scene. When shooting a white subject such as the museum, I dial in a +1/3 exposure to help protect the shadows.

- **White balance.** White balance I never touch because I find that the Auto White Balance of all modern-day cameras is pretty good.
- **ISO.** ISO should stay as low as possible unless you are handholding your camera. Adjust your ISO to get a shutter speed that is fast enough for you to hand hold a long lens.

Exposure

Set your exposure to +1/3 exposure compensation as the museum's white stone fools the camera into underexposing.

Ideal time to shoot

The Legion of Honor is open during normal business hours, so if you don't want to go inside the museum, then shooting the building late in the day when the sun is setting is your best bet. The sun is warm, low, and directly behind the museum, which creates wonderful light against the white stone.

Working around the weather

The spring and late fall are the ideal times to shoot. The sky is clear, and the city is treated to many colorful sunsets. These seasons also have little, if any, rain.

Getting creative

I like to use leading lines to draw the viewer into the scene. For figure 3.4, my leading line is a large red sculpture made of steel beams. A leading line can be almost anything: a road, path, sidewalk, fence, river, hedge, tree line, or shadow. You will not find a strong leading line around every subject, but you should look for them if they are there and take advantage of them. Lines in a picture should lead into, not out of, the picture, and they should lead your eye toward the main subject. Sometimes it is a matter of choosing the right angle or point of view to make leading lines lead into the picture. Starting a leading line from the corner of your picture will often improve composition. I also used a cranberry graduated density filter to create the wonderful red hue in the sky.

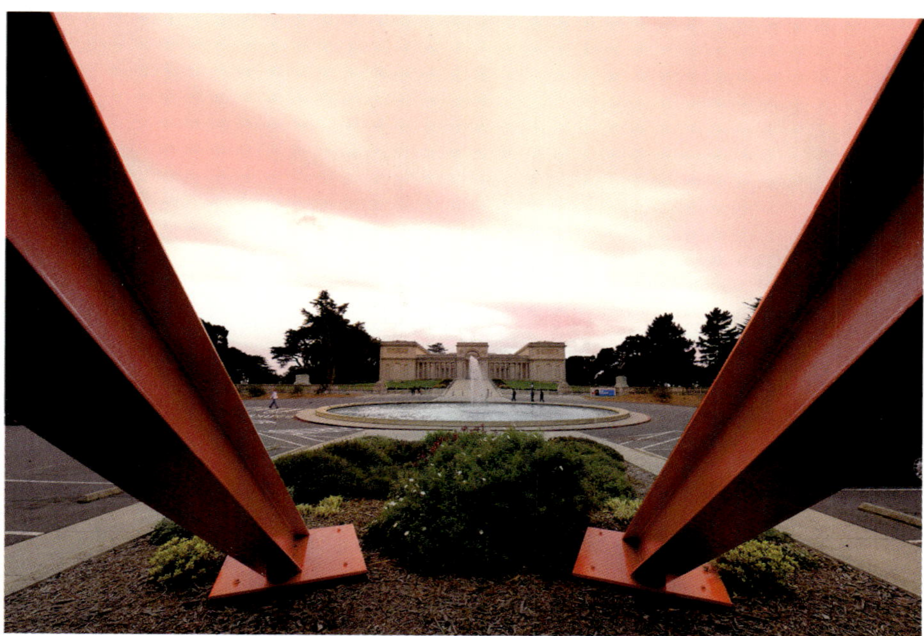

3.4 A view of the California Palace of the Legion of Honor on a clear autumn afternoon before the sun set. Taken at ISO 100, f/11, 1/125 second with a 14-24mm lens.

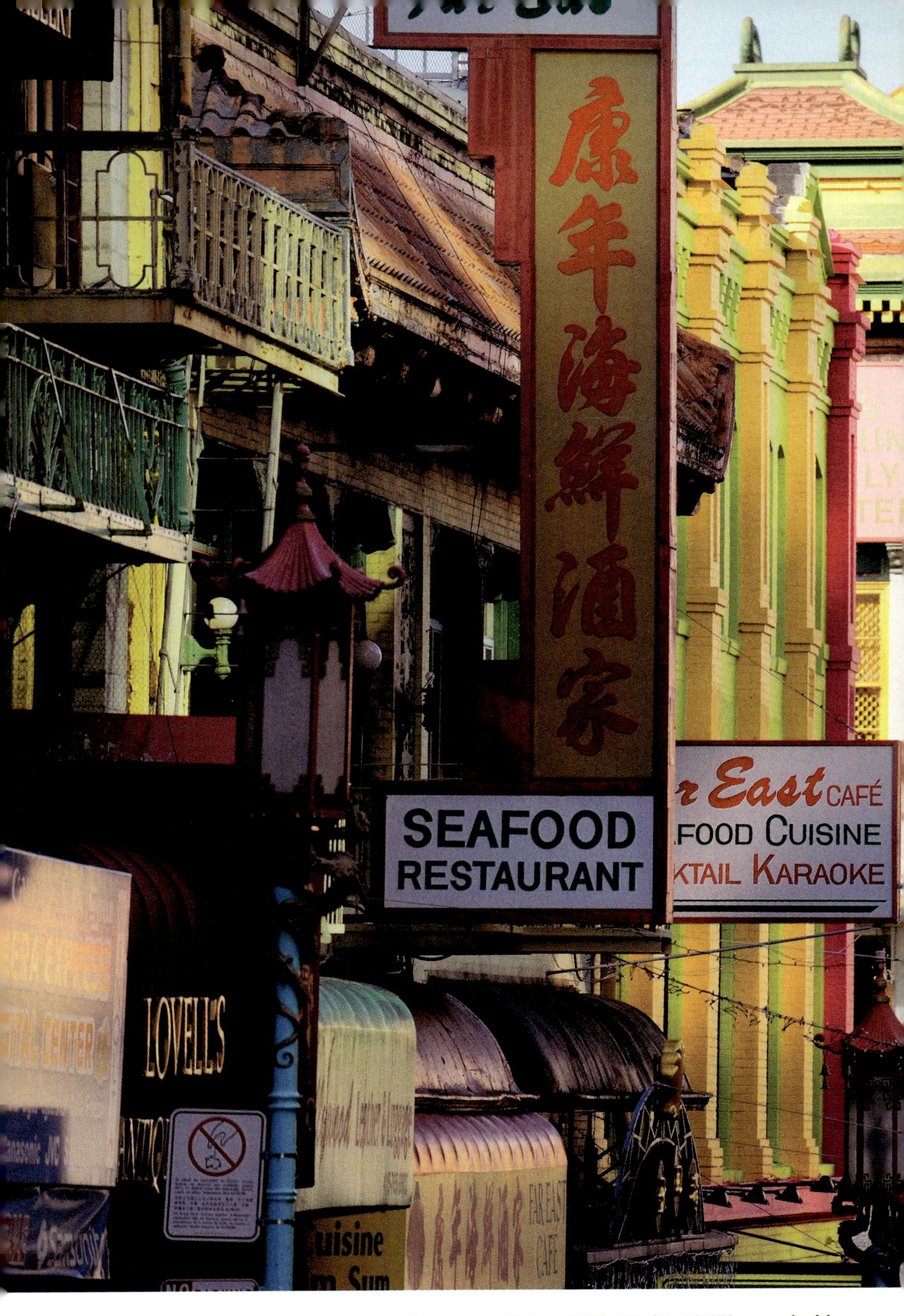

A view of Chinatown taken on a clear fall afternoon. Taken at ISO 200, f/4, 1/1250 second with a 70-200mm lens.

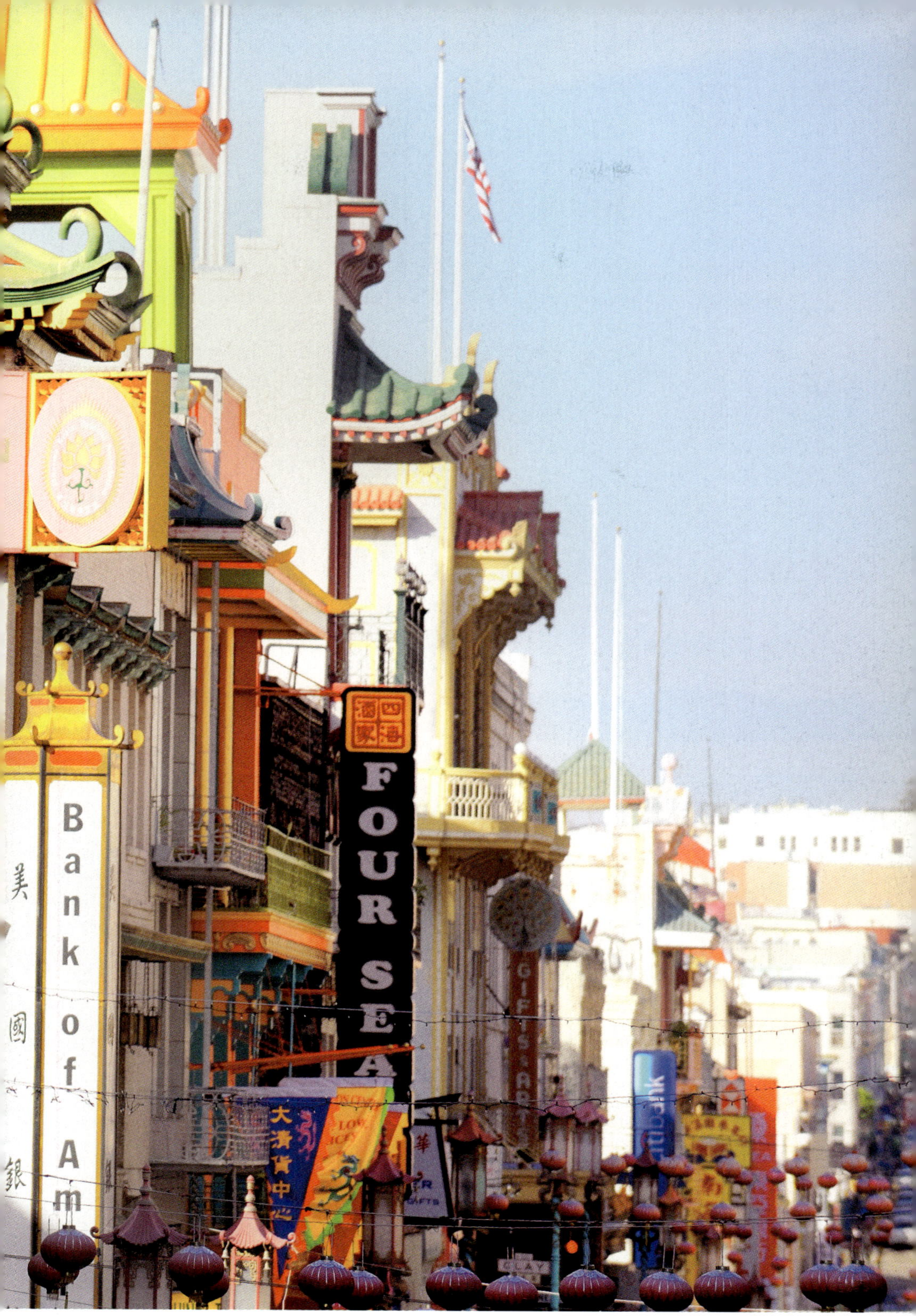

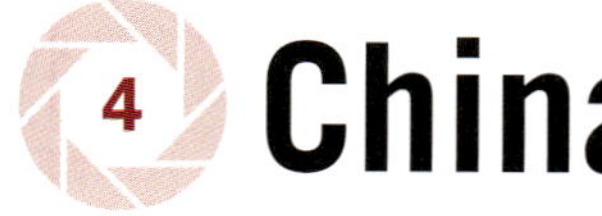

Chinatown

Why It's Worth a Photograph

San Francisco's Chinatown is the oldest Chinatown in North America and one of the largest Chinese communities outside Asia. Established in the mid-1840s, it is a center of Chinese culture and activity in North America. A city within a city, it has many venues for the arts, film, music, and literature. A tightly packed neighborhood that continues to grow, Chinatown offers visitors and residents hundreds of restaurants, booming fruit and fish markets, and shops of knickknacks and sweets on torturously narrow and overcrowded streets. Unlike many other mixed-Asian communities today, San Francisco's Chinatown retains its Chinese ethnic identity even after 160 years, and it is the largest Chinese community of its kind in the United States. The Asian-inspired architecture, food and souvenir markets, and wonderful colors are just a few of the things you can photograph. It is truly a street photographer's dream.

Where Can I Get the Best Shot?

There is one main street and two cross streets where you can photograph Chinatown. Grant Avenue at Bush Street is the primary entrance to Chinatown (see A on the map), and Grant Avenue at Sacramento Street (see B on the map) runs right in the heart of Chinatown and is a good place to capture many inspired images.

Grant Avenue and Bush Street

Grant Avenue at Bush Street is the main entrance to Chinatown and a wonderful place to begin your walk. Enjoy your stroll and stop often to photograph what you see. Chinatown is one of the few neighborhoods that you can spend an afternoon photographing just people. There are also many buildings, temples, and artwork that have a cultural significance and charm. Grant Avenue at Bush Street is the perfect place to capture an Asian-inspired entrance (see figure 4.1)

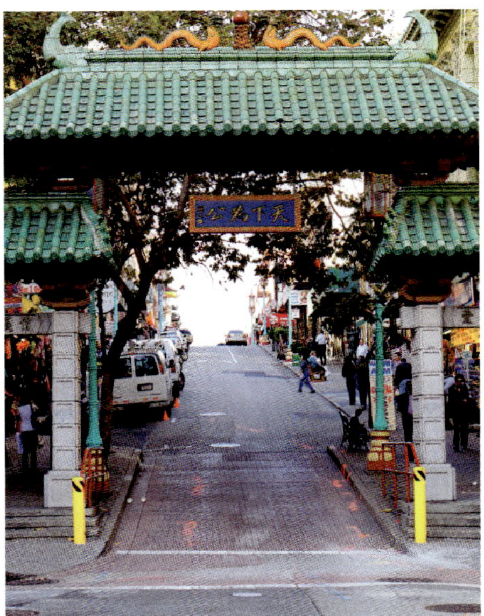

4.1 A view of the main entrance to Chinatown taken on a clear fall afternoon (see A on the map). Taken at ISO 200, f/4, 1/200 second with a 50mm lens.

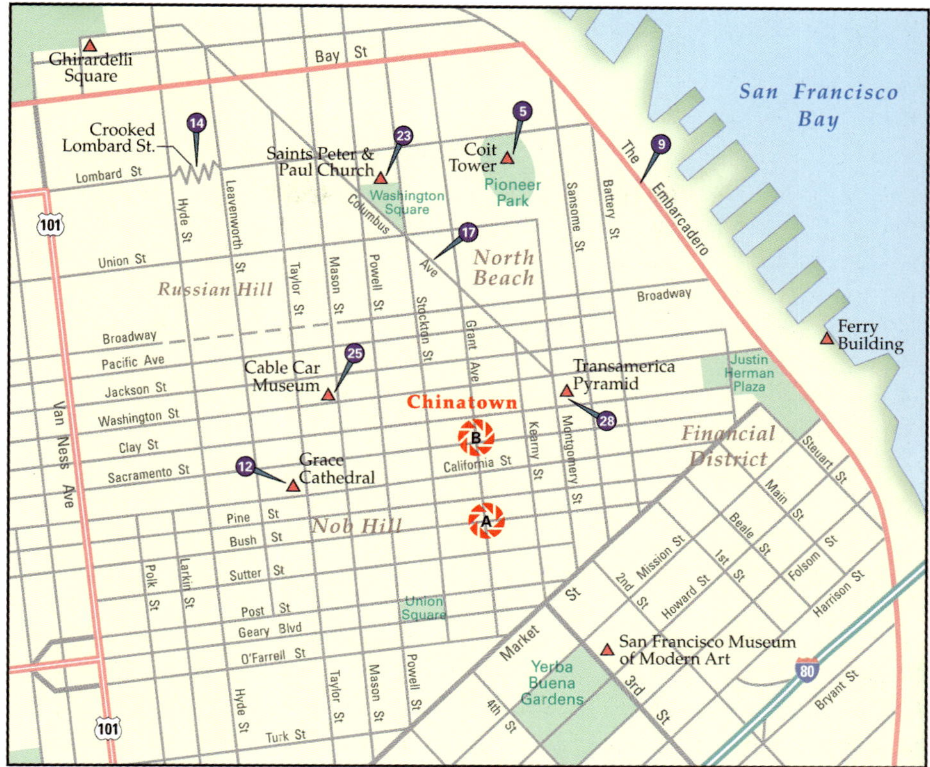

The best locations from which to photograph Chinatown: (A) Grant Avenue and Bush Street, (B) Grant Avenue and Sacramento Street. Other photo ops: (5) Coit Tower, (9) Embarcadero, (12) Grace Cathedral, (14) Lombard Street, (17) North Beach, (23) Saints Peter and Paul Church, (25) San Francisco cable cars, (28) Transamerica Pyramid.

Grant Avenue and Sacramento Street

As you continue your stroll north along Grant Street, eventually you reach Sacramento Street, which puts you right in the middle of Chinatown. This is where you can see and photograph the Chinese culture up close and personal (see figure 4.2). This is my favorite area of Chinatown — the architecture, hanging lanterns, light posts, and the hustle and bustle that is all around you make you forget you are in a Western country. This location is truly wonderful and a perfect place to capture Chinatown.

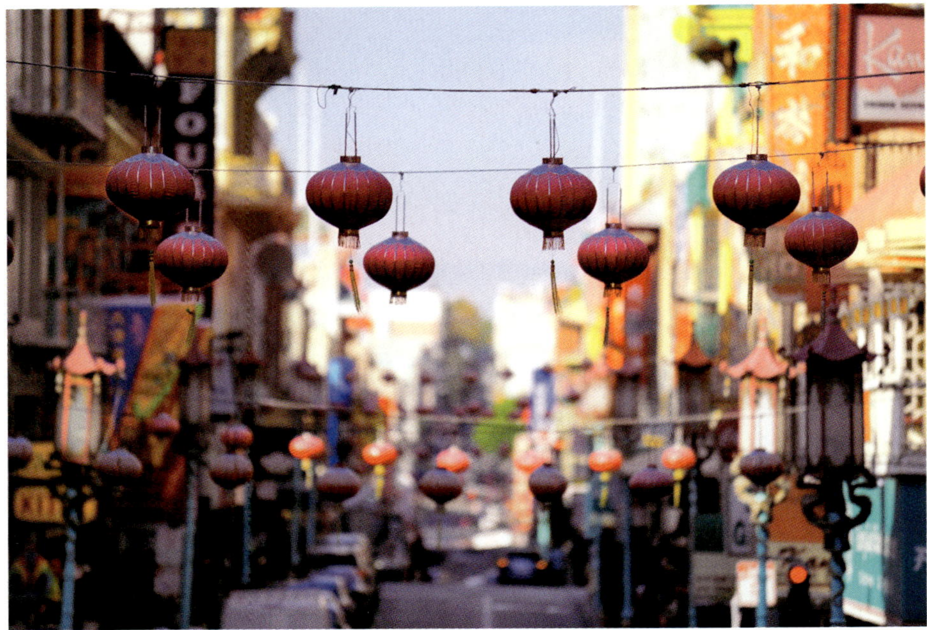

4.2 A view of Chinatown taken on a clear fall afternoon (see B on the map). Taken at ISO 500, f/2.8, 1/4000 second with a 70-200mm lens.

How Can I Get the Best Shot?

The fun thing about street shooting is that there are no rules. Early in the day is best because the sun is lower and the shadows are less harsh. Take your time when walking around, looking up and down. Look for bright colors, architecture, and people. Capture Chinatown as you see it. It is okay to include people in a shot as it helps give the viewer an awareness of the cultural aspects of Chinatown and how people live and work in this wonderful neighborhood.

Equipment

A medium telephoto zoom and a standard zoom lens are the two pieces of equipment that will make photographing Chinatown fun.

- **Medium telephoto zoom in the 70-300mm range.** A perfect lens for isolation, this lens can help capture photos that a shorter lens can't.
- **A standard zoom lens in the 24-100mm range.** This lens can give you much more versatility when traveling. This lens is the jack-of-all-trades and is best used for street shooting.

Camera settings

For shooting in Chinatown, you should shoot in Aperture Priority mode most of the time as it will allow you to focus on composition and capturing that quick shot. When shooting architecture, I use f/8 to f/11; when shooting people and street scenes, I like to isolate my subjects, so I will shoot at the largest aperture available. This however is not a perfect rule, and what you want to convey will ultimately determine your camera settings. The most important thing is to keep your shutter speed fast enough to hand hold your camera. You may want to increase your ISO to ensure you always have fast enough shutter speed.

- **Exposure mode.** Outside in narrow streets, I set my camera in Manual mode and adjust my aperture and shutter speed until I achieve the correct exposure. This may not be what the camera wants; the proper exposure is based on what I am trying to convey. Sometimes, I sacrifice the highlights to expose the shadows and vice versa. Most of the time, you want to balance your shadows and highlights.
- **White balance.** White balance I never touch because I find the Auto White Balance setting of all modern day cameras to be pretty good. This is especially true when shooting outside.
- **ISO.** Keep your ISO around 200 to 400; this will ensure you have a fast enough shutter speed when walking around during the day. At night you may want to increase it from 1600 to 3200.

Exposure

Metering can be tough on these narrow Chinatown streets because the bright sky can cause deep pockets of shade when shooting architecture. I recommend shooting in Manual mode. Doing this makes it easier to balance your highlights and shadows. Use the histogram on the back of your camera to help judge your exposure.

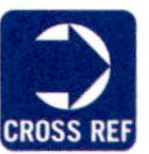

See Chapter 1 for more information about histograms.

Ideal time to shoot

The ideal time to shoot is in the early morning when no one is on the street. Chinatown can become extremely crowded, which makes setting up a shot nearly impossible.

Working around the weather

Chinatown is located in one of the warmest areas of the city situated just below Nob Hill. The weather stays relatively mild with very little fog and warmer than average city temperatures.

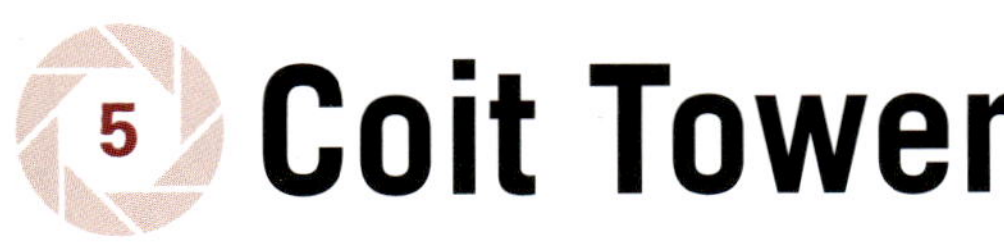

Coit Tower

A view of Coit Tower taken in the early morning on a warm summer day. Taken at ISO 400, f/22, 1/130 second with a 14-24mm lens.

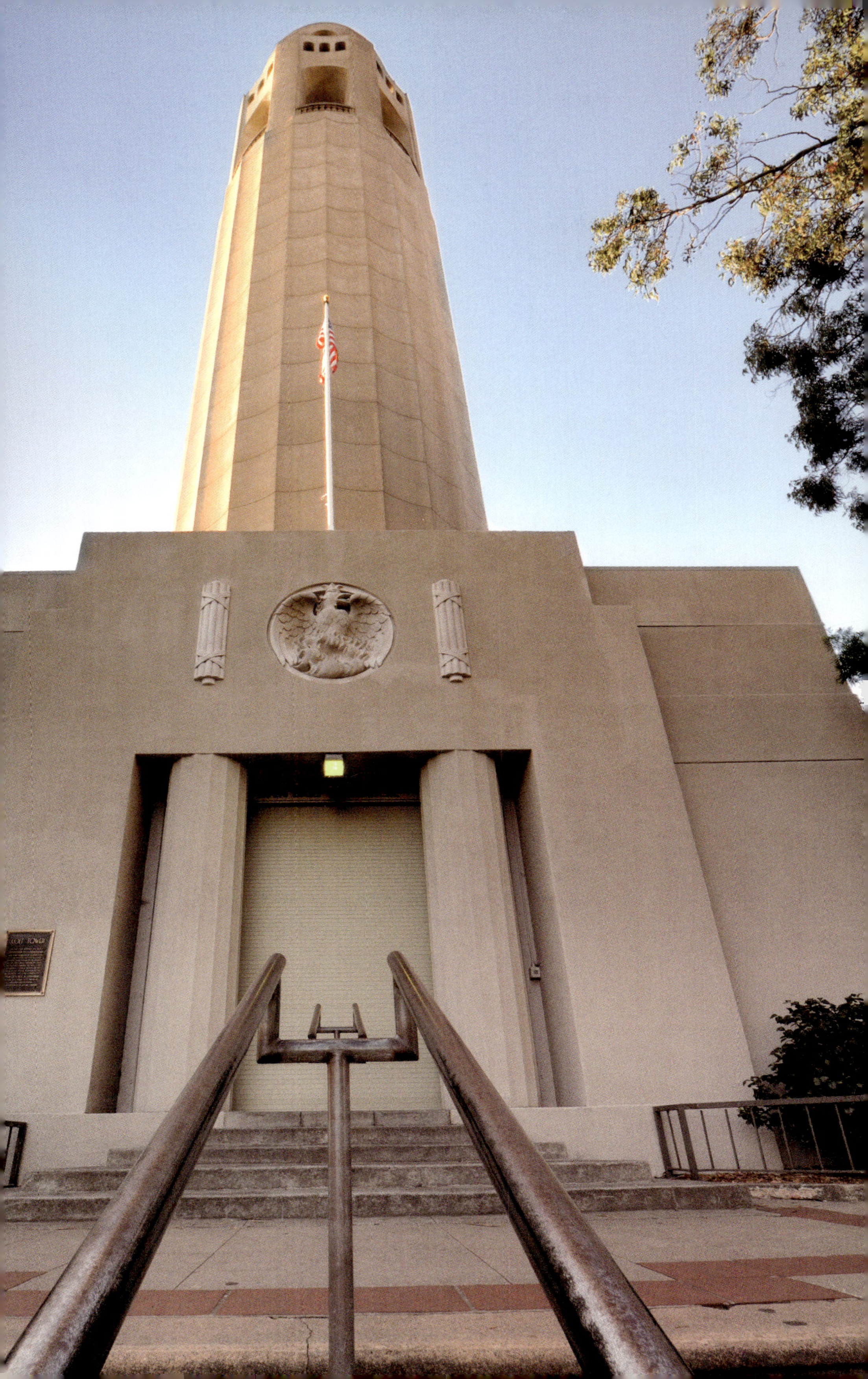

Why It's Worth a Photograph

Coit Tower was built in Pioneer Park atop Telegraph Hill in 1933. Contrary to popular opinion, the tower was not designed to resemble a fire hose nozzle. The Art Deco tower, which is 210 feet (64 m) of unpainted, reinforced concrete, stands alone on Telegraph Hill. The views from Coit Tower offer a 360-degree panoramic view of the city. Not to be missed are the murals decorating the lobby, considered to be one of California's best examples of Depression-era public art. What makes Coit Tower worth a photograph is the wonderful isolation this Art Deco tower has as it sits at the top of the hill with the sweeping waterfront on one side and the city on the other.

Where Can I Get the Best Shot?

There are a number of places around San Francisco you can photograph Coit Tower. The three most accessible and unobstructed views are from Lombard Street, Embarcadero Piers, and Fisherman's Wharf (see A, B, and C on the map).

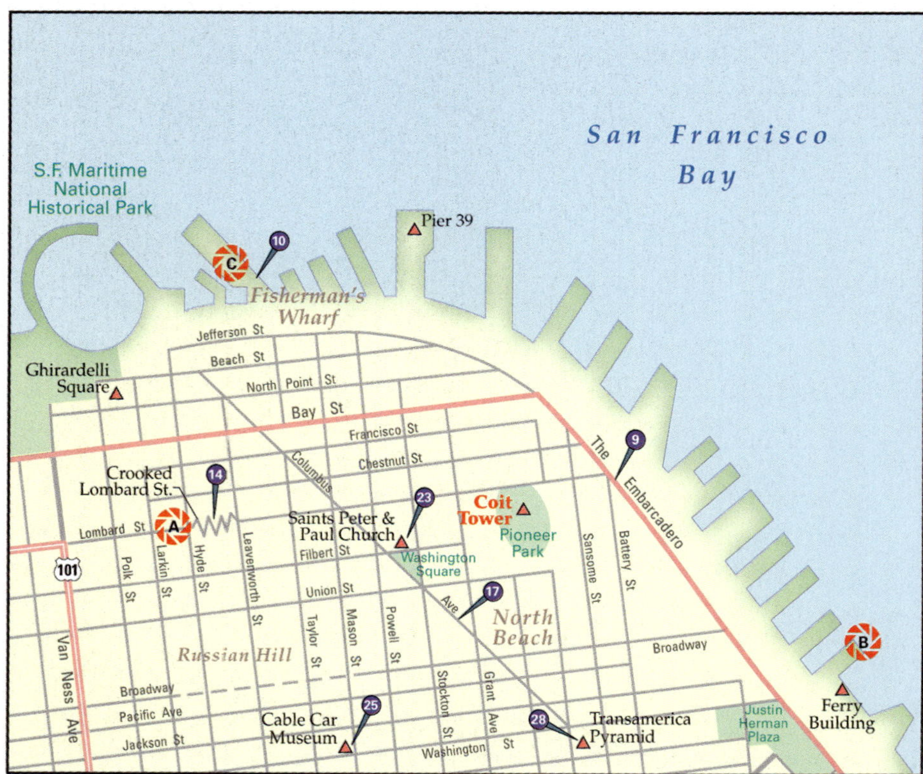

The best locations from which to photograph Coit Tower: (A) Lombard Street, (B) Embarcadero Piers, (C) Fisherman's Wharf. Other photo ops: (9) Embarcadero, (10) Fisherman's Wharf, (14) crooked Lombard Street, (17) North Beach, (23) Saints Peter and Paul Church, (25) San Francisco cable cars, (28) Transamerica Pyramid.

Lombard Street

The top of Lombard Street is my favorite vantage point of the three. This vantage point gives you an eye-level view of the tower. The easiest time to shoot from this vantage point is one hour before the sun sets. The sun will be behind and to your left creating a nice sidelit scene of Telegraph Hill with Coit Tower, the San Francisco-Oakland Bay Bridge, and the city of San Francisco as a backdrop. Bring a long lens — 200-300mm — to really isolate the tower (see figure 5.1). If you want to try a more challenging time to photograph Coit Tower, arrive at Lombard Street 30 minutes before the sun comes up and shoot the tower as the sun comes up from behind the horizon. If you nail your exposure, you should create a wonderfully colorful backlit photo of Coit Tower.

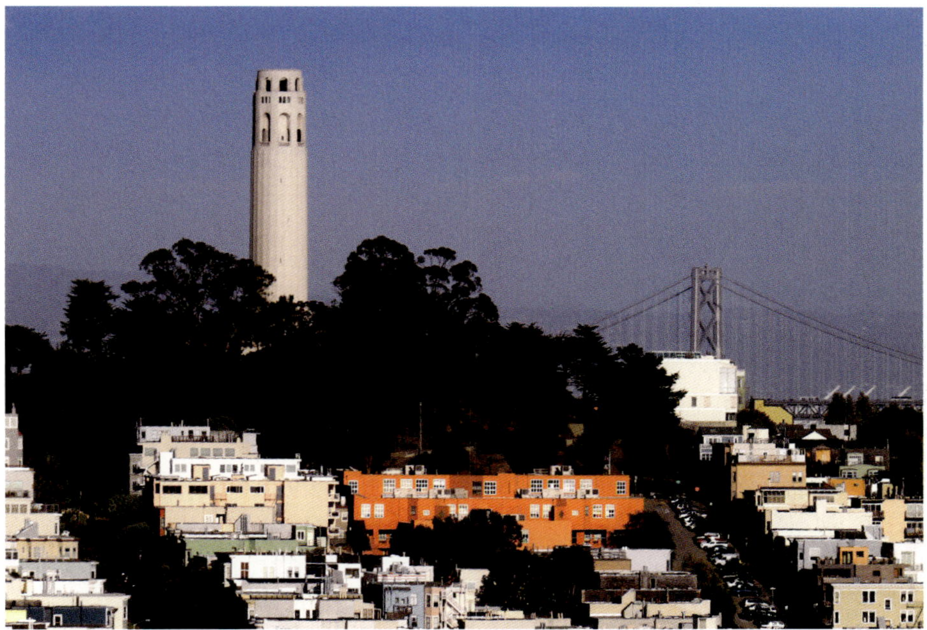

5.1 A view of Coit Tower taken in the early evening on a warm summer night (see A on the map). Taken at ISO 400, f/11, 1/1000 second with a 300mm lens.

Embarcadero Piers

Embarcadero Piers are a great vantage point to photograph Coit Tower. From the piers you are relatively close, so a lens of 200mm should be the perfect focal length. This vantage point gives a wonderful warm front-lit scene if shot one hour after sunrise. The advantage of shooting a front-lit scene is that there is very little to do from a camera settings and exposure perspective because the entire scene is evenly lit. Compose your picture and shoot (see figure 5.2).

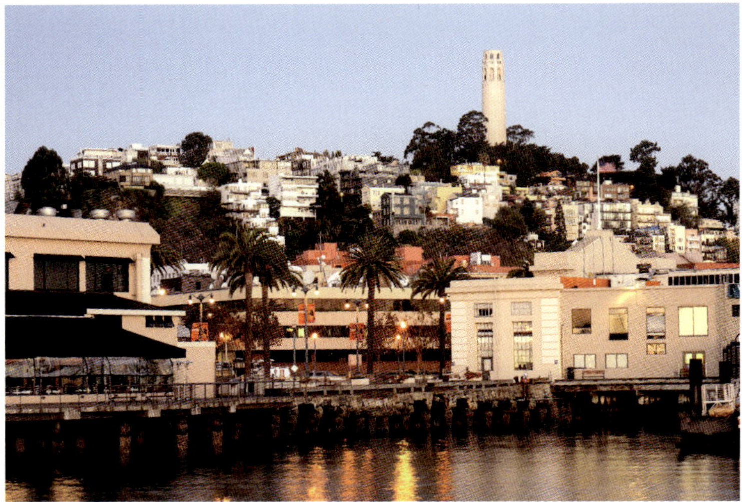

5.2 A view of Coit Tower taken in the early morning on a warm summer day (see B on the map). Taken at ISO 100, f/8, 1/6 second with an 85mm lens.

Fisherman's Wharf

Fisherman's Wharf like the Embarcadero Piers gives you an unobstructed shot of Coit Tower. The ideal time to shoot from this location is in the early morning at least 30 minutes after the sun has risen. What makes this the perfect time is the low warm sun striking the tower from the side creating a wonderful sidelit subject that has texture and form (see figure 5.3).

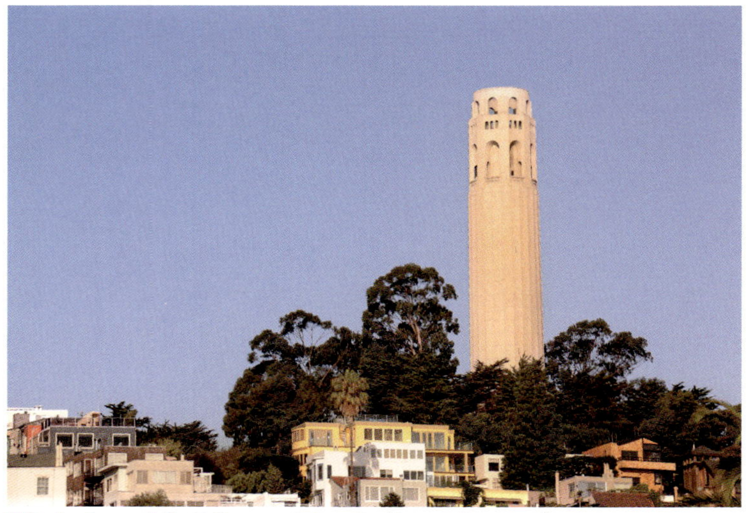

5.3 A view of Coit Tower taken in the early morning on a warm summer day (see C on the map). Taken at ISO 100, f/8, 1/200 second with a 70-200mm lens.

How Can I Get the Best Shot?

Good light is the key to making an average photo great. Shooting Coit Tower early or late in the day is the type of low, warm directional light that gives your photo form and texture.

Equipment

A good tripod, an ultrawide lens, and long telephoto lens are the three pieces of equipment that are critical for capturing sharp images of Coit Tower in low light.

Lenses

The choice of lens for shooting Coit Tower really comes down to two lens types. An ultrawide lens allows you to shoot close and still capture the entire tower. A long zoom lens gives you enough reach so you can shoot the tower from the waterfront or Lombard Street.

- **Ultrawide zoom lens in the 14-24mm range.** The ultrawide lens gives you the ability to create a unique perspective. By including something in the immediate foreground, you can create a sense of depth that can lead the person's eyes to the tower.
- **A zoom lens somewhere in the 70-400mm range.** This focal range allows you the ability to isolate Coit Tower from a distance. Due to the proximity of Coit Tower, a long lens is necessary to isolate the tower.

Extras

A tripod is useful when shooting Coit Tower with a long lens. A tripod can help stabilize the camera and lens when shooting in early morning or late evening light.

Camera settings

Setting up your camera will come down to time of day, amount of light, and composition. When shooting with a long lens from a distance, mount your camera on a tripod and set the aperture from f/8 to f/11; this will maximize your image quality. When shooting up close with your ultrawide lens where you have an immediate object in the foreground, set your aperture to f/22 to maximize your depth of field.

- **Exposure mode.** I set my camera in Aperture Priority mode and let my camera choose the shutter speed. I may dial in a plus exposure composition.
- **White balance.** I never touch white balance as I find the Auto White Balance of all modern day cameras to be pretty good.

- **ISO.** ISO should stay as low as possible unless you are handholding your camera. Increase your ISO to get a shutter speed that is fast enough for you to hand hold a long lens.

Exposure

Expose for the tower and sky because this is your main subject. A blown sky will more than likely mean a poorly exposed tower. Sacrifice the shadows and dark trees to capture the correct overall exposure.

Ideal time to shoot

The ideal time to shoot is in the early morning or late in the day when the sun is low. The perfect direction to shoot from is when the sun is at your back, and Coit Tower is being immersed in a low, warm, soft golden light. The sun rises in the east so be sure to shoot Coit Tower in the morning from the waterfront vantage points. Late in the day is the ideal time to photograph Coit Tower from Lombard Street.

Working around the weather

Weather is important for one reason: You don't want to be out shooting in the rain. My recommendation is any season but the winter is an ideal time to shoot. The winter months between late November and early March can have unpredictable rainstorms. Plan your days when it is clear and the sun is out. If it is foggy, the tower will not be worth a photograph.

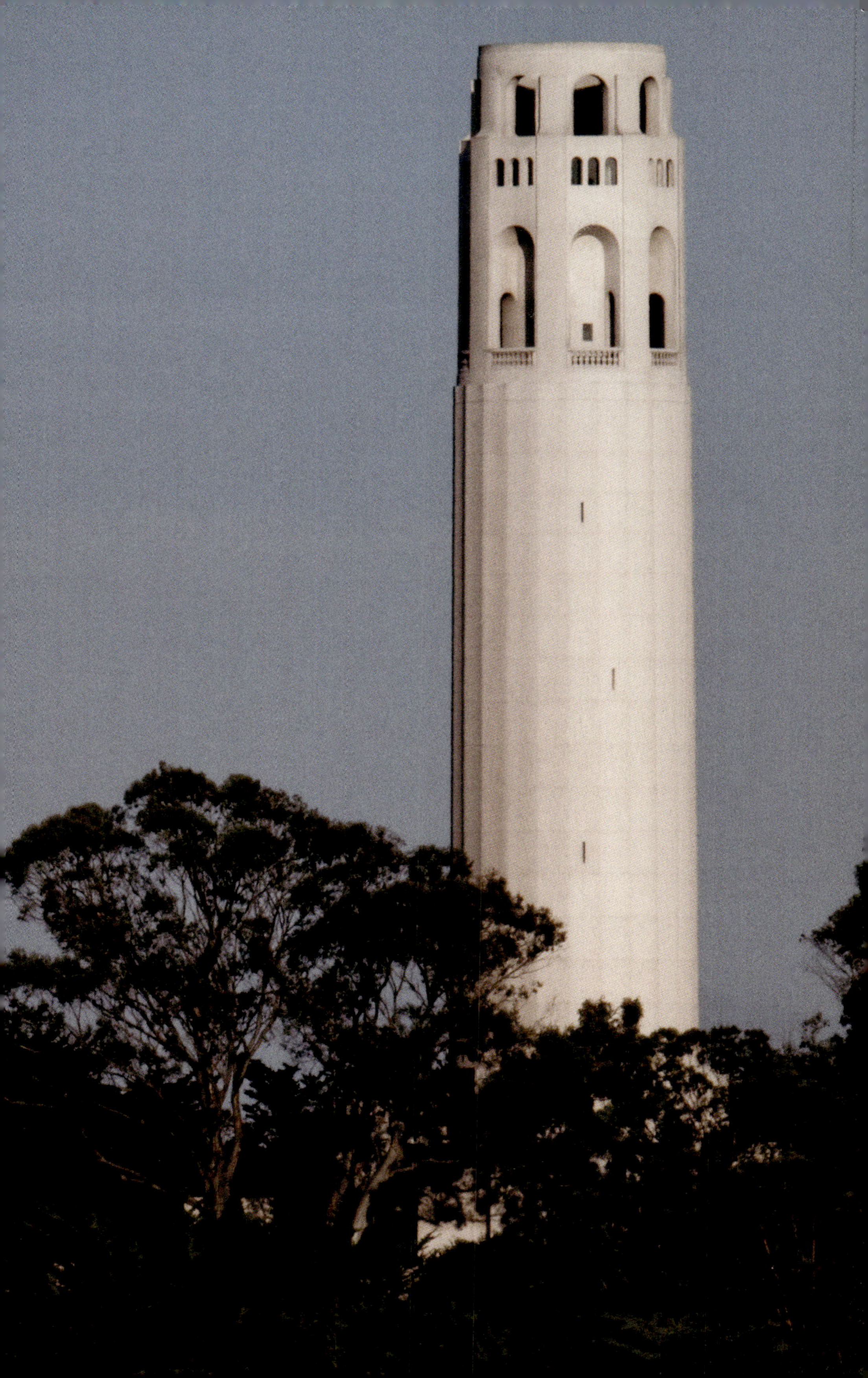

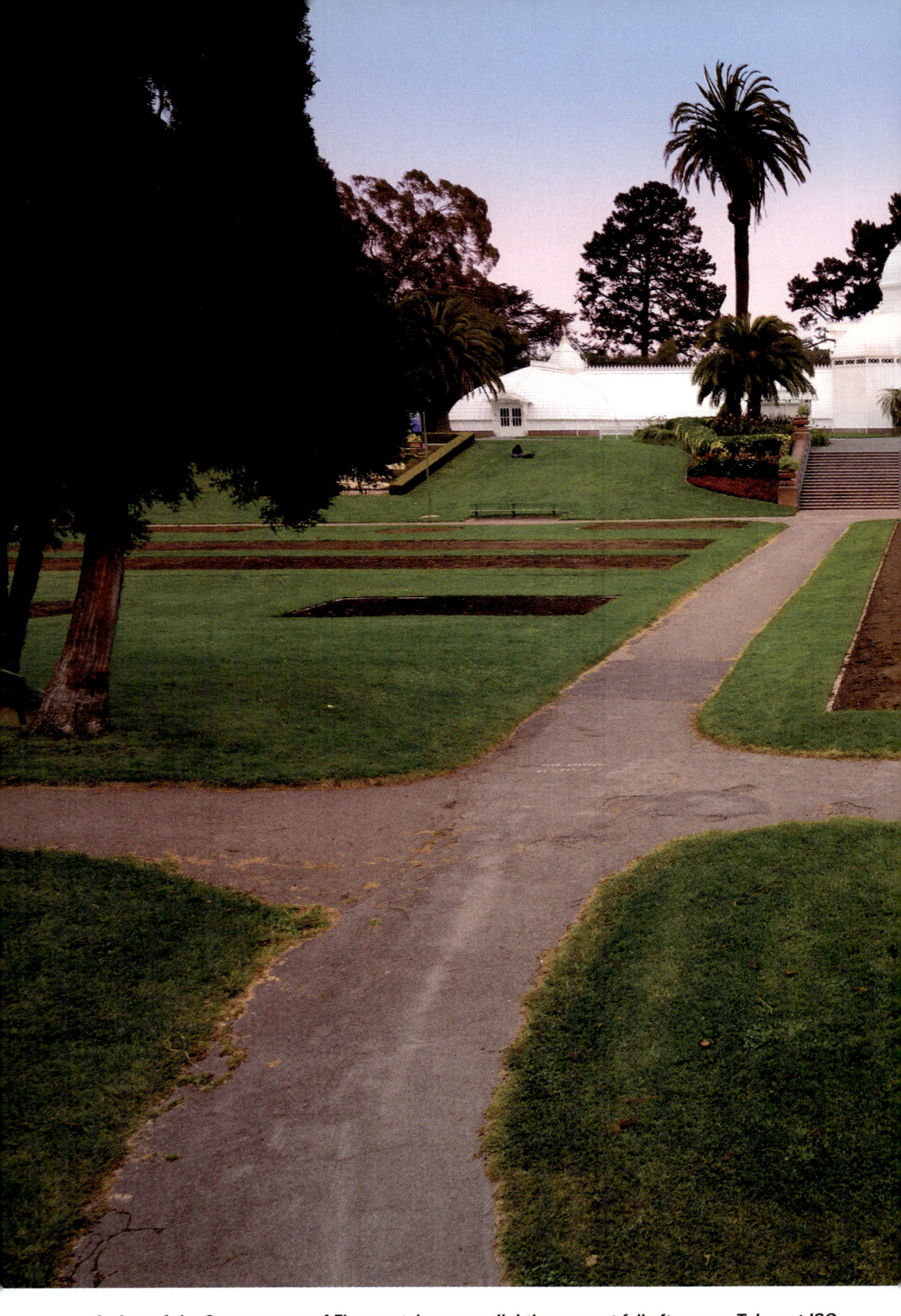

A view of the Conservatory of Flowers taken on a slightly overcast fall afternoon. Taken at ISO 200, f/8, 1/50 second with a 14-24mm lens.

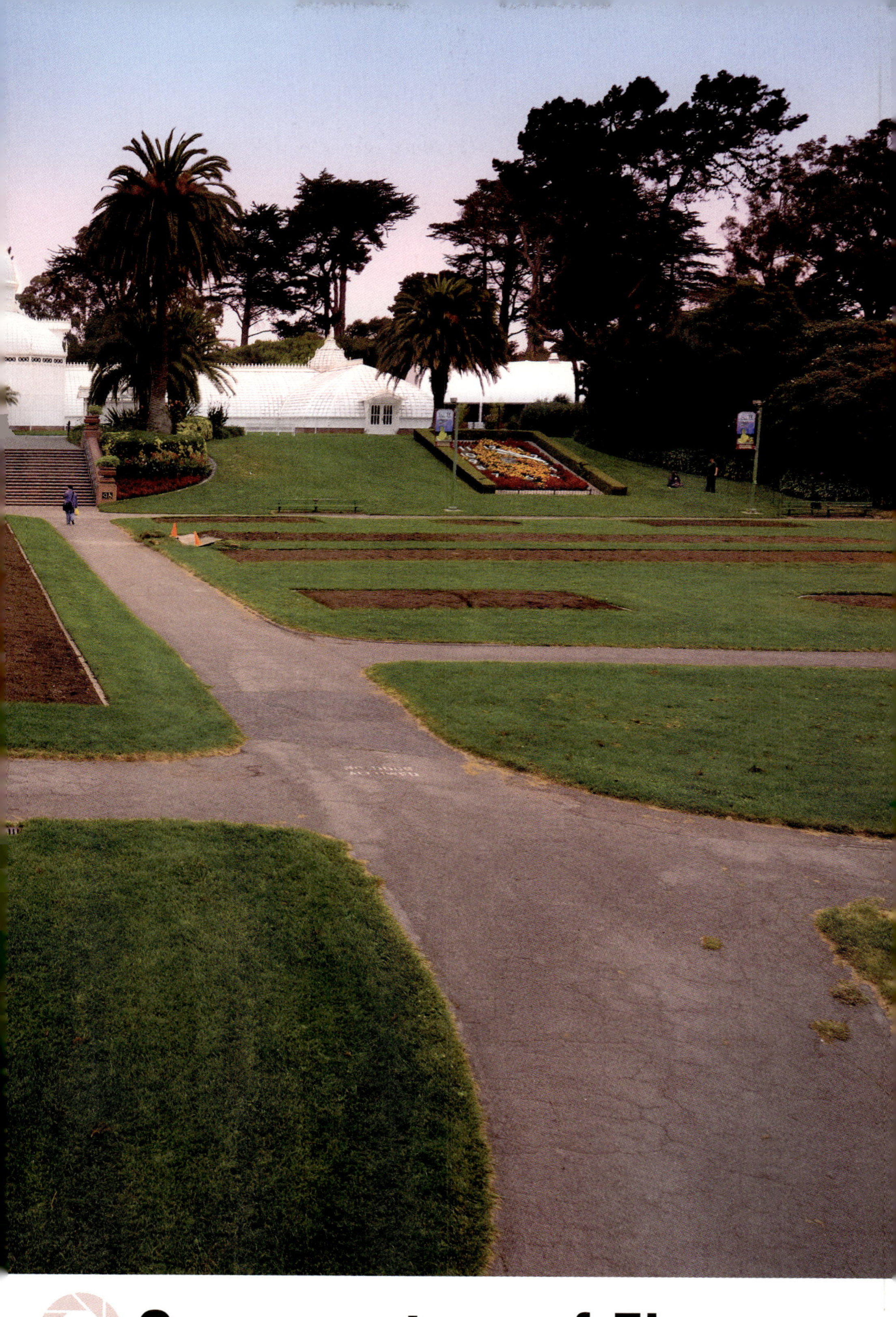

6 Conservatory of Flowers

Why It's Worth a Photograph

The Conservatory of Flowers is a large Victorian greenhouse in San Francisco's Golden Gate Park. The conservatory has a central dome rising nearly 60 feet high and arch wings extending from it for a length of 240 feet. It sits on top of a gentle slope overlooking Conservatory Valley. It is the oldest building in Golden Gate Park and the oldest wooden conservatory remaining in the United States. The Conservatory of Flowers is listed on the National Register of Historic Places. This conservatory houses hundreds of rare and exotic specimens that offer you a wonderful opportunity to photograph plants, flowers, and butterflies you may never see outside this location.

Where Can I Get the Best Shot?

To get the best shots, I recommend two places. The first is inside the Conservatory of Flowers (see A on the map); the second is on John F Kennedy Drive (see B on the map).

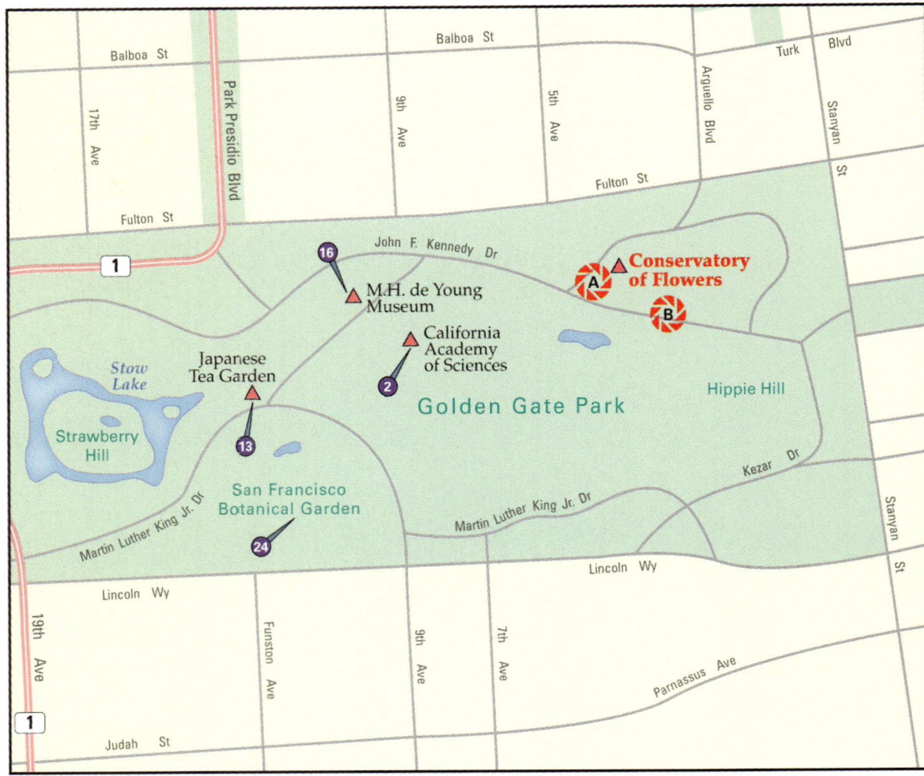

The best locations from which to photograph the Conservatory of Flowers: (A) inside the Conservatory, (B) John F Kennedy Drive. Other photo ops: (2) California Academy of Sciences, (13) Japanese Tea Garden, (16) M.H. de Young Museum, (24) San Francisco Botanical Garden.

Inside the conservatory

The Conservatory of Flowers features four permanent galleries. Plants are rotated into the galleries as they bloom, so you can always expect to be able to photograph the plants at their peak. The conservatory is also a host of special exhibits each year, giving photographers a wonderful opportunity to photograph something new each time they visit (see figures 6.1 and 6.2).

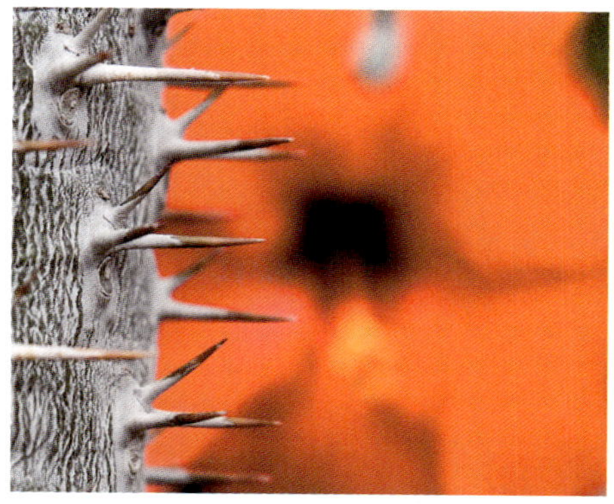

6.1 A photo of a wonderfully spiny cactus sitting in front of a colorful flower in the conservatory (see A on the map). Taken at ISO 100, f/4, 1/60 second with a 100mm lens.

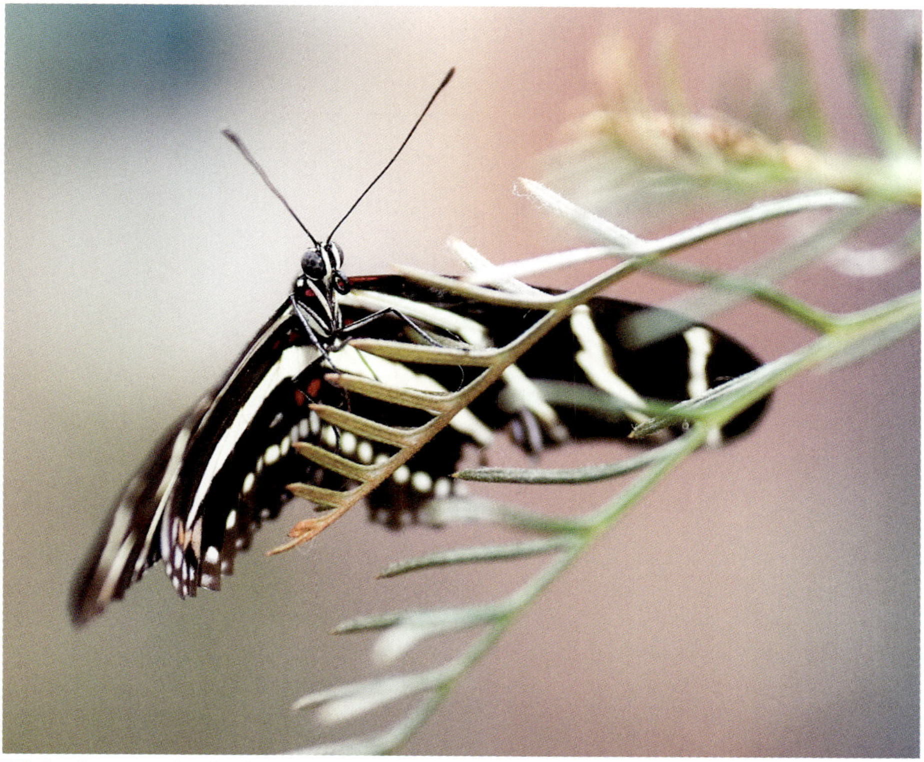

6.2 A photograph of a butterfly. Taken at ISO 100, f/2.5, 1/200 second with a 135mm lens.

John F Kennedy Drive

John F Kennedy Drive runs along the outside of the conservatory and can offer many wonderful angles to shoot from. The first and foremost is directly in front. During the spring and early summer months, the flower garden located between JFK drive and the conservatory offer a wonderful variety of colorful flowers to use as a foreground subject. A wonderful tunnel that leads under the road offers an interesting perspective when photographing the conservatory (see figure 6.3).

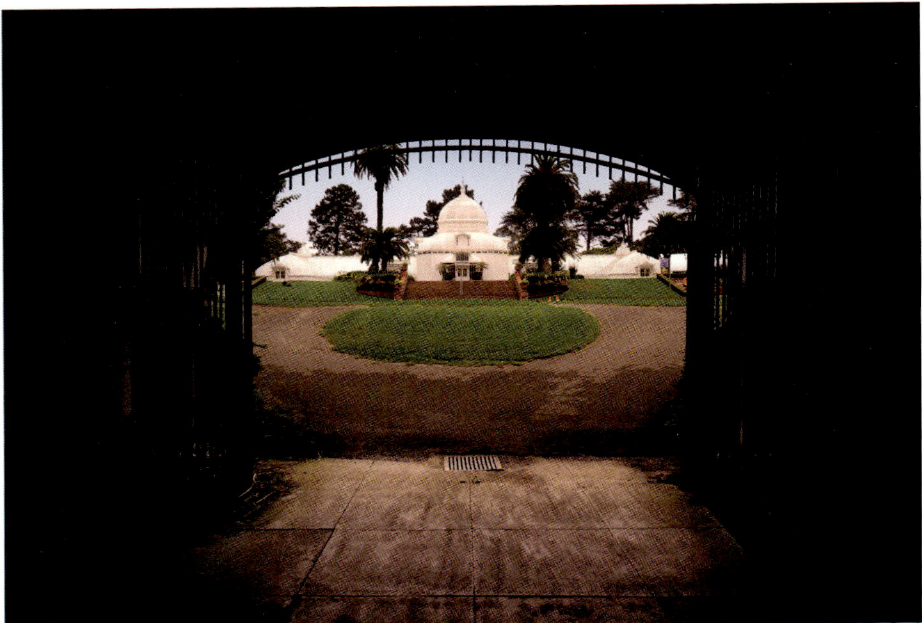

6.3 A view of the Conservatory of Flowers taken from a tunnel on an overcast autumn afternoon (see B on the map). Taken at ISO 200, f/11, 1/50 second with a 14-24mm lens.

How Can I Get the Best Shot?

Bring a macro lens to get in close, or a lens with a large aperture of f/1.2. to f/1.8 for a truly unique perspective. When photographing inside the conservatory, a tripod is not allowed, so crank up the ISO and use a larger aperture. The conservatory is made out of white frosted glass that acts as a big diffusion dome that softens the light. When shooting outside, use a wide lens and the wonderful landscaping that the flower garden offers to lead the viewer's eye to the conservatory.

Equipment

A macro lens and a prime lens with a large aperture or short zoom lenses are the pieces of equipment you want to bring.

Lenses

To photograph at the Conservatory of Flowers, I recommend the following lenses:

- **A macro lens.** This lens is specifically designed for close photography. A macro lens allows you to get extremely close to your subject creating a 1:1 life size image on your sensor. These lenses are extremely sharp and capture an enormous amount of detail.
- **A standard zoom lens in the 24-100mm range.** This lens can give you much more versatility when traveling. Most of these lenses come with some form of image stabilization and allow for a close working distance, which can be important when photographing flowers.
- **A fast prime/fixed focal length lens.** A fast prime/fixed focal length lens does not zoom. These lenses come in many focal lengths, and the most common lengths are 24, 35, 50, and 85mm. These lenses offer apertures much larger and come in a smaller package then most zooms. The benefit of these lenses is they allow you to shoot in much dimmer light due to the lens's light-gathering capability. These lenses tend to be very sharp and smaller than your average zooms.

Extras

A flash could be helpful when shooting inside. For the best results if using a pop-up flash, reduce the flash exposure so you don't have that flashed look. You want enough light to just fill in the shadows and still look natural. I recommend taking it down to 1/2 power. If using a removable speedlight flash, point the flash upward so that you can expose the entire area and not just the subject. Extension tubes are another handy tool that you can use instead of a macro lens. These tubes come in a variety of sizes and mount directly to the camera and a standard lens. The extension tubes allow you to focus much closer than normal, replicating what a macro lens does but at less cost.

Camera settings

Setting up your camera for shooting flowers comes down to what you want to achieve. I love the artsy look of a shallow depth of field and incredibly blurred background created by using a wide open aperture on a prime lens.

- **Exposure mode.** I set my camera in Aperture Priority mode and let my camera choose the shutter speed. I may dial in a plus or minus exposure compensation depending on the overall scene. When shooting inside the building, I dialed in a +1/3 to +2/3 exposure compensation to help expose the shadow areas.
- **White balance.** White balance I never touch as I find the Auto White Balance setting of all modern-day cameras to be pretty good.
- **ISO.** ISO needs to be bumped up to create shutter speeds that you can hand hold. A flash can help reduce your ISO to a lower number.

Exposure

Exposing inside can be tricky with or without a flash. Try to balance the ambient light or background light with the light that is on your subject, to create a photo that does not look flashed or underexposed.

Ideal time to shoot

The Conservatory of Flowers is open during normal business hours so shooting in the wee morning or late evening isn't going to happen unless you know someone. It's not as much about the time of day as it is about the light. Plan your trip when you have clear skies — the blue sky and the white building can look stunning together.

Working around the weather

If all you want to do is photograph the exterior of the building, plan your trip in the spring to early summer. The flowers that surround the building are in full bloom this time of year. If you're interested in shooting the wonderful specimens inside the conservatory, go during regular business hours.

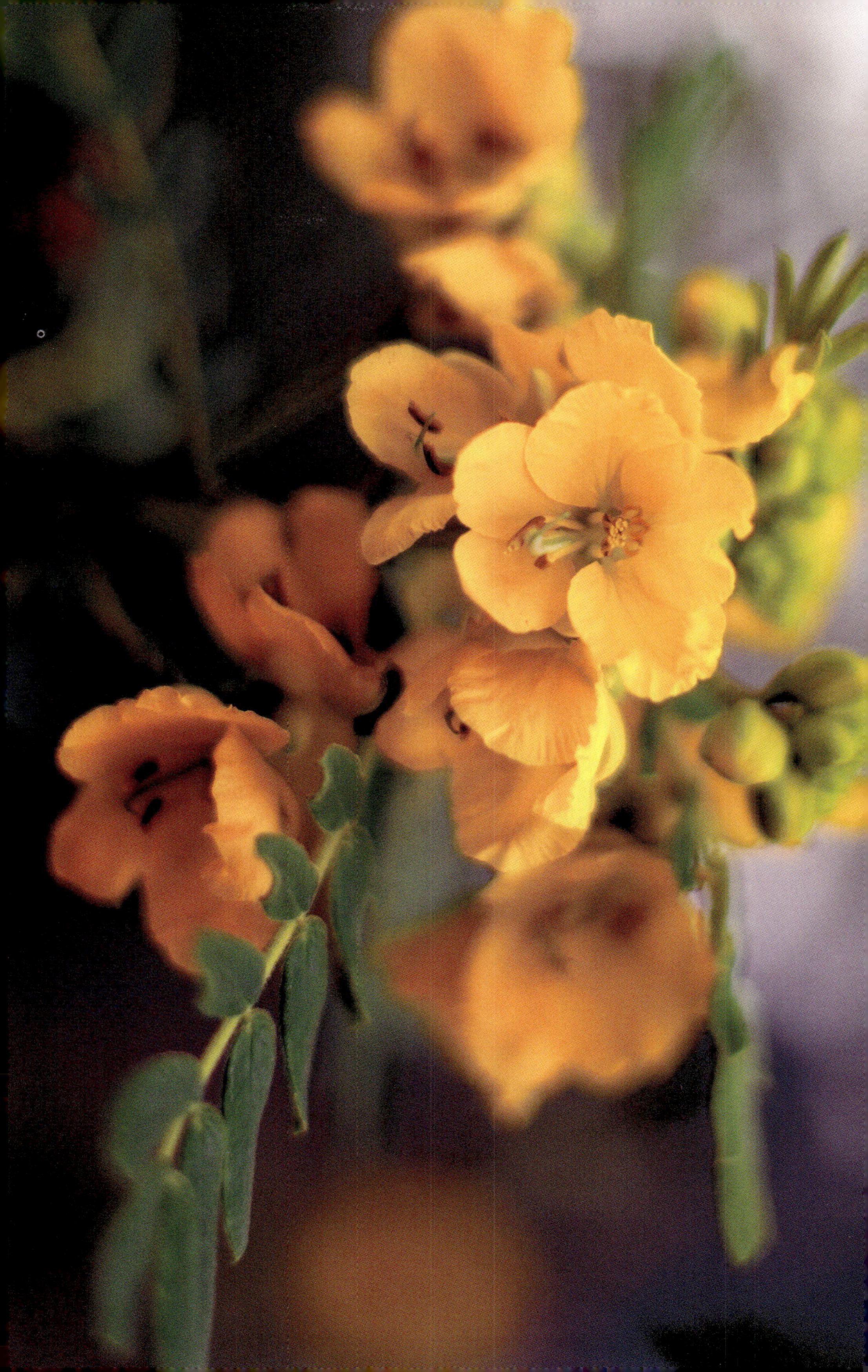

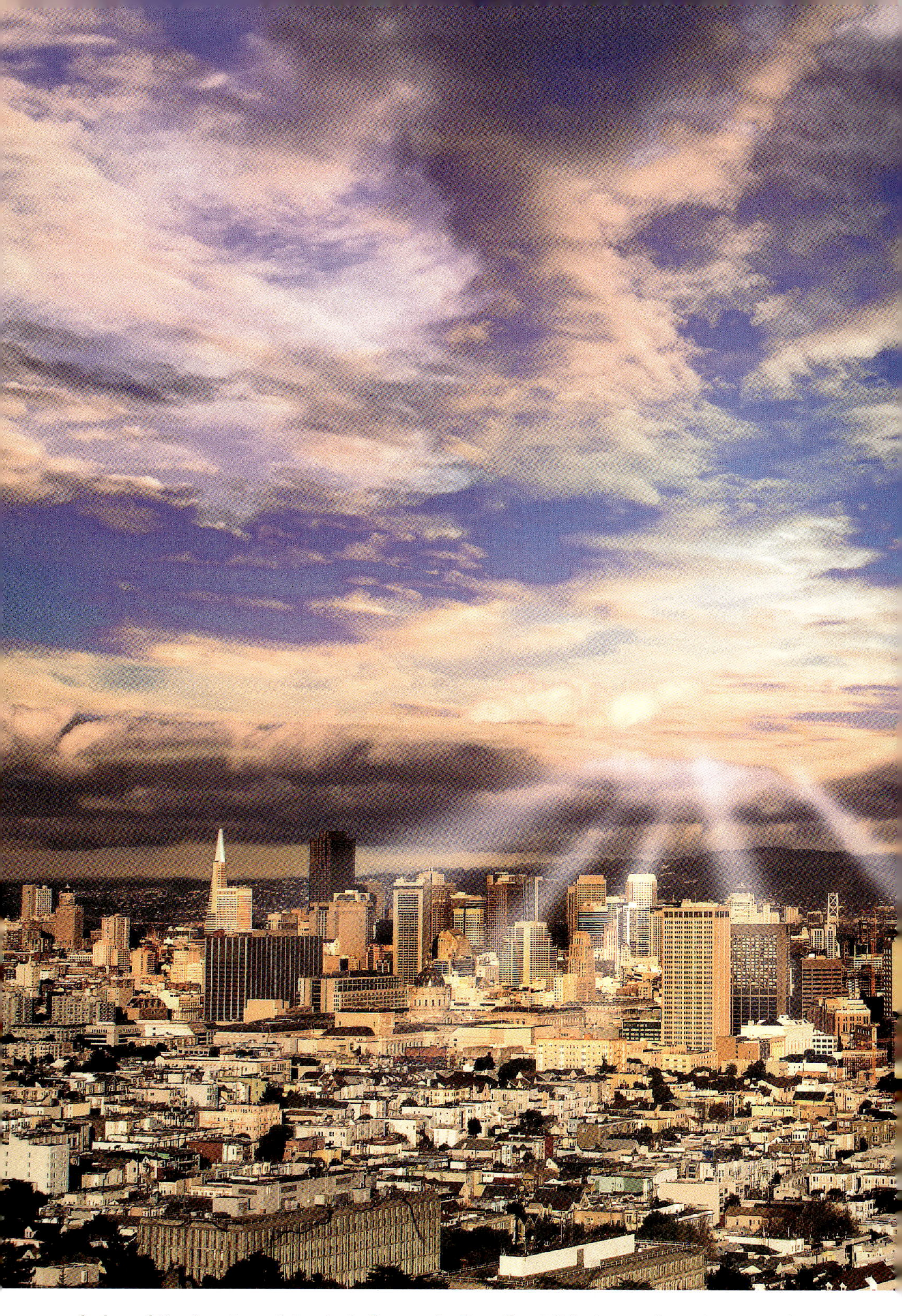

A view of the downtown taken just after sunrise from Randall Park on a clear winter morning. The sunburst effect was added in post-processing. Taken at ISO 100, f/11, 1/320 second with a 24-70mm lens.

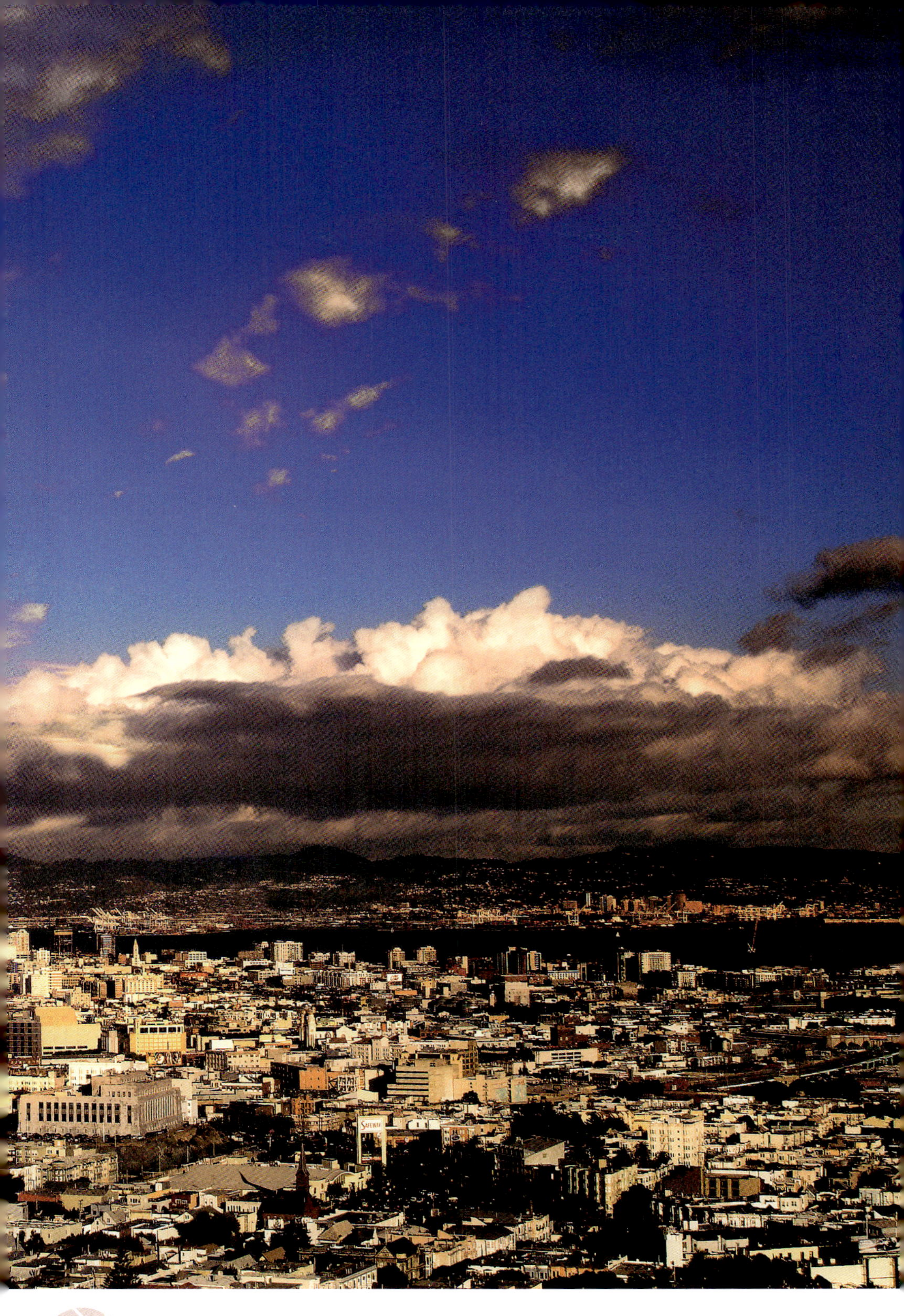

7 Downtown

Why It's Worth a Photograph

San Francisco is a unique and breathtaking city, known for its exquisite landscape, steep hills, and bay views. The city takes pride in its many unrivaled attractions, famous museums, and its unique neighborhoods that are like small towns within the city. Each of these small neighborhoods has a variety of sites, shops, and restaurants that reflect the city's great ethnic and cultural diversity. One of San Francisco's greatest assets is the combination of old and new architecture. If you have the time, spend an hour or so walking around downtown. Take your time and look around and take it all in. The city has so much to offer a photographer — breathtaking views, unparalleled skyline, a mixture of modern and Art Deco architecture — that you will have no shortage of inspiration.

Where Can I Get the Best Shot?

You can photograph downtown from many vantage points. Some of these places reside outside the downtown proper, allowing you to create beautiful photographs of the city skyline. A couple of the places involve short strolls around the downtown area, where you can find many great opportunities to photograph. Every time I go out, I find something new to photograph.

Use your imagination and look all around. You never know what you'll discover. What you may see may be entirely different from what I see. In all my years of living in San Francisco, the best locations to capture great photos of San Francisco's downtown include Market and Beale Street, Sacramento at Battery Street, Treasure Island, Twin Peaks, Randall Museum, and the Golden Gate Bridge Vista parking lot (see A–F on the map).

Market Street and Beale Street

Market Street at Beale Street is a great central location to capture your typical downtown photographs. Don't just focus on the buildings; look at the cable cars, light posts, and seasonal decorations that regularly dot the city. One of my favorite architectural features is the retro style light posts that are all along Market Street.

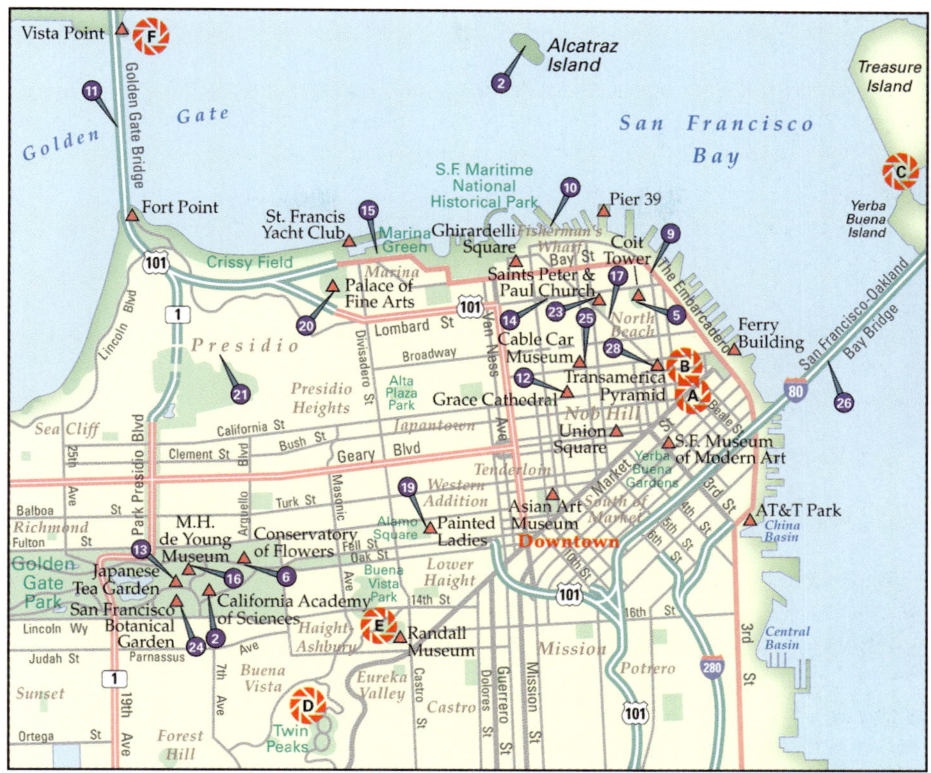

The best locations from which to photograph downtown: (A) Market Street and Beale Street, (B) Sacramento Street and Battery Street, (C) Treasure Island, (D) Twin Peaks, (E) Randall Museum, (F) Golden Gate Bridge Vista parking lot. Other photo ops: (2) California Academy of Sciences, (5) Coit Tower, (6) Conservatory of Flowers, (9) Embarcadero, (10) Fisherman's Wharf, (11) Golden Gate Bridge, (12) Grace Cathedral, (13) Japanese Tea Garden, (14) Lombard Street, (15) Marina Green, (16) M.H. de Young Museum, (17) North Beach, (19) Painted Ladies, (20) Palace of Fine Arts, (21) Presidio of San Francisco, (23) Saints Peter and Paul Church, (24) San Francisco Botanical Garden, (25) San Francisco cable cars, (26) San Francisco-Oakland Bay Bridge, (28) Transamerica Pyramid.

By using a long lens, you can isolate one of these light posts (see figure 7.1). The long lens combined with a large aperture helps create separation from the buildings behind. Every winter San Francisco, like many other cities, decorates the cityscape in festive seasonal decorations (see figure 7.2).

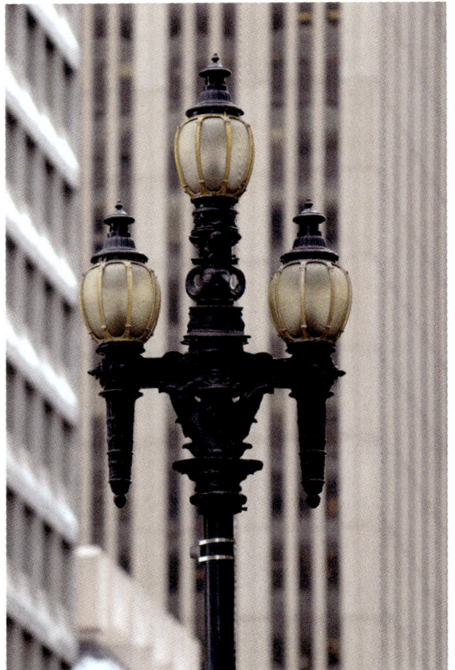

7.1 A view of downtown architecture taken on a fall day (see A on the map). Taken at ISO 100, f/2.8, 1/320 second with a 70-200mm lens.

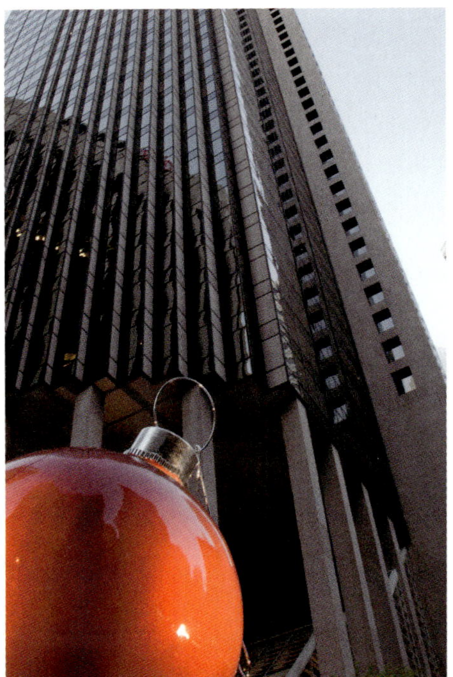

7.2 A view of a downtown building with holiday decorations taken on a winter morning. Taken at ISO 200, f/11, 1/6 second with a 24mm lens.

Sacramento Street and Battery Street

One of my favorite things to photograph in downtown San Francisco is a staircase located in the Embarcadero 3 building on Sacramento Street at Battery Street. This staircase has such an abstract presence when photographed from above. The straight lines of the bars, the spiraling staircase, checkered tile, and green fern create a photo with great lines, pattern, and color (see figure 7.3).

Treasure Island

Treasure Island is one of the premier locations to photograph the San Francisco skyline. Located halfway between Oakland and San Francisco, the only way to get to this location is by crossing the San Francisco-Oakland Bay Bridge. What makes Treasure Island the perfect location is the incredible full panoramic view you get of the city and its surrounding areas. If you decide to photograph the city in the morning, you can capture the incredible low, warm light that accentuates the details and creates wonderful depth and subtle shadows (see figure 7.4). If you are not available in the morning, early evening just before the sun sets can be perfect as the low, hot sun sets behind the city. Warm hues and intense saturation explode outward and upward from the city, creating a wonderful silhouette (see figure 7.5).

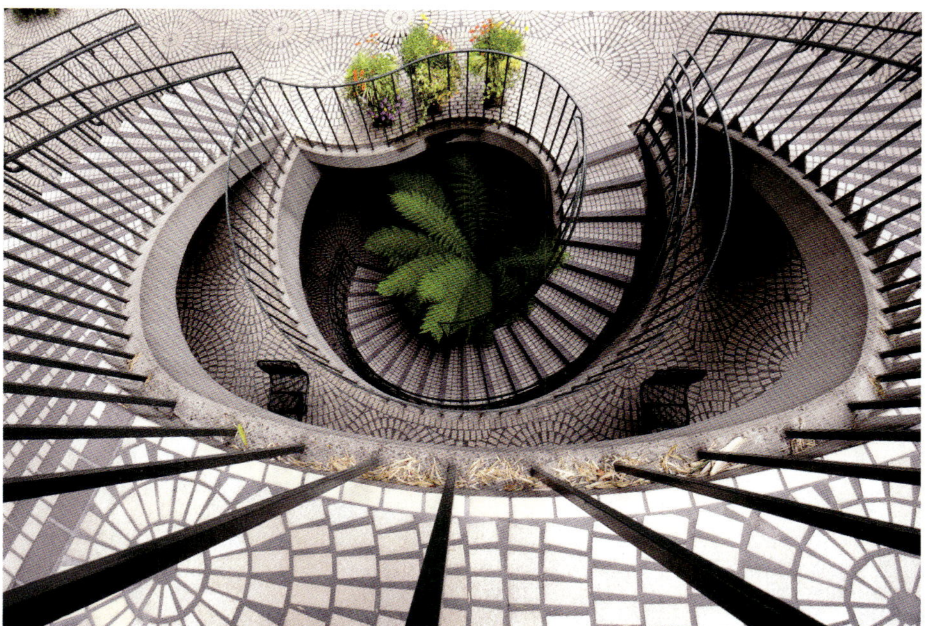

7.3 A photo of downtown architecture taken on an overcast summer afternoon (see B on the map). Taken at ISO 200, F22, for 1/20 second with a 14-24mm lens.

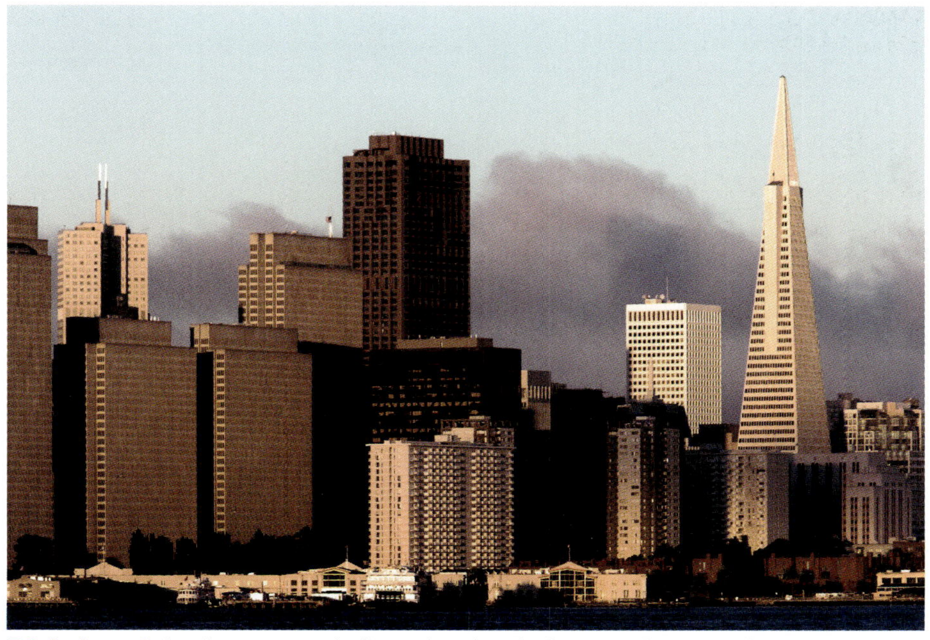

7.4 A view of the downtown skyline taken just before sunrise on a clear summer morning (see C on the map). Taken at ISO 100, f/8, 1/100 second with a 70-200mm lens.

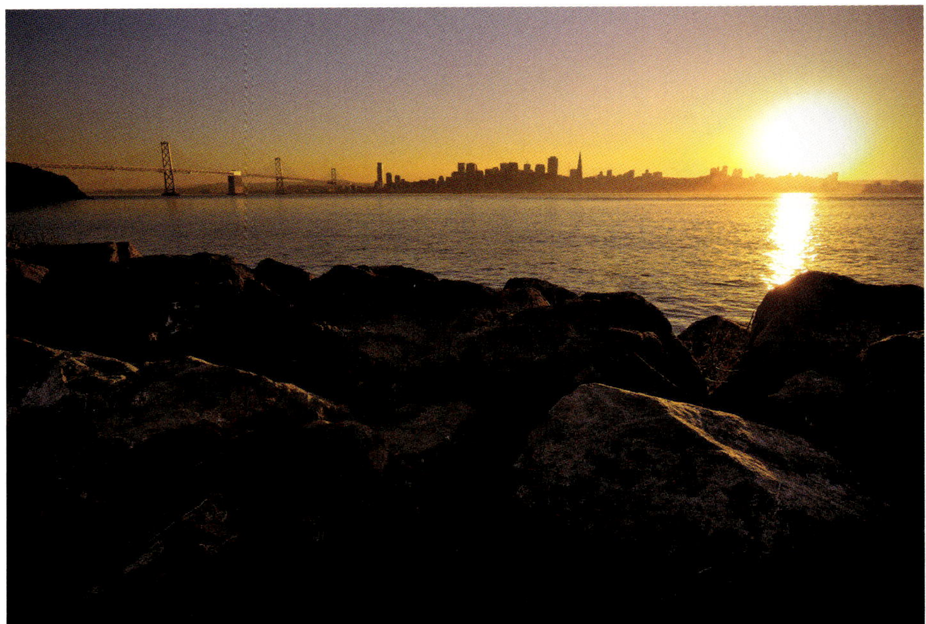

7.5 A view of an intensely lit downtown skyline taken on a clear fall evening just before sunset. Taken at ISO 80, f/16, 1/60 second with a 14-24mm lens.

Twin Peaks

Twin Peaks are two hills with an elevation of about 922 feet situated at the center of San Francisco. The two peaks have a north-south orientation and are divided by Twin Peaks Boulevard, which is the only road leading up to the summit. The elevation of the peaks makes this vantage point an ideal place to capture a panoramic of the entire city of San Francisco, the bay, and surrounding areas. This location is perfect at any time of the day, but early morning or late in the day seems to be the best because the sun is less harsh and casts a warm light on the city (see figure 7.6).

Randall Museum

This location is one of the best and most unknown locations in the city from which to capture an early morning sunrise. The Randall Museum is located in Corona Heights Park on a large hill between the Castro and Haight districts of San Francisco and boasts stunning views of the city, downtown financial district, and the bay. This premier photo location is a hidden gem with hardly a dog walker out before the sun comes up. The vantage point is perched high above the city and offers a 360-degree view of the entire city. The proximity makes this location perfect for early morning spring and fall sunrises. The early morning sky treats you to a soft diffused light of reddish hues that create a perfect contrast between the city below and the sky above. Bring your standard zoom and a tripod because this low-light night shooting is impossible to hand hold (see figure 7.7).

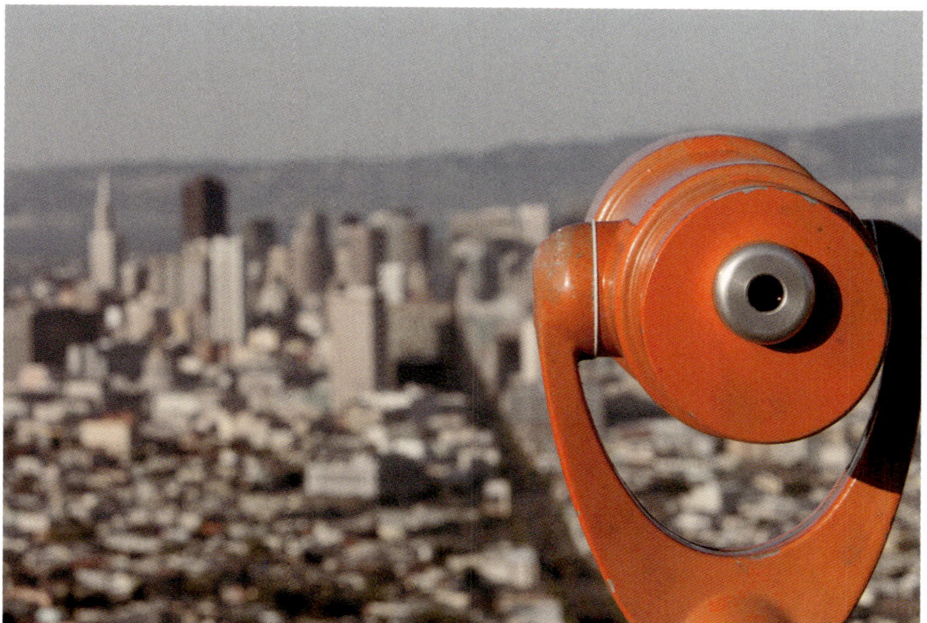

7.6 A view of the downtown skyline on a clear spring day (see D on the map). Taken at ISO 100, f/16, 1/100 second with a 70-200mm lens.

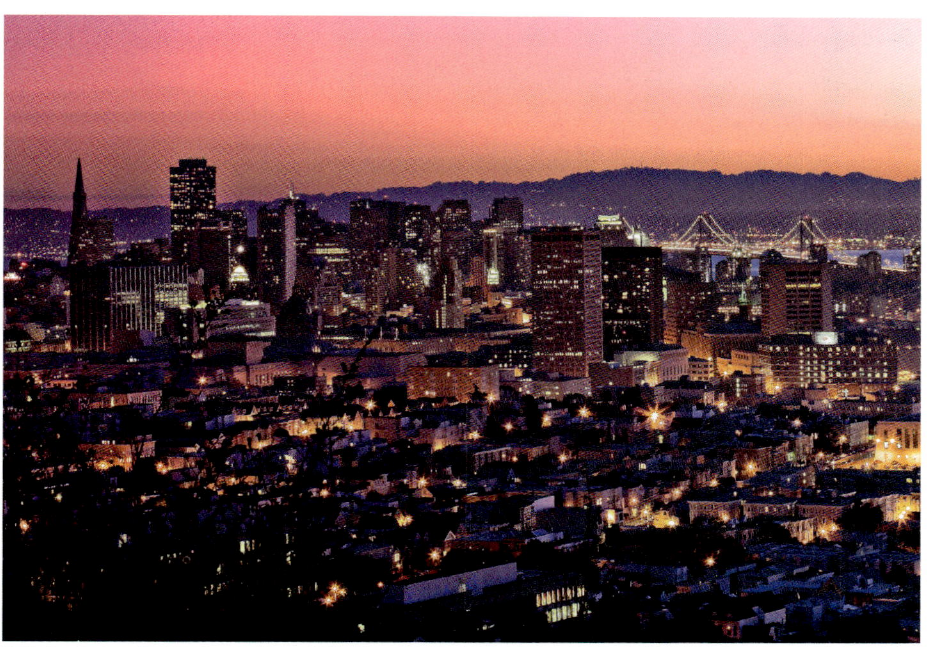

7.7 A view of the downtown skyline at sunrise on a clear fall morning (see E on the map). Taken at ISO 100, f/16, 30 seconds with a 24-70mm lens.

Golden Gate Bridge Vista Parking Lot

North Vista Point is located on the right side of the Golden Gate as you exit the Golden Gate Bridge in Marin. Take the first exit and pull into the parking lot. From this location, set your camera up along the stone wall at the rear of the parking lot. The vantage point is ideal for shooting back across the bay toward the city. If you shoot from here as the sun is coming up, in one image you can capture both a dramatic silhouette of San Francisco and an early morning fireball of exploding light flaring across the bay. I recommend that you bring a lens in the 70-300mm range and a sturdy tripod because the low-lighting conditions cause slower shutter speeds (see figure 7.8).

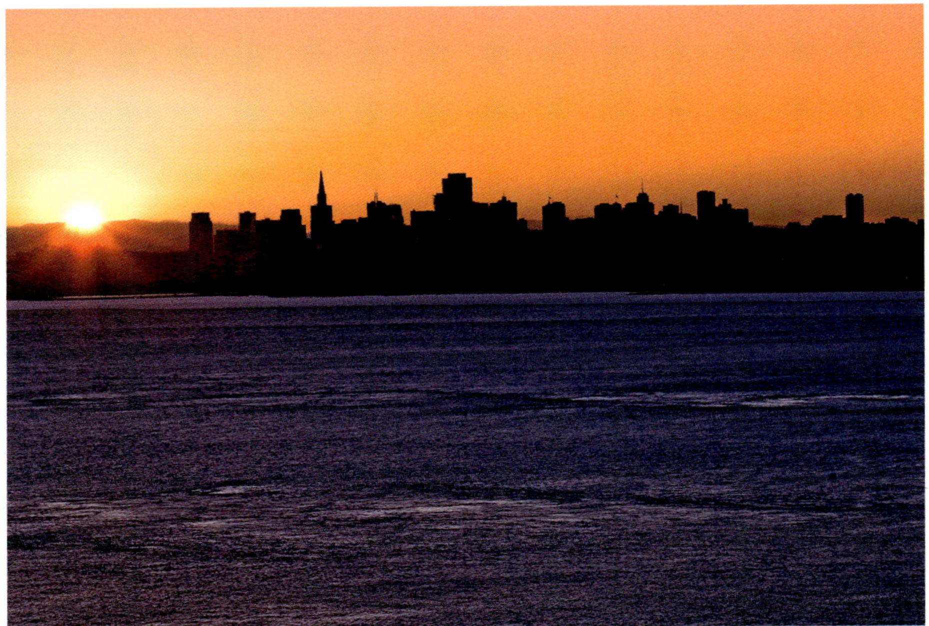

7.8 A view of the city of San Francisco immersed in a wonderful orange sunrise on a clear winter morning (see F on the map). Taken at ISO 100, f/8, 1/100 second with a 24-70mm lens.

How Can I Get the Best Shot?

Good light is the key to making an average photo great. Shooting images of the city is best done on clear mornings or evenings when the sun is low, soft, and warm. This light creates colorful dramatic skies when shooting the city from Treasure Island, Twin Peaks, Randall Museum, and the North Vista Point parking lot. When shooting from the downtown locations, foggy or slightly overcast conditions are ideal for creating soft diffused light void of harsh shadows.

Equipment

Most photographers like equipment (I know I do.) In addition to my dSLR, I bring an assortment of lenses, filters, and a sturdy tripod.

Lenses

Lens choice is important to ensure that you have the perfect focal length for each location. Whether you are shooting day or night, using the correct lens helps you create the ideal composition for any given subject.

- **Ultrawide-angle lens in the 14-24mm range.** The ultrawide lens gives you the ability to capture a downtown scene due to its wide field of view. When you are trying to capture tall buildings or entire cityscapes, this lens gives you more flexibility, which enables you to be more creative. When using an ultrawide lens, you must be wary about including elements on the outer edge of the frame that you may not want.
- **A standard zoom lens in the 24-100mm range.** This lens can give you much more versatility when traveling. A zoom lens in this range is generally considered the perfect walk-around lens for capturing anything from landscapes or cityscapes to pictures of the family.
- **A long telephoto lens somewhere in the 70-300mm range.** This lens allows you the ability to isolate a particular subject, such as San Francisco from Treasure Island or a lamp post on a street corner.

Filters

There are two primary filters I use when photographing San Francisco: a circular polarizing filter and a neutral density filter.

- **Circular polarizing filter.** A circular polarizing filter is a filter I suggest every photographer have in his bag. The polarizing filter's main purpose is to cut down or eliminate glare on water, glass, and metal. You can also use it to enhance color and contrast in your photos. I use it primarily to bring out the blue sky in my photos. A polarizer is best used on a lens that is not wider then 24mm because it can cause the sky to be unevenly polarized. A polarizer can come in handy downtown by preventing reflections from glass and metal.
- **Neutral density filter.** A neutral density (ND) filter allows you to shoot at a larger aperture when the sun is at its brightest but also allows you to slow your shutter speed by 2 or more stops. I have two neutral density filters: one is a 3-stop, while the other is a 10-stop. An ND filter is perfect for shooting the sun setting or rising behind the city because it allows you to expose the sky and city correctly.

Extras

A sturdy tripod is a must for night shots and low-light shooting. I also recommend a cable release. The advantage of using a cable release is that it allows you to shoot longer exposures and not have to trigger the shutter by touching the camera, which can cause camera shake and affect the quality of your photograph.

Camera settings

Capturing great images of sunsets and sunrises is achieved in Manual mode. Set your aperture and then dial in the correct shutter speed. You may need to tweak the shutter speed to get the desired exposure. Remember, exposure is not just about the correct light, it is also about creating a mood.

- **Exposure mode.** I shoot in Manual mode when a tricky lighting condition causes my meter to underexpose or overexpose. For all cityscapes, I set my camera to Manual and dial in the aperture and shutter speed, which can give me the creative exposure I am looking for. I check the histogram on the back of the camera until I achieve my correct exposure. When shooting downtown, I use Aperture Priority mode and adjust the exposure compensation when needed.

- **Exposure compensation.** Exposure compensation is a handy setting that you can use to adjust exposure — plus means more light and minus means less light. In general, most cameras allow at least a 3-stop difference either direction. I tend to use exposure compensation in many situations. In these situations, I dial in a +1 or +2 to allow more light into the camera to properly expose my subject. I dial in a minus exposure compensation when shooting silhouettes because this aids in darkening the sky and creates a wonderful silhouette.
- **White balance.** White balance stays on the Auto White Balance setting for all shooting. If I decide to change it, I will change it in post-processing.
- **ISO.** I keep my ISO as low as possible to maximize image quality. In general for shooting landscapes, lower ISO value is better.

Exposure

Exposing during the day should not be an issue for most modern cameras. After the sun gets low, metering becomes a bit trickier. At times like these, I switch to Manual mode. I set the aperture to my desired setting and adjust the shutter speed until I see on the histogram on the back of my camera the ideal balance between shadows and highlights. This balance is what makes the difference between a poorly exposed photo and one you want to show your friends.

For more information on histograms, see Chapter 1.

Ideal time to shoot

The ideal time to shoot is just before and just after the sun rises or sets. The hour just after the sun rises and just before the sun sets is known as the *golden hour* of light. Typically, lighting is softer and warmer in hue and shadows are longer. Just before the sun comes up and just after the sun goes down is also an ideal time to shoot because the night sky is a dusky blue, known as the *blue hour*. If you shoot the San Francisco skyline, doing so at these times you can capture some truly dramatic skies.

Working around the weather

San Francisco has a Mediterranean-like climate with mild, wet winters and dry, cool summers. Because it is surrounded on three sides by water, San Francisco's weather can be unpredictable at times. The best months to photograph the skyline are the spring and fall as the skies are clearer and the days are warmer.

Low-light and night options

Treasure Island is the best vantage point to photograph downtown San Francisco. A long lens is a must as you want to be able to get in real tight to show the detail of the city at night. What makes this a great low-light location is the sky behind the city and the water that lies between Treasure Island and downtown. When shooting with very little light, your camera is forced to use a longer shutter speed to properly expose the dark night scene. Setting your camera in Aperture Priority mode with an aperture of f/8 creates a shutter speed of less than 2 seconds. Using this slow shutter speed turns clouds into wisps of smoke and the rough ocean into a smooth glass-like surface (see figure 7.9).

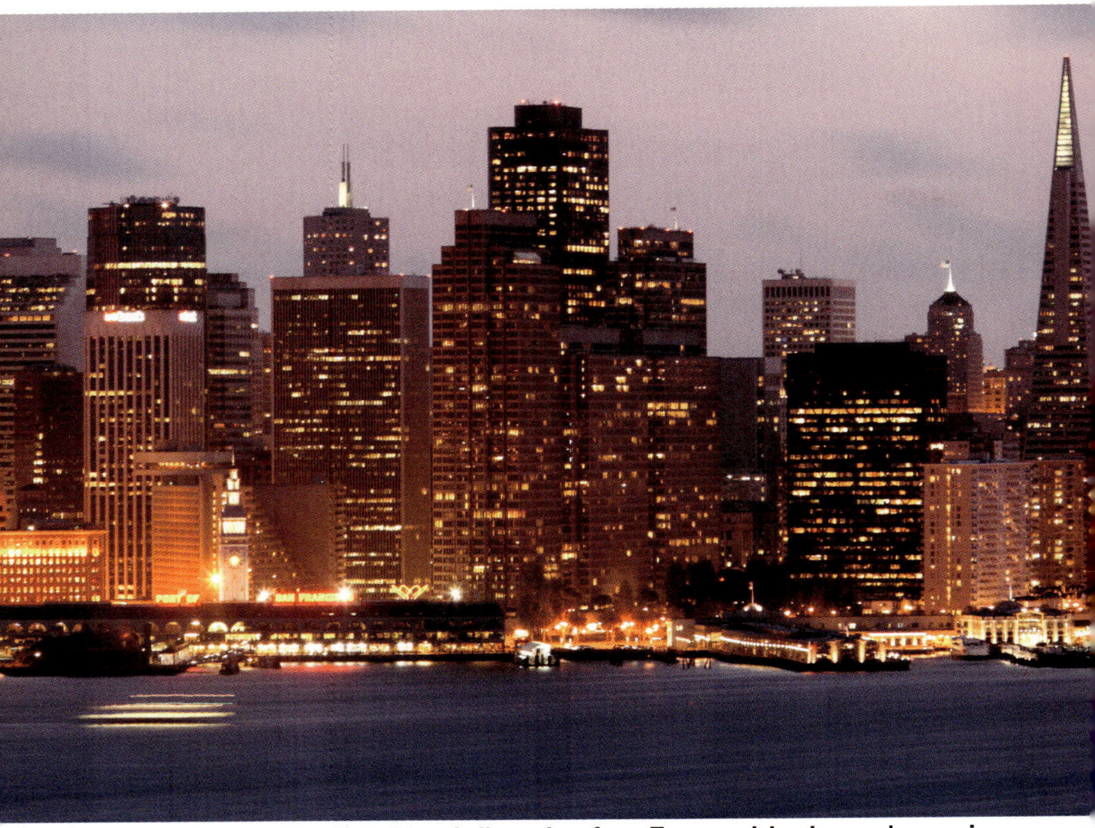

7.9 A view of the San Francisco skyline taken from Treasure Island on a clear spring evening (see C on the map). Taken at ISO 100, f/8, 13 seconds with a 70-200mm lens.

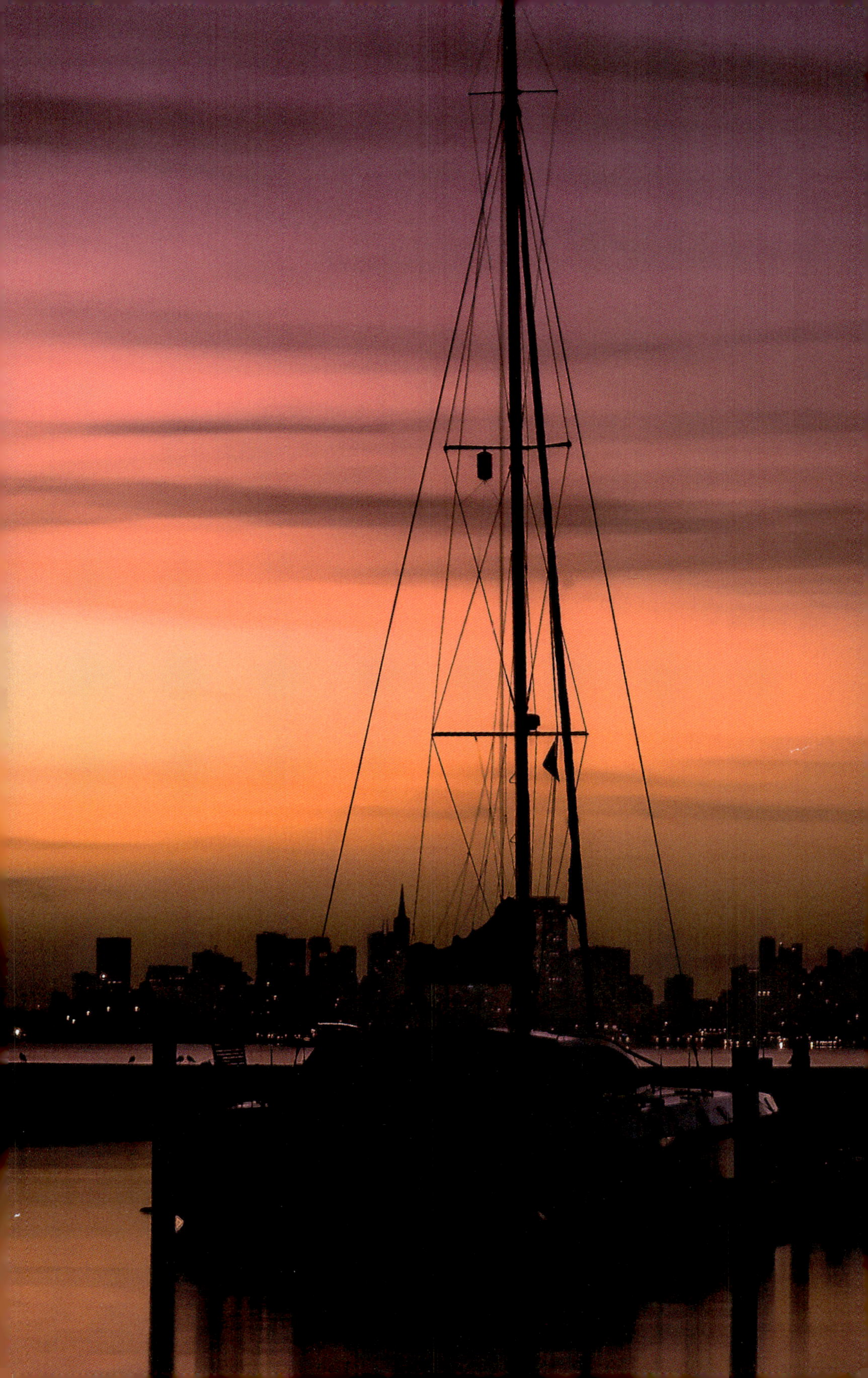

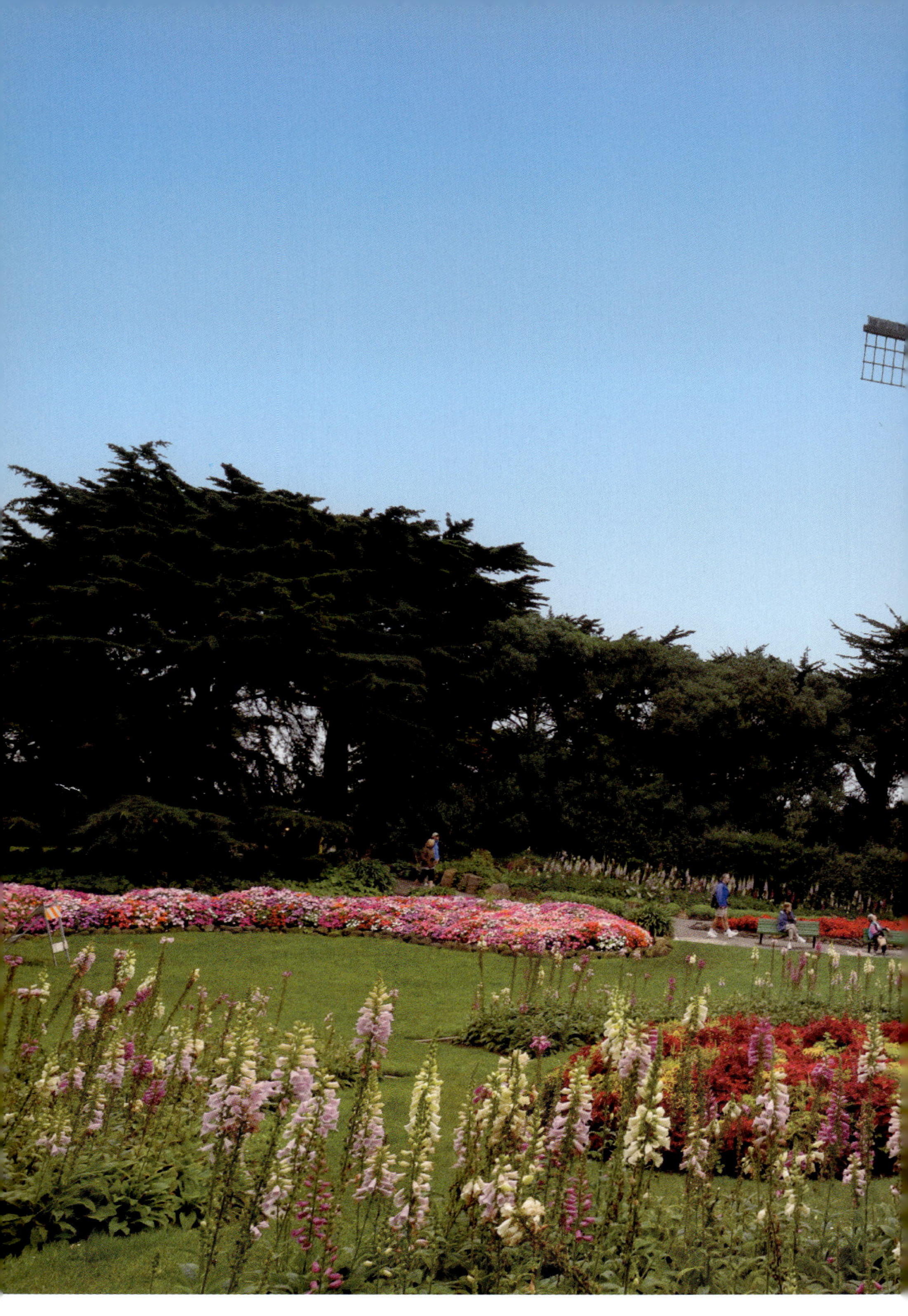

A view of the Dutch Windmill taken just before sunset on a clear summer evening. Taken at ISO 200, f/8, 1/125 second with a 14-24mm lens.

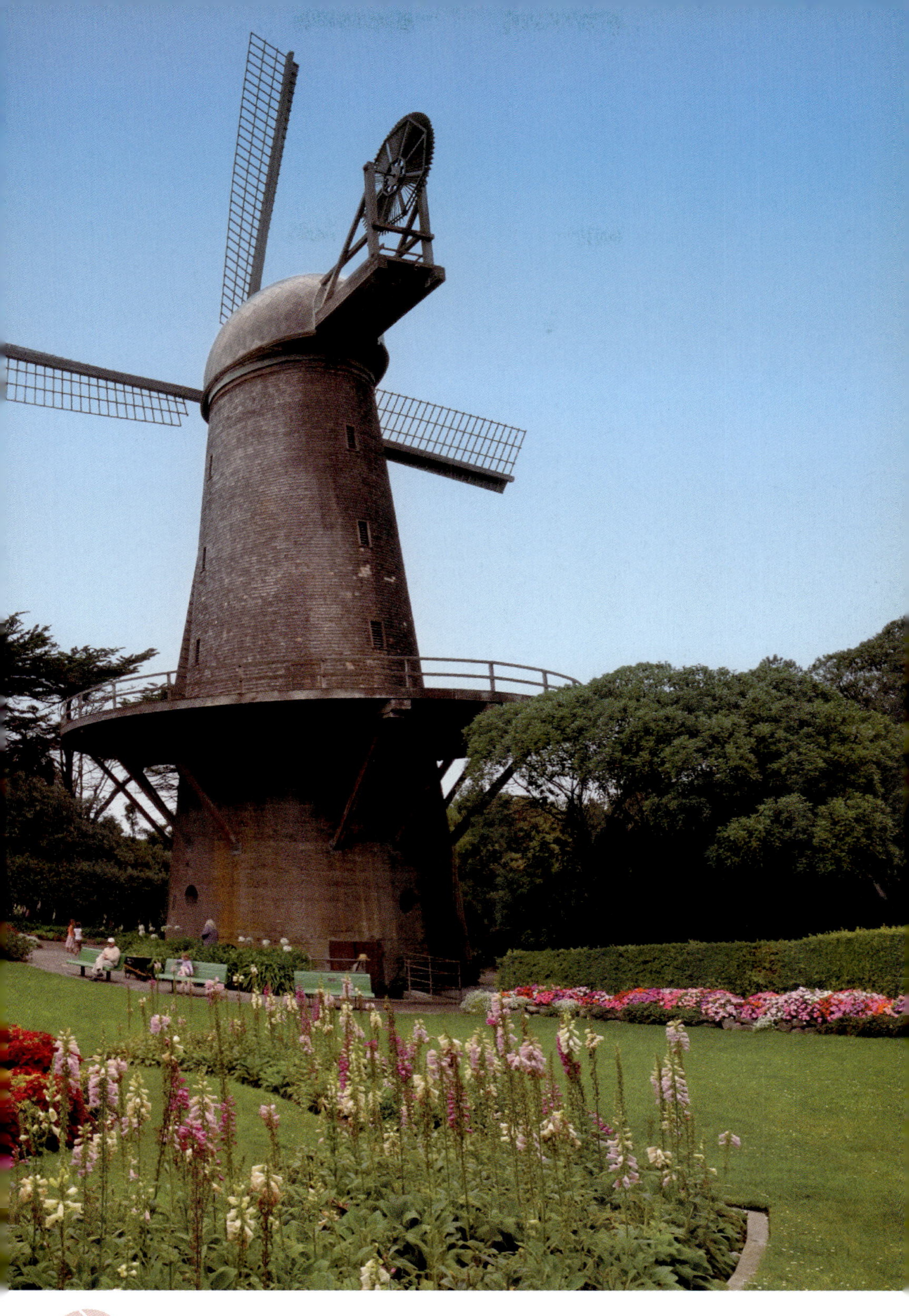

8 Dutch Windmill

Why It's Worth a Photograph

The world's largest Dutch windmill stands in Golden Gate Park just outside of San Francisco. The windmill is 75 feet tall with 102-foot long blades and was originally built in 1902 to pump fresh water to irrigate farms around the area. Surrounding the windmill is the Queen Wilhelmina Garden, which combined create one of the most picturesque spots in Golden Gate Park.

Where Can I Get the Best Shot?

Located at the western edge of Golden Gate Park, you find the Dutch Windmill a few hundred yards from the Pacific Ocean (see A on the map). The ideal place to photograph the windmill is from the small park where the windmill stands. From this vantage point, you have at least a half a dozen different locations to set up your tripod and photograph the windmill. What makes this such a wonderful location are the numerous flowers that lead up to and surround the windmill. Using an ultrawide-angle lens, you can create a wonderful leading line of colorful flowers that takes your eye right up to the windmill (see figure 8.1).

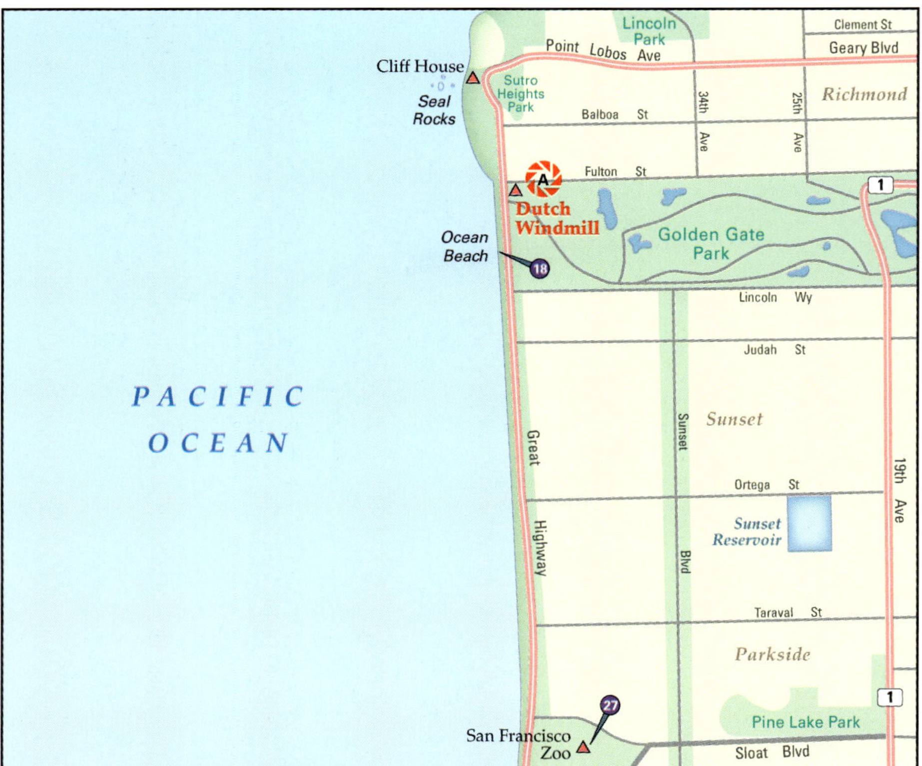

The best location from which to photograph the Dutch Windmill: (A) the grounds around the windmill. Other photo ops: (18) Ocean Beach, (27) San Francisco Zoo.

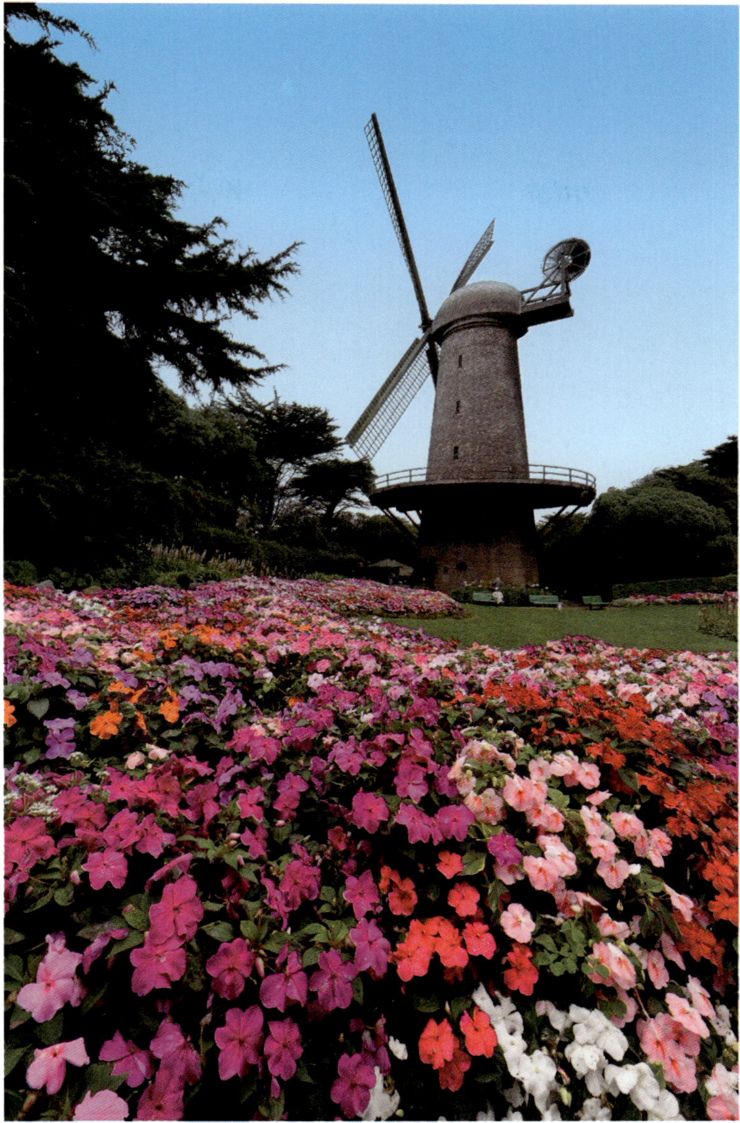

8.1 **A view of the Dutch Windmill taken just before sunset (see A on the map) on a clear summer afternoon. Taken at ISO 200, f/16, 1/60 seconds with a 14-24mm lens.**

How Can I Get the Best Shot?

Weather plays a huge part in capturing the best photo at this location. To ensure that you get the best shot, allow yourself enough time to set up your equipment. Make sure you arrive 30 minutes before the sun rises and plan to stay up to one hour after. Wander around the area to find the best composition. You can shoot the windmill from a half dozen different angles, each yielding a slightly different look.

Equipment

We photographers like having lots of gear, and for this location a tripod and a long telephoto or wide-angle lens are musts.

Lenses

Choosing which lens to use always comes down to your personal preference and what you want to convey in your photo. Whether you are shooting day or night, your lens choice is instrumental for creating the ideal composition for any given subject. My recommendations to photograph the Dutch Windmill are:

- **Ultrawide-angle lens in the 14-24mm range.** The ultrawide lens gives you the ability to create a composition in which you have something in the immediate foreground with the windmill in the background. Using this lens allows you to be more creative because you can include more elements in the final photograph. When using an ultrawide-angle lens, you must be wary about including elements on the outer edge of the frame that will distract from the composition.
- **A telephoto lens somewhere in the 70-300mm range.** By using this lens, you can isolate a particular subject, such as the mill, or you can shoot something far off in the distance.

Extras

A tripod is a must. Your shutter speed is slower due to the small f-stop (f/16-f/22) required to create a greater depth of field. I also recommend a cable release and bubble level. The advantage of using a cable release is it allows you to shoot longer exposures. A cable release will also allow you to trigger the shutter without touching the camera, which can cause camera shake and affect the quality of your photograph. A bubble level can help you level the camera so that you can prevent crooked shots.

Camera settings

How you set up your camera mostly depends on you and your shooting style or what you want to convey for that particular photo. The settings I have used for photographing the Dutch Windmill are based on the composition and the depth of field needed to capture the scene. When shooting the Dutch Windmill with an object in the immediate foreground, such as the flowers, you want to choose an aperture that renders sharpness from front to back. Therefore, choosing an aperture of f/16 to f/22 gives you enough depth of field to render the foreground and background sharp.

- **Exposure mode.** I set my camera in Aperture Priority mode and let the camera choose the shutter speed. I may dial in a plus exposure composition if the sky is so bright that the windmill is underexposing. In this situation, I may allow some of the sky to be overexposed in order to expose my main subject properly. I shoot in Manual mode when a tricky lighting condition causes my meter to under- or overexpose so much that I cannot correct it with exposure compensation.
- **White balance.** White balance I never touch because I find the Auto White Balance of all modern-day cameras to be pretty good.
- **ISO.** In general, to maximize the camera's image quality, I leave the ISO at 100 when shooting landscapes. The few times I have increased the ISO are to increase the shutter speed.

Exposure

Exposing the windmill and the sky evenly is the key to these photos. If the sky is foggy, then your camera will tend to underexpose from 1/3 to 2/3 of a stop. You will want to dial in a plus exposure compensation to expose the windmill correctly. This can be a bit of a balancing act as to what is more important, the sky or the windmill. On a clear blue day where the sun is low, exposing both the sky and windmill properly should not be difficult.

Ideal time to shoot

The ideal time to shoot is when the sun is low just after the sun rises or a day that is slightly overcast. When the sun is low, the top half of the windmill is lit with a soft, warm light, without creating any harsh shadow. A sky that is slightly overcast can help diffuse the harsh sun and create a soft lighting effect on the wonderful flowers that surround the windmill.

Working around the weather

Weather in San Francisco for the most part is not as much an issue as in other parts of the country. The weather at the Dutch Windmill is one of the exceptions. The windmill is located at the far west shore of San Francisco, adjacent to the Pacific Ocean. This is one of the coldest, windiest, and foggiest areas in San Francisco. November through February at the windmill is dominated by periodic rainstorms that blow in from the Pacific Ocean. As winter turns to spring, the weather can be much milder and quite pleasant. Summer months tend to have a combination of several clear and warm days, giving way to several foggy and cool days. July through October bring the highest average temperatures of the year to San Francisco and the longest series of clear skies. Plan your trip to the windmill accordingly. If it is foggy anywhere else in San Francisco, then you can be assured it will be foggy at the Dutch Windmill.

9 Embarcadero

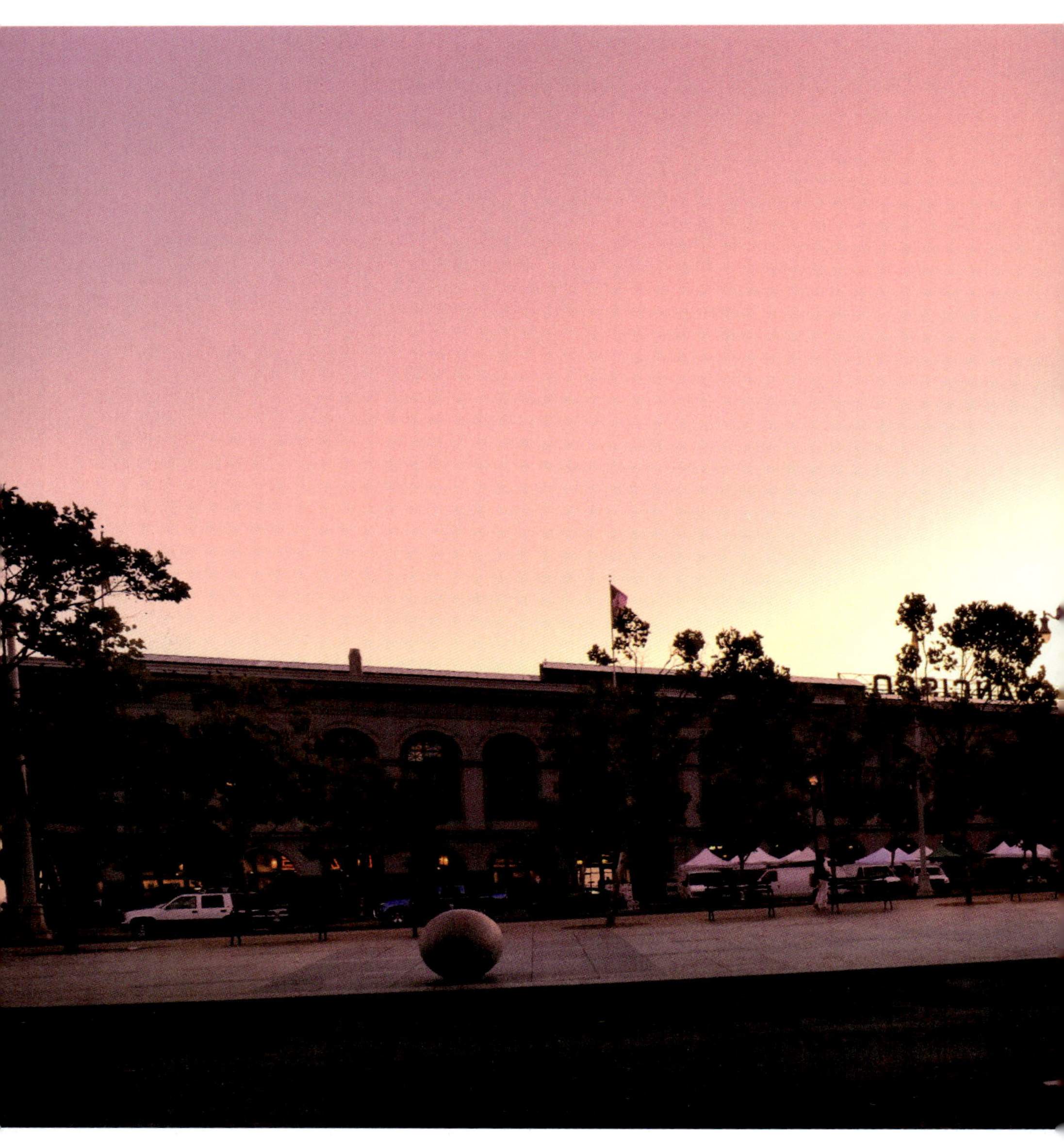

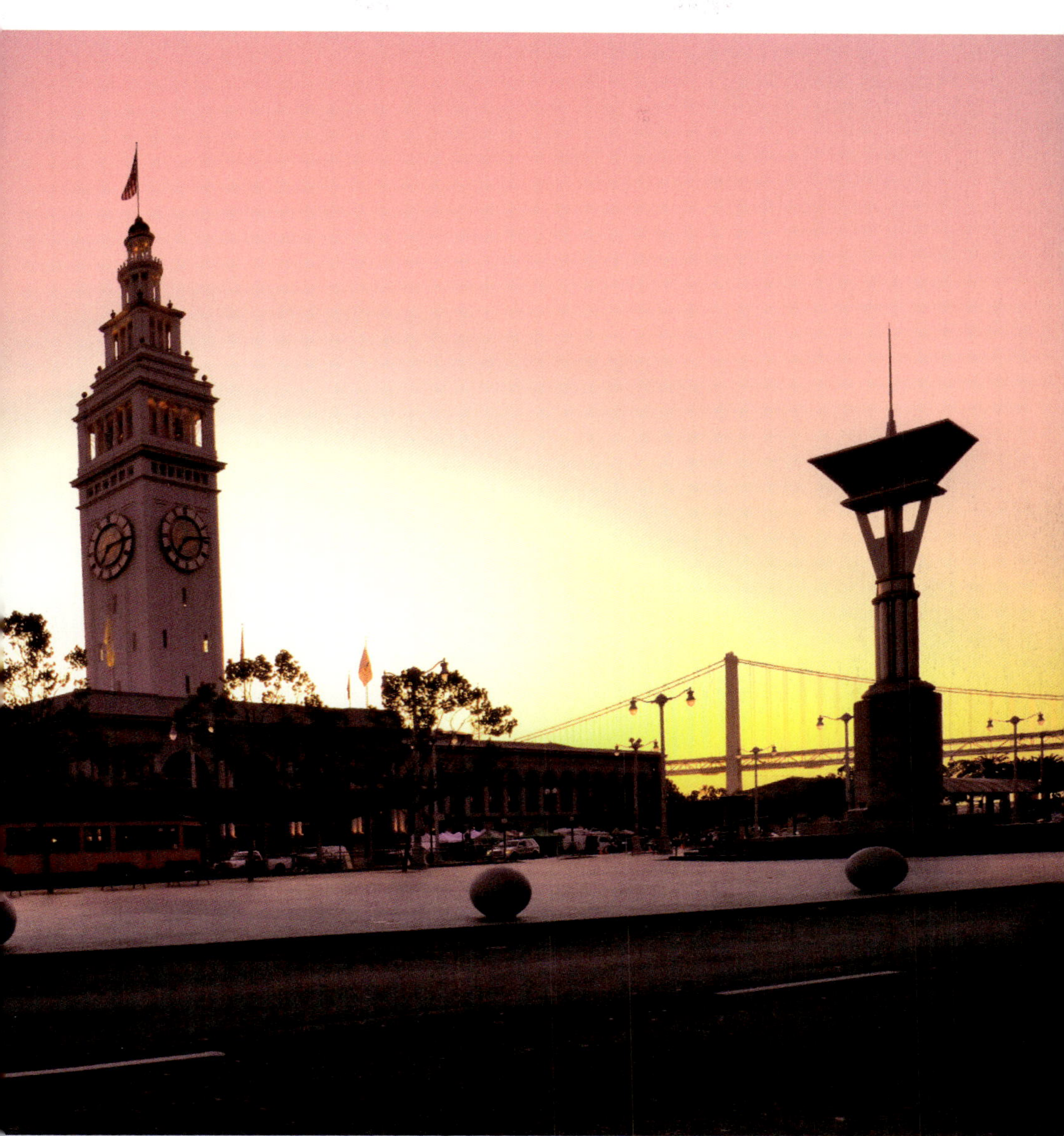

A view of the Embarcadero clock tower taken just after sunrise on a clear summer morning. Taken at ISO 400, f/8, 1/1250 second with a 14-24mm lens.

Why It's Worth a Photograph

The Embarcadero is the eastern waterfront section of the Port of San Francisco and runs along San Francisco Bay. It begins just south of the San Francisco-Oakland Bay Bridge and continues north, passing under it. The Embarcadero continues north along the waterfront past the Ferry Building and Fisherman's Wharf before ending at Pier 45. Many historical piers make up the Central Embarcadero Piers Historical District. Piers 1–5 were designed in the Beaux-Arts style, combining classical Greek and Roman architecture with Renaissance ideas. The San Francisco Ferry Building is modeled after La Giralda Cathedral in Seville, Spain, and is located in the busiest section of the Embarcadero. Once, many cable car lines converged in front of the Ferry Building, but these have now been replaced with streetcar lines. This area was also one of the busiest areas of foot traffic in the world. Today, the Embarcadero is a vital pedestrian, boat, automobile, and streetcar thoroughfare that takes advantage of its unique location in the City on the Bay. The Embarcadero is a wonderful spot to spend hours photographing the incredible sites down along the waterfront.

Where Can I Get the Best Shot?

You can photograph the Embarcadero from many vantage points, for starters the Ferry Building (see A on the map), but I also recommend an early morning stroll along the waterfront starting at Howard Street (see B on the map) and continuing north until you reach Pier 27. During your stroll, take the time to stop and photograph all the wonderful subjects that encompass the Embarcadero waterfront.

Embarcadero Ferry Building

This section of the Embarcadero is directly adjacent to downtown. Although one of the busiest places during the work week, this area is a wonderful place from which to capture the clock tower in a low, backlit light that can offer many wonderful colors. From Pier 7, you have the opportunity to capture the beautiful *San Francisco Belle*, the crown jewel of the San Francisco Bay. From bow to stern, her decks are a grand expression of Art Nouveau. The *Belle* is a San Francisco landmark. From the end of the pier, you have an opportunity to capture her grandeur and style that is uniquely San Francisco. Bring an ultrawide-angle lens so that you can include the water and the San Francisco skyline (see figure 9.1). While out on the pier, take note of the wonderful lamps that are along the pier. Try to isolate one or more against the dusky blue sky (see figure 9.2). Finally, if you continue your walk, you will pass many piers where on occasion you may be lucky enough to photograph a large cruise liner docked at one of the many ports. For this shot, you can use an ultrawide-angle lens to help you capture the ship and the rising sun on the bay (see figure 9.3).

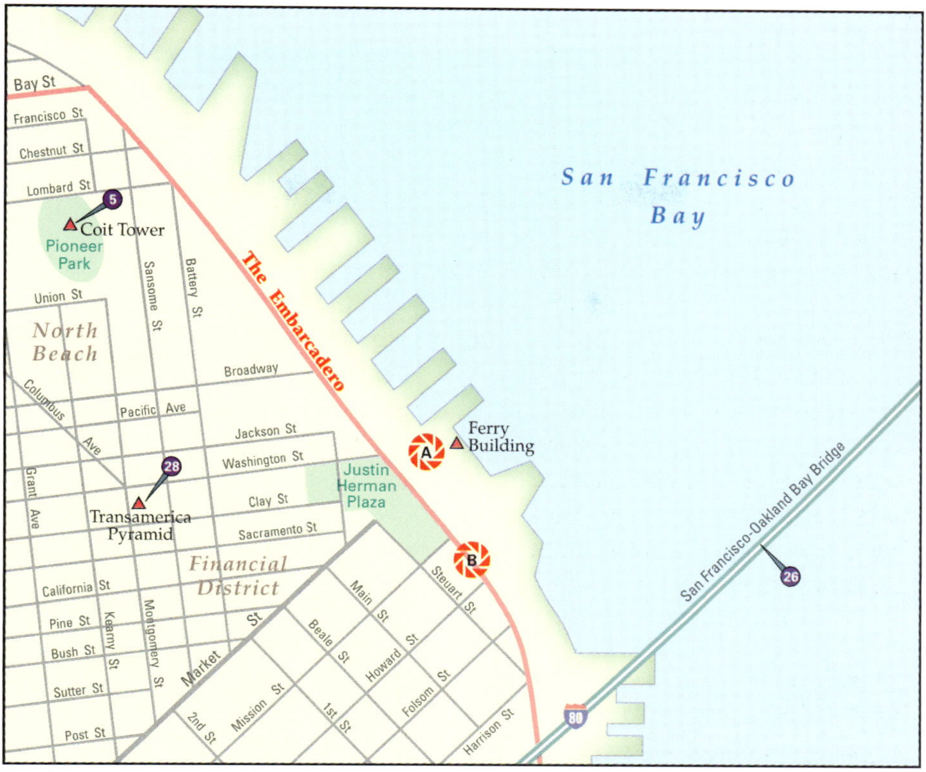

The best locations from which to photograph the Embarcadero: (A) Embarcadero Ferry Building, (B) Embarcadero between Mission Street and Howard Street. Other photo ops: (5) Coit Tower, (26) San Francisco-Oakland Bay Bridge, (28) Transamerica Pyramid.

9.1 A view of the *San Francisco Belle* taken from the Embarcadero on a clear summer morning (see A on the map). Taken at ISO 100, f/11, 10 seconds with a 14-24mm lens.

9.2 A photo of an old lamp taken from the Embarcadero on a clear summer morning. Taken at ISO 100, f/10, 1/4 second with a 24-70mm lens.

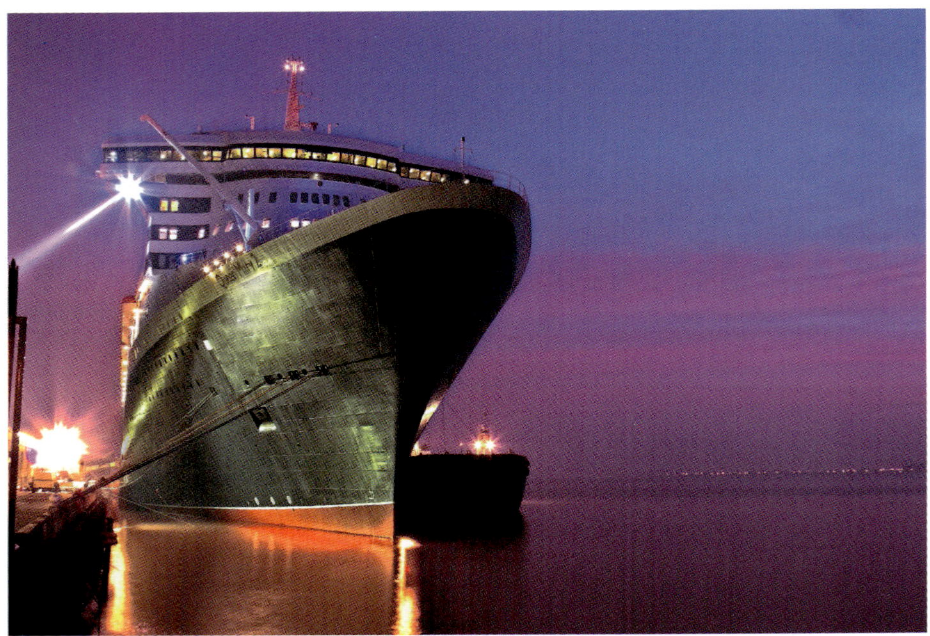

9.3 A view of the *Queen Mary* in port on the Embarcadero taken on a clear spring morning. Taken at ISO 100, f/8, 1/20 second with a 14-24mm lens.

Embarcadero between Mission Street and Howard Street

This section of the Embarcadero offers views of the Embarcadero waterfront, enormous sculptures, great views of the San Francisco Bay, and the Embarcadero buildings. This area enables you to capture these subjects with a warm, front-lit light that creates soft colors and long shadows. Along the city side of the Embarcadero, you see a path that stretches for a half mile. Don't miss this opportunity to look up and see the soft, leafy palm trees, which are a stark contrast from the tall, hardened buildings that make up the Embarcadero waterfront. With a warm, morning light and an ultrawide-angle lens, you can capture a unique perspective of these soft, tropical palm trees blending together with the tall, hard steel of the city (see figure 9.4).

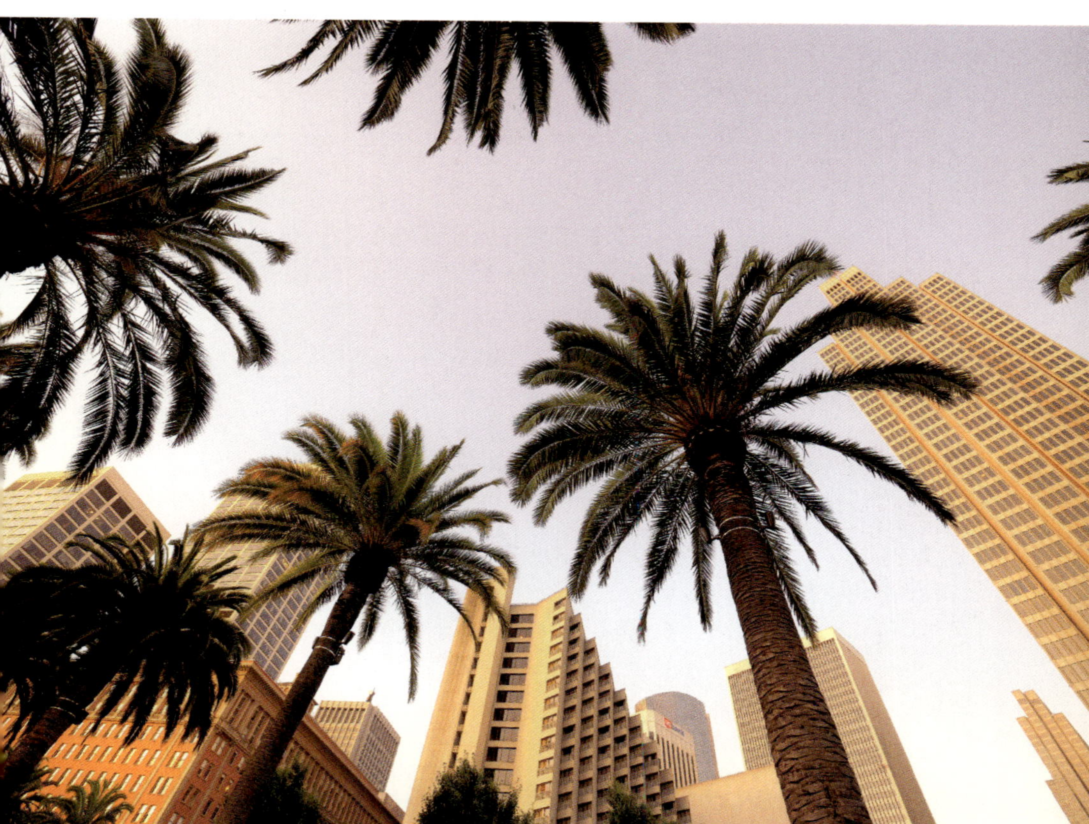

9.4 A view looking up from the Embarcadero on a clear summer morning (see B on the map). Taken at ISO 200, f/8, 1/20 second with a 14-24mm lens.

How Can I Get the Best Shot?

Much like Fisherman's Wharf, early morning light can really enhance the mood of the Embarcadero waterfront. Shooting early helps you avoid large crowds of people and harsh light that the midday sun can produce. A clear, dusky blue sky is ideal for shooting because you can produce vibrant images, which can include the city and water. A tripod is a must while shooting in low light with slow shutter speeds. Dress warmly and try to avoid the many joggers that will thunder past you as you are setting up for that perfect shot.

Equipment

A good tripod, an ultrawide-angle lens, and a medium telephoto lens are the three pieces of equipment that are critical for capturing sharp images of the Embarcadero waterfront.

Lenses

An ultrawide-angle lens and a long telephoto lens are the two lenses that are critical for capturing creative images of the Embarcadero.

- **Ultrawide-angle lens in the 14-24mm range.** The ultrawide-angle lens gives you the ability to create a unique perspective. This type of lens comes in handy when trying to shoot the ferry or large ships in port.
- **A zoom lens somewhere in the 70-300mm range.** This focal range gives you the ability to isolate the architecture and buildings, such as the clock tower.

Extras

Due to the low light at this time of day, your shutter speeds will be too slow to hand hold, so a tripod is necessary for capturing the Embarcadero before sunrise. A cable release to trigger the shutter and a bubble level to level the horizon can come in handy for these types of shots.

Camera settings

Setting up your camera comes down to the time of day, amount of light, and composition. When shooting with a long lens from a distance, mount your camera on a tripod and set the aperture from f/8 to f/11 to maximize your image quality. When shooting up close with your ultrawide-angle lens, if you have an immediate object in the foreground, set your aperture to f/22 to maximize your depth of field. When photographing the ships in dock or the clock tower, you want to shoot from f/8 to f/22 depending on your composition. You want to create enough depth of field to have a sharp photo from front to back.

- **Exposure mode.** Aperture Priority is best used on most occasions except when the light is difficult or you want to over- or underexpose one area. In those cases, dial in exposure compensation or switch to Manual mode if you feel comfortable. I may dial in a plus or minus exposure compensation to help balance out the bright sky and darker city. Many times this can end up being a balancing act, sacrificing shadows for a properly exposed sky or highlights for properly exposed city.
- **White balance.** I never touch white balance because I find the Auto White Balance of modern day cameras to be pretty good.
- **ISO.** ISO should stay as low as possible unless you are handholding your camera. Raise your ISO to create a shutter speed that is fast enough for you to hand hold your camera. Remember everyone is different in this regard, and a good rule of thumb is your shutter speed should equal your focal length.

Exposure

Let your camera have first crack at the exposure. If the camera cannot deliver what you want, switch to Manual mode or dial in the appropriate exposure compensation. I am happy with the way my camera chooses to expose the photo 90 percent of the time. Understand there are situations when no matter what mode you're in, you will have to sacrifice sky or land to capture the overall best exposure.

Ideal time to shoot

The ideal time to shoot is in the early morning when the sun is low, and the waterfront is lit by the soft, warm light that creates brilliant colors, long shadows, and a surreal mood.

Working around the weather

Weather conditions are important for one reason: You don't want to be out shooting in a rainstorm. The late spring, late summer, and early fall are the ideal months to photograph the waterfront. These months of year tend to have the most dramatic sunrises and sunsets with very little fog.

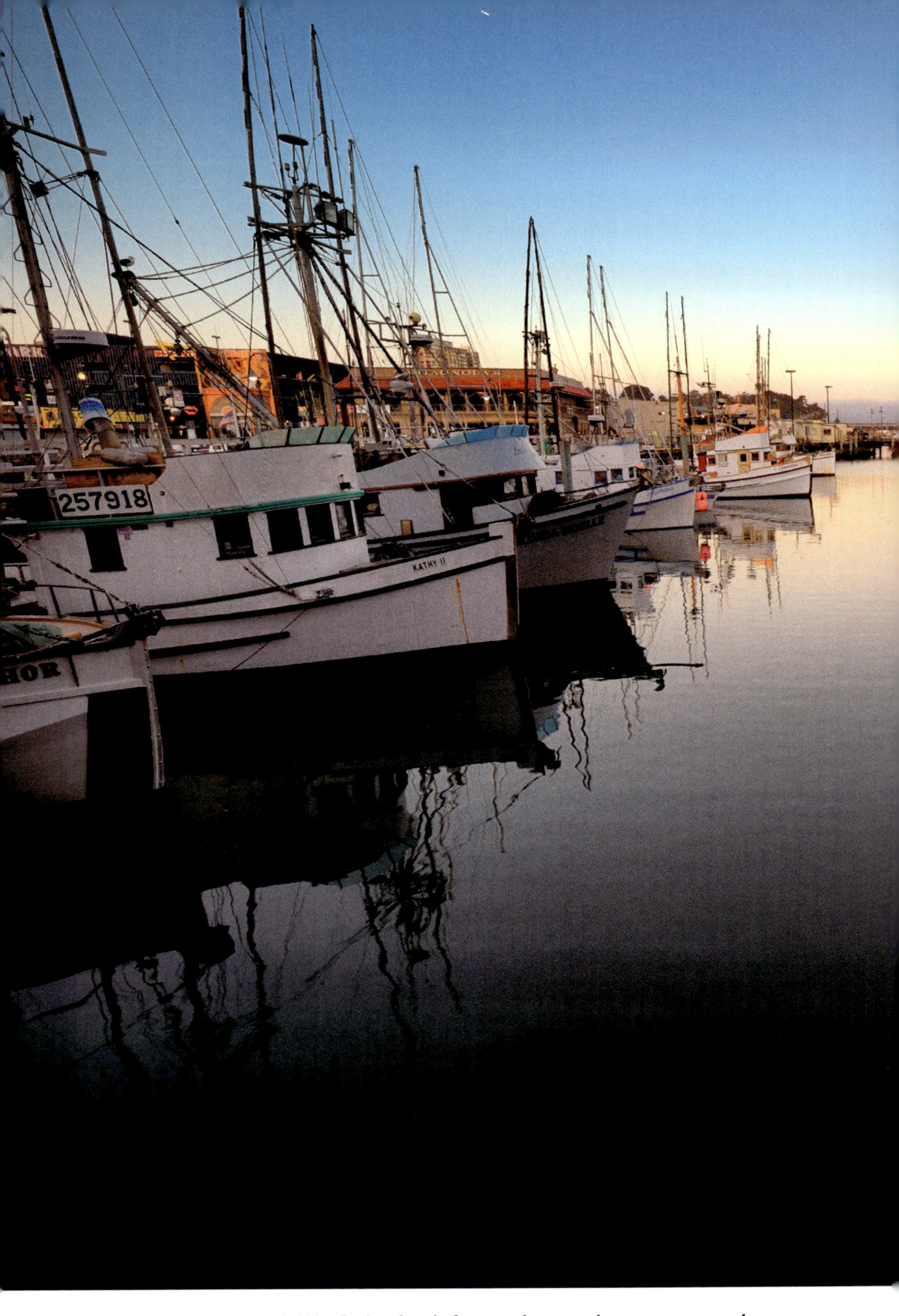

A view of the Fisherman's Wharf taken just before sunrise on a clear summer morning. The photo was taken at ISO 100, f/11, 1/13 second with a 14-24mm lens.

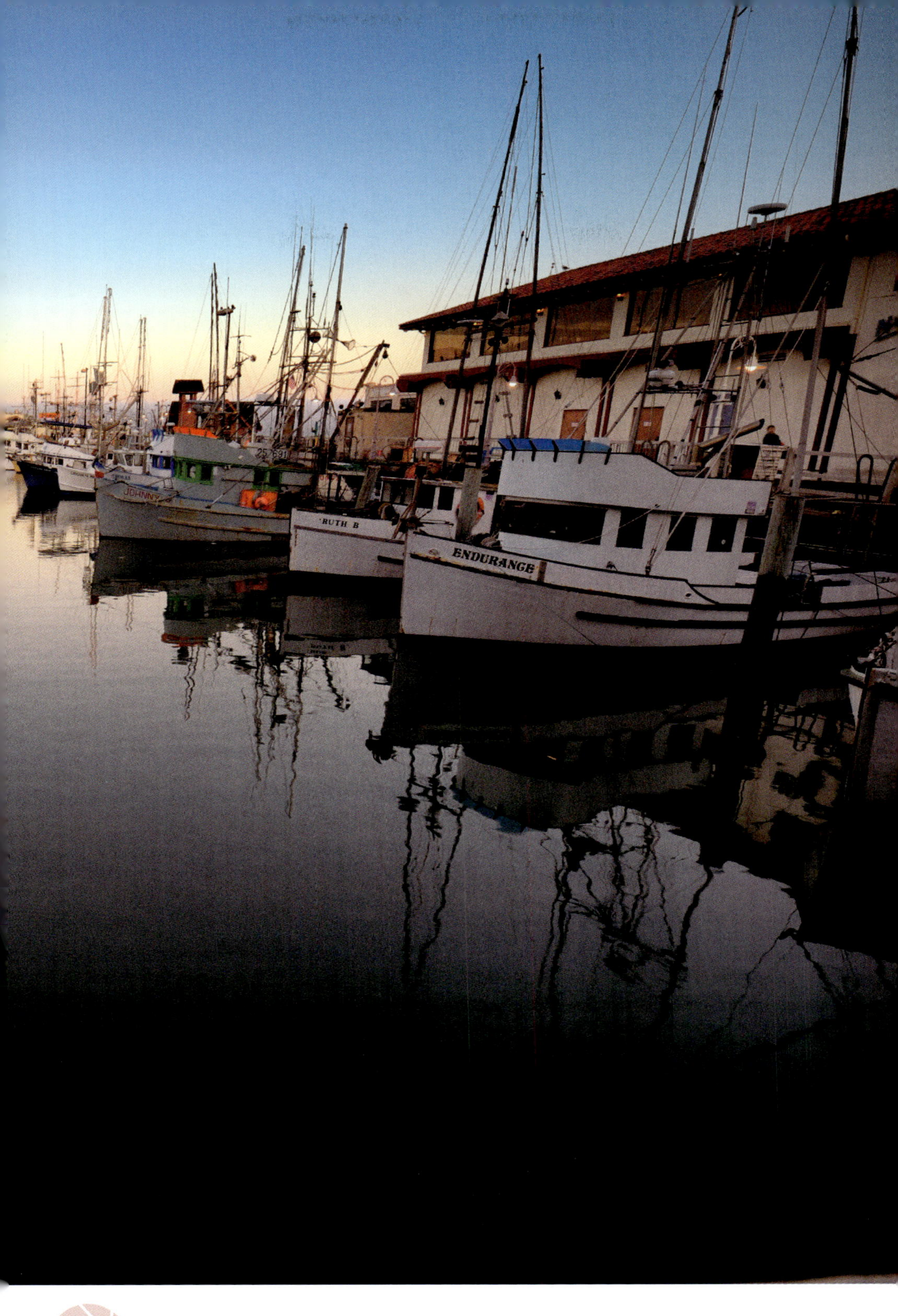

10 Fisherman’s Wharf

Why It's Worth a Photograph

Fisherman's Wharf is a neighborhood and popular tourist attraction in San Francisco. The wharf area roughly encompasses the northern waterfront area of San Francisco and stretches from Ghirardelli Square east to Pier 35. Fisherman's Wharf has been the home of San Francisco's colorful fishing fleet for over a century and is world famous for its wide variety of seafood. One of the great pleasures of visiting San Francisco is an early morning walk along this historic Fisherman's Wharf. Here, you find numerous subjects to photograph, from the fishing crafts riding in the calm water to the fishermen rigging their boats or the barking seals of Pier 39.

Where Can I Get the Best Shot?

There are so many locations from which to photograph Fisherman's Wharf that I recommend you stroll down Jefferson Street starting at Hyde Street. If you follow Jefferson east from Hyde, you eventually end up at Pier 39. Take the time to stop and photograph what you see. Arrive before the sun comes up and you will see wonderful color in the sky and silky smooth reflections on the water.

Jefferson Street between Powell Street and Hyde Street

The walk along the wharf brings you to many interesting places that you may want to stop and photograph. The first area I recommend is the old fishing boat marina, where you find colorful fishing boats left over from another generation. The boats make a wonderful subject to photograph with early morning light. I recommend bringing a wide-angle lens and a tripod. Expect your shutter speed to be at least 5 seconds long when shooting from f/8 to f/11 (see figure 10.1). As you continue on Jefferson Street, you eventually come to Pier 39. Stop and photograph the sea lions camped out at Pier 39's West Marina. The boisterous, barking sea lions started arriving in bunches, taking over the docks, in early 1990 shortly after the 1989 Loma Prieta earthquake. At first they came in small numbers, but due to the abundance of herring and available dock space, the population grew to more than 300 within a few months. Every winter, the population can increase up to 900 sea lions. To capture the sea lions, a long lens of at least 300mm is necessary (see figure 10.2). After you photograph the sea lions, continue east to the other side of Pier 39 where you can photograph the lovely sailboats against the early morning sky (see figure 10.3).

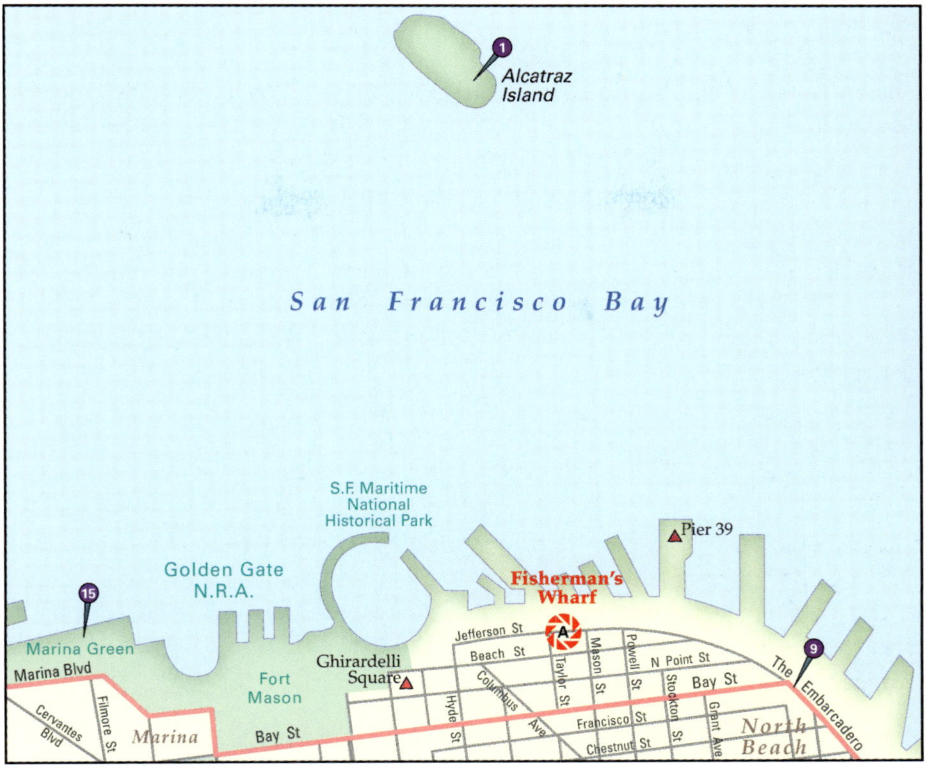

Alcatraz Island
San Francisco Bay
S.F. Maritime National Historical Park
Pier 39
Golden Gate N.R.A.
Fisherman's Wharf
Marina Green
Marina Blvd
Ghirardelli Square
Fort Mason
Jefferson St
Beach St
N Point St
Bay St
Cervantes Blvd
Fillmore St
Marina
Hyde St
Columbus Ave
Taylor St
Mason St
Powell St
Stockton St
Grant Ave
Francisco St
Chestnut St
North Beach
The Embarcadero

The best locations from which to photograph Fisherman's Wharf: (A) Jefferson Street between Powell Street and Hyde Street. Other photo ops: (1) Alcatraz, (9) Embarcadero, (15) Marina Green.

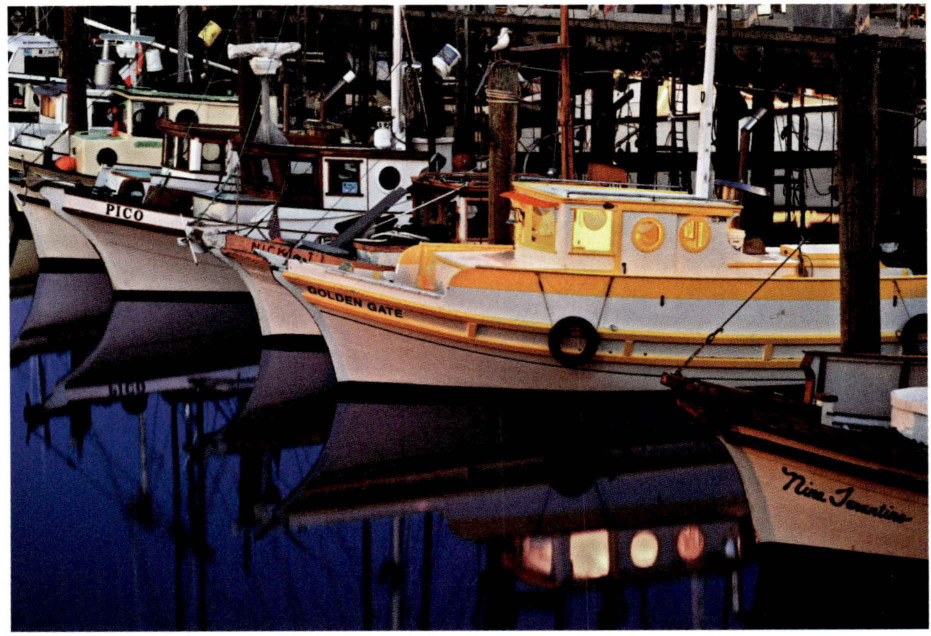

10.1 A view of fishing boats taken at Fisherman's Wharf on a clear winter morning (see A on the map) on a clear fall morning. Taken at ISO 100, f/8, 5 seconds with a 17-35mm lens.

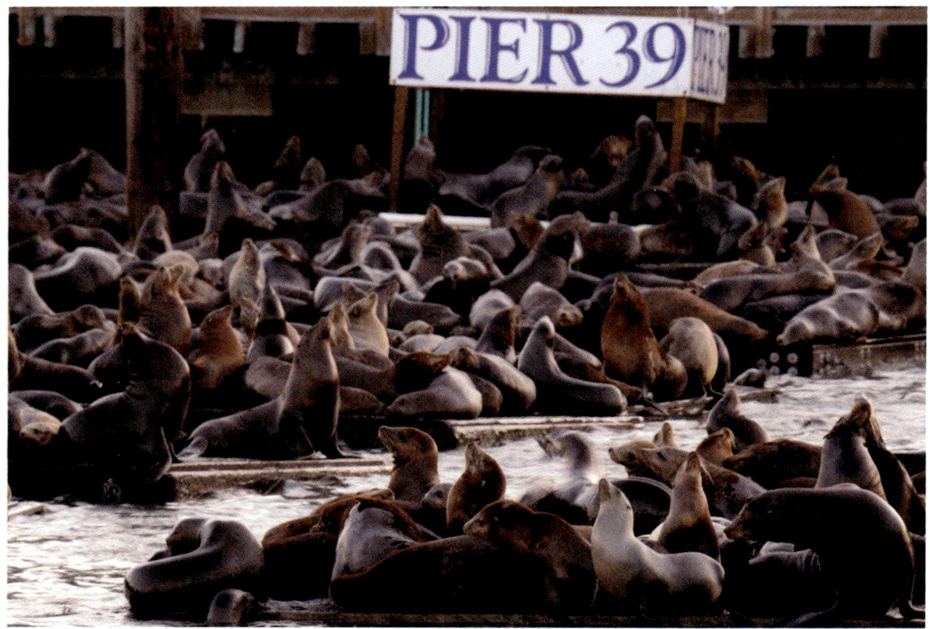

10.2 A view of the Pier 39 sea lions taken just after sunrise from Fisherman's Wharf on a clear summer morning. Taken at ISO 100, f/8, 1/13 second with a 400mm lens.

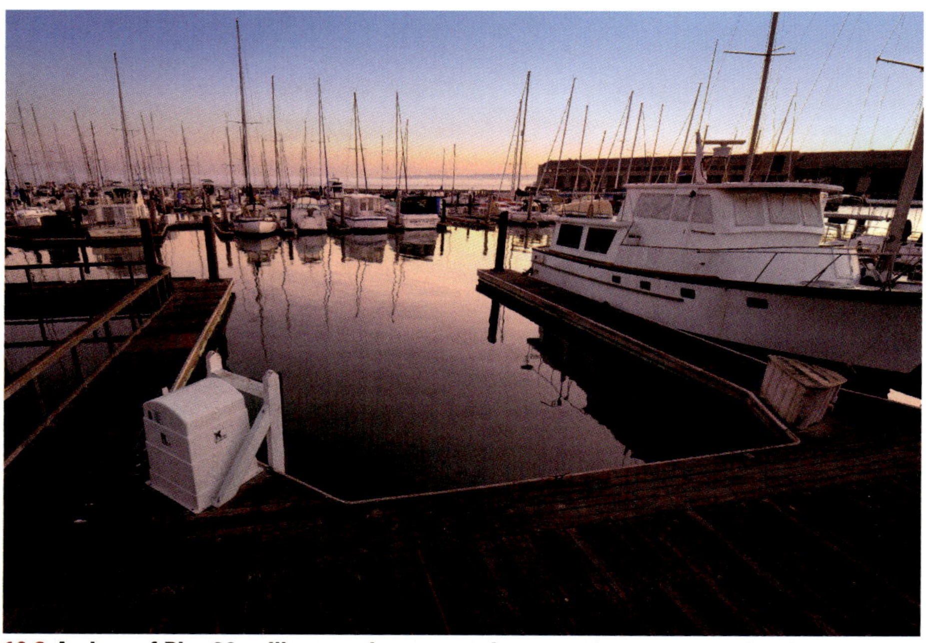

10.3 A view of Pier 39 sailboats taken at sunrise on a clear summer day. Taken at ISO 100, f/11, 1/10 second with a 14-24mm lens.

How Can I Get the Best Shot?

Early morning light can really enhance the mood at Fisherman's Wharf. Shooting early helps you avoid large crowds of people and harsh light that the midday sun can produce. A clear blue sky is great, but you can also create wonderful mood with dense fog. A tripod is a must while shooting with slow shutter speeds during the wee hours of the morning. Dress warm and bring a cup of coffee (see figure 10.4). If you're shooting into fog, your camera will tend to underexpose by at least –2/3 and sometimes up to –1.5. This is caused by the camera meter being fooled by the bright white fog. Be sure to add plus exposure compensation to your camera to account for this underexposure.

Equipment

A good tripod, an ultrawide lens, and a medium telephoto lens are the three pieces of equipment that are critical for capturing sharp images on Fisherman's Wharf.

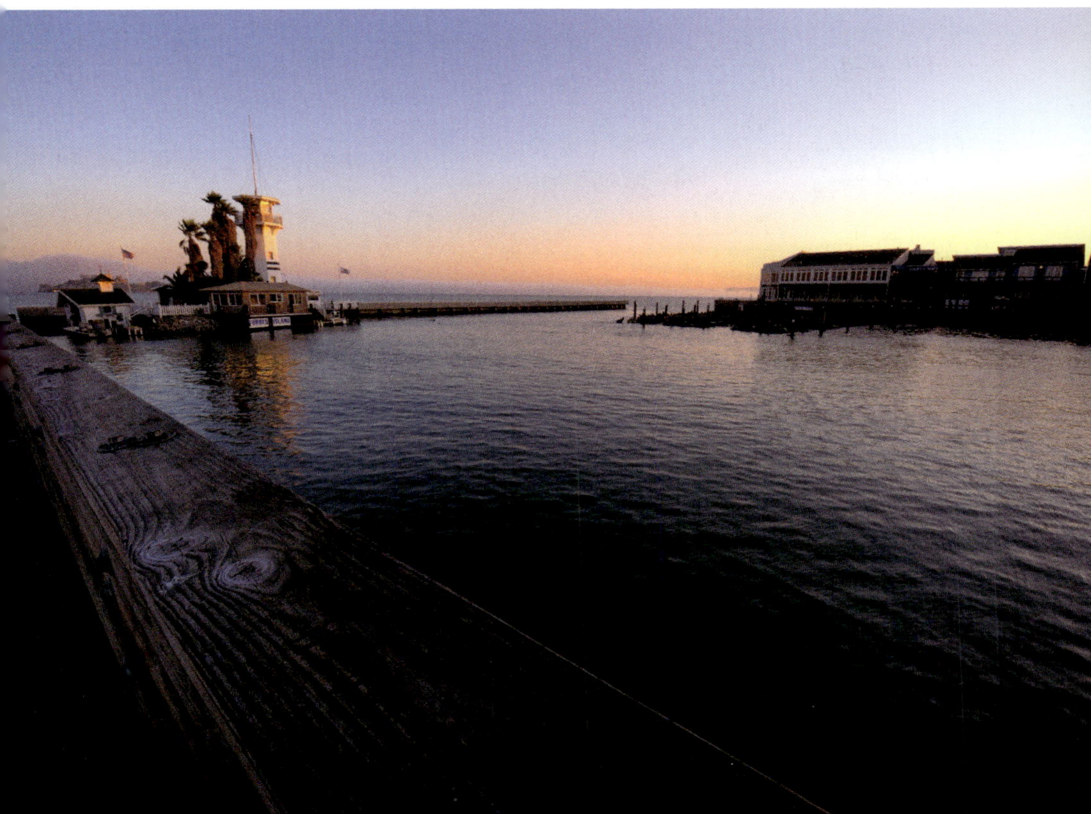

10.4 A view of Fisherman's Wharf taken just before sunrise on a clear fall morning. Taken at ISO 100, f/22, 1/13 second with a 14-24mm lens.

Lenses

An ultrawide-angle lens and a long telephoto lens are the two lenses that are critical for capturing the perfect images and composition at Fisherman's Wharf.

- **Ultrawide-angle lens in the 14-24mm range.** The ultrawide lens gives you the ability to create a unique perspective. This type of lens comes in handy when trying to include many boats in the marina shot.
- **A zoom lens somewhere in the 70-300mm range.** This focal range gives you the ability to isolate the sea lions from across the Pier 39 marina.

Extras

A tripod is absolutely necessary for shooting the Fisherman's Wharf. Your shutter speeds will be too slow to hand hold the camera. A cable release to trigger the shutter and a bubble level to level the horizon can come in handy for these types of shots.

Camera settings

Setting up your camera comes down to time of day, amount of light, and composition. When shooting with a long lens from a distance, mount your camera on a tripod and set the aperture from f/8 to f/11, which maximizes your image quality. When shooting up close with your ultrawide lens, if you have an immediate object in the foreground, set your aperture to f/22 to maximize your depth of field. To photograph the boats in the marina, you want to shoot from f/8 to f/22 depending on your composition. You want to create enough depth of field to have a sharp photo from front to back. To photograph sea lions, I recommend f/8, which gives you plenty of depth of field and the sharpest results.

- **Exposure mode.** I set my camera in Aperture Priority mode and let my camera choose the shutter speed. I may dial in a plus or minus exposure composition to help balance a bright sky and dark foreground. I will also add a plus exposure compensation when shooting into fog.
- **White balance.** White balance I never touch because I find the Auto White Balance of all modern day cameras to be pretty good.
- **ISO.** ISO should stay as low as possible to help maximize image quality. I will raise the ISO to increase my shutter speed when handholding a lens. By increasing the shutter speed, it will help combat camera shake.

Exposure

During this time of day, Aperture Priority will give you the proper exposure most of the time. Understand there are situations where no matter what mode you're in you will have to sacrifice sky or land to capture the overall best exposure. When you are presented with a situation like this, when you are shooting into the sun, you will need to dial in minus exposure compensation to keep the sky from overexposing. Use your histogram or check the back of your camera to see if the image has large areas of overexposure. If so, you will need to compensate by dialing in a minus exposure compensation until you have balanced the exposure. There is no single correct setting; each situation can render a different amount of exposure compensation. If you feel confident enough, switch to Manual and choose the best combination of aperture and shutter speed to render a proper exposure.

Ideal time to shoot

The ideal time to shoot is in the early morning when the sun is low and Fisherman's Wharf is being bathed with soft, warm light, creating wonderful colors and long shadows.

Working around the weather

The worst months to be out and about on Fisherman's Wharf are the early summer and winter months. The wind, thick fog, and cold rain make miserable conditions for photographers. The spring, late summer, and early fall can offer wonderful weather with low-lying fog, dramatic skies, warm temperatures, and moody sunsets.

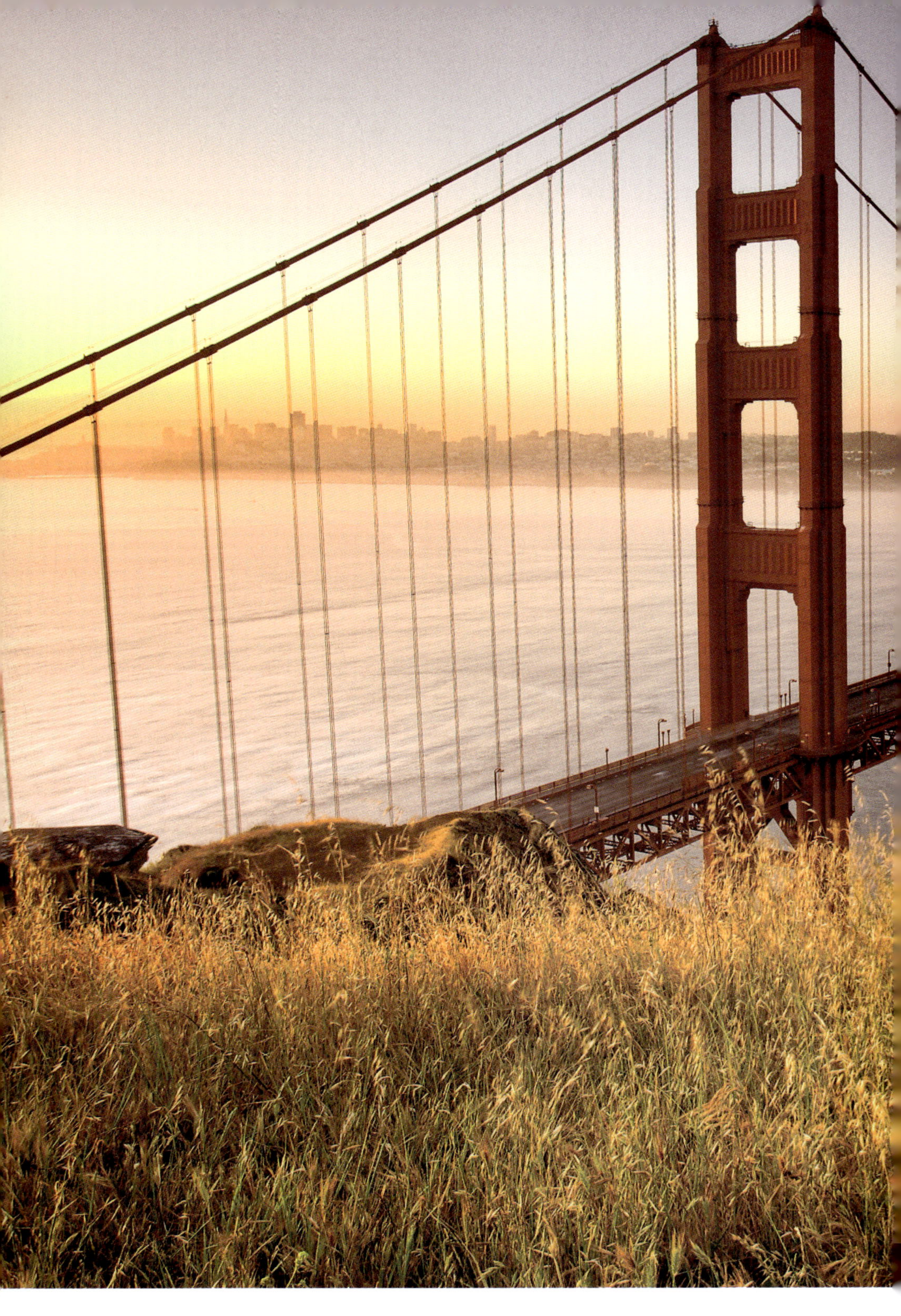

A view of the Golden Gate Bridge taken just after sunrise from the Marin Headlands on a clear spring morning. Taken at ISO 100, f/8, 1 second with a 17-35mm lens.

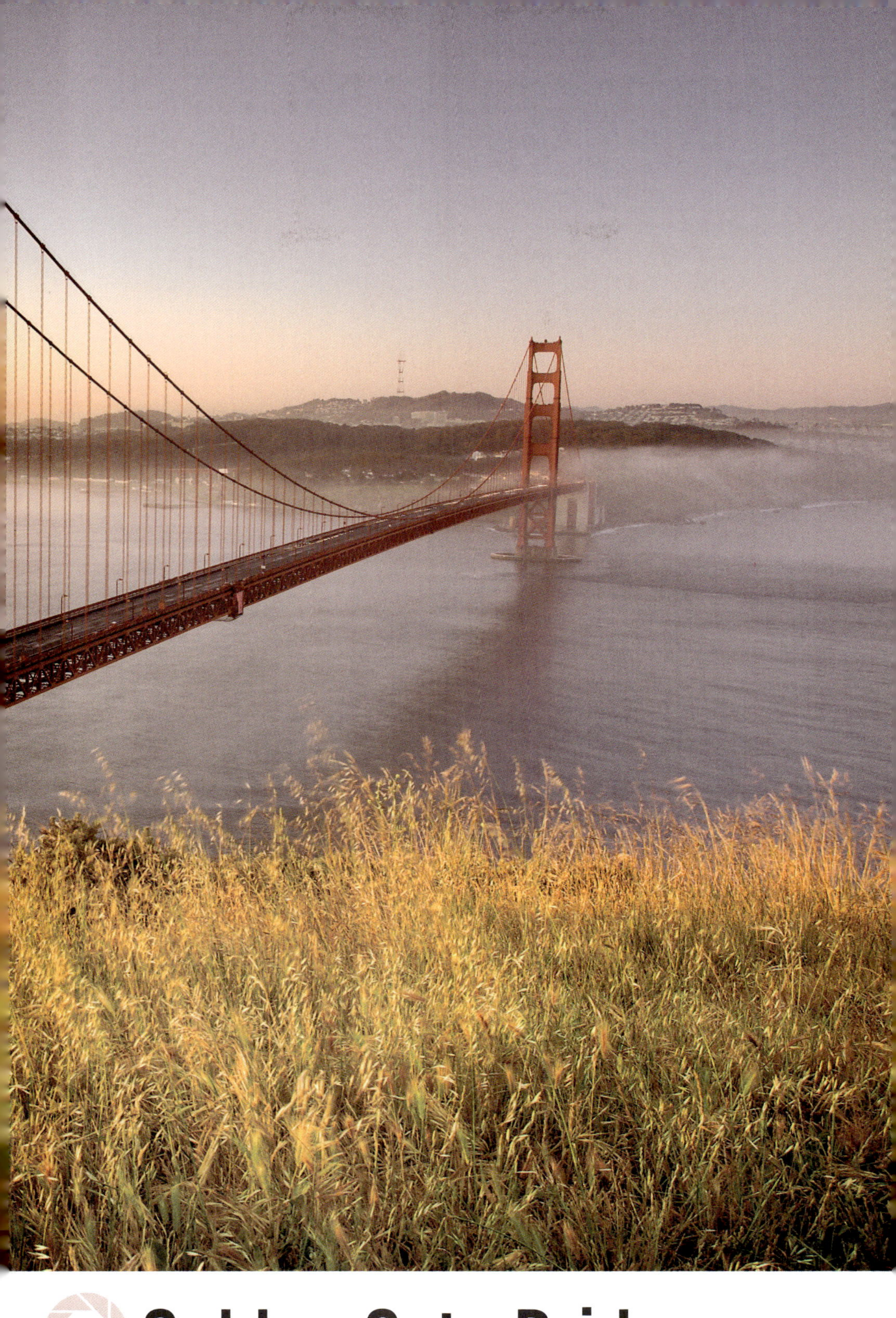

11 Golden Gate Bridge

Why It's Worth a Photograph

The Golden Gate Bridge, a symbol of San Francisco, spans two of the most beautiful areas in the world: the city of San Francisco and the Sausalito-Marin Headlands. Built in 1937, the bridge is considered one of the most remarkable structures in the world, and the surrounding areas offer many vantage points to photograph. The Golden Gate Bridge's 4,200-foot long span set a world record, which stood for about 27 years. The bridge's two towers rise 746 feet above the water making them 191 feet taller than the Washington Monument. The Golden Gate Bridge has an Art Deco style with wide, vertical ribbing on the horizontal towers that help catch the sun's light at both sunrise and sunset. This feature alone makes it worth a photograph.

The Marin Headlands also offers you breathtakingly beautiful views of the Golden Gate Bridge together with one of the most beautiful cities. To top it off, you have the San Francisco Bay and the Pacific Ocean crashing together 200 feet below. Taking a photo at daybreak gives you a wonderfully colorful sidelit scene of the bridge and San Francisco. A photo taken at sunset can offer you a beautiful, golden silhouette of the bridge, the water, and surrounding cliffs. And a photograph at night offers up a vibrant, dusky blue sky with the bridge and city all lit up and wonderful reflections on the water below.

Where Can I Get the Best Shot?

You can photograph the Golden Gate Bridge from many places around San Francisco. I have photographed the bridge every which way, from the early morning to late at night. I have photographed the bridge when the sky was a crystal clear, vibrant morning blue, only to see it turn into a cold, dense, wet fog one hour later. In over 15 years of exploring and seeking out new locations, Marin Headlands, Baker Beach, Crissy Field, Fort Point, North Vista Point, the Visitor Center, and Conzelman Road Headlands (see A–G on the map) seem to offer the best light and best perspective to capture a photo that is truly worth hanging on a wall.

Marin Headlands

The Marin Headlands is arguably the most popular location to photograph the Golden Gate Bridge. Located just north of San Francisco on Conzelman Road, it's just a short drive, hike, bike ride, or bus trip over the Golden Gate Bridge. The Marin Headlands is best known for its gentle rolling hills, high cliffs, and military history. After you have crossed the Golden Gate Bridge, follow Conzelman Road up the hill a few hundred yards until you see military bunkers on the left; these bunkers are called Battery Spencer. Wear comfortable shoes and bring a camera backpack or shoulder bag to carry your gear. You have a 5- to 10- minute walk, depending on

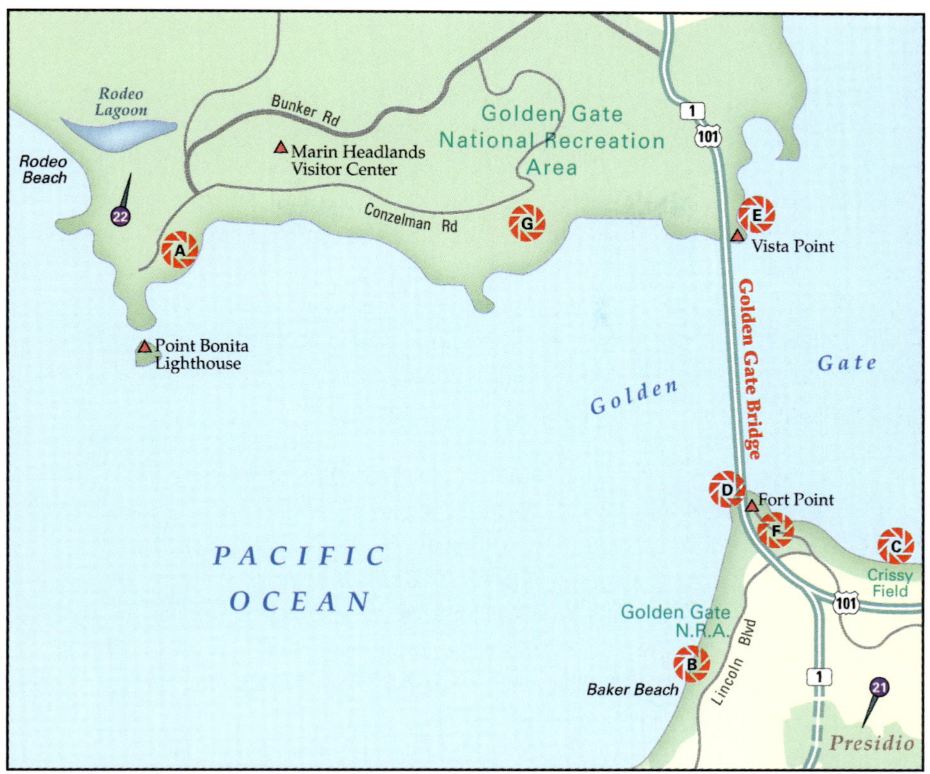

The best locations from which to photograph the Golden Gate Bridge: (A) Marin Headlands, (B) Baker Beach, (C) Crissy Field, (D) Fort Point, (E) North Vista Point, (F) Visitor Center, (G) Conzelman Road Headlands. Other photo ops: (21) Presidio of San Francisco, (22) Rodeo Beach/Marin Headlands.

wind and weather, up a path to the main gun battery installation where there are numerous places to set up and photograph the bridge from. In my experience, the perfect angle to shoot — the angle that gives you the best vantage point of the bridge and city — is directly between the far-left fence and the far-right cliff. From here, you are looking directly back at the bridge from approximately a 25- to 30-degree angle. Make sure that you bring a sturdy tripod because the wind can blow upwards of 30 mph. A wide-angle lens between 14-24mm is a must if you want to be able to shoot the entire length of the bridge with the city as its backdrop.

From this location, you have the opportunity to photograph the Golden Gate Bridge at any time of day, up close and personal, with the city of San Francisco as a backdrop and the Pacific Ocean directly below (see figure 11.1). My favorite times to photograph the bridge from this vantage point are 20 minutes before the sun comes up and 20 minutes after the sun goes down. What makes these two times so ideal is the dark blue, magenta, and orange sky interlaced with the effect your shutter speed has on the traffic coming across the bridge. When your shutter speed gets below 5 seconds, you can expect to see numerous red and white streams of light from the headlights and taillights of cars caused by the slow shutter speed.

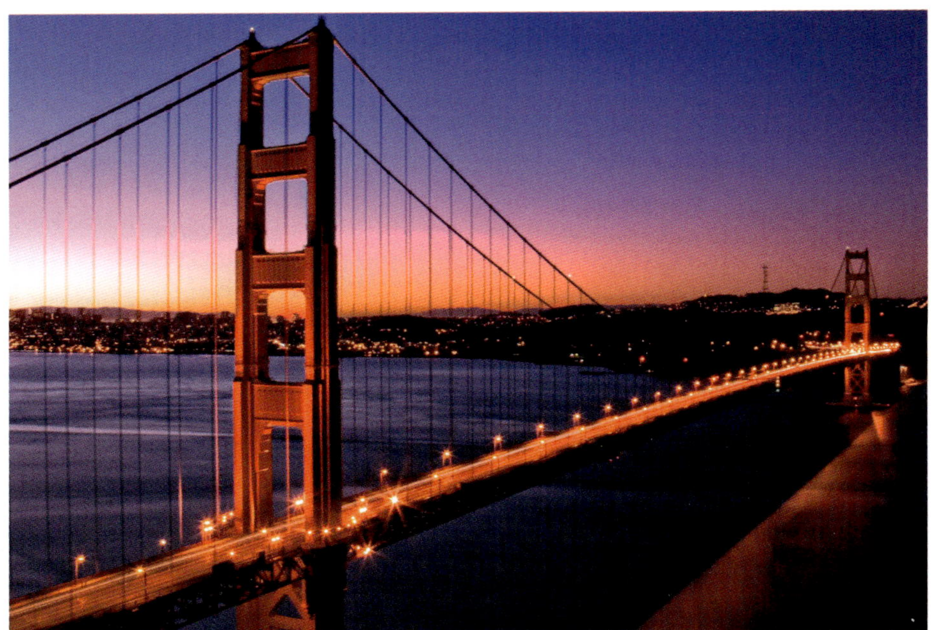

11.1 A view of the Golden Gate Bridge taken just before sunrise from the Marin Headlands (see A on the map) on a clear fall morning. Taken at ISO 100, f/22, 30 seconds with a 24mm lens.

Baker Beach

Baker Beach offers a wonderful vantage point to photograph the bridge. The ideal time of day to shoot from this location is 20 minutes before and 20 minutes after sunset (see figure 11.2). The sun at your back offers a warm, vibrant light that accentuates the orange color of the bridge. Baker Beach, on the ocean side of the Golden Gate Bridge, is a west-facing beach that is one mile long and lies at the foot of the high cliffs on the western shoreline of the Presidio. The view from the beach with the cliffs of the Marin Headlands and the Golden Gate Bridge is spectacular. The beach is primarily visited by locals who want to enjoy a peaceful afternoon. This spot is very popular with San Franciscans of all kinds, and because it's on federal land where nudity is allowed, you'll almost always find a few unclothed folks up by the rocks. So when setting up your gear, be wary of this possibility.

Crissy Field

Crissy Field offers a number of prime locations from which you can photograph the Golden Gate Bridge. The most popular spot is along the beach that leads up to the bridge. Crissy Field is linked to the early history of aviation in the United States and was the military's first Air Coast Defense Station on the Pacific coast. Crissy Field

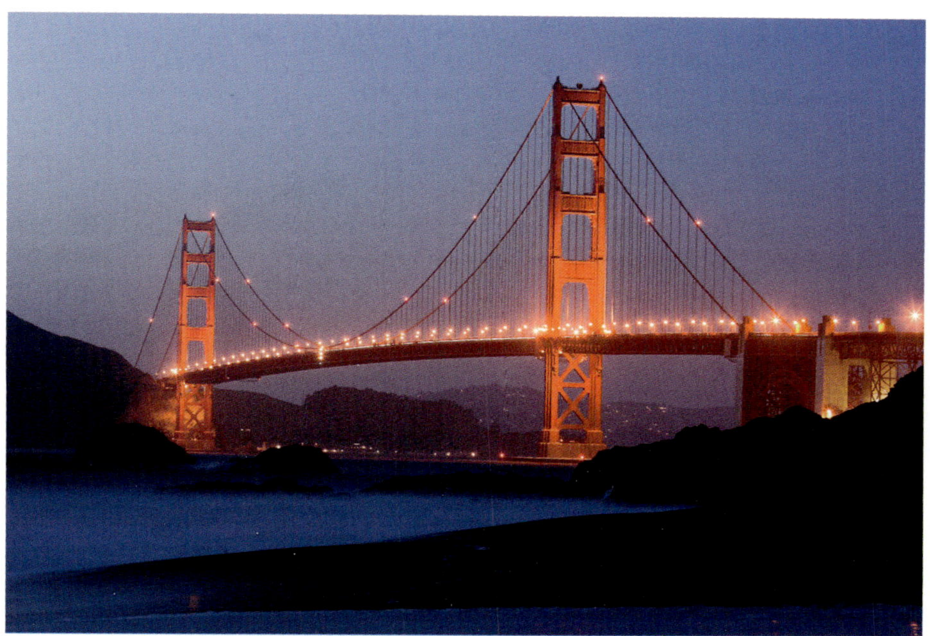

11.2 A view of the Golden Gate Bridge taken just after sunset from Baker Beach (see B on the map) on a clear spring night. Taken at ISO 100, f/11, 30 seconds, +0.3 exposure compensation with a 70-200mm lens.

is the area along the northern shoreline of the Presidio of San Francisco. It is southeast of the Golden Gate Bridge between the Palace of Fine Arts and the bridge. I recommend parking in the West Bluff Picnic Area parking lot at the end of Mason Street. The best time to shoot from this vantage point is just before sunrise when the sun is at your back, the bridge glows from the low, warm light striking the bright orange structure, and the early morning sky is dusky blue (shown in figure 11.3). Another wonderful but less popular time is as the sun is setting directly behind the bridge. The bridge is immersed in a low, bright orange light that creates a wonderful silhouette of the Golden Gate Bridge, Fort Point, and the Marin Headlands. I tend to favor shooting from this location as the sun is setting, because it offers a dramatic photographic moment. When shooting a silhouette of the Golden Gate Bridge, I set my camera aperture while metering in Manual exposure mode. I point the camera just to the left or right of the sun, being careful not to include the sun as part of my exposure. I then adjust my shutter speed until my camera indicates the correct exposure. In this case, it was 1/1600 second at f/13 (see figure 11.4)

For more information on Rodeo Beach/Marin Headlands, see Chapter 22.

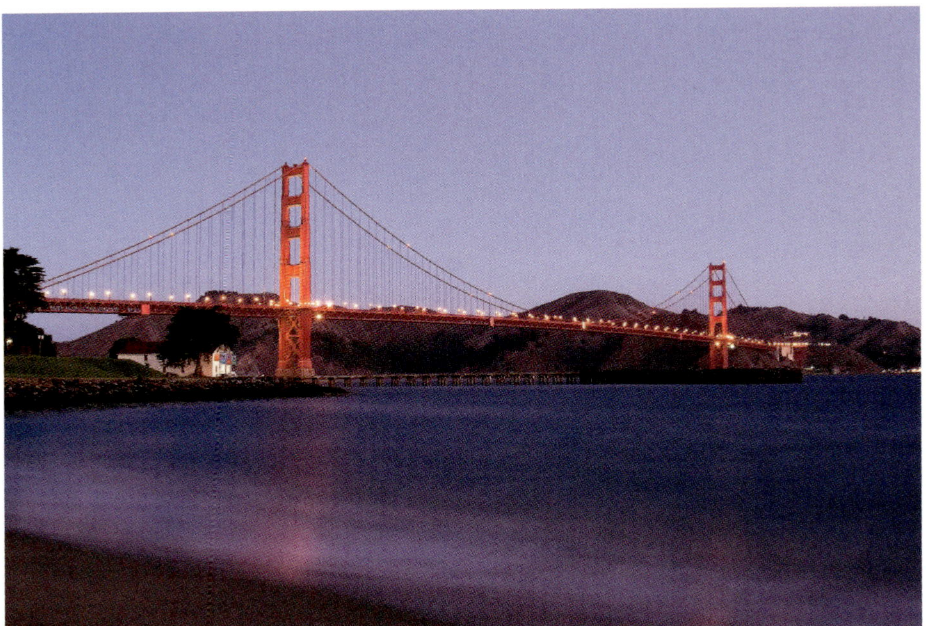

11.3 A view of the Golden Gate Bridge taken just before sunrise from Crissy Field (see C on the map) on a clear fall morning. Taken at ISO 200, f/11, 30 seconds with a 17-35mm lens.

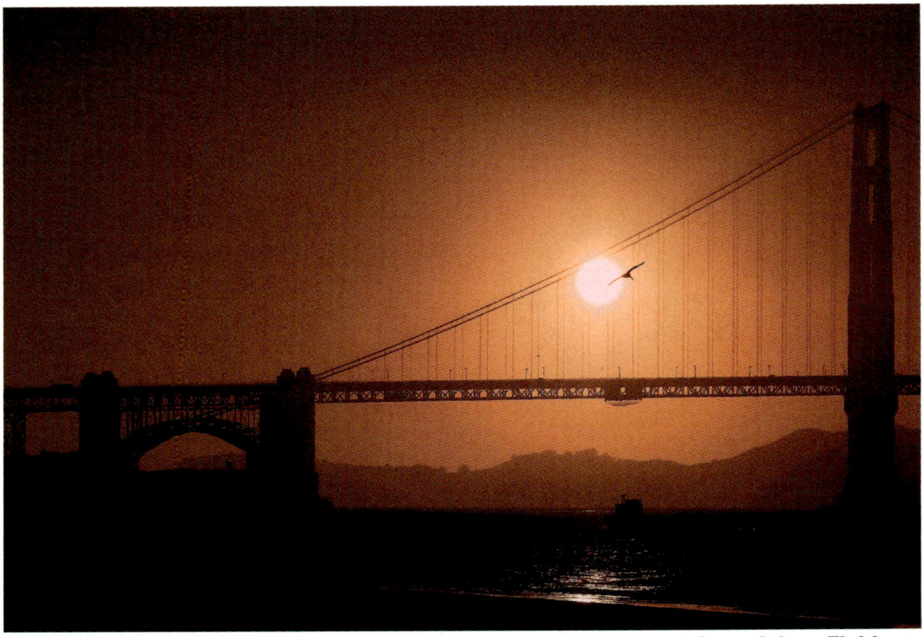

11.4 A view of the Golden Gate Bridge taken just before sunset from Crissy Field on a clear summer night. Taken at ISO 100, f/13, 1/1600 second with a 24-105mm lens.

Fort Point

Fort Point is an old Civil War fort that sits at the base of the Golden Gate Bridge and offers numerous photographic opportunities. From this vantage point, the angle at which to photograph the bridge is pretty severe because you are literally at the base of one of the bridge's piers; however, it is well worth your time to capture the bridge from this view because it adds a really fantastic artistic element to your photo (see figure 11.5). The fort itself is only open from 10 a.m. to 5 p.m., so low-light shooting from this location can only happen from outside the fort. A wide-angle lens is a must to capture the bridge along with ocean and sky. A lens in the 14-24mm range is highly recommended.

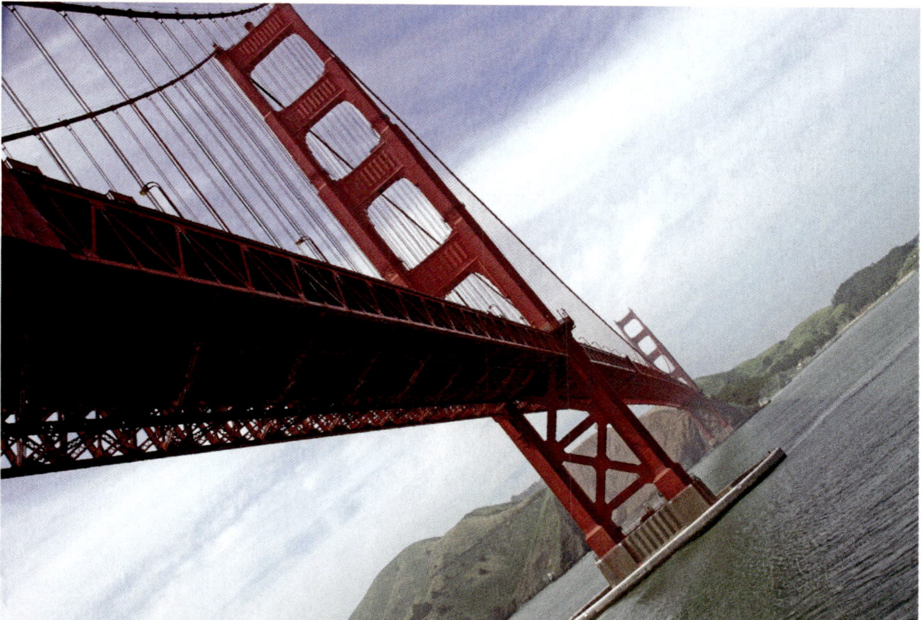

11.5 A view of the Golden Gate Bridge taken late afternoon from the roof of Fort Point (see D on the map) on a clear spring day. Taken handheld at ISO 100, f/10, 1/200 second with a 24-105mm lens.

North Vista Point

North Vista Point is located on the right side of the Golden Gate Bridge as you exit the bridge in Marin. Take the first exit and pull into the parking lot. From this location set your camera up along the stone wall at the right rear of the parking lot. This vantage point is ideal for shooting back through the arches of the bridge. The only time of day I shoot from this location is either before the sun comes up or after the sun goes down (see figure 11.6). The combination of the dusky night sky and glowing bridge with arches and streaming lights makes for a photograph with great lines, pattern, and color. What more could you want? I recommend bringing a lens in the 200-300mm range and a sturdy tripod as you will likely shoot this scene with a shutter speed of greater than 5 seconds. The advantage of a lens in the 200-300mm range is you can isolate the bridge without introducing any unwanted foreground into your photograph.

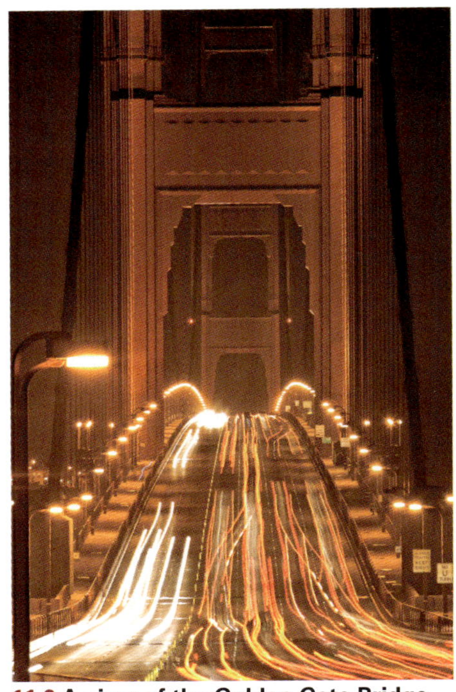

11.6 A view of the Golden Gate Bridge taken at night from North Vista Point (see E on the map) on a clear winter night. Taken at ISO 100, f/8, 10 seconds with a 70-200mm lens.

Visitor Center

This location enables you to capture a wonderful shot of the Golden Gate Bridge and the incredible cliffs that make up the Marin Headlands. Early evening and early morning are the best times to photograph the bridge from this vantage point because the sun is either due west or due east and casts a beautiful sidelight on the bridge. On the right side of the bridge directly adjacent to the Visitor Center are walking paths that lead down to a wonderful garden. From here, you can capture a unique perspective of the Golden Gate Bridge (see figures 11.7 and 11.8). Another popular choice for photographers is to walk onto the bridge itself and photograph the bridge from the walking/biking path that runs along the bridge. This location can offer a unique perspective of arches and cables converging to the blue sky above. I recommend a moderate to long zoom lens, something that can cover 17-200mm range.

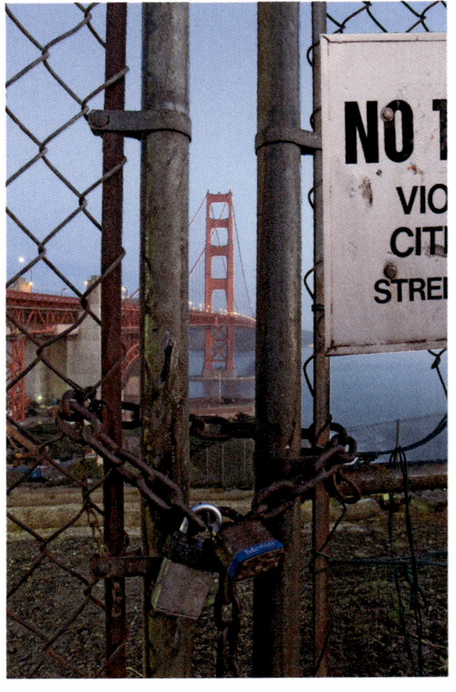

11.7 A view of the Golden Gate Bridge taken just after sunrise from the Visitor Center (see F on the map) on a clear winter day. Taken at ISO 100, f/16, 8 seconds with a 17-35mm lens.

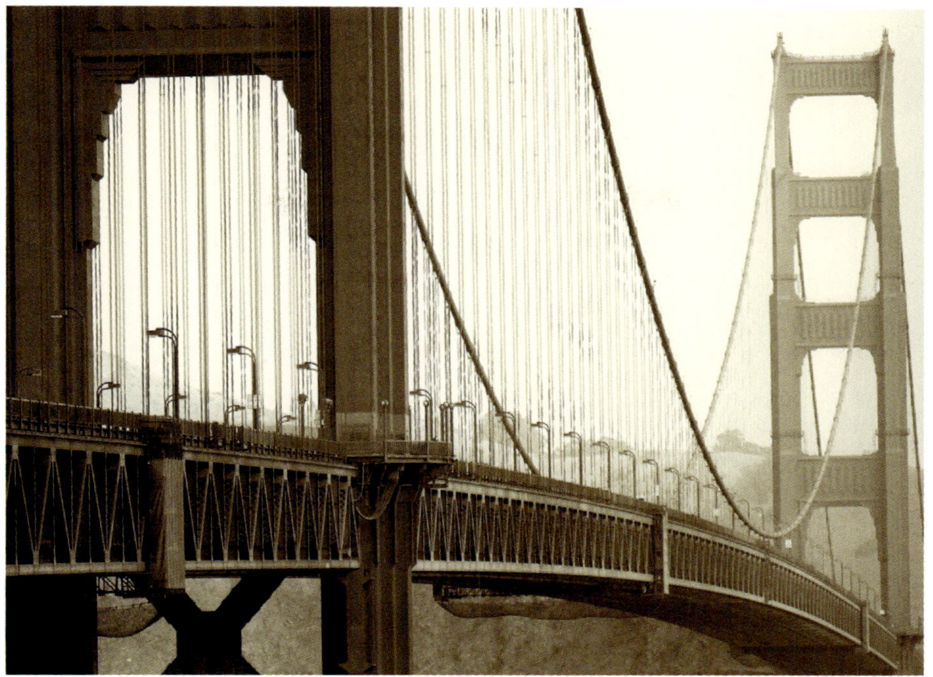

11.8 A view of the Golden Gate Bridge taken midmorning from the Visitor Center on a clear winter day. Taken at ISO 100, f/2.8, 1/1000 second with a 100mm lens.

Conzelman Road Headlands

Conzelman Road has two popular places to photograph the Golden Gate Bridge from: Kirby Cove and Hawk Hill. Conzelman Road is the main road that runs along the Marin Headlands (perpendicular to the Golden Gate Bridge). Follow the road along the cliffs until you reach an area called Kirby Cove. You can see a little area to pull off onto and plenty of places to set up your tripod. This location gives you a wonderful eye-level view of the bridge towers and the city of San Francisco as a backdrop. What makes this such a unique vantage point is the ability for you to isolate the left tower of the Golden Gate Bridge with the city of San Francisco behind. I recommend a lens in the 200-300mm range — Kirby Cove is a half mile from the bridge. The best time to shoot is late in the day as the sun is behind you and casts a warm, low, golden light on the bridge (see figure 11.9). Continuing up Conzelman Road, you arrive at Hawk Hill. This vantage point gives a superb place to photograph the bridge and all the surrounding areas. On a clear day, you can see the Golden Gate Bridge, San Francisco, Alcatraz, and the San Francisco-Oakland Bay Bridge. On a foggy morning, you can expect a blanket of fog to coat the ocean below (see figure 11.10). The ideal lens for Hawk Hill can be anything from 14-300mm. A wide lens gives you a wonderful shot of the entire San Francisco area. A long lens allows you to isolate a specific subject.

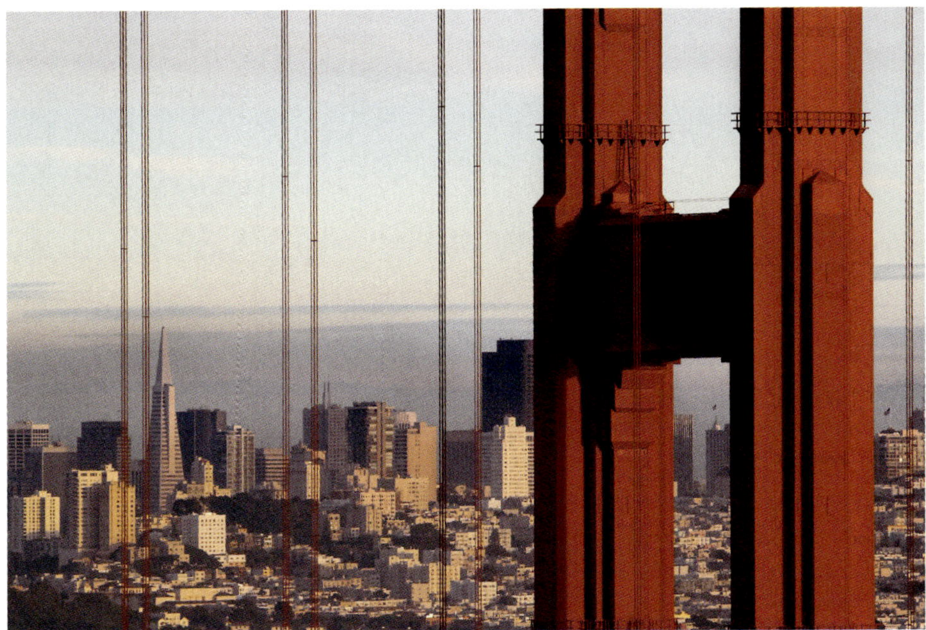

11.9 A view of the Golden Gate Bridge taken late afternoon from Conzelman Road (Kirby Cove) (see G on the map) on a clear winter day. Taken at ISO 100, f/9, 1/60 second with a 200mm lens.

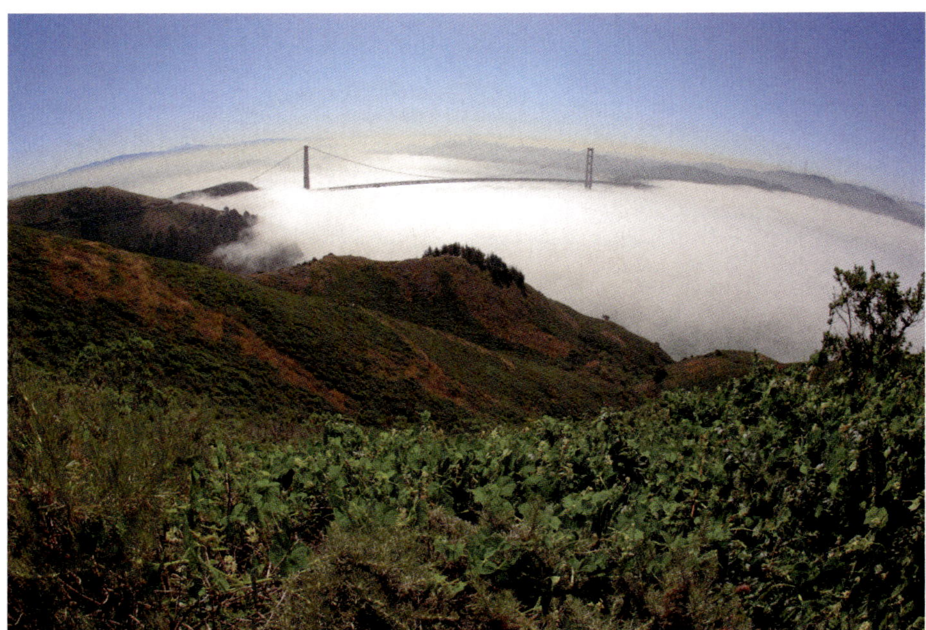

11.10 A view of the Golden Gate Bridge taken midmorning from Conzelman Road (Hawk Hill) on a clear spring day. Taken at ISO 100, f/11, 1/120 second with a 15mm lens.

How Can I Get the Best Shot?

Time of day and weather play a huge part in capturing the best photo. To ensure that you get the best shot, I recommend that you arrive at all locations 15 to 20 minutes prior to the time you actually want to start shooting. Doing so allows you time to walk to the locations that are not accessible by car and the freedom to scout additional locations to shoot from. This also ensures you have plenty of time to set up your gear and dial in your settings.

Equipment

Most photographers are a bit of equipment junkies. I know I am. So I want to cover a little bit about equipment, which can help you capture the best image for a given location. Along with my camera, I bring an assortment of lenses, filters, and a sturdy tripod. A point-and-shoot camera rounds out my assortment of equipment.

Lenses

The choice of lens always comes down to your personal preference and what you want to convey in your photo. Whether you are shooting day or night, your lens choice is critical to creating the ideal composition for any given subject. To photograph the Golden Gate Bridge, I recommend the following lenses:

- **Ultrawide zoom lens in the 14-24mm range.** The ultrawide lens gives you the ability to frame the Golden Gate Bridge from one end to the other. You can be more creative because more things can be included in the final photograph. When using an ultrawide lens, you must be wary about including elements on the outer edge of the frame that you may not want.
- **A standard zoom lens in the 24-100mm range.** This lens can give you much more versatility when traveling. A zoom lens in this range is generally considered the perfect walk-around lens for capturing anything from landscape/cityscapes to pictures of the family.
- **A super-telephoto lens somewhere in the 70-300mm range.** This lens allows you the ability to isolate a particular subject, such as a tower, or gives you the extra reach when shooting subjects that are too far off to shoot with a standard zoom lens.

Filters

I primarily use two filters when photographing the Golden Gate Bridge: a circular polarizing filter and neutral density filter.

- **Circular polarizing filter.** A circular polarizing filter is a filter I suggest every photographer have in his bag. The polarizing filter's main purpose is to cut down or eliminate glare on water, glass, and metal. It can also be used to enhance color and contrast in your photos. I use it primarily to bring out the blue sky in my photos. The maximum effect of polarization can be seen when used at a 90-degree angle from the sun. A polarizer is best used on a lens that is not wider than 24mm because it can cause the sky to be unevenly polarized.
- **Neutral density filter.** A neutral density filter allows you to shoot at a larger aperture when the sun is at its brightest but also allows you to slow your shutter speed 2 or more stops. I have two neutral density filters: One is a 3-stop and the other is a 10-stop filter.

Extras

A sturdy tripod is a must. If you don't own one, buy one. Without a tripod, night shots and low-light shooting are out of the question. I also recommend a cable release and a point-and-shoot camera. A cable release allows you to shoot longer exposures and not have to trigger the shutter by touching the camera, which can cause camera shake and affect the quality of your photograph. A point-and-shoot comes in handy for those quick shots when you don't have your dSLR ready. It also comes in handy when you need to throw in a few pictures of you or the family posing in front of that plaque in front of each monument. Hey, if you're traveling with the family, you need a few shots to show that you really care.

Camera settings

You can choose from many camera settings. How you set up your camera mostly depends on your shooting style and what you want to convey for that particular photo. The settings I use tend to be fairly consistent because I want to capture the maximum resolution the lens and camera combo can achieve. These settings are mostly determined by what I am trying to convey. I usually set my camera in Aperture Priority mode and set the aperture between f/8 and f/16 at ISO 100. In general most camera/lens combinations perform best at these apertures and ISO. I increase or decrease my aperture within this range to increase or decrease my shutter speed. When shooting night or low-light photographs, I tend to opt for the aperture that gives me the slowest shutter speed. Slowing your shutter speed allows you to turn water into a frothy, cotton candy-like surface, or make headlights and taillights on automobiles turn into streaming lasers of light.

In many cases you may want a greater depth of field, meaning that a greater area from front to back will be in perfect focus. This can be achieved in general by shooting at a smaller aperture (larger f-number). Briefly, depth of field is controlled by aperture, focal length, and distance from the subject. So generally if you want the flowers 3 feet in front and the bridge 500 yards behind the flowers to be in perfect focus, you need to select an aperture in the f/16 to f/22 range. If depth of field is not important, say, in the case of shooting the Golden Gate Bridge where you are already focusing at infinity, set the aperture from f/8 to f/11, which maximizes resolution.

- **Exposure mode.** I generally shoot in Aperture Priority mode. To set my exposure, I choose the ideal aperture, which for me tends to be between f/8 and f/16. My camera then chooses the correct shutter speed. I adjust my aperture to raise or lower the shutter speed to create the desired effect. I shoot in Manual mode when a tricky lighting condition causes my camera's meter to under- or overexpose.
- **Exposure compensation.** Exposure compensation is a handy setting that you can use to adjust exposure; plus for more light or minus for less light. In general most cameras allow at least a 3-stop difference either direction. I tend to use exposure compensation in many situations. In these situations, I dial in a +1 or +2 to allow more light into the camera to properly expose my subject. I dial in a minus exposure compensation when shooting silhouettes because doing this aids in darkening the sky and creates a wonderful silhouette.
- **White balance.** White balance I never touch because I find the Auto White Balance of all modern day cameras to be pretty good.
- **ISO.** In general, to maximize your camera's image quality, leave the ISO at 100 when shooting landscapes. The few times I may have increased the ISO was to increase the shutter speed or to allow me to use a smaller or larger aperture.

Exposure

Understanding exposure is the key to all photography. If you underexpose your photo, you can introduce unwanted noise and artifacts by trying to recover the photo in post-processing. Overexposing can add blown highlights that are areas of unrecoverable data. All modern day cameras have some form of matrix (Nikon) or multi-zone metering system (Canon) that are darn near perfect. My recommendation is to let the camera do the metering.

Ideal time to shoot

The ideal time to shoot is just before and just after the sun rises or sets, known as the golden hour of light. Typically, lighting is softer (more diffuse) and warmer in hue, and shadows are longer. Just before the sun comes up and just after the sun goes down are also ideal times to shoot because the night sky is a dusky blue. With the Golden Gate Bridge, this is no exception.

Working around the weather

Weather in San Francisco is not as much an issue as in other parts of the country. You can expect moderate weather, where cool summers and mild winters and warm spring and fall almost blend into one. Morning and evening fog is common during summer months for San Francisco, but it rarely remains throughout the day. September and October tend to be the warmest and clearest months, whereas rain can be common in late November through March. San Francisco weather literally varies from neighborhood to neighborhood; it may be sunny and pleasant in one area and foggy and cool in another. No season in San Francisco is really out of the question for photographing the Golden Gate Bridge.

However, if you wake up one morning planning to photograph the Golden Gate only to look outside and see the city blanketed in a thick, wet fog, don't hit the snooze and go back to bed; use this opportunity to photograph the Golden Gate Bridge protruding through the fog. Not only can this be the most beautiful time to photograph the Golden Gate Bridge, but also it can result in the most dramatic image. When shooting into a thick blanket of fog, you need to apply a little plus exposure compensation to account for the amount of underexposure your camera will do when exposing against the thick white fog. Camera metering systems tend to underexpose when shooting at white and overexpose when shooting at black. If you shoot fog at night, you need to dial in +2/3 exposure compensation to get the correct exposure (see figure 11.11).

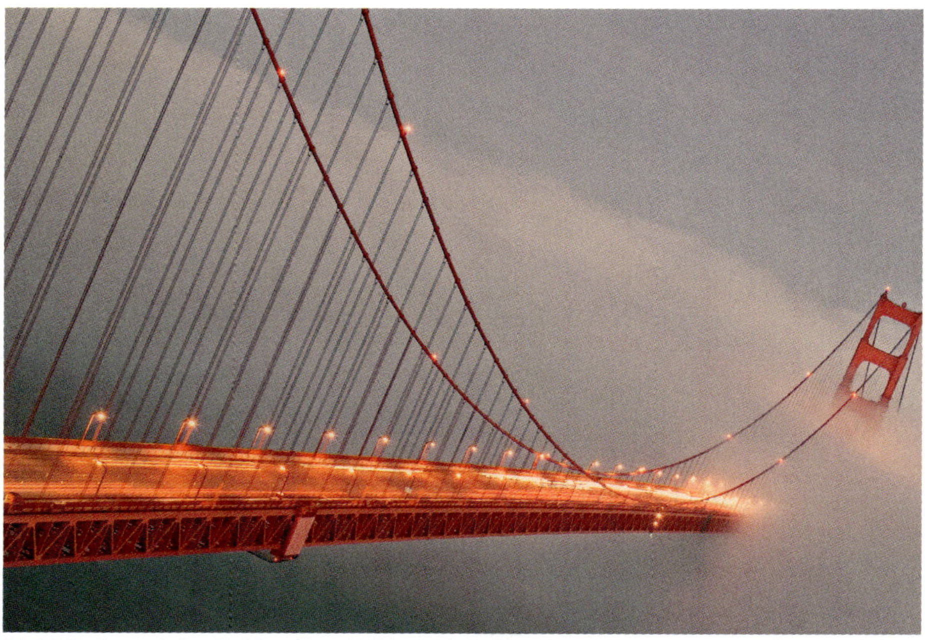

11.11 A view of the Golden Gate Bridge taken from the Marin Headlands (see A on the map) on a foggy summer night. Taken at ISO 100, f/9, 5 seconds with a 35mm lens.

Low-light and night options

If you're going to photograph the Golden Gate Bridge and you have a choice between day or night, I recommend night. Shooting the Golden Gate Bridge at night is a must for any photographer because it can allow you to create some very dramatic lighting effects. When shooting night shots of the bridge, a sturdy tripod and cable release is a must. You put your camera in Aperture Priority mode with an ISO of 100. You can expect your shutter speed to be in the area of 5 to 30 seconds with an aperture between f/8 and f/16. These slow shutter speeds and small apertures create streams of light from automobiles, starburst from the bridge lamps, and a glow of light blanketing the ocean below the bridge. If the proper shutter speed cannot be achieved by using the above settings, bump up your ISO until the desired shutter speed is achieved (see figure 11.12)

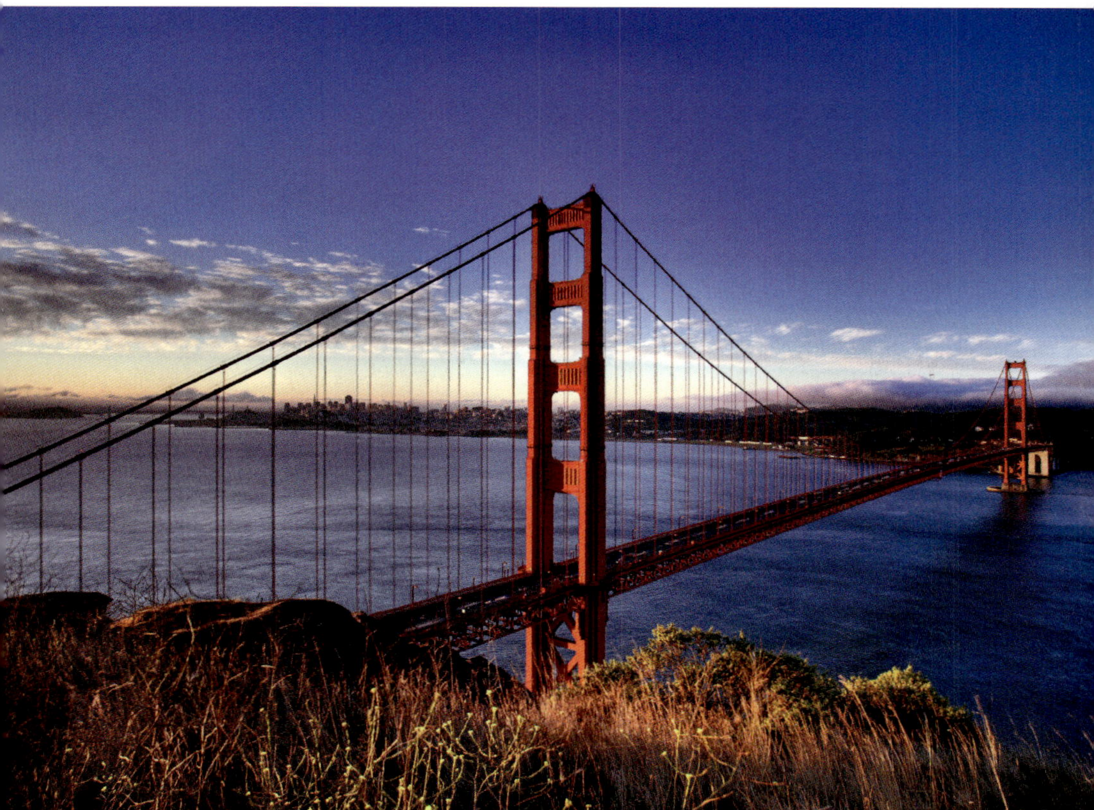

11.12 A view of the Golden Gate Bridge taken after sunrise from the Marin Headlands on a clear summer morning. Taken at ISO 100, f/8, 1/6th second with a 17-35mm lens.

Getting creative

If you want to try something a little more creative, I recommend shooting the bridge with a fisheye lens. The 180-degree angle the lens provides can create unique and intriguing effects on the bridge and horizon (see figure 11.13). A fisheye lens is a wide-angle lens that takes in an extremely wide, hemispherical image. I like to use a fisheye when shooting broad landscapes to suggest the curve of the earth. Using a fisheye is about the same as using other wide lenses with one exception: The more you tilt the lens above and below the horizon, the more you can exaggerate the fisheye effect.

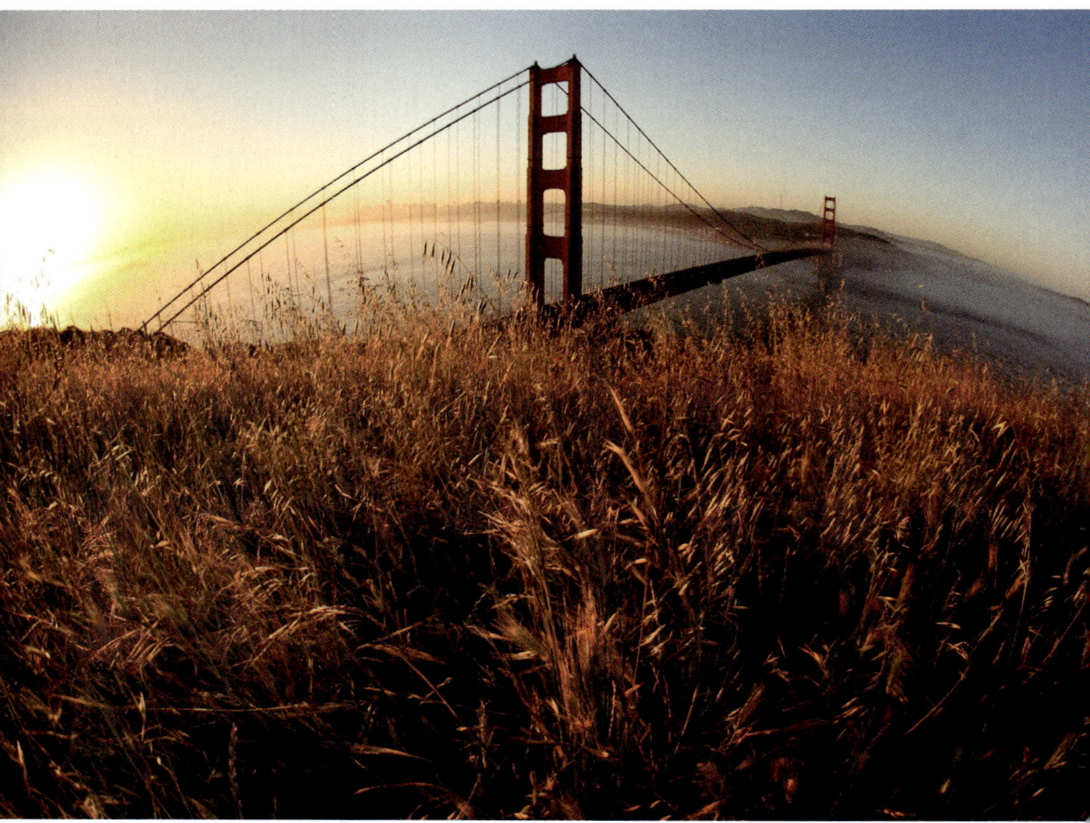

11.13 A view of the Golden Gate Bridge taken from the Marin Headlands on a clear spring morning. Taken at ISO 100, f/8, 1/180 second with a 15mm fisheye lens.

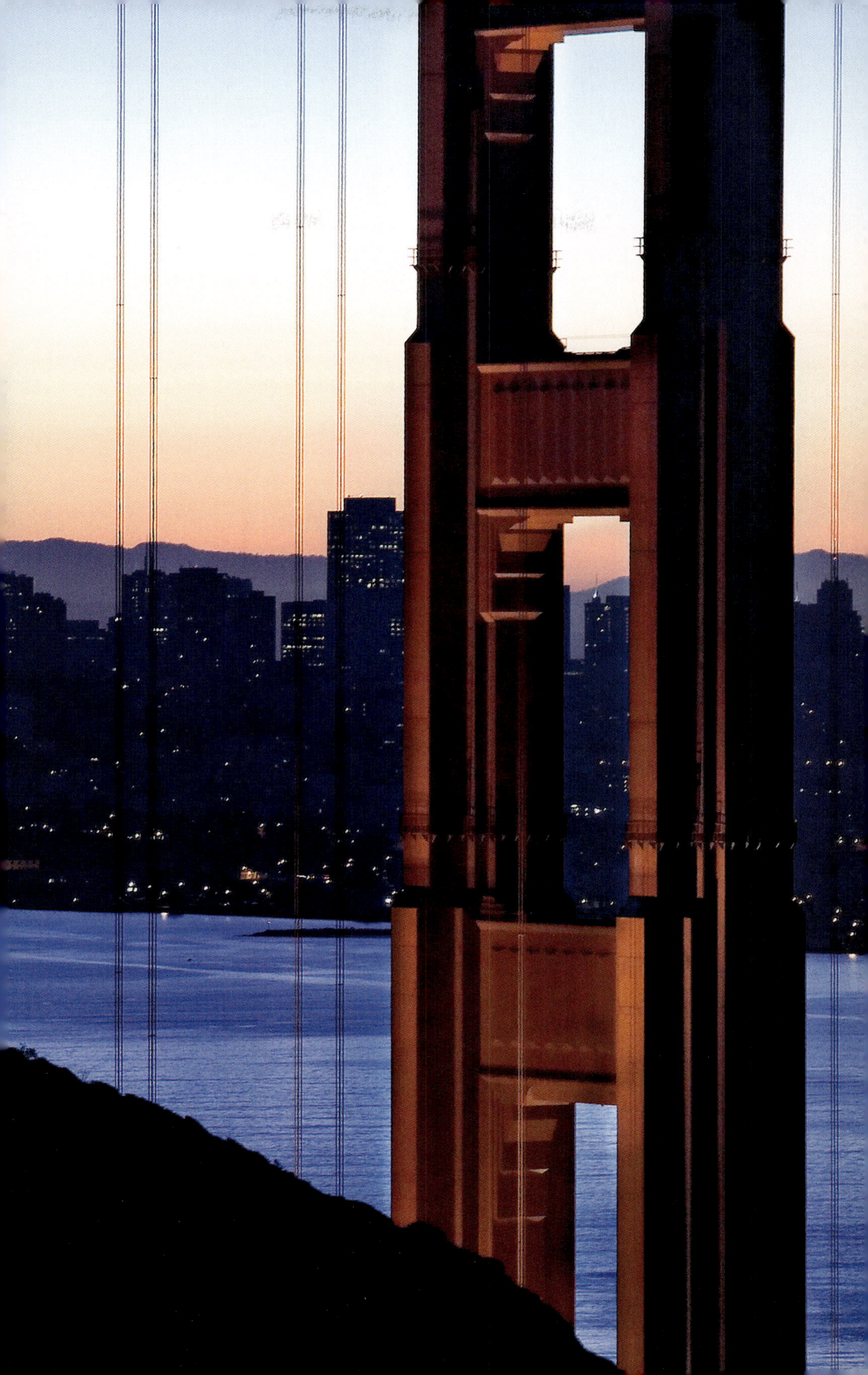

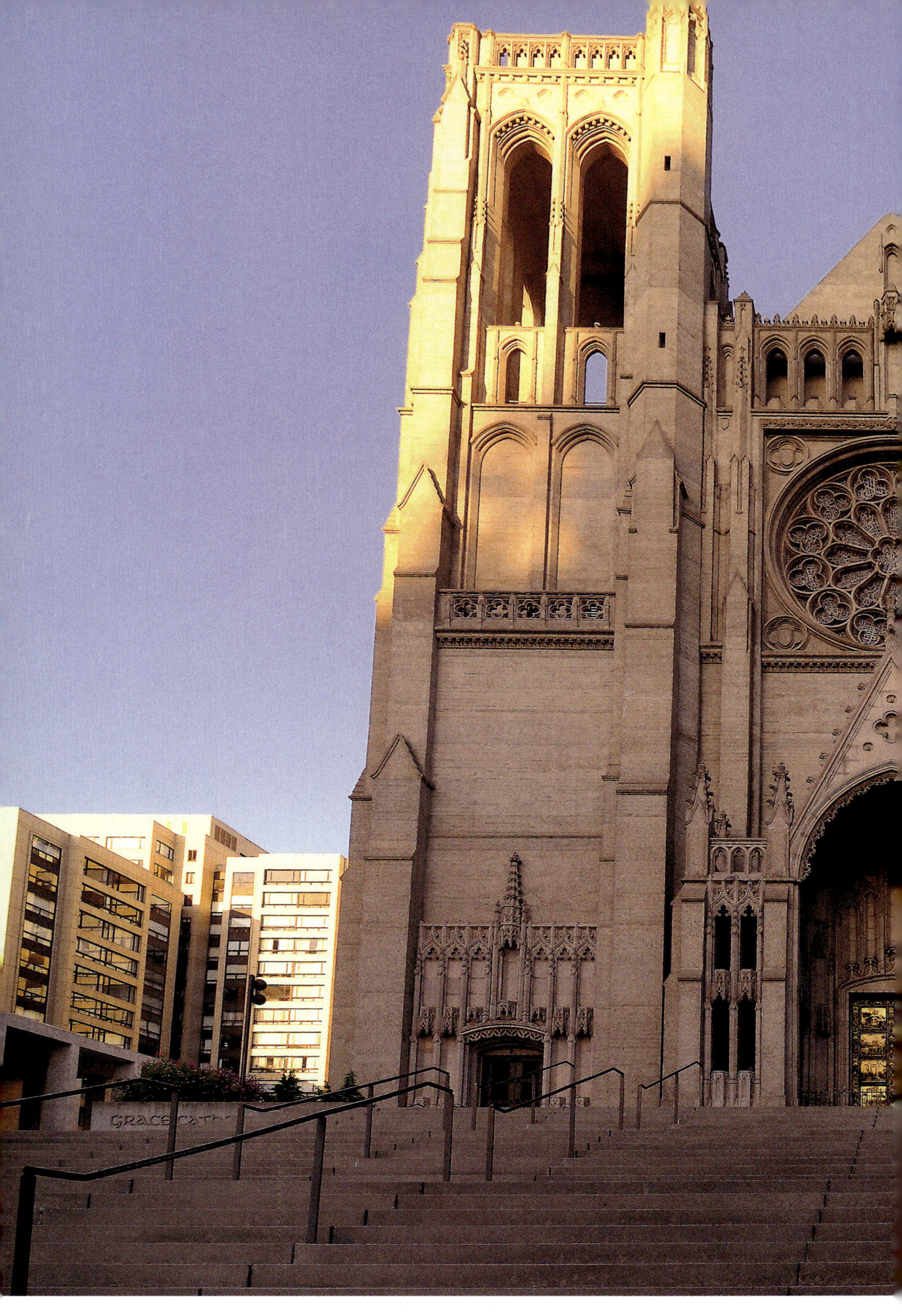

A view of the Grace Cathedral taken just after sunrise on a clear summer day. Taken at ISO 100, f/8, 1/60 second with a 14-24mm lens.

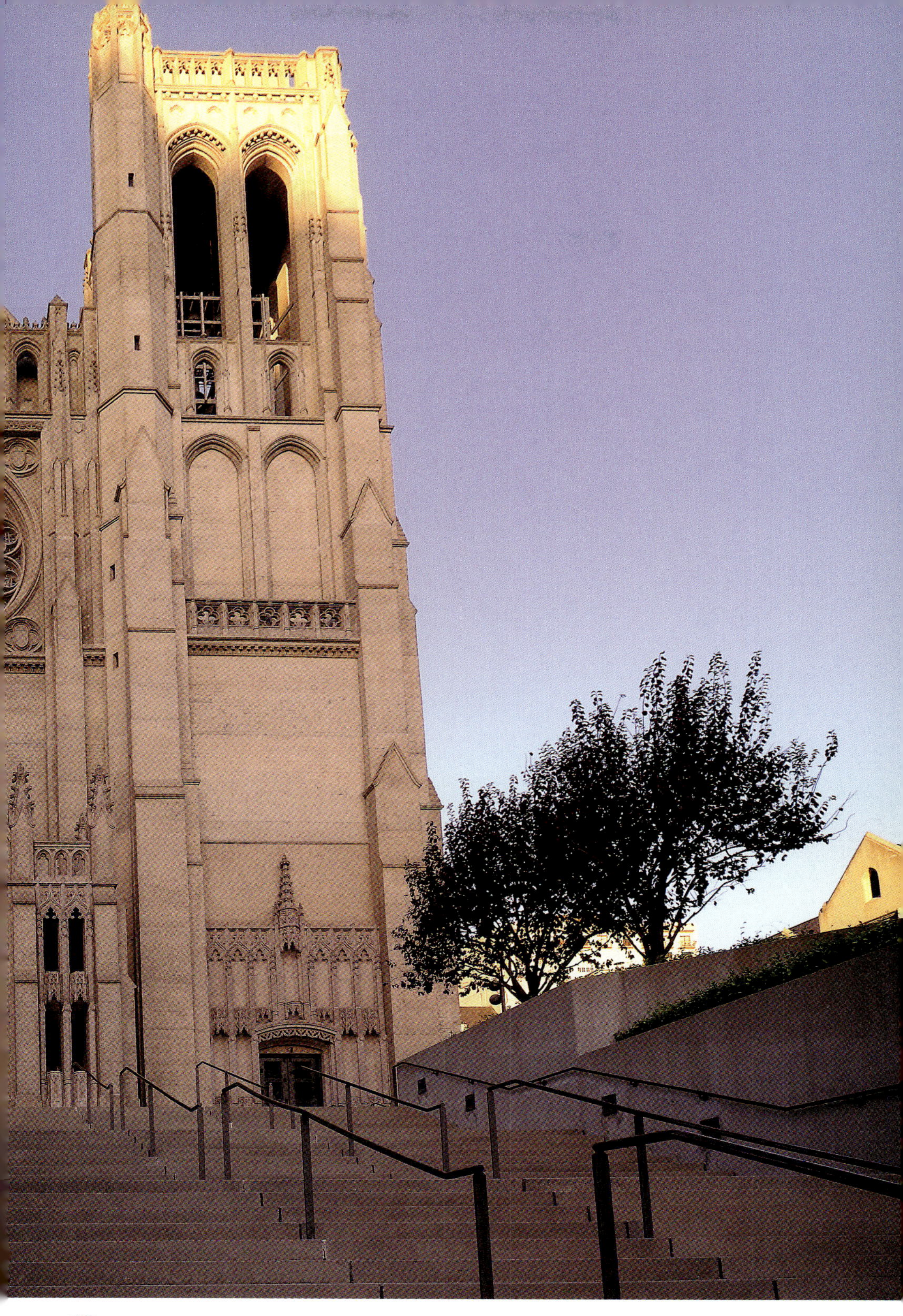

12 Grace Cathedral

Why It's Worth a Photograph

Grace Cathedral is an Episcopal cathedral located on Nob Hill in San Francisco. The church was founded during the gold rush year of 1849. Grace Cathedral is the daughter of historic Grace Church. The cathedral community is known for its open-mindedness. All kinds of people walk through these doors every day. Many come to participate in worship services, walk the labyrinths, seek a peaceful place, or pray. Famed as a destination for visitors from all over the world, the cathedral is known for its striking gothic architecture, amazing collection of art, beautiful stained-glass windows, and its medieval and contemporary furnishings. The cathedral entrance has an impressive pair of doors, often called the Ghiberti doors. They are a copy of the doors of the Florence Baptistry, also dubbed Gates of Paradise. Laid out on the floor of Grace Cathedral is a labyrinth that is based on the famous medieval labyrinth of Cathédrale Notre-Dame de Chartres (the Cathedral of Our Lady of Chartres) located in Chartres, France. It is said that if a visitor walks the pattern of the labyrinth, it will bring him to a meditative state. Why is this worth a picture? The beautiful gothic architecture, the medieval-style furnishings, and the wonderfully colorful stained-glass windows make this a wonderful place to capture and show the essence of one of the most beautiful churches in America.

Where Can I Get the Best Shot?

California Street at Taylor Street offers you the best vantage point to photograph this wonderful Gothic-style church (see A on the map).

California Street

There are many angles to shoot from at this location, and the first and foremost is from the bottom of the steps. This angle along with a wide-angle lens gives you a direct shot of the church with the stairs and handrails leading the eye straight to the front door. Shoot this in the early morning when the sun is low and warm, creating wonderful soft shadows on the white stone. Also bring a medium telephoto lens so that you can isolate the wonderful detail inlaid on the stone (see figure 12.1). If you want to photograph the inside of the church, you need to arrive after 7 a.m. The interior architecture and furnishings are stunning. Bring a wide lens to photograph the massive hall and the wonderful stained-glass windows (see figure 12.2).

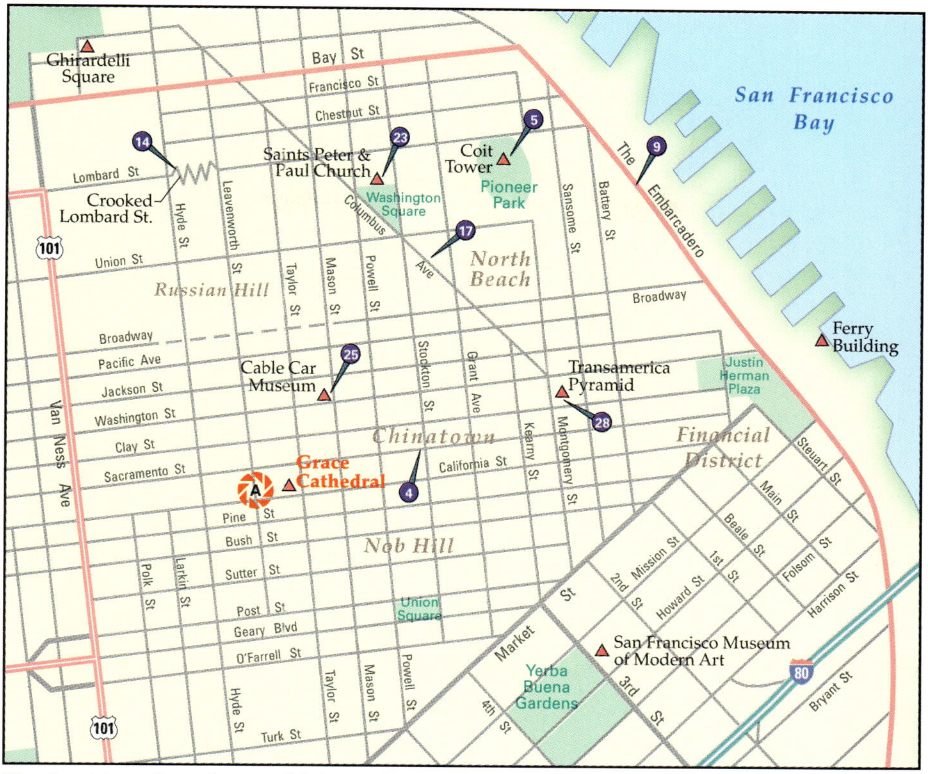

The best locations from which to photograph Grace Cathedral: (A) California Street. Other photo ops: (4) Chinatown, (5) Coit Tower, (9) Embarcadero, (14) Lombard Street, (17) North Beach, (23) Saints Peter and Paul Church, (25) San Francisco cable cars, (28) Transamerica Pyramid.

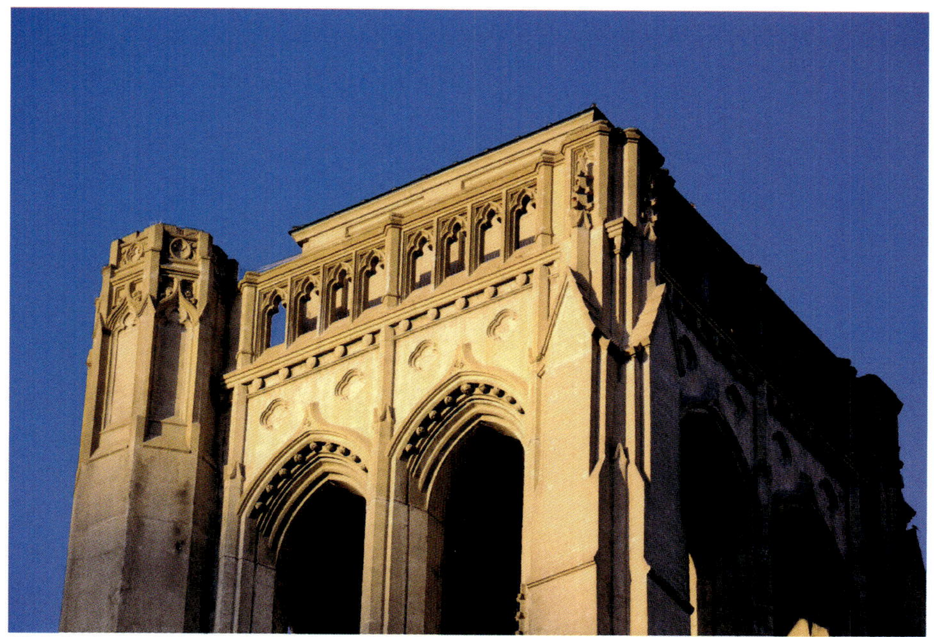

12.1 A view of Grace Cathedral taken just after sunrise on a clear summer day (see A on the map). Taken at ISO 100, f/8, 1/125 second with a 70-200mm lens.

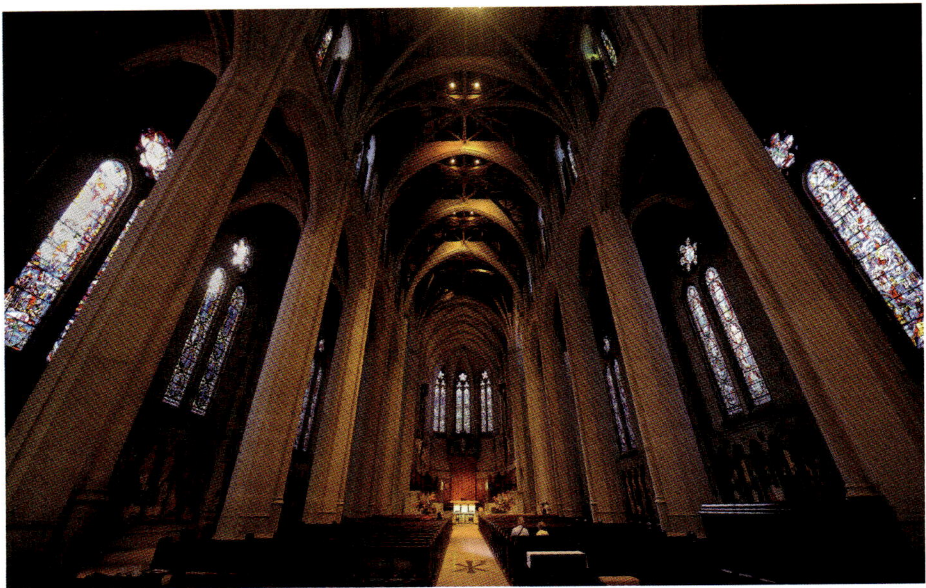

12.2 **A view of the interior of Grace Cathedral taken on a clear autumn day. Taken at ISO 1600, f/2.8, 1/40 second with a 14-24mm lens.**

How Can I Get the Best Shot?

Early morning light can really enhance the detail in the stone. This is the easiest time of day to shoot and produces some of the nicest images (see figure 12.3). A clear blue sky is a must because the white stone blends into a gray sky. You want to create contrast between the stone and a blue morning sky to really make the church stand out.

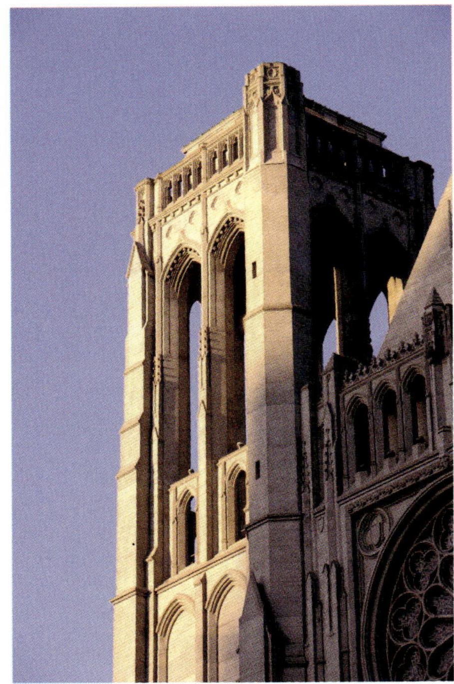

12.3 **A view of Grace Cathedral taken just after sunrise on a clear summer day. Taken at ISO 100, f/8, 1/80 second with a 70-200mm lens.**

If you have a clear evening, a photo taken just before sunset, glowing with warm colorful hues, can create a stunning photo. This time of day can be a very tricky time to shoot because the church will tend to cause the camera to underexpose against the bright sunset. Use an ultrawide-angle lens if you are shooting inside the church to capture the enormous space. Slightly overcast skies will benefit you here because the stained-glass windows allow light in from the outside, making it difficult to expose the entire space without blown highlights if it's not overcast.

A flash would help with exposure inside the church, but the cathedral does not allow it.

Equipment

A good tripod, an ultrawide lens, and a medium telephoto lens are the three pieces of equipment that are critical for capturing sharp images of Grace Cathedral.

Lenses

An ultrawide and medium telephoto lens are the two lenses that are critical for capturing the perfect images of Grace Cathedral.

- **Ultrawide zoom lens in the 14-24mm range.** The ultrawide lens gives you the ability to create a unique perspective. By including something in the immediate foreground, you can create a sense of depth that can lead the person's eyes to the church. Using this lens also gives you the ability to capture the interior of the church.
- **A zoom lens somewhere in the 70-200mm range.** This focal range allows you the ability to isolate the church's towers against the blue sky.

Extras

A tripod is useful when shooting Grace Cathedral. A tripod can help stabilize the camera and lens when shooting in early morning or late evening light. It is also useful for shooting the interior of the church where your shutter speed will be too slow to hand hold.

Camera settings

Setting up your camera comes down to time of day, amount of light, and composition. When shooting with a long lens from a distance, mount your camera on a tripod and set the aperture from f/8 to f/11; this will maximize your image quality. When shooting up close with your ultrawide lens where you have an immediate object in the foreground, set your aperture to f/22 to maximize your depth of field.

- **Exposure mode.** I set my camera in Aperture Priority mode and let my camera choose the shutter speed. I dial in a minus exposure compensation to help protect the highlights from blowing out on the windows inside the church.

- **White balance.** White balance I never touch as I find the Auto White Balance of all modern day cameras to be pretty good.
- **ISO.** ISO should stay as low as possible unless you are handholding your camera. Adjust your ISO to get a shutter speed that is fast enough for you to hand hold a long lens. The day I shot inside Grace Cathedral, I did not have a tripod, so I bumped up the ISO to 1600 and shot at f/2.8 to give me a 1/40 second. This was fast enough for me to hand hold.

Exposure

I allow my camera's metering system to make most of the tough decisions for me. On occasion, I have to dial in exposure compensation or shoot in Manual mode to create the desired effect. Use your histogram on the back of your camera to help judge whether the exposure fits what you see and what you want to convey.

Ideal time to shoot

The ideal time to shoot is in the early morning when the sun is low and the church is being bathed with soft, warm light, creating wonderful light and shadows that accentuate form and detail.

Working around the weather

The winter months between late November and early March can have unpredictable rainstorms. During the summer months, the city can be blanketed in thick fog. Plan your mornings when it is clear and the sun is out. The best times are late spring, late summer, and early fall.

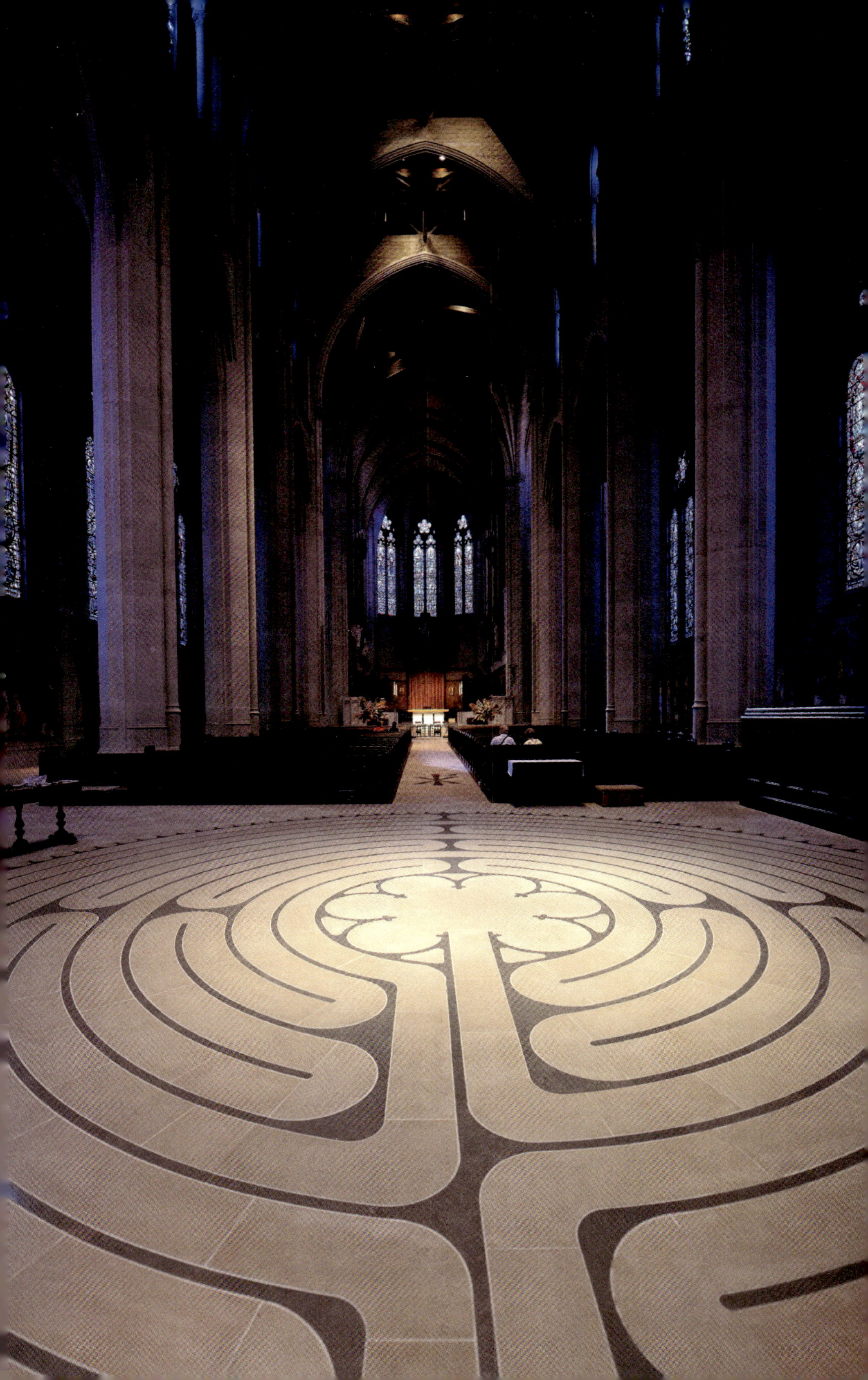

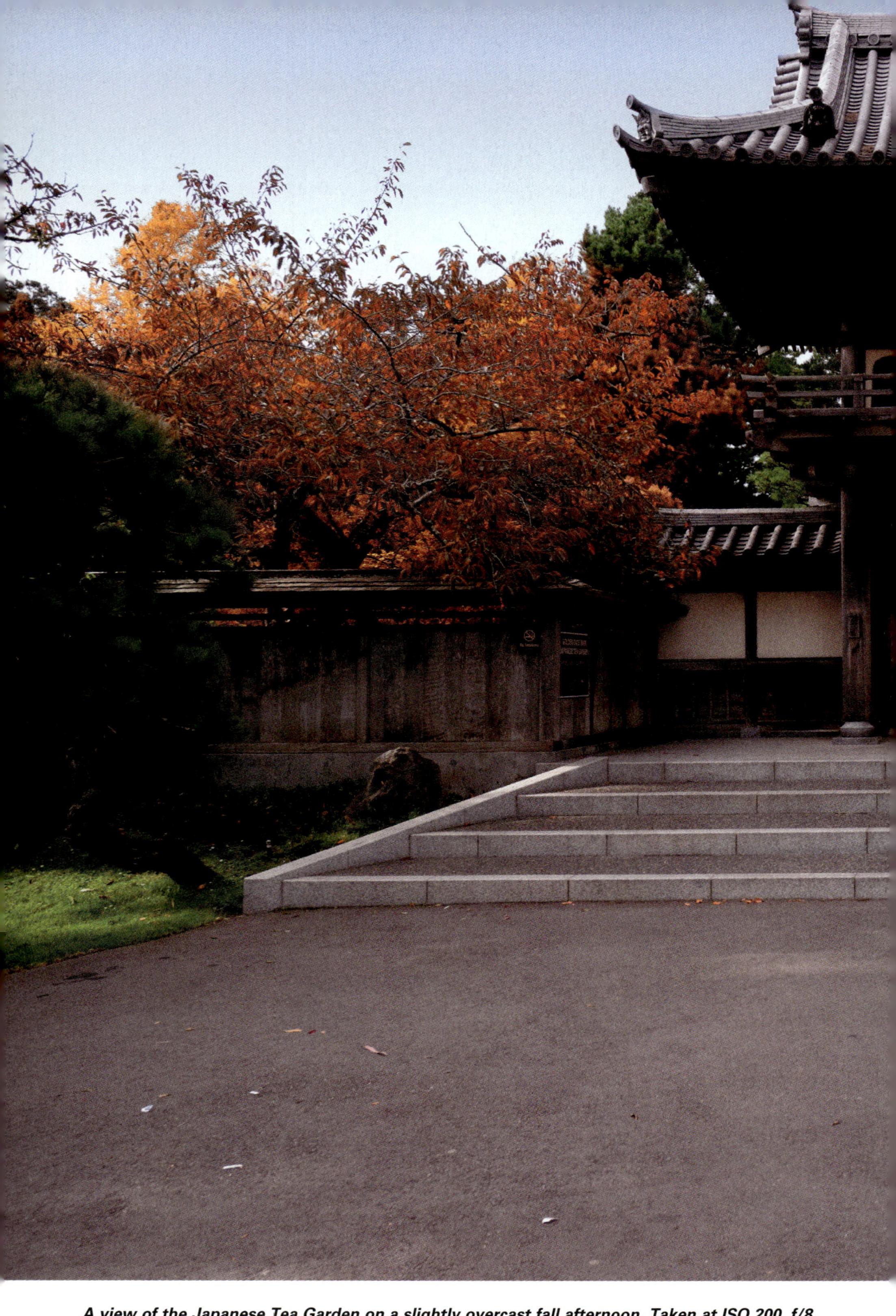

A view of the Japanese Tea Garden on a slightly overcast fall afternoon. Taken at ISO 200, f/8, 1/160 second with a 14-24mm lens.

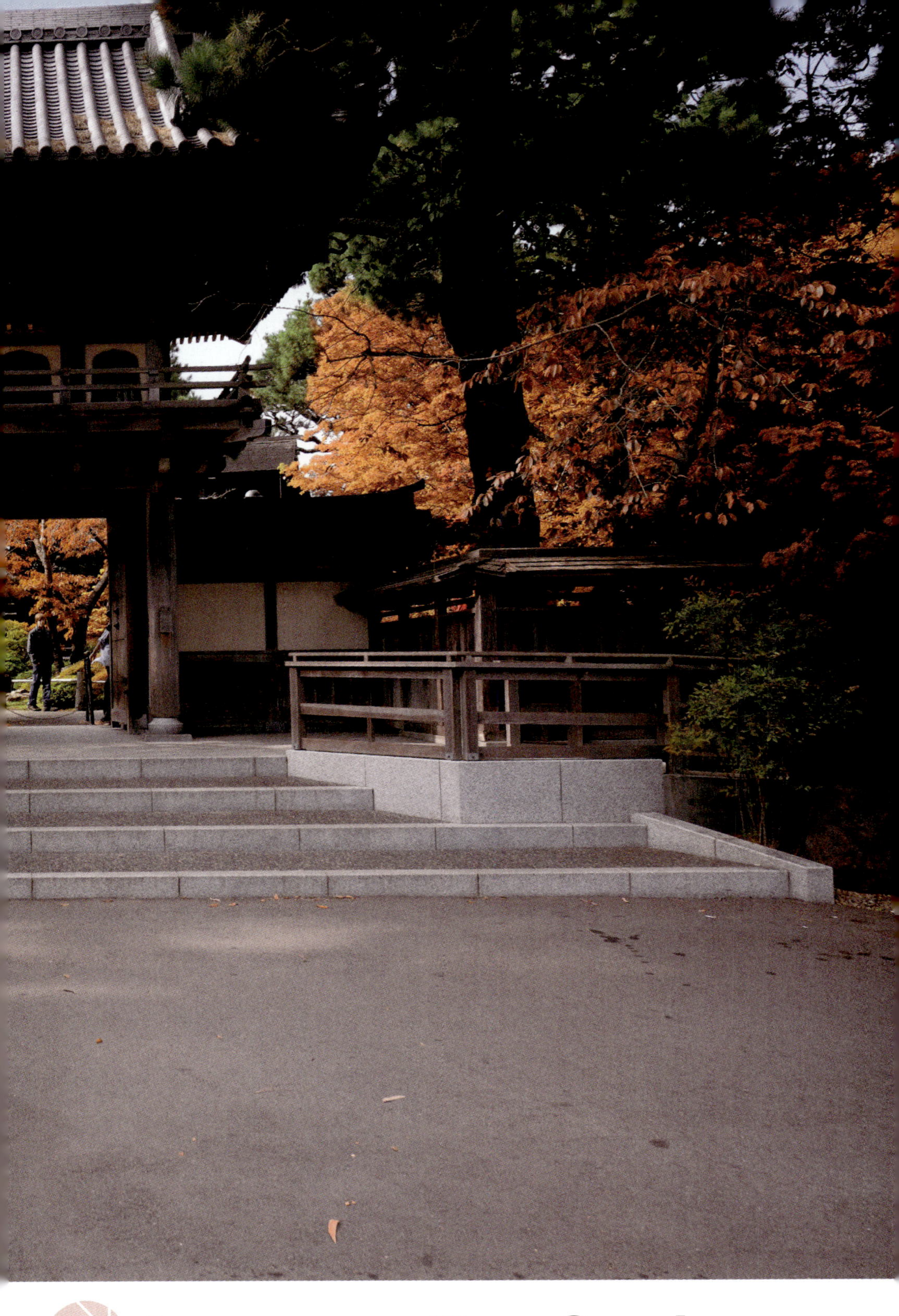

13 Japanese Tea Garden

Why It's Worth a Photograph

The Japanese Tea Garden, located in Golden Gate Park, is the oldest public Japanese garden in the United States. The garden is wonderfully landscaped complete with quaint bridges, sunken ponds, waterfalls, and statues. The two main seasons to visit the tea garden are the spring and fall months. The spring months delight you with cherry trees in full bloom, along with many other tree varieties and flowers. The fall season is another wonderful time to photograph the tea garden. When the weather turns cold in late October, the garden's greenery is kindled by the glow of fleeting fall color. The red fiery tones of maple leaves and the golden foliage of ginkgoes serve as reminders that fall is a vibrant season in Golden Gate Park. What makes the Japanese Tea Garden worth a photograph? The garden is made up of colorful landscaping: winding paths, atmospheric bridges, ornamental lanterns, ornate gateways, gentle slopes, and tranquil water. All these things combined with soft overcast light can create a wonderful photo filled with vibrant colors, textures, and form.

Where Can I Get the Best Shot?

The best place to photograph the Japanese Tea Garden is from Tea Garden Drive in Golden Gate Park (see A on the map).

Tea Garden Drive

There are many places inside the tea garden to photograph the wonderful colors and textures offered by the garden. The first location I recommend is directly in front of the entrance. This is a great spot to get the Asian-inspired architecture, surrounded by the lush, colorful vegetation that makes up the garden. Once inside the garden, take a walk along the winding concrete path until you reach an arching bridge. Set up your tripod and photograph back across the pond, capturing the maple trees, cherry blossom trees, and tea garden structure that gets swallowed up in the lush yet controlled garden vegetation (see figure 13.1). Following the path past the bridge, you come across another pond with incredible colors and depth. The pond as the foreground leads you to the background, a wonderfully colorful Asian-inspired pagoda that gets swallowed on all sides by the advancing garden and steep terrain (see figure 13.2). Continuing through the garden, you encounter numerous other tranquil areas you may want to photograph. Enjoy your walk and remember to not just look down but to also look up. You might see something worth a photograph (see figure 13.3).

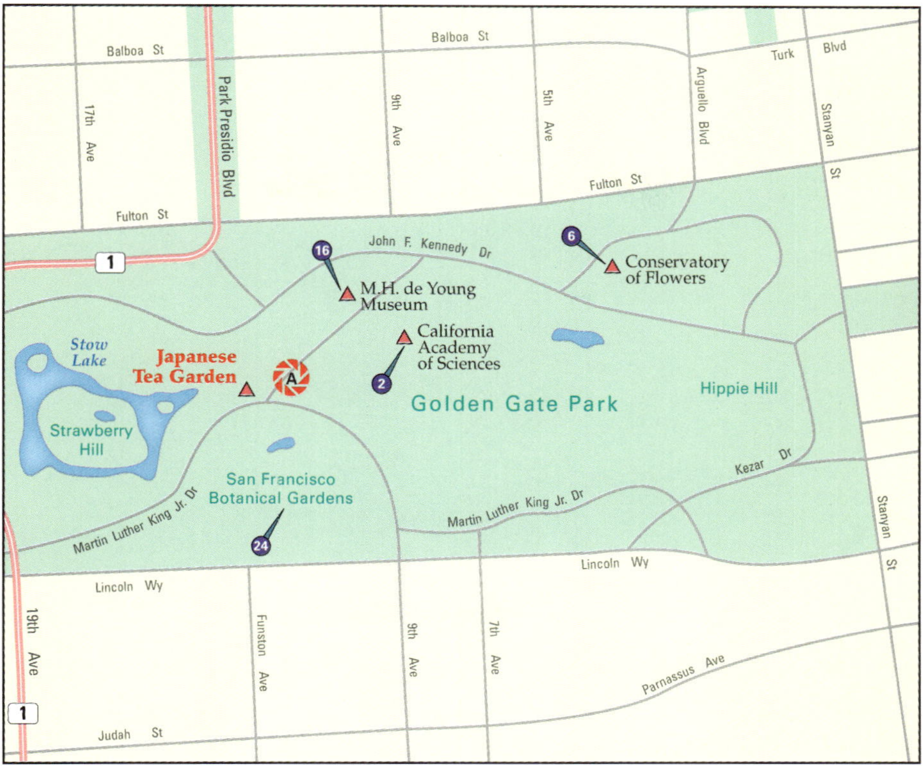

The best location from which to photograph the Japanese Tea Garden: (A) Tea Garden Drive. Other photo ops: (2) California Academy of Sciences, (6) Conservatory of Flowers, (16) M.H. de Young Museum, (24) San Francisco Botanical Garden.

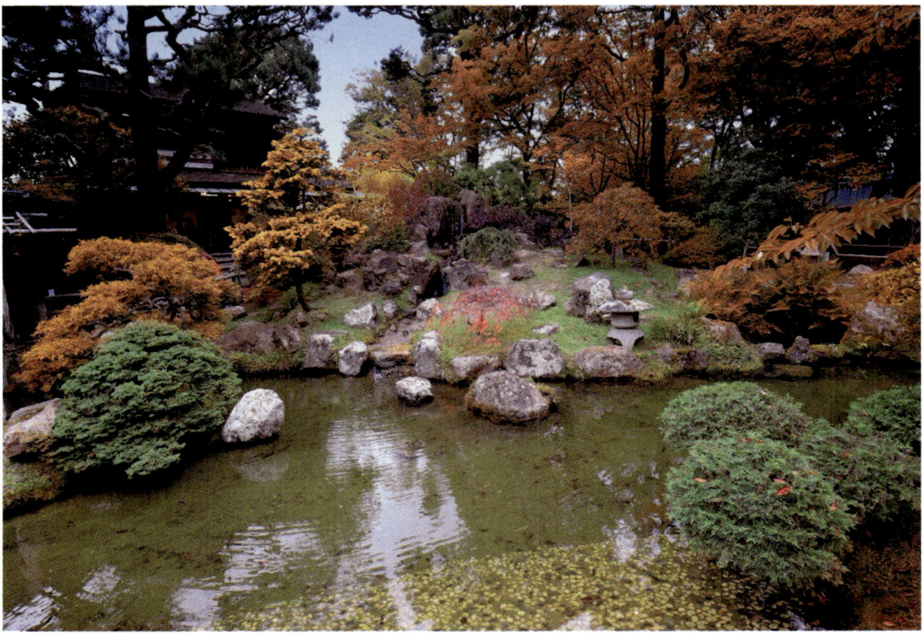

13.1 A view of the Japanese Tea Garden taken on an overcast autumn afternoon (see A on the map). Taken at ISO 400, f/8, 1/40 second with a 14-24mm lens.

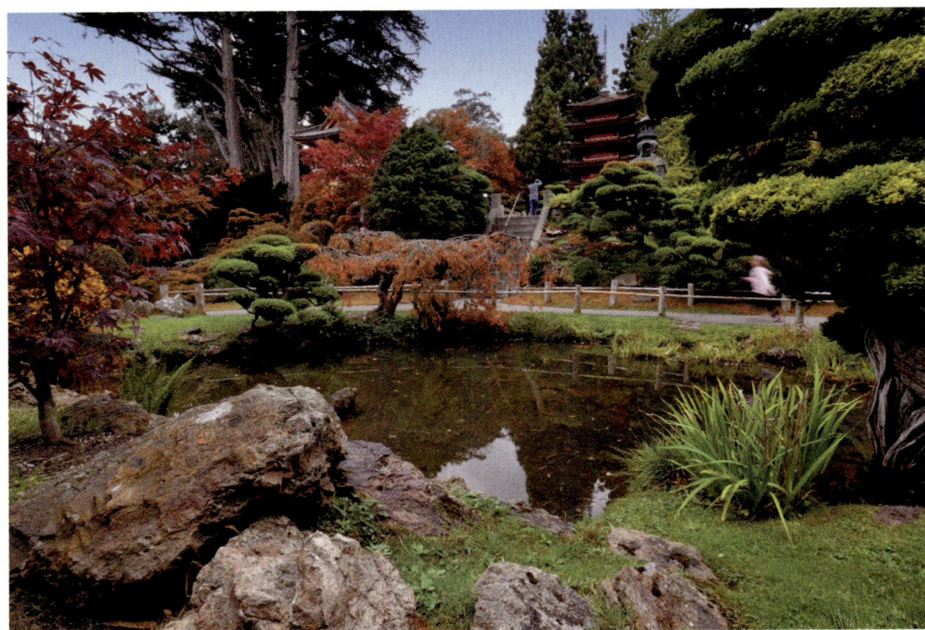

13.2 A view of the Japanese Tea Garden with a pagoda in the background taken on an overcast autumn afternoon. Taken at ISO 500, f/22, 1/13 second with a 14-24mm lens.

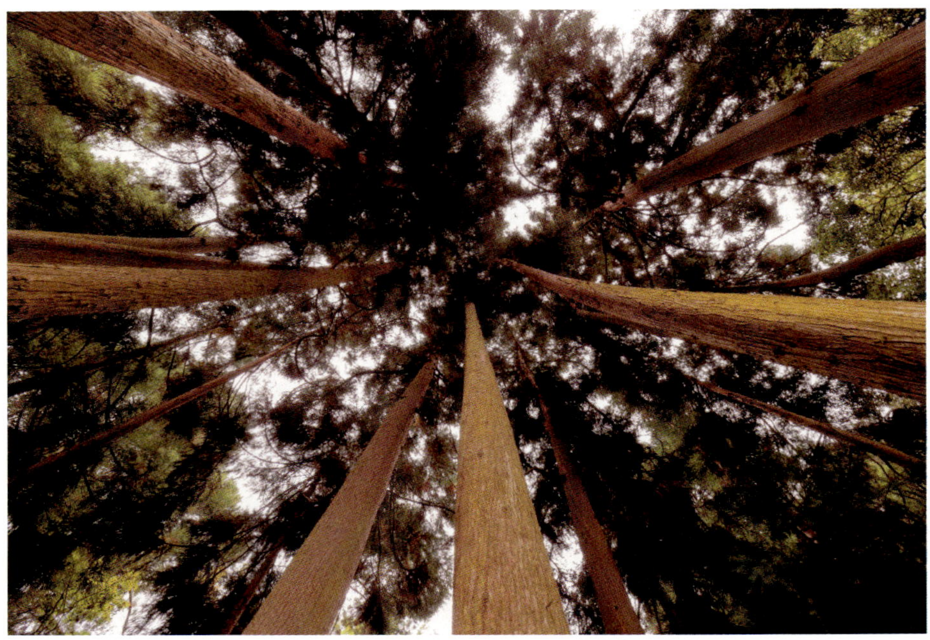

13.3 A view of wonderful tall trees in the Japanese Tea Garden on an overcast autumn afternoon. Taken at ISO 100, f/8, 1/25 second with a 14-24mm lens.

How Can I Get the Best Shot?

Unlike many of the other locations in this book, time of day is less important than the weather. Plan your trip to the tea garden when the sky is slightly overcast or foggy. The overcast sky helps create an even, diffused lighting void of any harsh shadows. Try not to include too much of the sky, because you want the photo to appear as a bright, sunny, warm day. Bring a tripod when shooting with slow shutter speeds to ensure that you have a crisp photo with a straight horizon.

Be prepared for large crowds on narrow paths — they can disrupt your composition.

Equipment

A good tripod, an ultrawide lens, and a standard zoom lens are the three pieces of equipment that are critical for capturing sharp images at the Japanese Tea Garden.

Lenses

An ultrawide and a standard zoom lens are the two lenses you should carry to ensure that you can cover the proper focal range.

- **Ultrawide zoom lens in the 14-24mm range.** The ultrawide lens gives you the ability to create a unique perspective. This type of lens comes in handy for creating an ultrawide perspective of the tea garden's landscape.
- **A standard zoom lens in the 24-100mm range.** This lens can give you much more versatility when traveling. This lens is the jack-of-all-trades and is best used for street shooting and inside buildings. This is a great lens for the garden because it gives you a wide perspective in conjunction with a longer focal length for isolating subjects.

Filters

I primarily use two filters when photographing the Golden Gate Bridge: a circular polarizing filter and a neutral density filter.

- **Circular polarizing filter.** A circular polarizing filter is one I suggest every photographer have in his bag. The polarizing filter's main purpose is to cut down or eliminate glare on water, glass, and metal. It can also be used to enhance color and contrast in your photos. I would recommend using it here as it can really help enhance the reds, oranges, greens, and yellows.
- **Neutral density filter.** A neutral density filter allows you to shoot at a larger aperture when the sun is at its brightest but also allows you to slow your shutter speed 2 or more stops. I generally use either a 3-stop or a 10-stop filter.

Extras

Because your shutter speeds will likely be too slow to hand hold, a tripod is essential for capturing sharp photos in the garden. A cable release to trigger the shutter and a bubble level to level the horizon can come in handy for these types of shots.

Camera settings

Setting up your camera comes down to the time of day, amount of light, and composition. When shooting up close with your ultrawide lens, if you have an object in the immediate foreground, set your aperture from f/16 to f/22 to maximize your depth of field.

- **Exposure mode.** I set my camera in Aperture Priority mode and let my camera choose the shutter speed. I may dial in a plus or minus exposure compensation depending on the overall scene. When shooting in the garden, I dialed in a –1/3 to –2/3 exposure to help protect the highlighted areas.
- **White balance.** White balance I never touch because I find the Auto White Balance of all modern day cameras to be pretty good.
- **ISO.** ISO should stay as low as possible unless you are handholding your camera. Adjust your ISO to get a shutter speed that is fast enough for you to hand hold your camera.

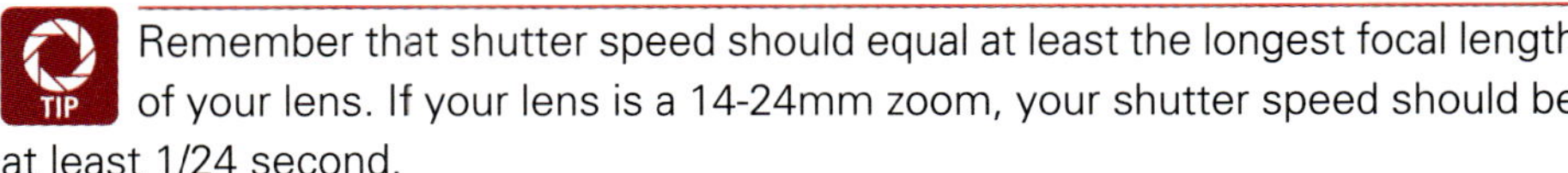

Remember that shutter speed should equal at least the longest focal length of your lens. If your lens is a 14-24mm zoom, your shutter speed should be at least 1/24 second.

Exposure

When you have harsh lighting conditions, expose for your foreground as the tea garden should be your primary subject. On days when it is foggy or overcast, try not to include the sky as it can cause underexposure, and you want to convey that warm, sunny experience. Remember you may have to add in a bit of exposure compensation to compensate for the underexposure caused by the white overcast sky.

Ideal time to shoot

The Japanese Tea Garden is open during normal business hours so shooting in the wee morning or late evening isn't going to happen unless you know someone. It's not as much about the time of day as it is about the light. Plan your trip around a slightly overcast day.

Working around the weather

The spring and late fall are the ideal times to shoot. The spring and fall colors are the most vibrant and will add that extra pop to your photo. Coincidentally, these are the best months as far as the weather is concerned. You can expect little if any rain and warmer temperatures.

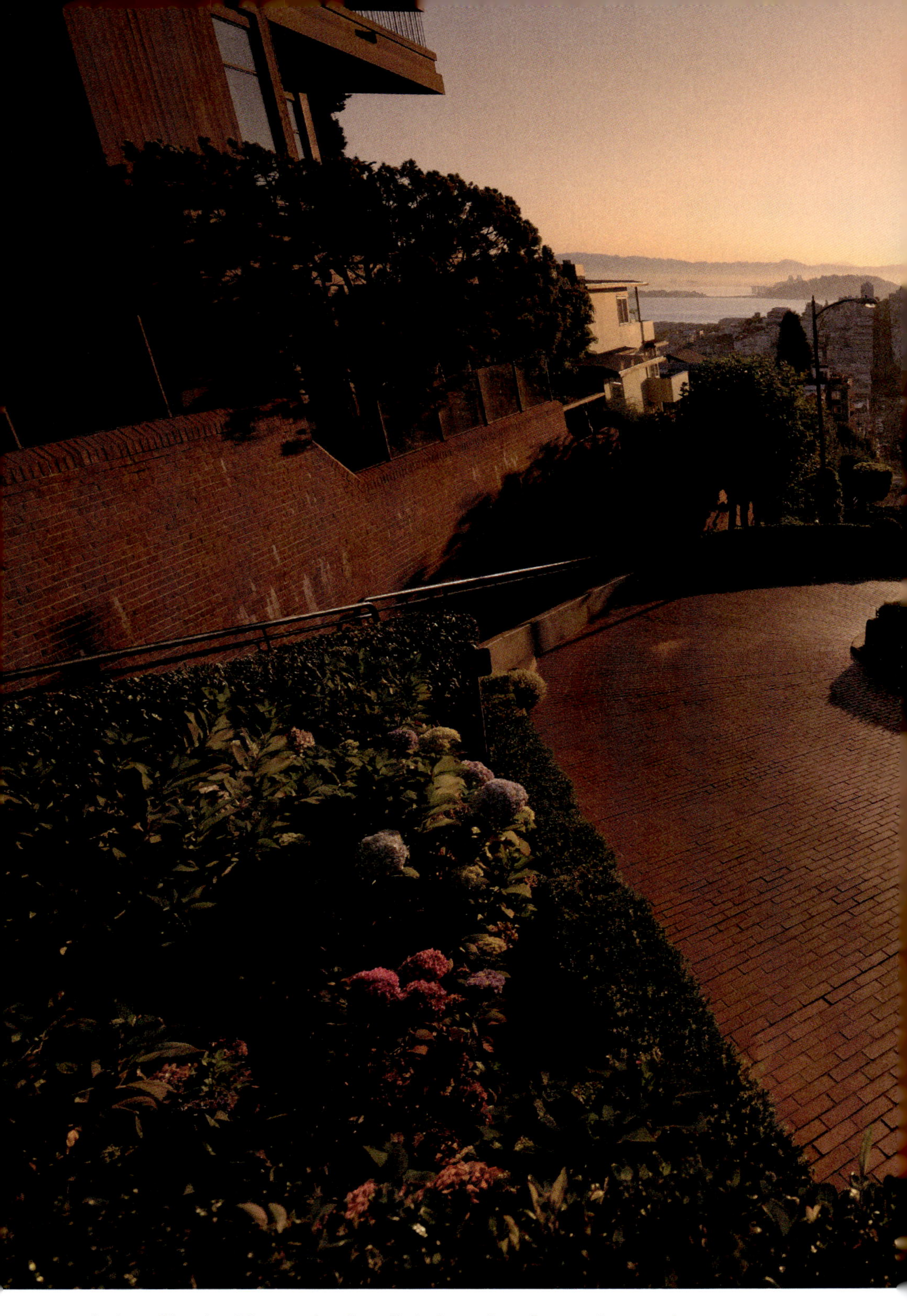

A view of Lombard Street taken from Hyde Street just after sunrise on a clear summer morning. Taken at ISO 100, f/8, 1/250 second with a 14-24mm lens.

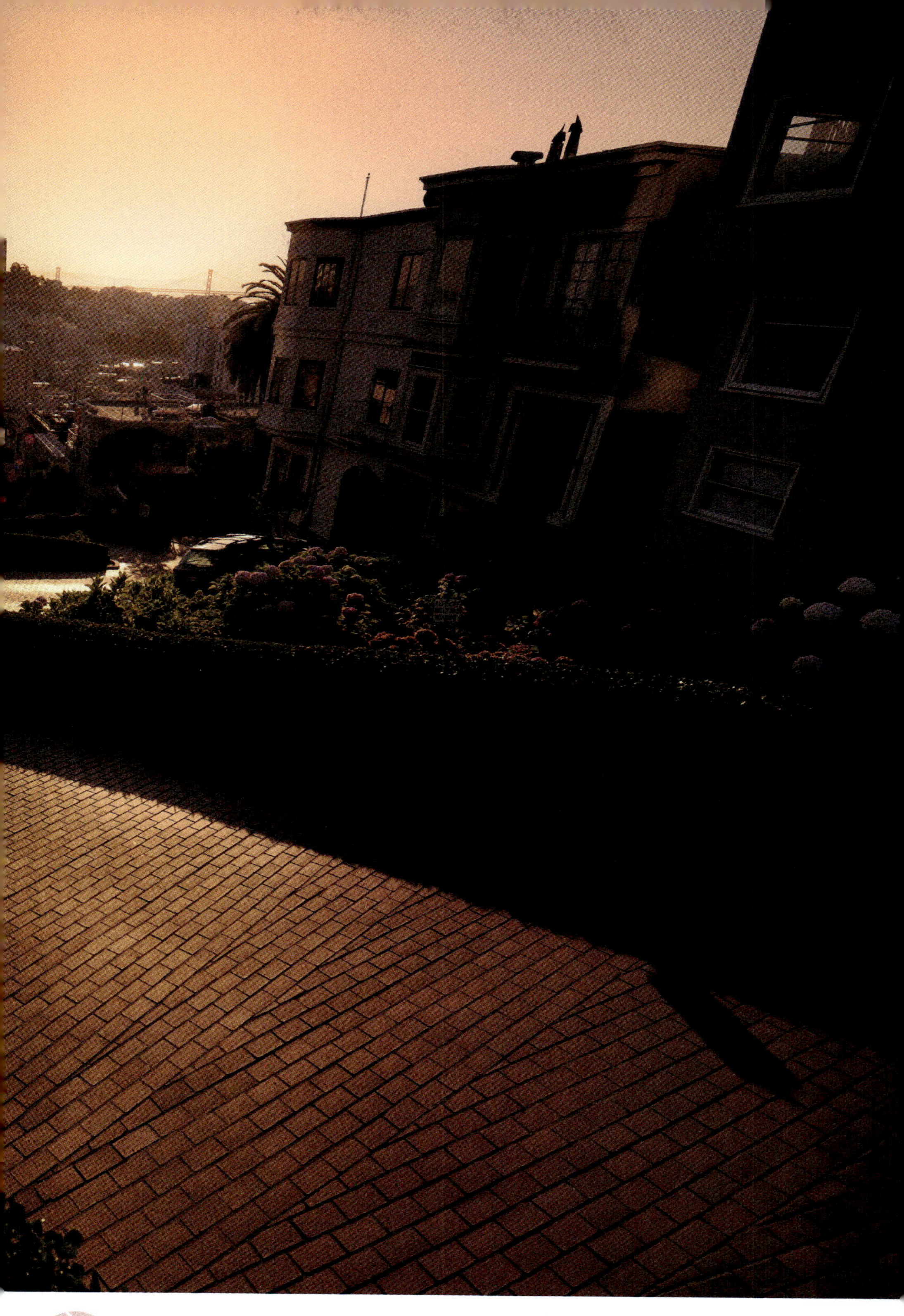

14 Lombard Street

Why It's Worth a Photograph

Lombard Street is best known for the one-way section on Russian Hill between Hyde and Leavenworth Streets. This section of roadway has eight sharp turns that have earned the street the distinction of being "the crookedest in the world." The switchback design was created out of necessity to reduce the hill's natural 30-percent grade, which was too steep for vehicles and pedestrians to climb. The crooked sections are ¼-mile long and are reserved for one-way traffic traveling downhill. Lombard Street's curves and turns are world famous, and it has appeared in numerous movies, television shows, and printed materials. Despite all the publicity, you still must see it.

Where Can I Get the Best Shot?

The best locations to capture this unique landmark are Lombard Street at Hyde Street, Coit Tower at Lombard Street and Grant Street, and Lombard Street at Leavenworth Street (see A, B, and C on the map).

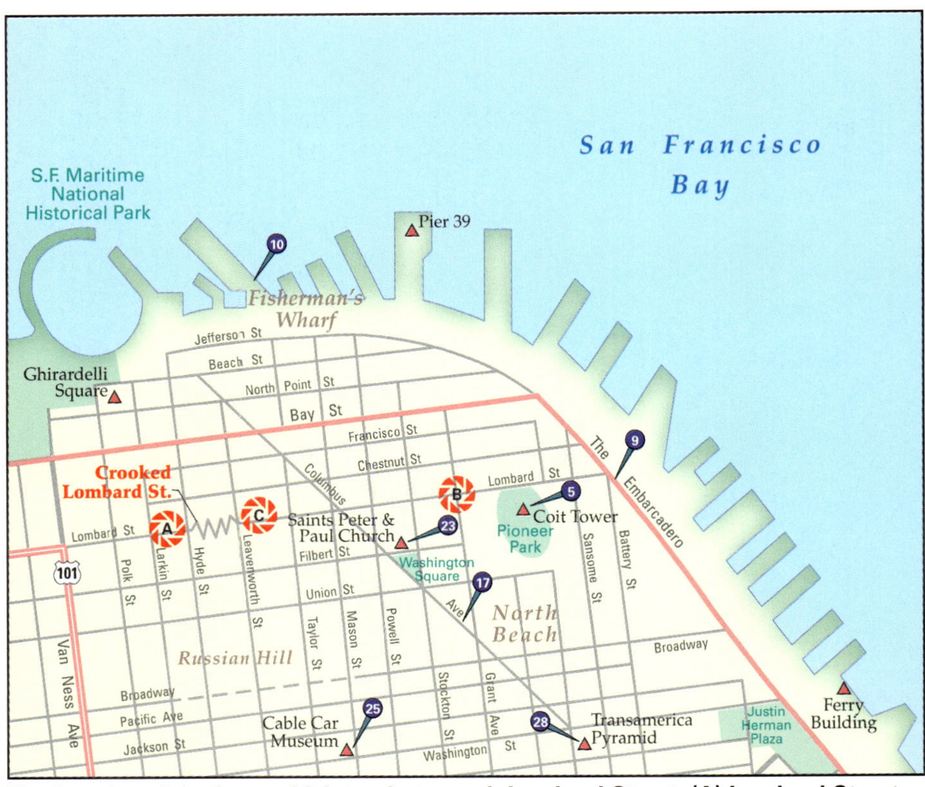

The best locations from which to photograph Lombard Street: (A) Lombard Street at Hyde Street, (B) Coit Tower at Lombard Street and Grant Street, (C) Lombard Street at Leavenworth Street. Other photo ops: (5) Coit Tower, (9) Embarcadero, (10) Fisherman's Wharf, (17) North Beach, (23) Saints Peter and Paul Church, (25) San Francisco cable cars, (28) Transamerica Pyramid.

Lombard Street at Hyde Street

The top of Lombard Street is my favorite vantage point to photograph the crooked street. This vantage point gives you a downward view of Lombard Street. You can capture the small sections of the bending street along with the wonderful flowers and buildings that surround the street. The ideal time to shoot is 30 minutes after the sun comes up. The sun is in front of you and to your right, which creates a wonderful front and sidelit scene where shadows and highlights blend into one. The entire scene will be basked in this hot orange sunlight creating wonderful form and textures against the brick road and blooming flowers. Another favorite time to shoot is at night when you can photograph the street with a wide lens using a slow shutter speed. This slow shutter speed creates trails of auto lights speeding down the hill (see figure 14.1).

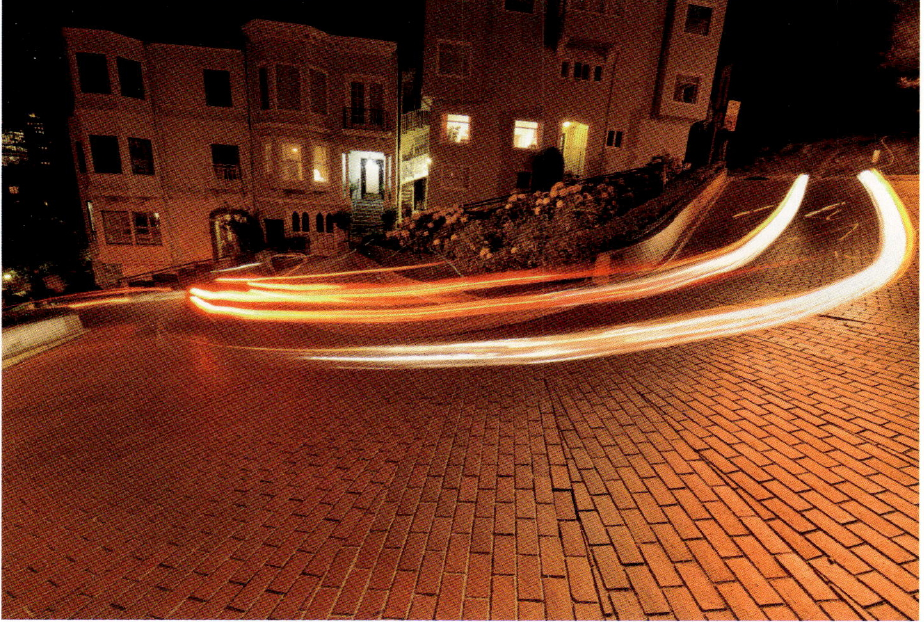

14.1 A view of Lombard Street taken from Hyde Street just after sunrise on a clear summer morning (see A on the map). Taken at ISO 100, f/8, 1/250 second with a 14-24mm lens.

Lombard Street and Grant Street

This is the only vantage point where you can capture each twist and turn of Lombard Street. Bring the longest lens you have because you need at least a 400mm lens to capture this scene. The only time of day to photograph from this vantage point is between 7 a.m. and 10 a.m. when the sun is high enough to clear the skyscrapers behind you, but not so high as to create dark pockets of shadows along the street (see figure 14.2).

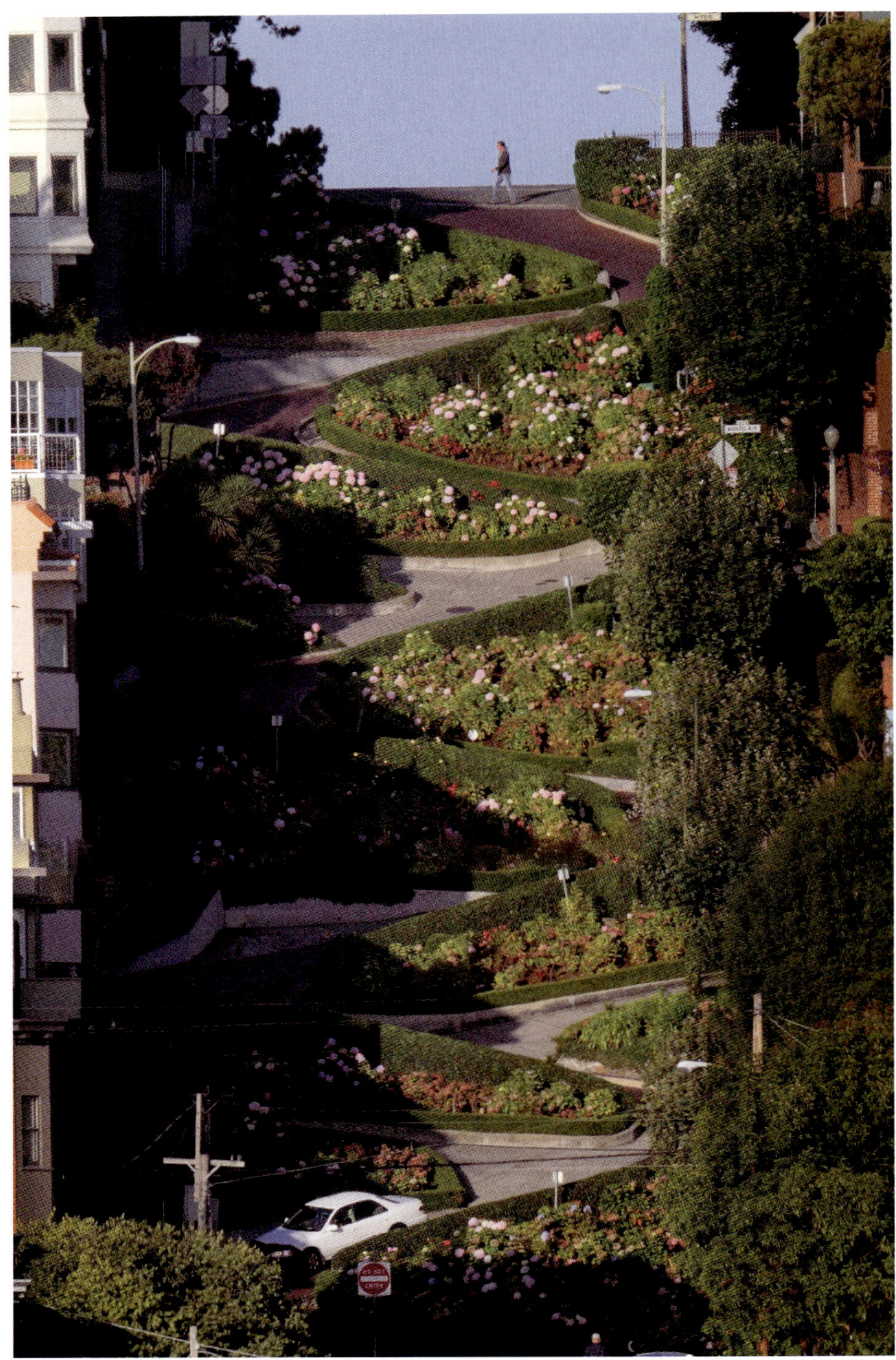

14.2 **A view of Lombard Street taken after sunrise from Grant Street (see B on the map) on a clear summer morning. Taken at ISO 200, f/11, 1/250 second with a 120-300mm lens and 2X teleconverter.**

Lombard Street at Leavenworth Street

This vantage point is located at the base of Lombard Street. The key to capturing this location is to use the widest lens you have. Your composition should include the wonderful flowers that surround the road. Capturing each twist and turn from this angle is impossible, but much like the photo from Hyde Street and Lombard Street, you want to create a composition where a curve is shown while using the flowers to add color and interest to the photo. These flowers also act as a leading line, which draws your viewer's eye to the curve in the road (see figure 14.3).

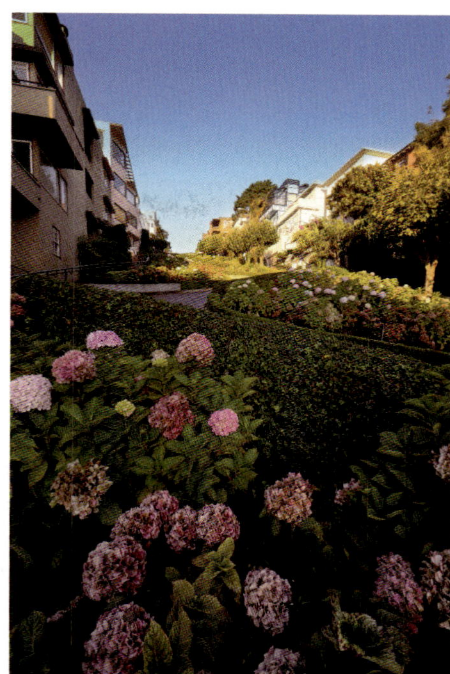

14.3 A view of Lombard Street taken from Leavenworth Street just after sunrise (see C on the map) on a clear summer morning. Taken at ISO 400, f/16, 1/50 second with a 14-24mm lens.

How Can I Get the Best Shot?

Good light is the key to making an average photo great. Shooting Lombard Street early in the day is the type of low, warm, directional light that gives your photo form and texture.

Equipment

A good tripod, an ultrawide lens, and a long telephoto lens are the three pieces of equipment that are critical for capturing sharp images of Lombard Street in the early morning light.

Lenses

Ultrawide and long telephoto lenses are critical for capturing sharp images of Lombard Street in low light.

- **Ultrawide zoom lens in the 14-24mm range.** The ultrawide lens gives you the ability to create a unique perspective. By including something in the immediate foreground, you can create a sense of depth that can lead the person's eyes to the main subject. In this case, the flowers would be in the immediate foreground and the street would be in the background.

- **A zoom lens somewhere in the 70-400mm range.** This focal range allows you the ability to isolate Lombard Street from the surrounding buildings.

Extras

A tripod is useful when shooting Lombard Street with a long lens. A tripod can help stabilize the camera and lens when shooting in early morning or late evening light.

Camera settings

Setting up your camera to shoot Lombard Street can vary depending on lens and time of day. When shooting with your ultrawide lens from Lombard Street and Hyde Street, maximize your depth of field and image quality by using an aperture of f/11 to f/16. Dial in some minus exposure compensation on those early morning shots when the sun is in front of you. Doing this helps protect against blown highlights and creates a wonderful moody light. When shooting with a long lens from a distance, mount your camera on a tripod and set the aperture from f/8 to f/11, which helps maximize your image quality.

- **Exposure mode.** I set my camera to Aperture Priority mode and dial in some plus or minus exposure compensation to create a certain mood and to ensure that I do not under- or overexpose in tricky lighting situations. If you feel confident, you can also set your camera to Manual mode and adjust the aperture and shutter speed until the ideal exposure is achieved.
- **White balance.** White balance I never touch because I find the Auto White Balance of all modern day cameras to be pretty good.
- **ISO.** I keep my ISO as low as possible because I am shooting from a tripod and the best image quality is important. For the night shot, it is imperative to keep the ISO low because the dark shadows and low light can develop more noise than a day shot at the same ISO.

Exposure

I let my camera do most of the metering. When shooting into the sun, I dial in a minus exposure compensation to help create a warmer, moodier light. Use the histogram on the back of your camera or look at the picture taken of the scene to help determine if you are over- or underexposing parts of the picture. Make adjustments to your exposure based on this. There are times when you have to sacrifice part of the sky to expose the rest of the photo correctly.

Ideal time to shoot

The ideal time to shoot is in the early morning when the sun is low and Lombard Street is immersed in a soft, golden light that accentuates its curves.

Working around the weather

The late summer/early fall and spring months bring you the best weather. These months have the most dramatic sunrises and sunsets with little or no fog.

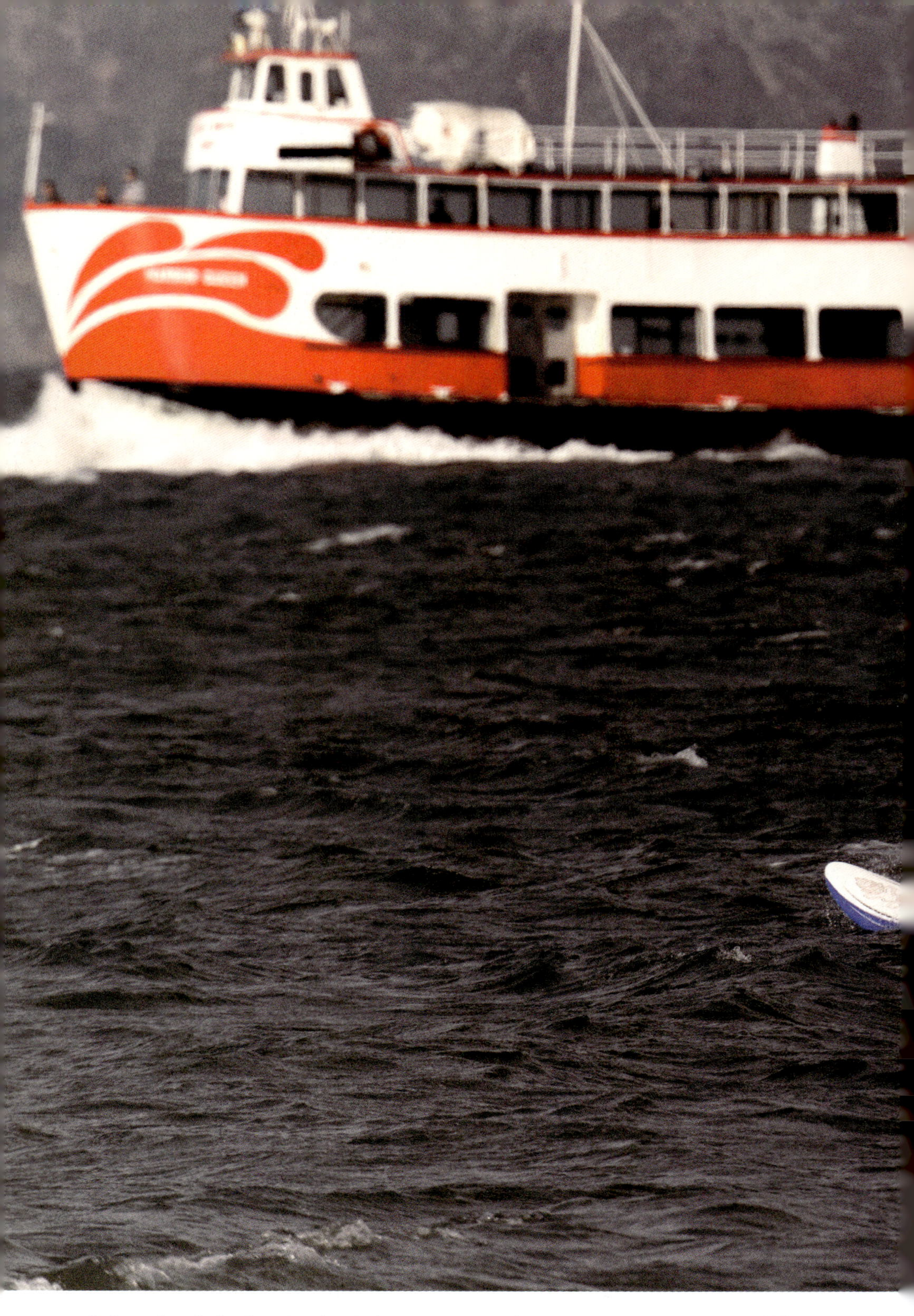

A view of a windsurfer taken just before sunset on a clear summer evening. Taken at ISO 400, f/8, 1/1600 second with a 400mm lens.

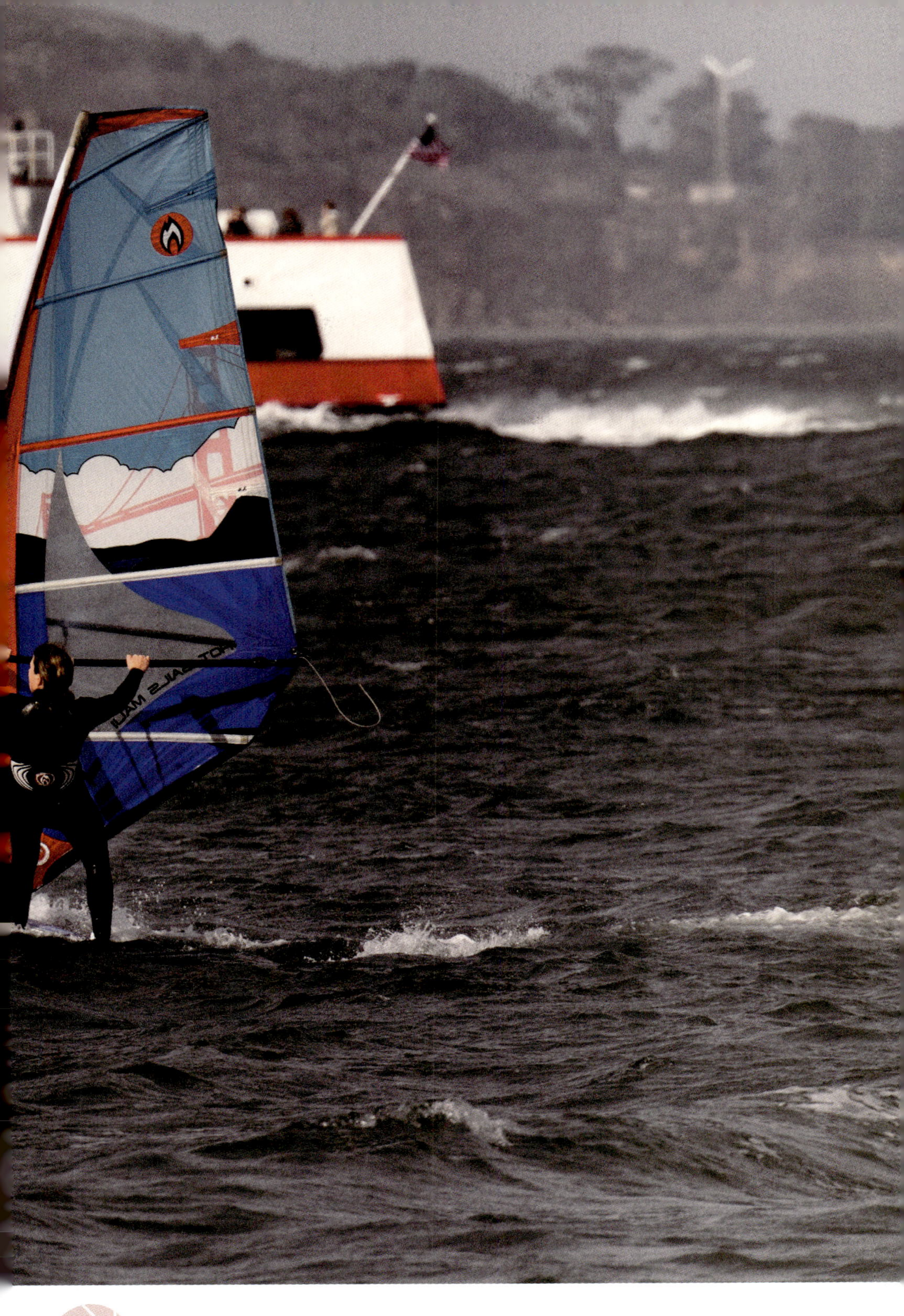

15 Marina Green

Why It's Worth a Photograph

The Marina Green in San Francisco, California, is a 74-acre expanse of grass between Fort Mason and the Presidio. It is adjacent to San Francisco Bay, and this location provides incredible views of the Golden Gate Bridge, Angel Island, Alcatraz Island, and parts of Marin County. Prior to the 1906 earthquake, this area was a tidal marsh. After the earthquake, much of the resulting rubble was dumped here. Later, to provide land for the 1915 Panama-Pacific International Exposition, this site and the adjacent neighborhood (now the present day Marina District) was filled in. The Marina Green is one of the most popular areas in the city for people who like to spend time outdoors. On any given day, you can witness activities including jogging, biking, sailing, windsurfing, kite boarding, and informal games of football and soccer. The locals come out in numbers as do the tourists. All this activity makes for inspiring images.

Where Can I Get the Best Shot?

The best shots can be had at the west end of the green where the Saint Francis Yacht Club resides (see A on the map).

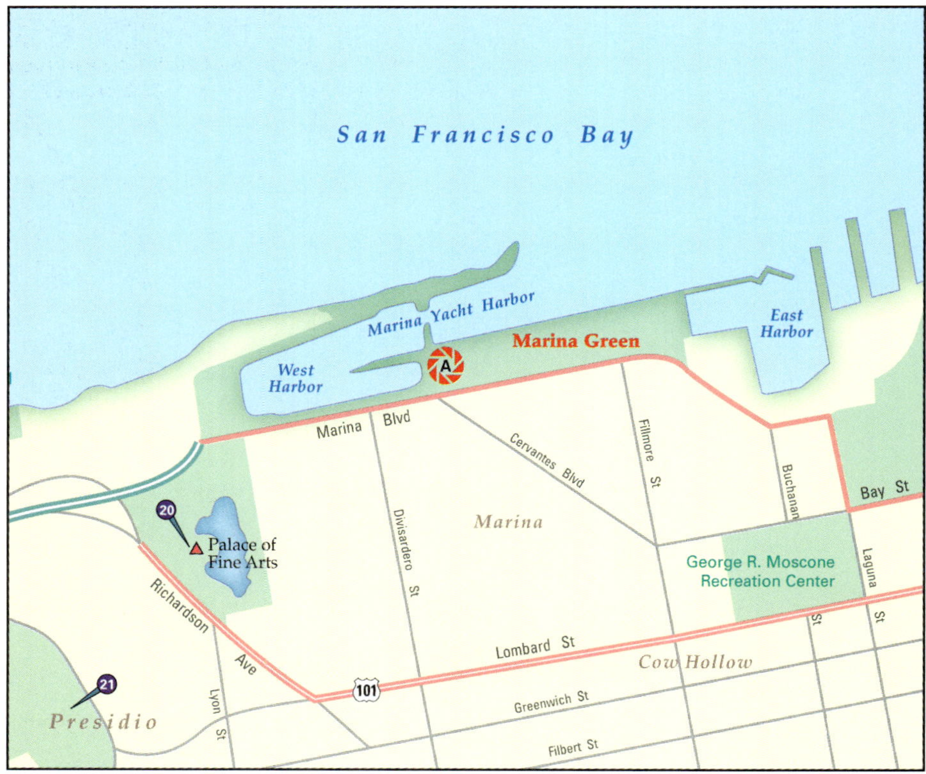

The best location from which to photograph the Marina Green: (A) the west end of the grounds. Other photo ops: (20) Palace of Fine Arts, (21) Presidio of San Francisco.

This area offers numerous opportunities to photograph the marina at sunset (see figure 15.1). Also popular to photograph are the hundreds of windsurfers and kite boarders that are out on the bay every evening around sunset. This time of day combined with a long lens and great subject makes for a dramatic photo (see figure 15.2).

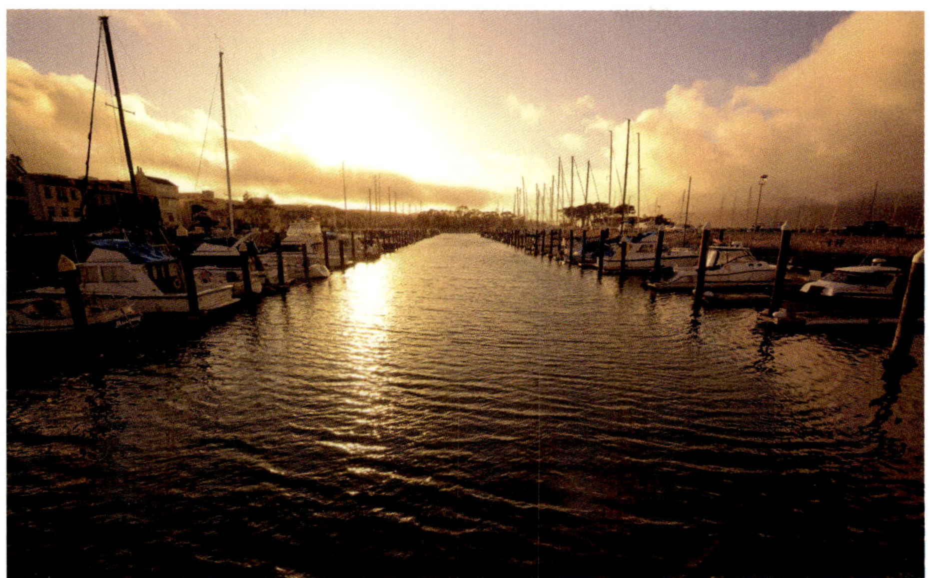

15.1 A view of the Saint Francis Yacht Club Marina located on the Marina Green (see A on the map) on a clear summer afternoon. Taken at ISO 400, f/11, 1/800 second with a 14-24mm lens.

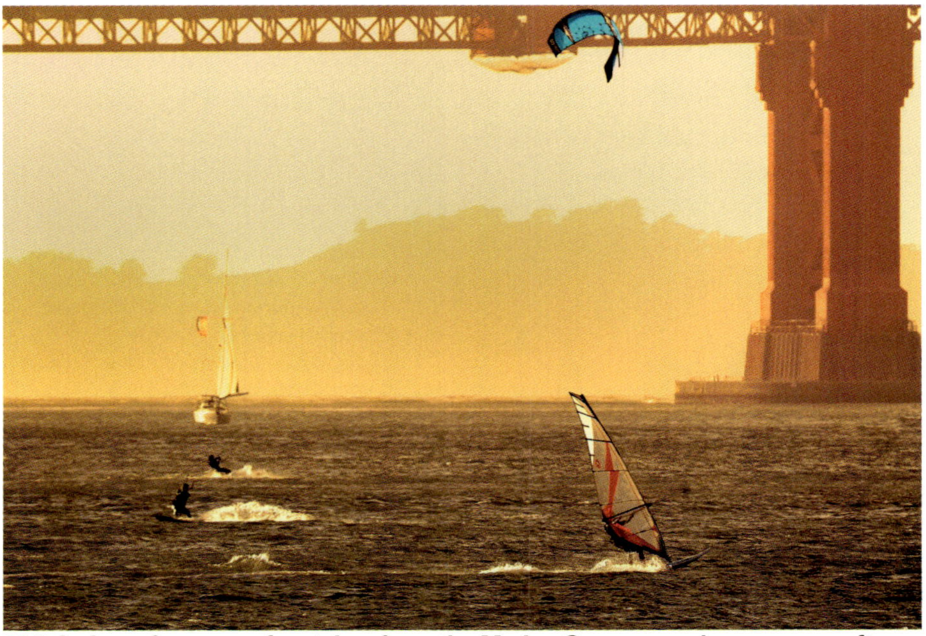

15.2 A view of many surfers taken from the Marina Green on a clear summer afternoon. Taken at ISO 100, f/7.1, 1/500 second with a 400mm lens.

How Can I Get the Best Shot?

The sunlight and equipment play a huge part in capturing the best photo at this location. To ensure that you get the best shot, bring a wide and a long lens. Arrive one hour before the sun goes down and be ready to capture images of boats and surfers (see figure 15.3) bathed in this low, warm, golden light.

Equipment

We photographers like having lots of gear. For this location, a tripod and a long telephoto and wide-angle lens are must-haves.

Lenses

The choice of lens always comes down to your personal preference and what you want to convey in the photo. Whether you are shooting day or night, your lens choice is instrumental for creating the ideal composition for any given subject. I recommend using an ultrawide lens and a long telephoto lens.

- **Ultrawide zoom lens in the 14-24mm range.** The ultrawide lens gives you the ability to create a composition that pulls the viewer's eye to the main subject.
- **A telephoto lens somewhere in the 70-400mm range.** This lens allows you the ability to isolate a surfer hundreds of yards off the shore.

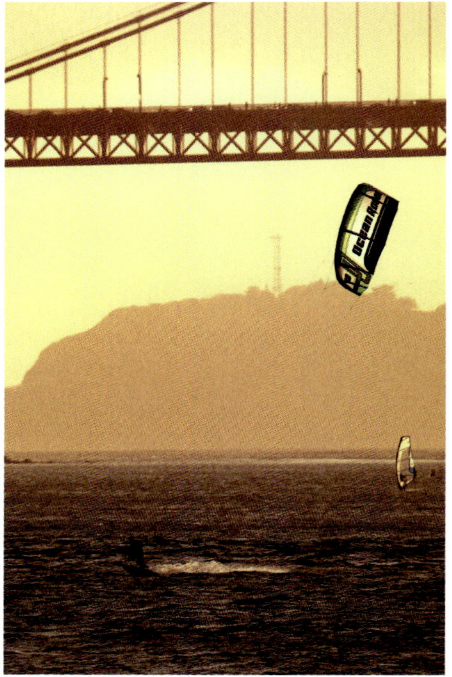

15.3 A view of a lone kite surfer taken from the Marina Green on a clear summer afternoon. Taken at ISO 400, f/7.1, 1/2500 second, –1/3 exposure compensation with a 400mm lens.

Extras

A tripod is important to help stabilize the camera when using a long lens.

Camera settings

For a wide-angle lens, set the aperture from f/8 to f/22 depending on your composition. For the marina photo, I used f/11 because I was able to create enough depth of field from front to back to render a sharp photo throughout. For long lenses, set the aperture from f/5.6 to f/8 because you want to maximize sharpness while keeping your shutter speed fast. Bump up your ISO as it gets darker to ensure that you have a fast enough shutter speed.

- **Exposure mode.** Set your camera in Aperture Priority mode and dial in the aperture you need. Let the camera choose the shutter speed. Dial in a minus exposure compensation to protect the bright sky from overexposing.
- **White balance.** I never touch white balance because I find the Auto White Balance setting of all modern day cameras to be pretty good.
- **ISO.** Adjust your ISO to ensure that you have at least a shutter speed of 1/500 second when shooting the windsurfers and kite boarders.

Exposure

Exposing the sky in all these photos was the trickiest part, so I made sure to meter off the sky so that I would not overexpose it. Use the histogram on the back of your camera to help judge if your exposure is spot on or you need more or less exposure compensation.

Ideal time to shoot

The ideal time to shoot is when the sun is low just before the sun sets. When the sun is low, it creates a wonderful warm, soft light that makes your photo so much more appealing.

Working around the weather

The weather can be cold and miserable on the Marina Green due to the proximity of the bay. The late spring, late summer, and fall provide the warmest temperatures and clearest skies. Plan your days when there is no fog as the Marina Green is best photographed in the late, warm, setting sun.

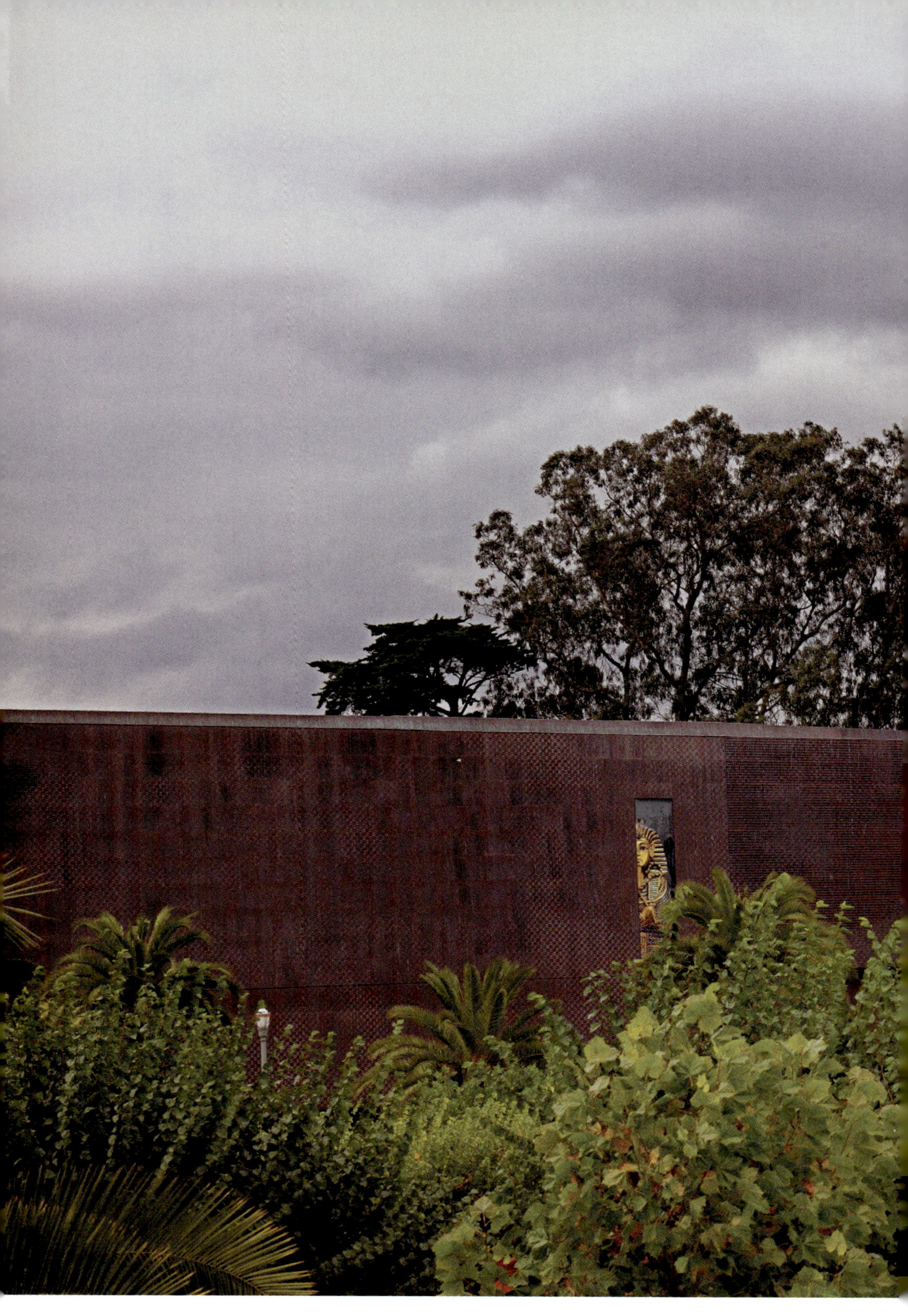

The M.H. de Young Museum taken on a cloudy autumn afternoon. Taken at ISO 200, f/11, 1/80 second with a 70-200mm lens.

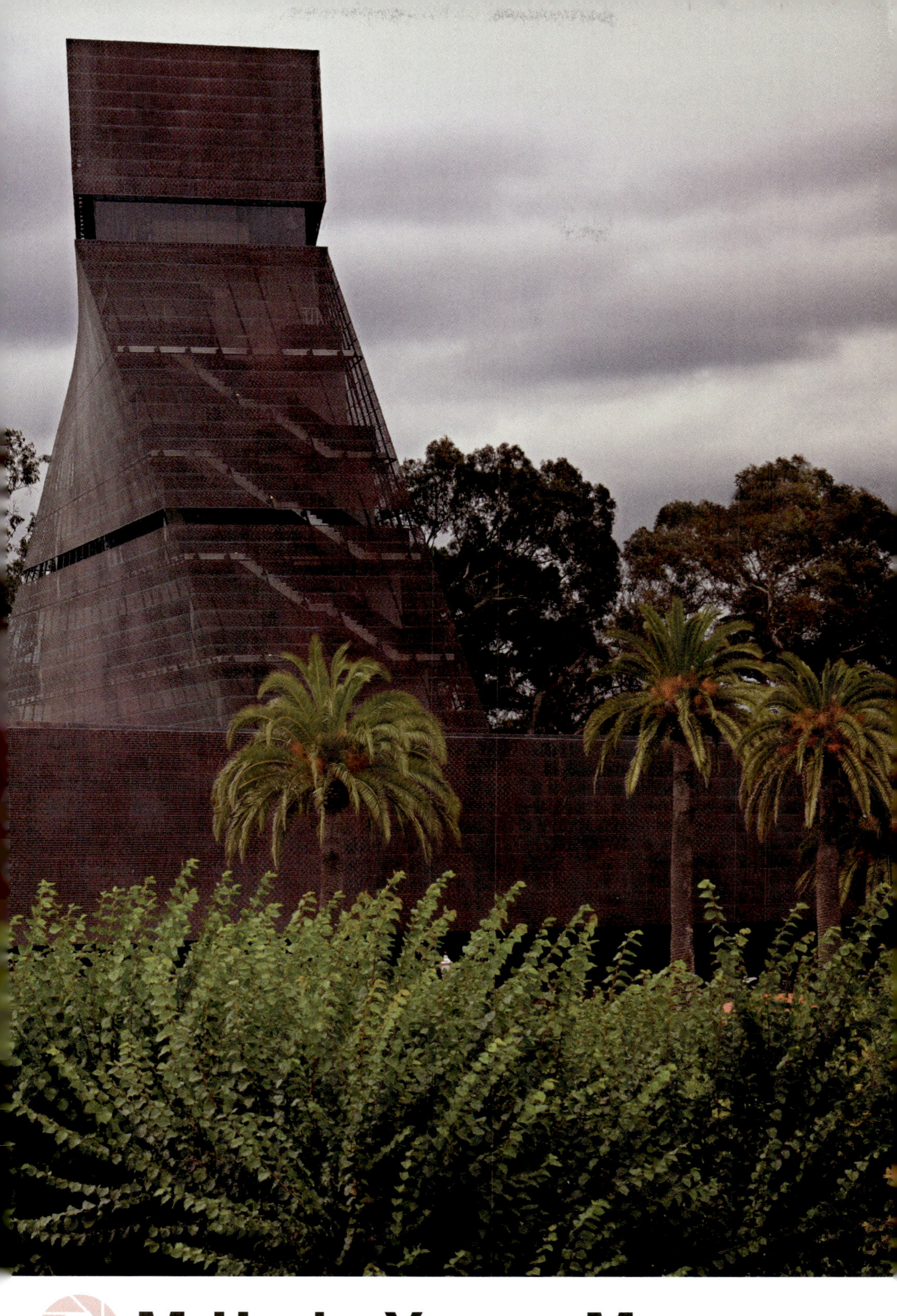

16 M.H. de Young Museum

Why It's Worth a Photograph

The M.H. de Young Museum has been a favorite of both San Francisco locals and visitors since 1895 and is an integral part of San Francisco culture. Originally housed in a building from an international exposition, the De Young, as it's commonly called, was rebuilt and reopened in 2005 as a state-of-the-art facility that integrates art, architecture, and the natural landscape in one multifaceted museum. Designed by Swiss architecture firm Herzog & de Meuron and Fong & Chan Architects in San Francisco, the De Young provides San Francisco with a landmark art museum to showcase priceless collections of American, African, and Pacific art from the seventeenth through the twentieth centuries. The ultramodern museum, constructed of copper, stone, and glass, complements its natural surroundings.

Where Can I Get the Best Shot?

The De Young Museum is located in Golden Gate Park (see A on the map), and its dramatic copper facade is the showcase for any photographer.

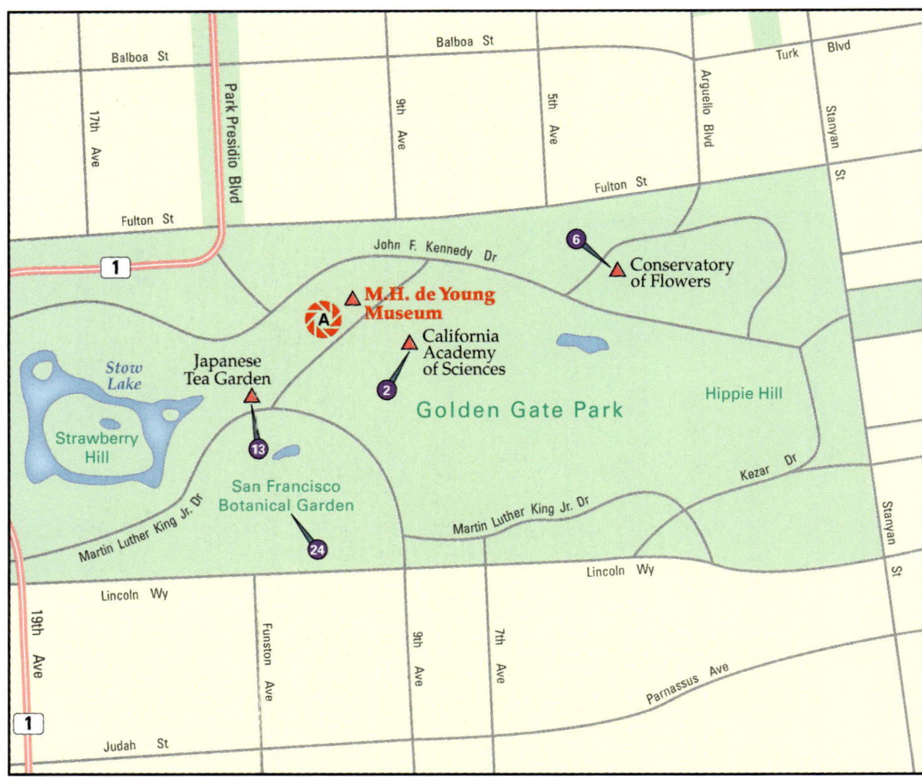

The best location from which to photograph the M.H. de Young Museum: (A) the grounds of the museum. Other photo ops: (2) California Academy of Sciences, (6) Conservatory of Flowers, (13) Japanese Tea Garden, (24) San Francisco Botanical Garden.

When warm light strikes the perforated and textured skin, it replicates the impression that light makes when filtering through a tree canopy. This creates a wonderful artistic impression that is well worth a photo (see figures 16.1 and 16.2).

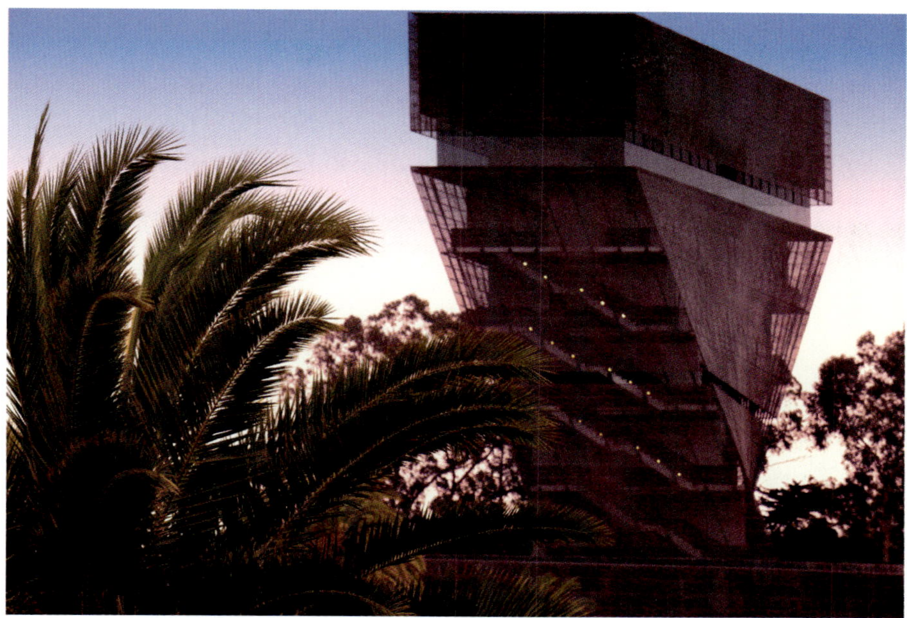

16.1 A view of the M.H. de Young Museum on a clear autumn afternoon (see A on the map). Taken at ISO 400, f/8, 1/60 second, –1/3 exposure compensation with a 70-200mm lens.

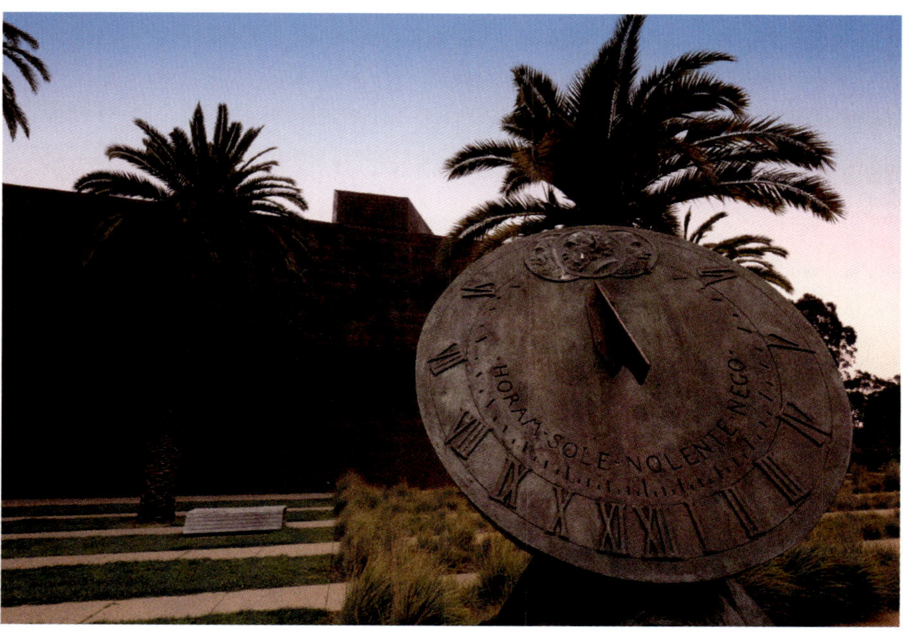

16.2 A view of a sundial in front of the M.H. de Young Museum on a clear autumn afternoon. Taken at ISO 800, f/22, 1/25 second, – 2/3 exposure compensation with a 14-24mm lens.

Another gorgeous attribute to the incredible design is the building's copper skin that was selected because of its unique qualities. Over time, more and more oxidation sets in and creates a rich patina that blends gracefully into its surrounding environment (see figure 16.3).

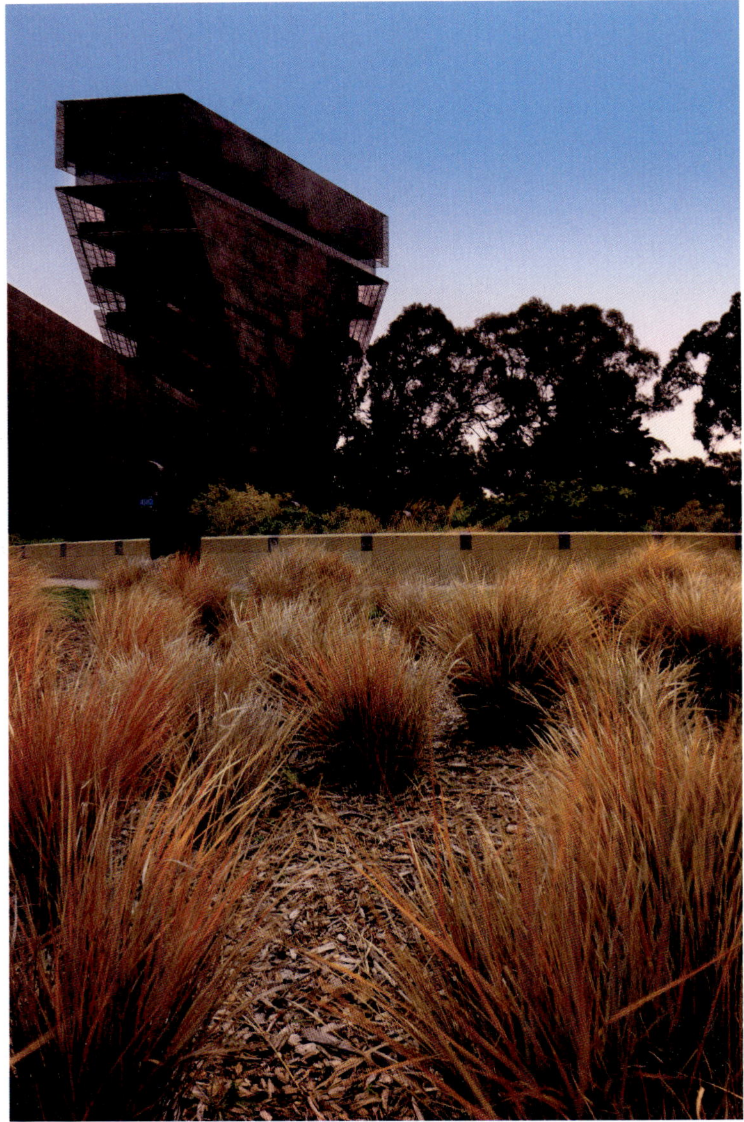

16.3 A view of the M.H. de Young tower on a clear autumn afternoon. Taken at ISO 800, f/22, 1/25 second, –1/3 exposure compensation with a 14-24mm lens.

How Can I Get the Best Shot?

Plan your trip to the De Young late in the day when the sky is clear, the sun is going down, and the warm tones are in the sky. Let this warm, colorful, low light enhance your photos by creating wonderful long, soft shadows and turning the copper facade into a warm abstract piece of art (see figure 16.4). An ultrawide-angle lens and medium telephoto will give you the ability to capture many wonderful pictures of this remarkable building and its incredible architecture.

Equipment

A tripod, ultra wide-angle lens, and a medium telephoto lens are the three pieces of equipment you should consider bringing when photographing the De Young Museum.

Lenses

Ultrawide and medium telephoto lenses are the two lenses that can help capture the essence of the De Young Museum. The wide lens creates a wide perspective while the longer lens allows you to isolate detail.

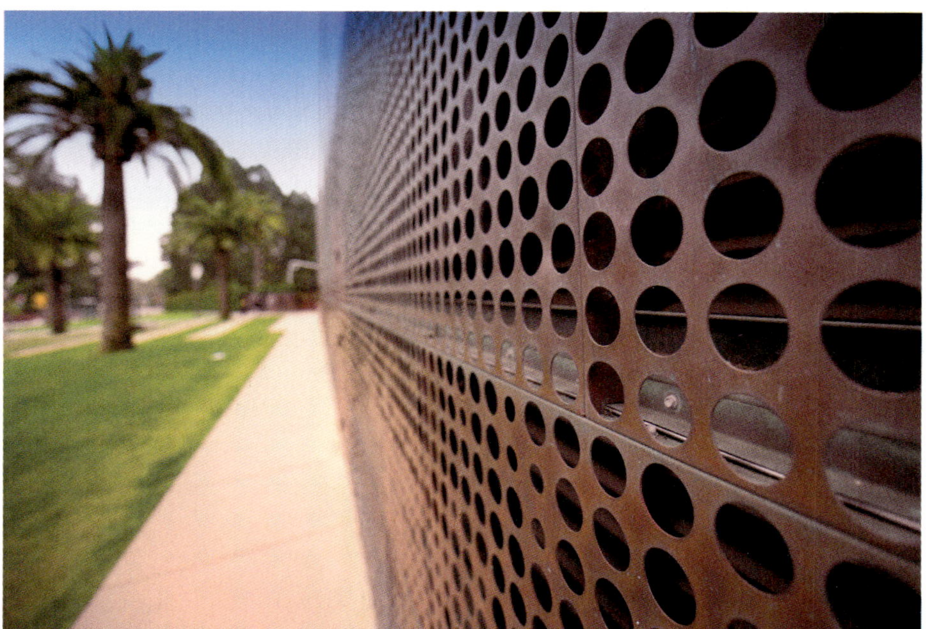

16.4 A view of the De Young Museum's perforated copper skin taken on a clear autumn afternoon. Taken at ISO 800, f/2.8, 1/400 second, –1/3 exposure compensation with a 14-24mm lens.

- **Ultrawide zoom lens in the 14-24mm range.** The ultrawide lens gives you the ability to create wonderful photos that have a unique perspective. Try to include something in the foreground because doing so gives the viewer a sense of depth as well as draws the viewer in.
- **Medium telephoto lens 70-200mm range.** This allows you the ability to isolate the De Young Museum's tower and create perspective from a much farther distance.

Extras

A tripod is helpful to stabilize the camera when using a long lens.

Camera settings

I set my camera to Aperture Priority mode with a –1/3 exposure compensation for the wide-angle shots. This helps protect the brightly lit sky from overexposing against the dark copper museum. You can shoot these at either f/2.8 to create an emphasis on a specific spot, such as the copper facade, or f/22 to create maximum depth of field and to create perfect focus from front to back. For your longer lens, set the camera to Aperture Priority mode with a –1/3 to –2/3 exposure compensation to protect your highlights. You can set the aperture from f/8 to f/11 to maximize image quality.

- **Exposure mode.** I set my camera to Aperture Priority mode and let my camera choose the shutter speed. Dial in a minus exposure composition to help balance the bright sky with the dark copper building.
- **White balance.** Auto White Balance is your best bet for 95 percent of outdoor shooting.
- **ISO.** Keep the ISO between 200 and 800 because you want to ensure that you have a fast enough shutter speed if you hand hold the camera for these shots.

Exposure

Because my exposure settings were pretty consistent, I let the camera take the initial reading. I dialed in a bit of exposure compensation based on what the histogram was showing me on the back of the camera. You can also check the LCD and judge how the camera is exposing the image, which gives you a good idea how your picture will turn out. I tend to use this in conjunction with the histogram to select the correct exposure. Make your adjustments based on these. It will never be 100 percent perfect, so you may need to try a few settings until you get a satisfactory exposure.

Ideal time to shoot

The De Young is open during normal business hours, so if you don't want to go inside the museum, then shooting the building late in the day when the sun is setting is your best bet. The sun is warm, low, and to the left and behind the museum, creating wonderful light against the copper skin. If you plan to go inside the museum, plan your trip for the afternoon so that when you leave the building, the sun is low, warm, and just right.

Working around the weather

Weather is important for one reason: You don't want to be outside shooting in a rainstorm. Spring and late fall are the ideal seasons to shoot. The sky is clear and we are treated to many colorful sunrises and sunsets. Coincidentally, these are the best months you can expect little, if any, rain and warmer temperatures.

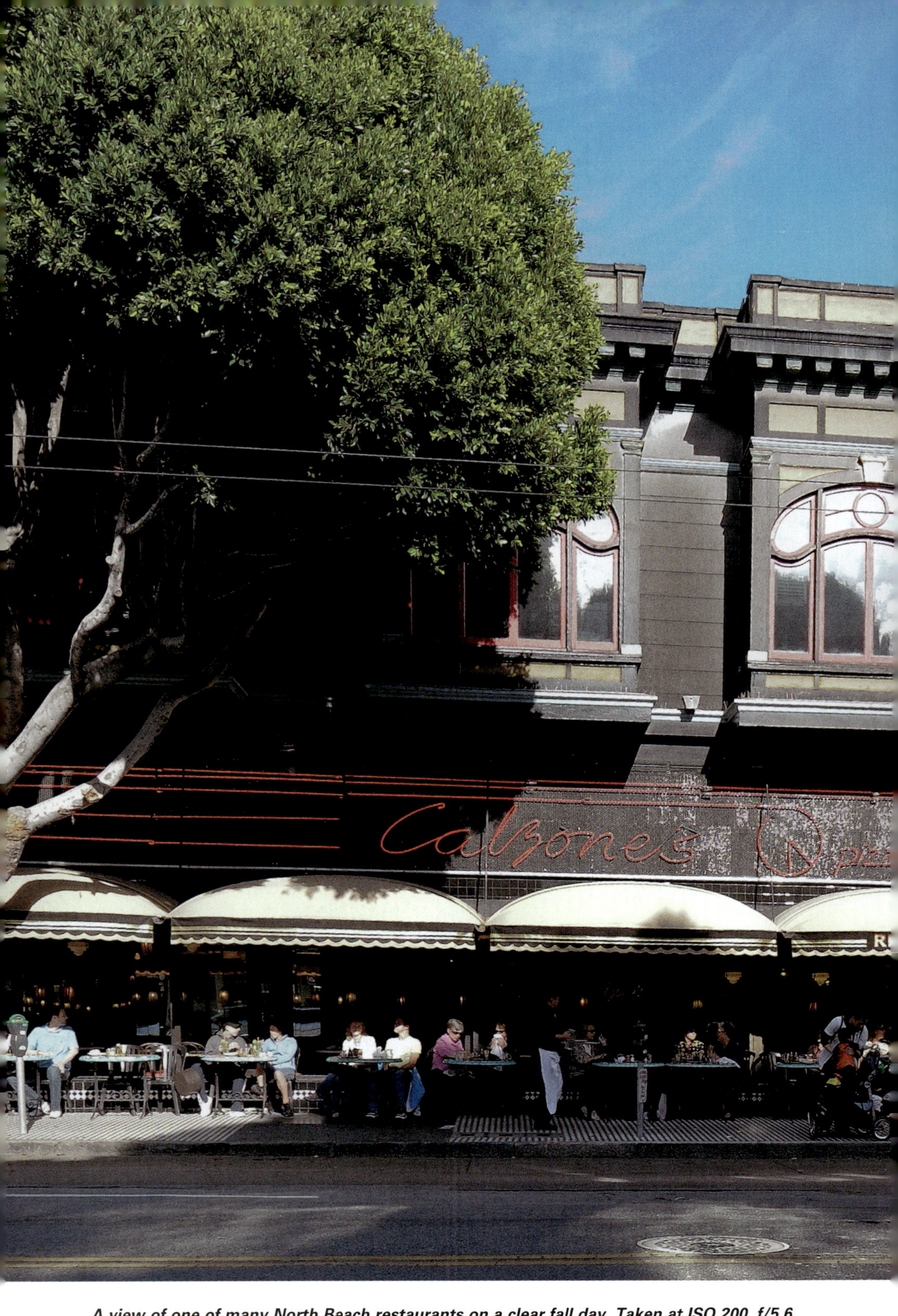

A view of one of many North Beach restaurants on a clear fall day. Taken at ISO 200, f/5.6, 1/160 second with a 50mm lens.

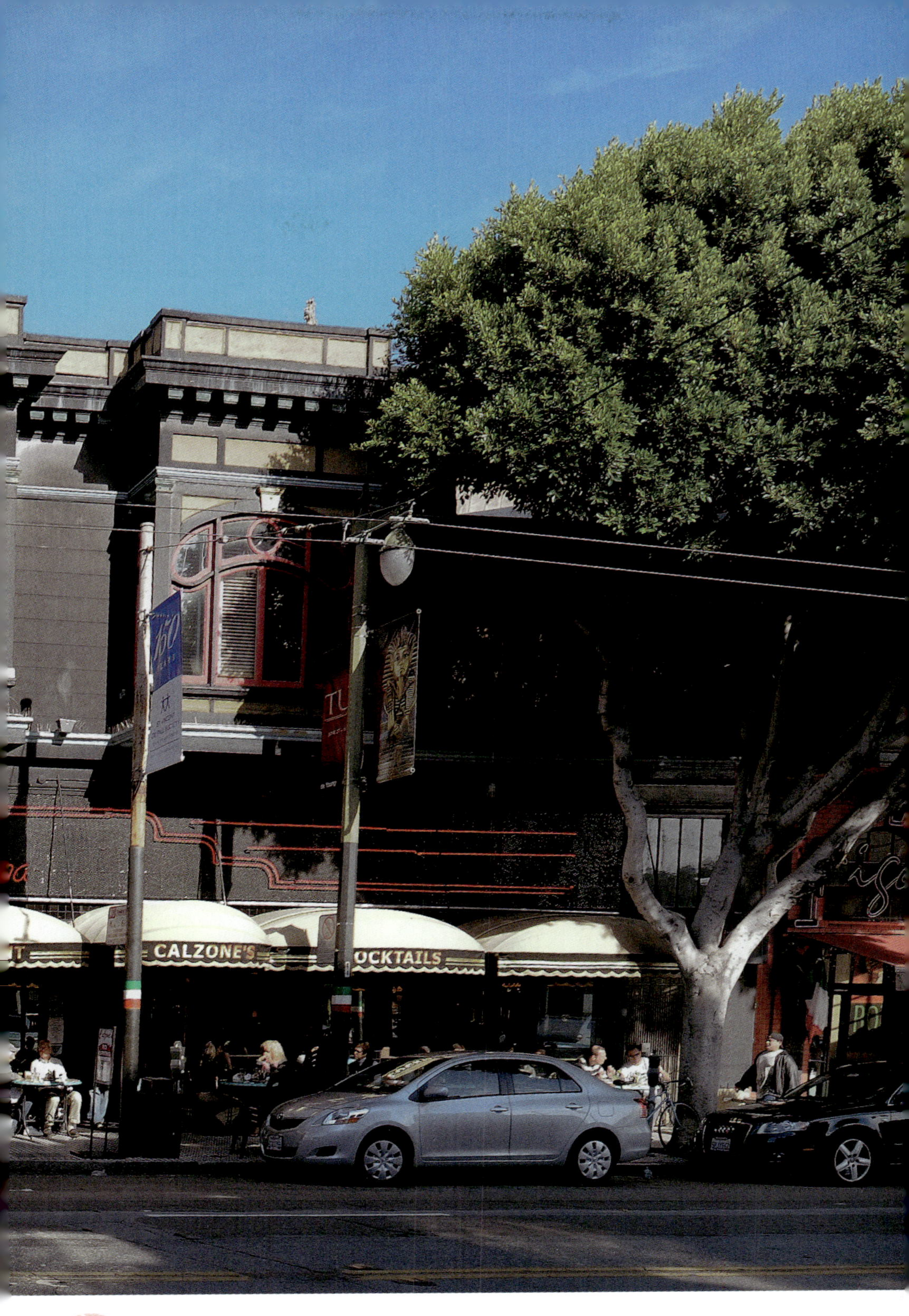

17 North Beach

Why It's Worth a Photograph

There is no longer a beach in North Beach. The name was established in the 1850s when an inlet of the bay extended far inland between Telegraph Hill and Russian Hill, and the neighborhood was a stretch of shoreline. What was once known as Little Italy has become a melting pot of Italian, Chinese, Hispanic, Japanese, Indian, and other pocket communities. If you love to eat, drink, and hang out in a friendly urban neighborhood complete with phenomenal restaurants, dive bars, cafes, trendy nightclubs, and off-the-wall, one-of-a-kind shops, then North Beach is a place you must visit.

Where Can I Get the Best Shot?

North Beach has it all: romantic cable cars, Lombard Street, Coit Tower, historical buildings, the steep slopes of Russian Hill and Telegraph Hill, and fantastic bay and downtown views. It's all in a small, self-sustained area on or off Columbus Street between Filbert Street and Washington Street. Although North Beach extends out many blocks from these streets, the heart and soul of this Little Italy can be found here.

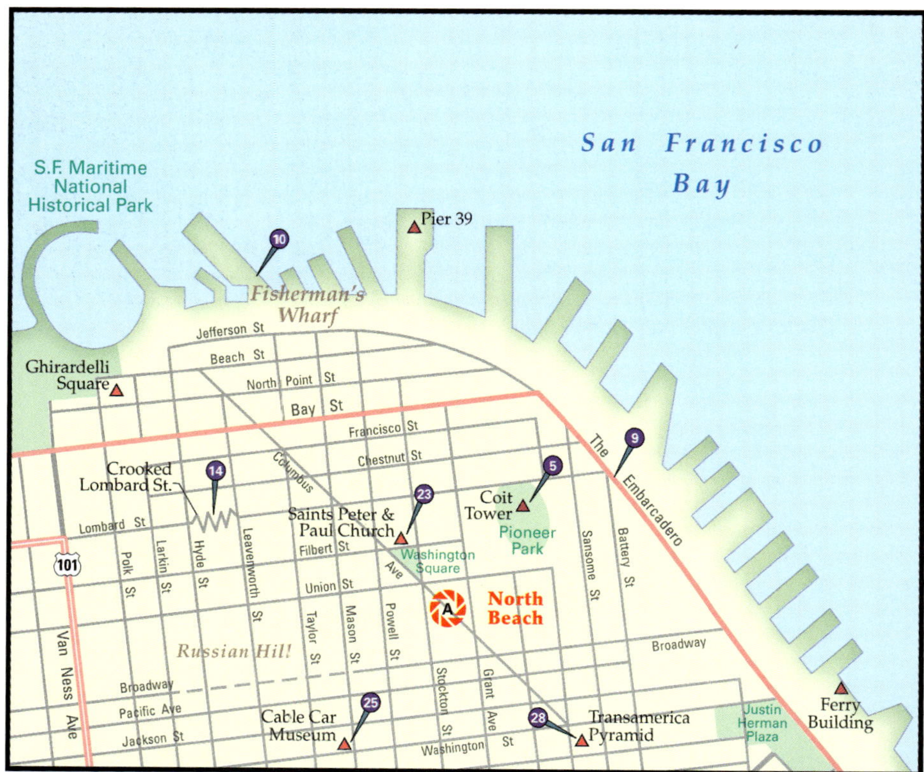

The best locations from which to photograph North Beach: (A) Columbus Street between Filbert Street and Washington Street. Other photo ops: (5) Coit Tower, (9) Embarcadero, (10) Fisherman's Wharf, (14) Lombard Street, (23) Saints Peter and Paul Church, (25) San Francisco cable cars, (28) Transamerica Pyramid.

Columbus Street between Filbert Street and Washington Street

Columbus Street is the main street that cuts North Beach in half (see A on the map). This street on any day or evening can be flowing with people enjoying street-side seating at any one of the hundred or so restaurants or cafes (see figure 17.1). North Beach is the premiere location to people watch and catch a relaxing afternoon or evening enjoying your favorite libation. This area is a great place for you to walk around and work on your street photography.

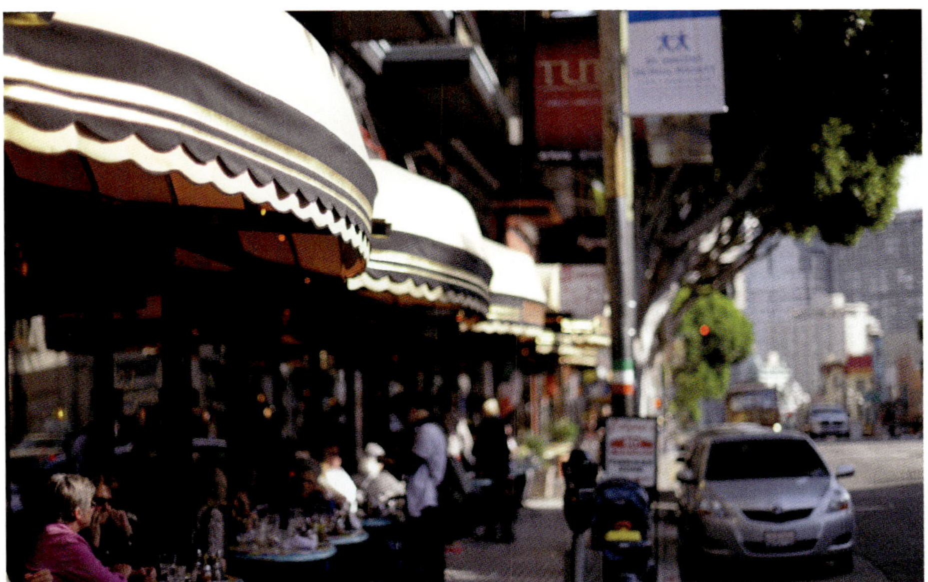

17.1 A cafe in North Beach on a clear fall day (see A on the map). Taken at ISO 100, f/1.4, 1/2500 second with a 50mm lens.

How Can I Get the Best Shot?

Street shooting has no rules. Early in the day or late into the evening can be prime times to capture a mood. Take your time when walking around; photography is not just about landscapes and sunsets. Some of the most compelling photographs are of people in their own environment (see figure 17.2).

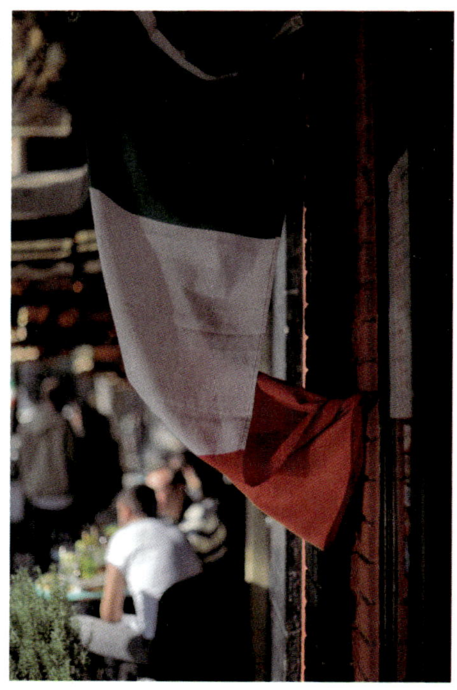

17.2 A view of an Italian flag as people are enjoying lunch at one of the many cafes on a clear fall day. Taken at ISO 100, f/1.4, 1/2500 second with a 50mm lens.

One or two lenses are all you need, preferably a standard zoom or fast prime. If you have room for one more lens in your bag, throw in a medium telephoto to help you shoot people or architecture from a distance (see figure 17.3).

Equipment

A medium telephoto zoom, a standard zoom, and fast prime lens are the three pieces of equipment that make capturing the streets of North Beach a snap.

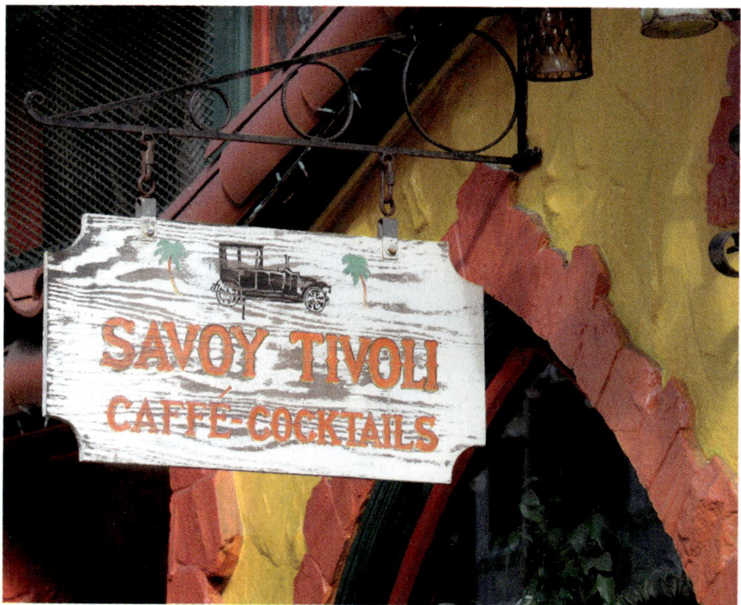

17.3 A view of one of the many famous clubs in North Beach taken on a clear fall day. Taken at ISO 100, f/7.1, 1/125 second with a 70-200mm lens.

Two to three lenses are all you need to cover a wide variety of focal ranges.

- **Medium telephoto zoom in the 70-200mm range.** A perfect lens for isolation, this lens can help capture photos that a shorter lens can't.
- **A lens in the 24-100mm range.** This lens can give you much more versatility when traveling. This lens is the jack-of-all-trades and is best used for street shooting. This lens gives you the perfect balance of wide to long with a relatively fast aperture.
- **A fast prime lens.** Not only is a prime lens smaller and lighter to carry, but it allows you to shoot at a much larger aperture. This capability can be an advantage when shooting people in low light.

Camera settings

For shooting in North Beach, you should shoot in Aperture Priority mode most of the time as it will allow you to focus on composition and capturing that quick shot. When shooting architecture, I use f/8 to f/11 when shooting people and street scenes. I like to isolate my subjects so I shoot at the largest aperture available. This however is not a perfect rule and what you want to convey will ultimately drive your camera settings. The most important thing to keep in mind is that your shutter speed needs to be fast enough to hand hold your camera. You may want to increase your ISO to ensure you always have fast enough shutter speed.

- **Exposure mode.** In the narrow streets, when shooting buildings or places of interest, I set my camera in Aperture Priority mode and adjust my exposure compensation when needed. If the scene is tricky, I switch to Manual and adjust my shutter speed until I get the appropriate exposure for that scene. I set my camera in Aperture Priority mode when shooting street scenes such as people enjoying an afternoon at a cafe. Shooting in this mode allows me the freedom to focus on the composition while the camera chooses the exposure. Many times you won't have time to do both, and to me the composition is more important.
- **White balance.** White balance I never touch because I find the Auto White Balance setting of all modern day cameras to be pretty good. This holds especially true when shooting outside.
- **ISO.** I keep my ISO around 200 to 400 to help keep my shutter speed fast enough when shooting on the street without a tripod.

Exposure

I recommend using Aperture Priority mode when shooting people in North Beach because you do not have much time to fiddle with settings while capturing a moment. I dial in a –1/3 exposure compensation to protect against blown highlights when the sun is high. After hours or in lower light, I adjust accordingly.

Ideal time to shoot

Plan your trip around what you want to capture — there really is no perfect time when shooting in North Beach. Early in the day the cafes are filled with patrons enjoying their coffee. As the day moves into night, the restaurants and bars begin to fill.

Working around the weather

North Beach is located in one of the warmest areas of the city and is situated just below Nob Hill, Telegraph Hill, and Russian Hill. The weather stays relatively mild with very little fog and warmer than average city temperatures.

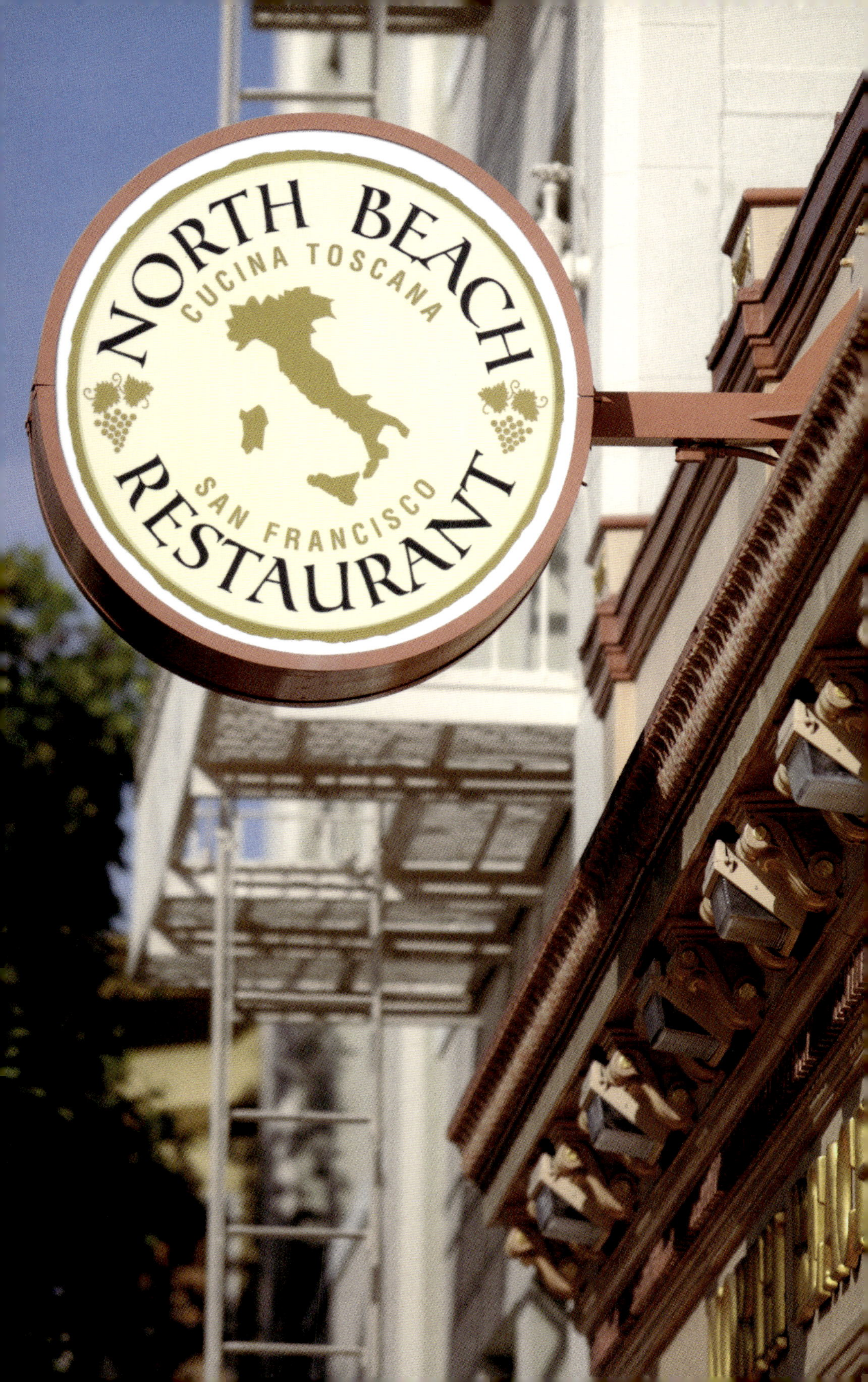
NORTH BEACH
CUCINA TOSCANA
SAN FRANCISCO
RESTAURANT

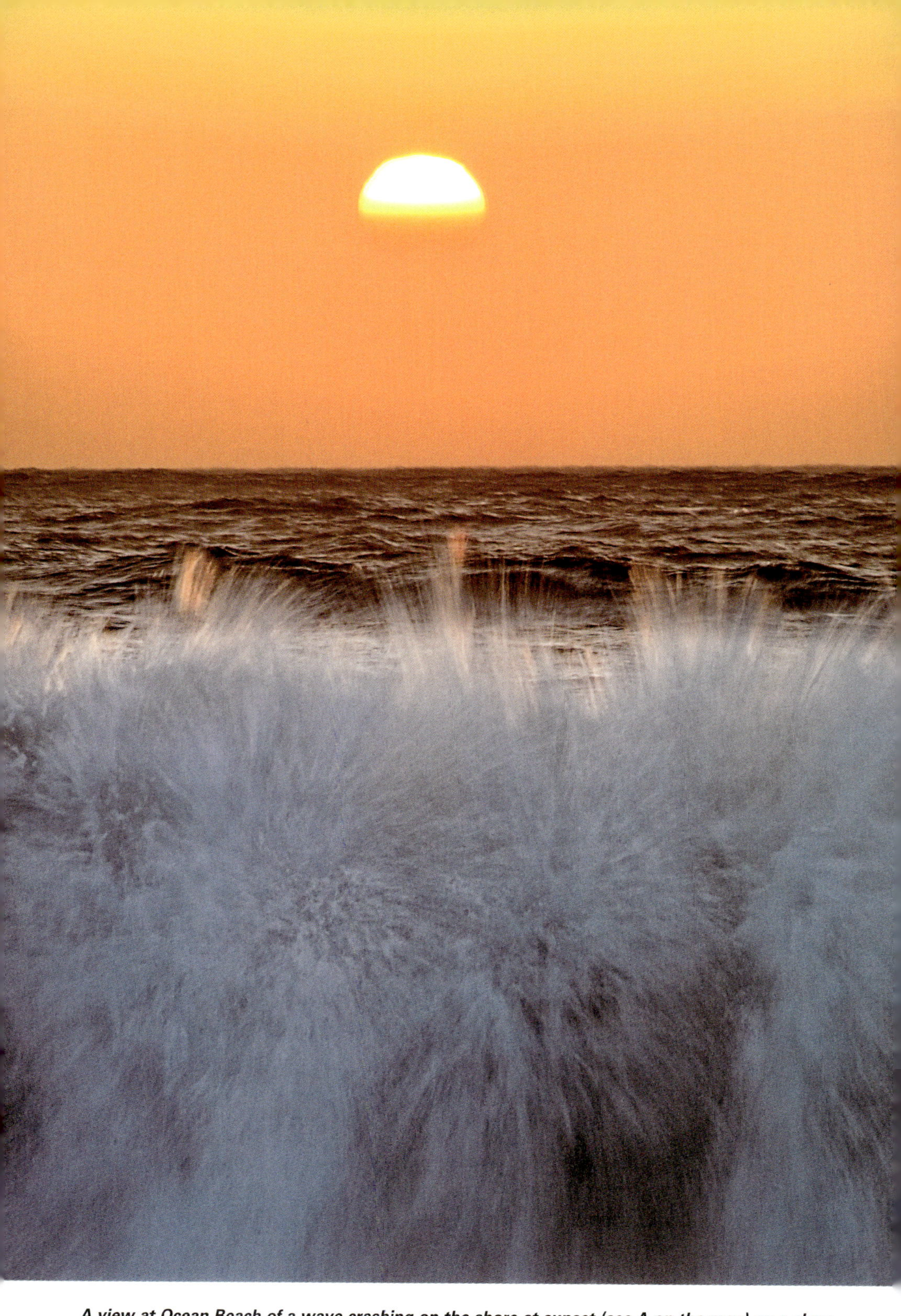

A view at Ocean Beach of a wave crashing on the shore at sunset (see A on the map) on a clear spring night. Taken at ISO 100, f/20, 1/10 second, -2/3 exposure compensation with a 70-200mm lens.

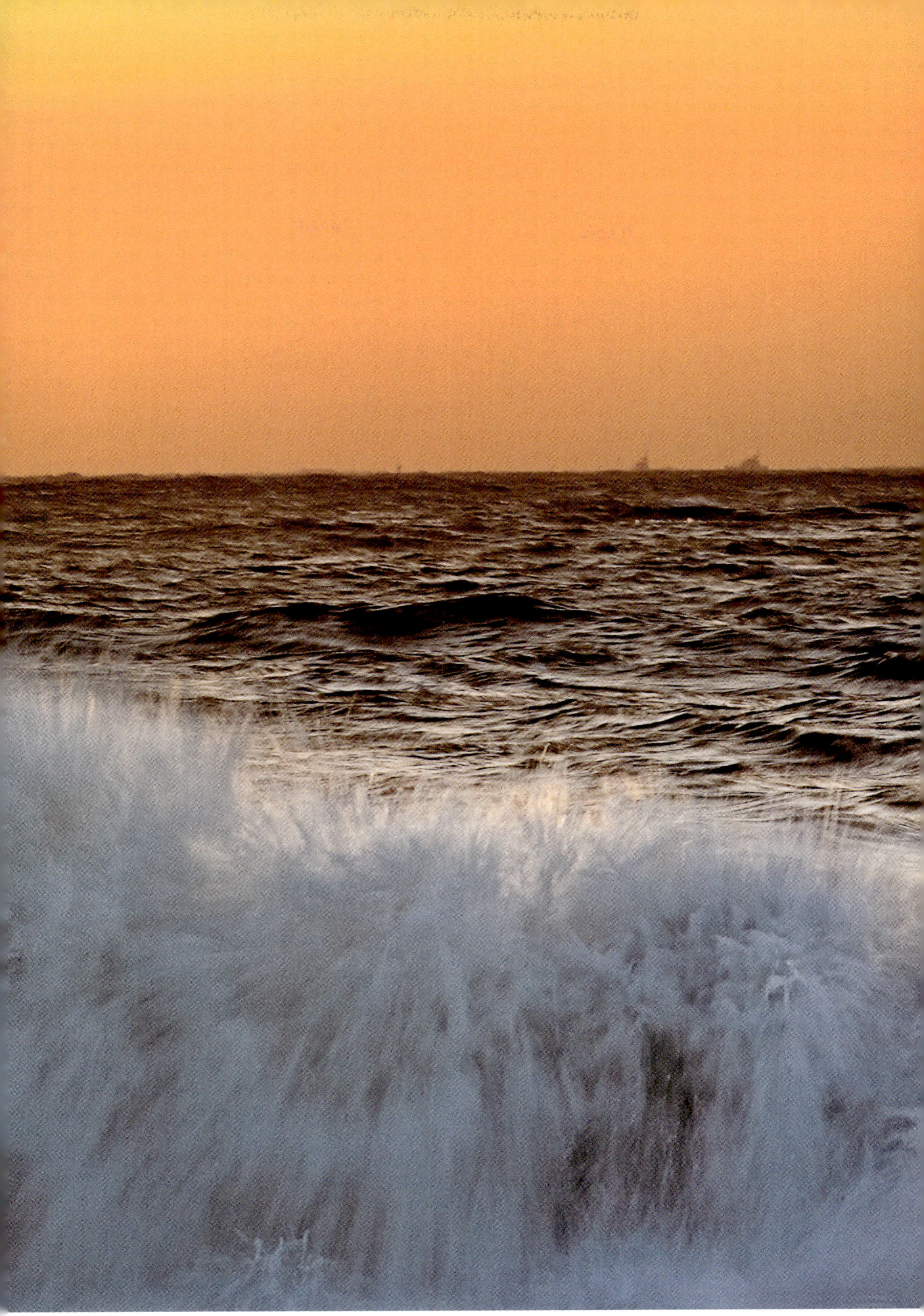

18 Ocean Beach

Why It's Worth a Photograph

Ocean Beach is located on the western shoreline of San Francisco and has a unique and untamed presence. The view from the beach with the cliffs to the left and the jagged rocks just off the shore is simply breathtaking at sunset. With the sun directly in front of you, a warm, intense light creates wonderful colors and reflections off the crashing waves.

Where Can I Get the Best Shot?

The best area to photograph from is located at the northern end of the beach adjacent to Golden Gate Park, at Fulton Street and Great Highway (see A on the map).

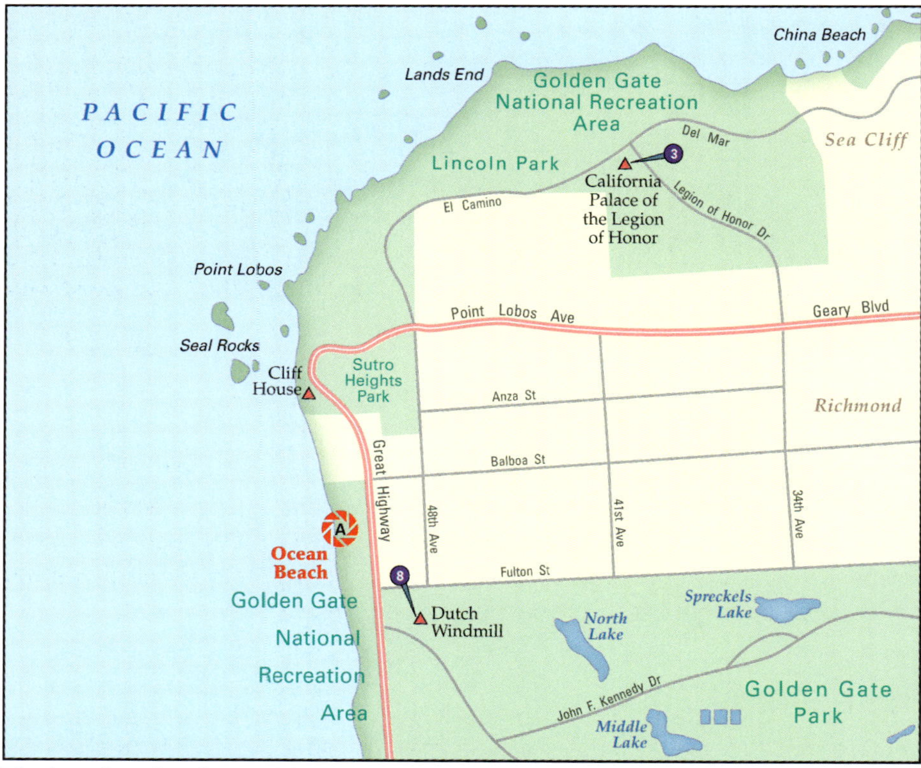

The best location from which to photograph Ocean Beach: (A) the north end of the beach. Other photo ops: (3) California Palace of the Legion of Honor, (8) Dutch Windmill.

Ocean Beach offers a wonderful vantage point to photograph the ocean at sunset. What you can create with an ocean generating such power and a sky made up of wonderful hues of pink and orange can be stunning (see figure 18.1).

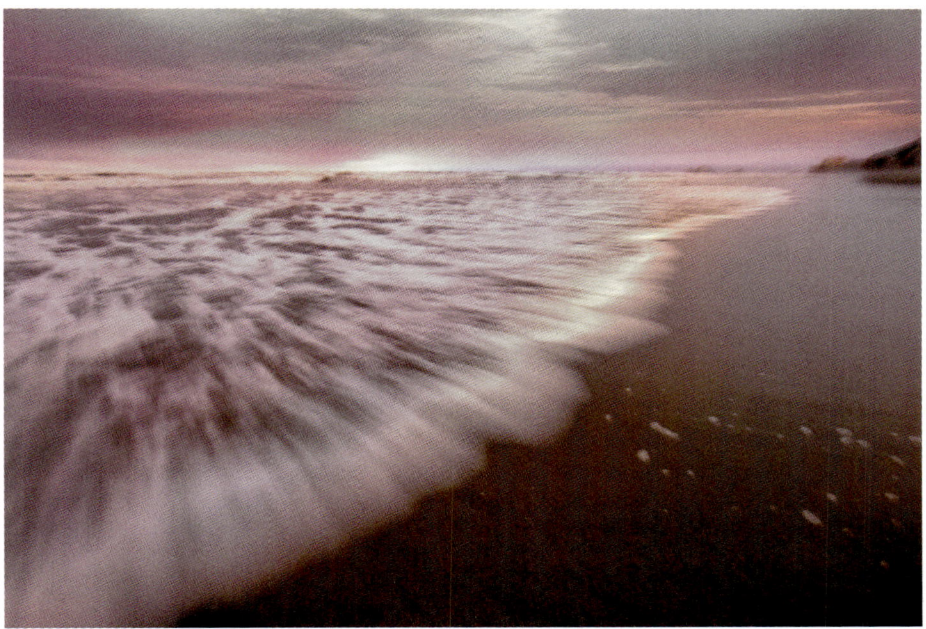

18.1 A view of Ocean Beach taken at sunset. Taken at ISO 50, f/22, 1/10 second with a 14-24mm lens.

How Can I Get the Best Shot?

Time of day and weather play a huge part in capturing the best photo. If the city is fogged in, don't bother making the trip. If weather is good, an ultrawide or telephoto lens, a filter, and a tripod will help ensure that you get the best shot. I recommend you arrive at this location one hour before the sun sets, which allows you time to walk on to the beach and set up your equipment.

Equipment

For Ocean Beach, an ultrawide-angle lens, medium telephoto lens, graduated neutral density filter, and a tripod are the equipment you will want to bring to help you photograph the waves, sun, and sand.

Lenses

The choice of lens comes down to your personal preference and what you own. Whether you are shooting day or night, your lens choice is the key to creating the ideal composition for any given subject. I recommend using the following lenses to photograph Ocean Beach:

- **Ultrawide zoom lens in the 14-24mm range.** The ultrawide lens gives you the ability to capture the beach from one end to the other. It allows you a much more creative aspect because more things can be included in the final photograph. When using an ultrawide-angle lens, you must be wary about including elements on the outer edge of the frame that you may not want.
- **Medium telephoto lens somewhere in the 70-300mm range.** This lens allows you the ability to isolate a particular subject such as a wave crashing on the beach or tide coming in.

Filters

The one filter I recommend for shooting Ocean Beach sunsets is a graduated neutral density filter. One of the trickiest aspects of landscape photography is to capture the wide range of brightness values that are typical of the most interesting and attractive scenes. How can you expose correctly for both the foreground and sky at the same time? Using a graduated neutral density filter, often known as the ND Grad, can help you solve this problem. The filter allows you to take a photograph when the sky is much brighter than the rest of your scene. How this works is the filter is half neutral density (darker) and half clear. The darker half allows you to darken the sky so that you can expose the sky and the rest of the scene properly.

To use an ND Grad filter, set up your camera on a tripod and meter the scene for the foreground, which in this case is the water or beach. Because the sky is much brighter than the water, the sky can become overexposed. Hold the filter in front of the lens while looking through the viewfinder. Position the filter so the darker half is covering the area of the sky that is overexposing and take the picture. The sky now should be exposed properly.

Extras

A tripod is important, but for many of us with the sun directly in front of us, and our shutter speeds pretty high, handholding the camera is not out of the question. If you are planning on shooting with a slower shutter speed, which you may want to when the sun dips below the horizon, then a tripod and cable release are a must.

Camera Settings

For shooting sunsets at the beach, I use Aperture Priority mode and dial in a minus exposure compensation when needed. I set the aperture between f/8 and f/16 at ISO 100. These settings give me the best overall image quality while also producing the perfect amount of depth of field for these subjects.

- **Exposure mode.** I generally shoot in Aperture Priority mode. To set my exposure, I choose the ideal aperture, which for me tends to be between f/8 and f/16. My camera then chooses the correct shutter speed. I adjust my aperture to raise or lower the shutter speed to create the desired effect. I shoot in Manual mode when there is a tricky lighting condition that is causing my meter to under- or overexpose so much that I cannot correct it with exposure compensation.
- **Exposure compensation.** Exposure compensation can come in handy when shooting extremely bright beach scenes when the sun is setting. I usually dial in a minus exposure compensation to help combat the bright sun.
- **White balance.** I never touch white balance because I find the Auto White Balance of all modern day cameras to be pretty good.
- **ISO.** If you are shooting landscapes off a tripod, you have little reason to set your ISO above the lowest setting. Most camera brands offer a low setting of 100 or 200.

Exposure

Shooting a sunset scene late at Ocean Beach can be very challenging to expose correctly. I recommend that you set the meter off the sky just to the right or left of the sun; this ensures that you do not blow out the sky when shooting the scene. Be careful not to include the sun when you meter off the sky.

Ideal time to shoot

The best time to be at Ocean Beach is one hour prior to and just after the sun sets. This is known as the golden hour of light. This time of day is ideal because the sun will be setting directly in front of you.

Working around the weather

Ocean Beach throughout the late spring and early summer is almost always enveloped in San Francisco's characteristic foggy weather, leaving average temperatures on the cooler side. August through October offers the most consistent weather and best time to photograph sunsets.

Low-light and night options

My recommendation is to shoot the sunset as the sun is just above the horizon line. The sun at this angle creates a wonderful light, and it is a great time to shoot silhouettes. To capture a skim boarder skipping across the surf (see figure 18.2), I used Aperture Priority mode and dialed in a minus exposure compensation to help create the silhouette you see. I made sure to fire off a sequence of shots as he passed in front of the sun, creating the wonderful ring light surrounding him.

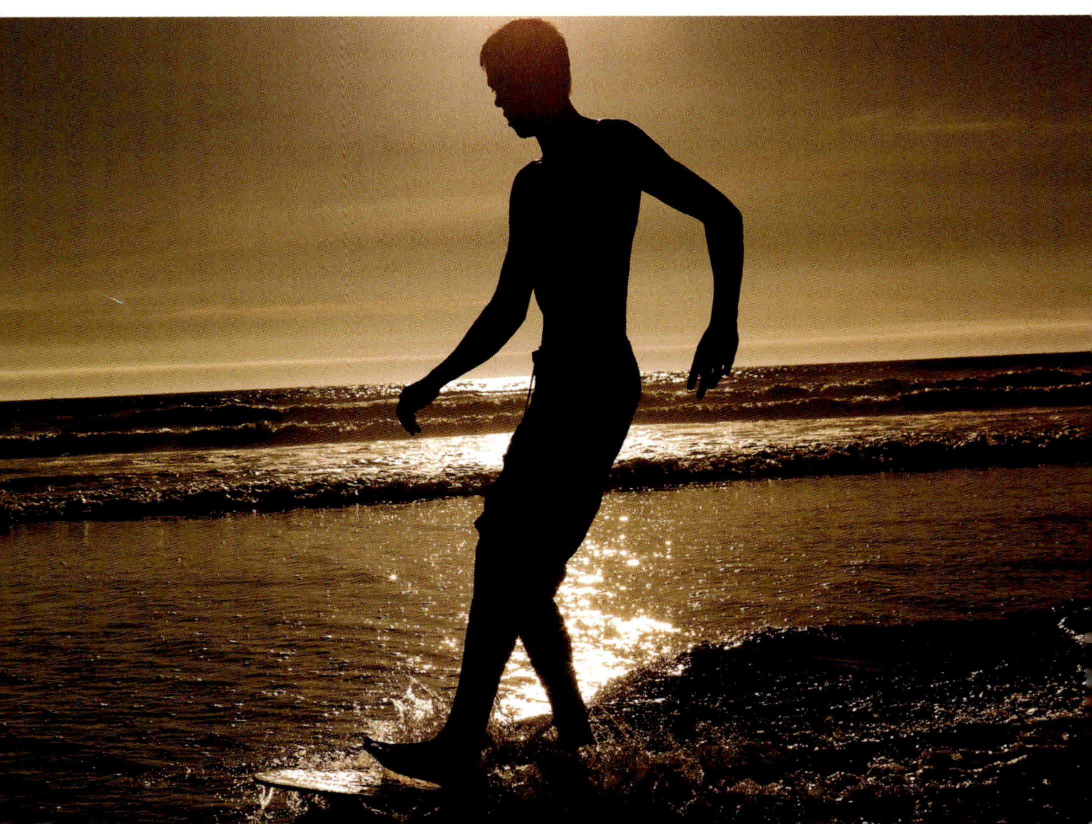

18.2 A view of a skim boarder at Ocean Beach on a clear summer evening. Taken at ISO 100, f/16, 1/1250 second with a 24-70mm lens.

Getting creative

Photography also can be about creating something special and abstract. A colorful sun setting against calm surf can offer you a unique opportunity to create a photograph with lines, color, and texture. You can create a cool, abstract image by shooting the glowing surf against dark, wet sand. Place your camera in Aperture Priority mode and dial in an aperture that gives you 1/4 second or slower. The slow shutter speeds combined with the advancing surf and reflective water create a colorful tidal abstract (see figure 18.3).

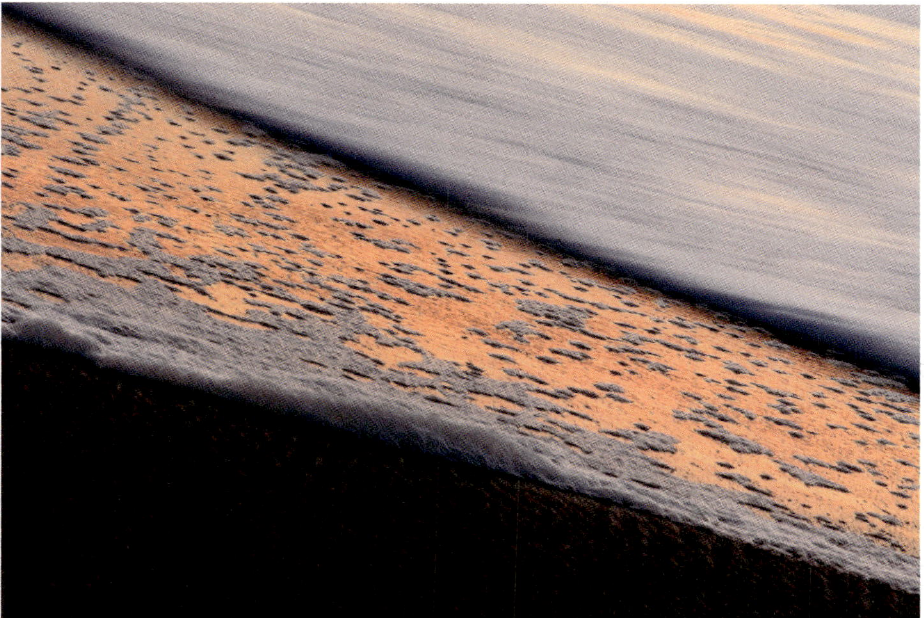

18.3 A view of the tide coming in at Ocean Beach on a clear spring evening. Taken at ISO 100, f/22, 1/4 second with 70-200mm lens.

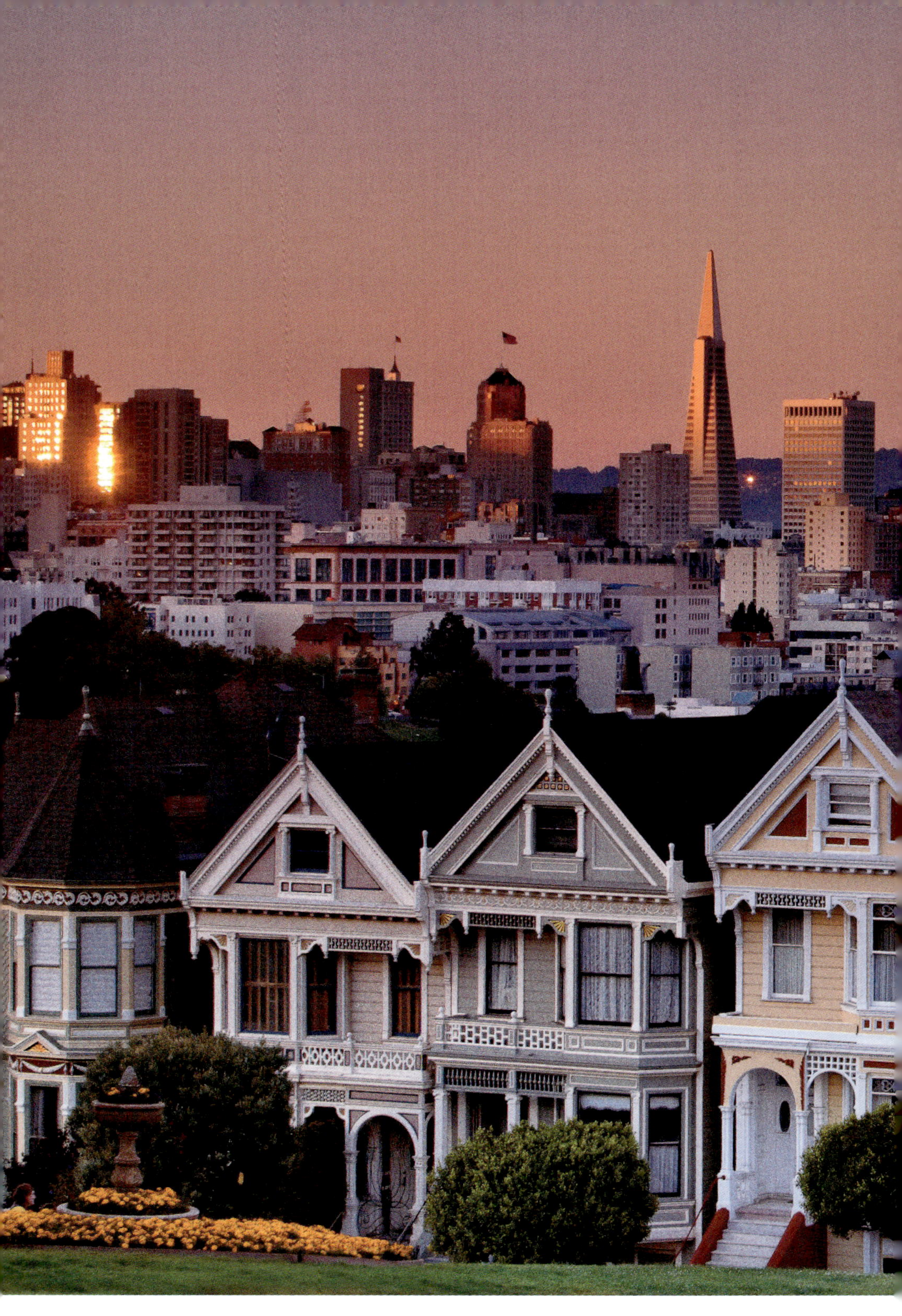

A view of the Painted Ladies taken just after sunset from Alamo Square on a clear summer evening. Taken at ISO 100, f/8, 1/13 second with a 70-200mm lens.

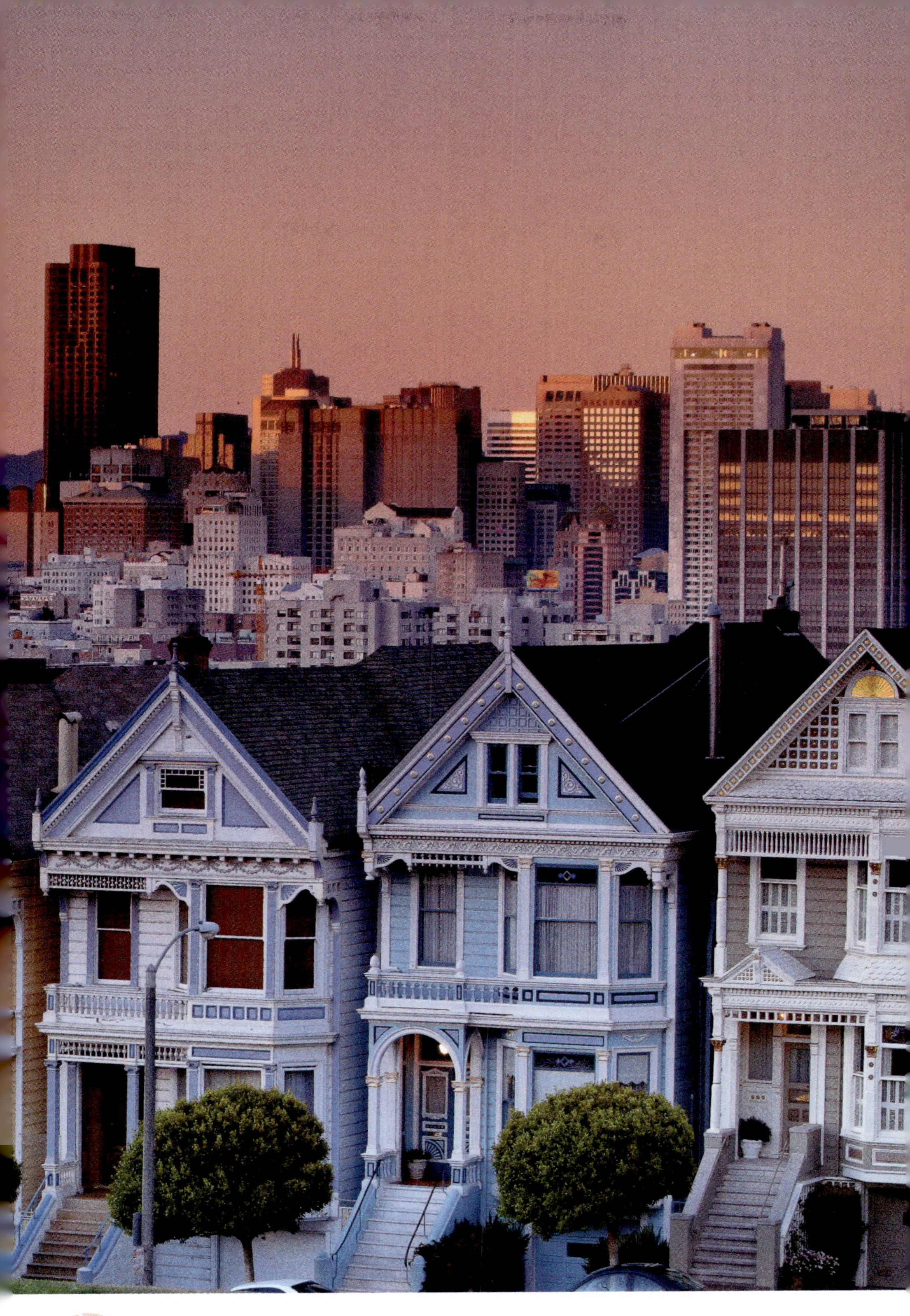

19 Painted Ladies/Postcard Row

Why It's Worth a Photograph

The San Francisco Painted Ladies — also known as Postcard Row or the Seven Sisters — are a row of Victorian homes that have become synonymous with San Francisco. *Painted Ladies*, a term used for Victorian and Edwardian houses and buildings, are known to be painted in three or more colors that embellish or enhance their architectural details. About 48,000 of these homes were built in San Francisco between 1849 and 1915. They are not known for their beauty but rather their setting with the backdrop of downtown behind them. The view from Alamo Square is always stunning but never better than at sunrise, sunset, and dusk. The late nineteenth century architecture combined with the modern twentieth century skyline of San Francisco as a backdrop is simply stunning. This contrast between the Victorian and the Modern era makes the Painted Ladies worth a photograph. A photo at daybreak gives you a wonderfully colorful front-lit scene of the Painted Ladies and the city. A photo taken at sunset can offer you a beautiful backlit scene. And a photograph at night offers up a vibrant, dusky blue sky with the Painted Ladies and San Francisco all lit up.

Where Can I Get the Best Shot?

The best vantage point to photograph the Painted Ladies is from Alamo Square (see A on the map).

Alamo Square

Located directly adjacent to the Painted Ladies, the park is one square block. The corner of Hayes Street at Scott Street is the best vantage point in the park to set up your gear. I have photographed the Painted Ladies from the early morning to late evening. I have photographed these homes when the sky was crystal clear and the warm morning hues from the sun were rising behind. And I have photographed these homes in the middle of the day when the sun was directly above casting long, harsh shadows. By far, my favorite times to photograph these homes are one hour before and up to one hour after sunset. At sunset, the sun is setting behind you, and the light will be soft and warm. The sky, 20 minutes after sunset, will be a dark blue, sometimes with a magenta tint. This blue combined with the San Francisco skyline is absolutely stunning (see figure 19.1).

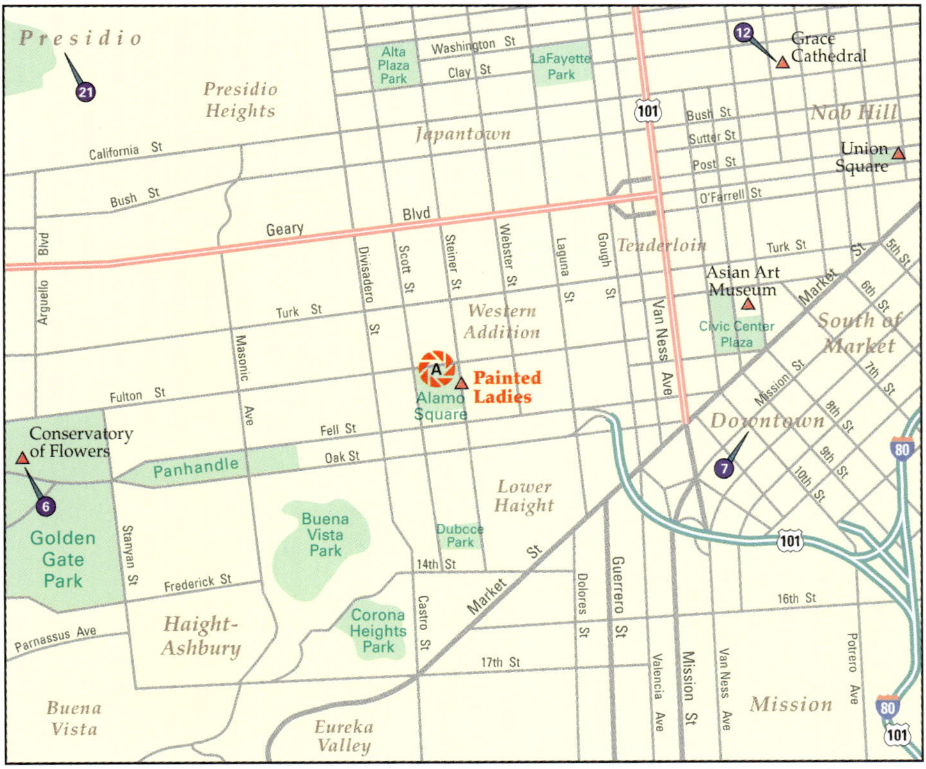

The best location from which to photograph the Painted Ladies: (A) Alamo Square. Other photo ops: (6) Conservatory of Flowers, (7) Downtown, (12) Grace Cathedral, (21) Presidio of San Francisco.

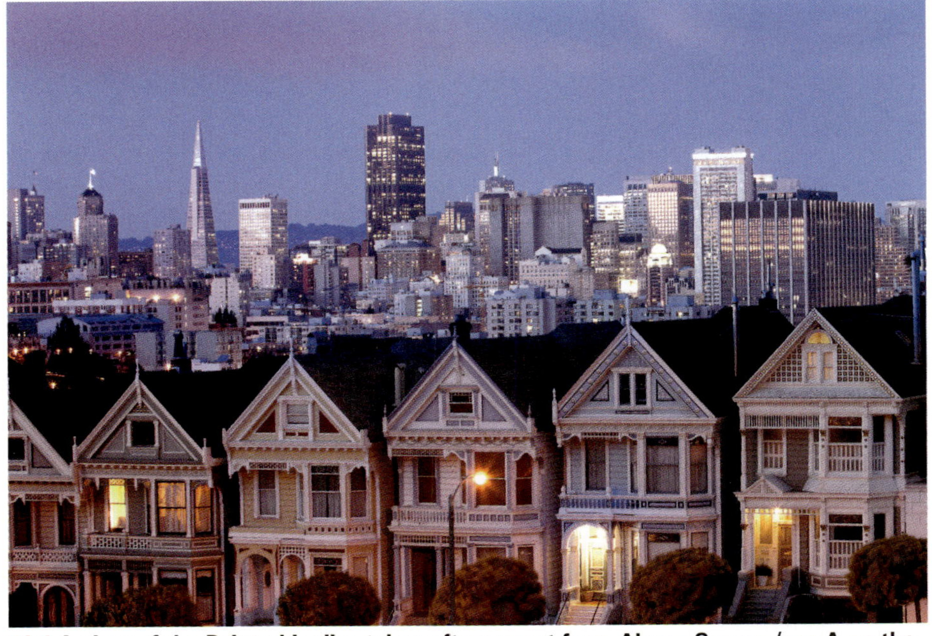

19.1 A view of the Painted Ladies taken after sunset from Alamo Square (see A on the map) on a clear summer night. Taken at ISO 100, f/8, 8 seconds with a 70-200mm lens.

How Can I Get the Best Shot?

The time of day and weather play a huge part in capturing the best photo. To ensure that you get the best shot, I recommend you arrive to this location 15 to 20 minutes prior to the time you actually want to start shooting. Doing this ensures that you have plenty of time to set up your gear and dial in your settings. Pay careful attention to composition when setting up the shot of the Painted Ladies. Due to the severe slope of the park, getting the camera aligned with the horizon line can be a bit of a chore. If you have a bubble level, this can help.

Equipment

There are three primary pieces of equipment you should have to successfully photograph these beautiful Victorians. A standard zoom lens, a tripod, and cable release are critical for capturing good quality photos of the Painted Ladies.

Lenses

The choice for this location is pretty simple. You want be able to cover a focal range between 24-100mm. Whether you are shooting the Painted Ladies during the day or at night, your lens choice is instrumental in capturing them along with the city of San Francisco. To photograph the Painted Ladies, I recommend a lens or lenses that can cover a 24-200mm range. This range can give you much more versatility when photographing the Painted Ladies. The focal length can vary based on the type of camera you use and how close you are to the homes.

Extras

A sturdy tripod is a must. Without a tripod, low-light shooting is out of the question. I also recommend a cable release and a point-and-shoot camera. A cable release allows you to shoot a longer exposure without having to trigger the shutter by touching the camera, which can cause camera shake and affect the quality of your photograph. If you do not own a cable release, you can use your camera's timer function. Most cameras have a 3-second or 10-second delay. Using the camera's timer can help prevent camera shake. A bubble level is another piece of equipment you should have with you. A bubble level slides on the flash hot shoe and helps to show whether your camera is level to the ground. Having a bubble level is particularly important in Alamo Square because the park is severely sloped.

Camera settings

You can choose from many camera settings. How you set up your camera mostly depends on you and your shooting style or what you want to convey for that particular photo. For the Painted Ladies and the typical shot from Alamo Square, the settings I tend to use are pretty consistent because I want to capture the maximum resolution the lens and camera combo can achieve. I set my camera in Aperture Priority mode and set the aperture between f/8 and f/11 at ISO 100. In general, most camera/lens combinations perform best at these apertures and ISO. I let the camera choose the shutter speed, because I am not really concerned about trying to freeze or convey motion. Depth of field is not an issue for this photo as you are approximately 100 yards from the Painted Ladies and are already focusing at infinity. Your foreground, the Painted Ladies, and your background, the city, should be in perfect focus from front to back at these apertures.

- **Exposure mode.** I generally shoot in Aperture Priority mode. To set my exposure, I choose the ideal aperture, which for the Painted Ladies is between f/8 and f/11. My camera then chooses the correct shutter speed. I shoot in Manual mode when there is a tricky lighting condition that causes my meter to underexpose or overexpose so much that I cannot correct it with exposure compensation.
- **Exposure compensation.** Exposure compensation can come in handy when photographing the Painted Ladies. Sometimes you need a bit more light to expose the homes properly; in this case, you want to add more light or dial in a plus (+) setting on your camera. If you want to lower your exposure so that you do not blow out any of the bright lights or sky, you may need to dial in a minus (–) setting, meaning less light. Most cameras allow at least a 3-stop difference either direction.
- **White balance.** White balance I never touch because I find the Auto White Balance setting of all modern day cameras to be pretty good. This holds true when shooting the Painted Ladies.
- **ISO.** Set your ISO to 100 because you want the best image quality. You can bump up the ISO if you are handholding the camera and need a faster shutter speed to render a sharp image.

Exposure

Exposing the Painted Ladies in setting light is very easy if you allow your camera to meter off the sky. This should provide you the ideal exposure. When shooting during sunrise, be careful not to underexpose the houses as the sun gets higher in the sky.

Ideal time to shoot

The ideal times to shoot the Painted Ladies are just before and just after the sun sets. The hour before the sun sets is known as the golden hour of light. Typically, lighting is softer (more diffuse) and warmer in hue, and shadows are longer. Just after the sun goes down is my favorite time to shoot, because the night sky is a dusky blue, which accentuates the Painted Ladies and the city behind.

Working around the weather

Plan your trip to the Painted Ladies around good weather. The ideal months that offer the best sunrises, sunsets, and warmest temperatures are the spring and fall months. There is no point in planning to photograph these Victorian beauties if the fog has covered the downtown.

Low-light and night options

If you're going to photograph the Painted Ladies and you have to choose between day or night, I recommend night. Shooting the Painted Ladies at night is a must for any photographer because you can create some very dramatic lighting effects. When shooting night shots of the Painted Ladies, a sturdy tripod, a cable release, and your camera's self-timer are essential. The settings for shooting at night will be no different than shooting during the day. Set your camera to Aperture Priority with an aperture of f/8 to f/11 and ISO 100.

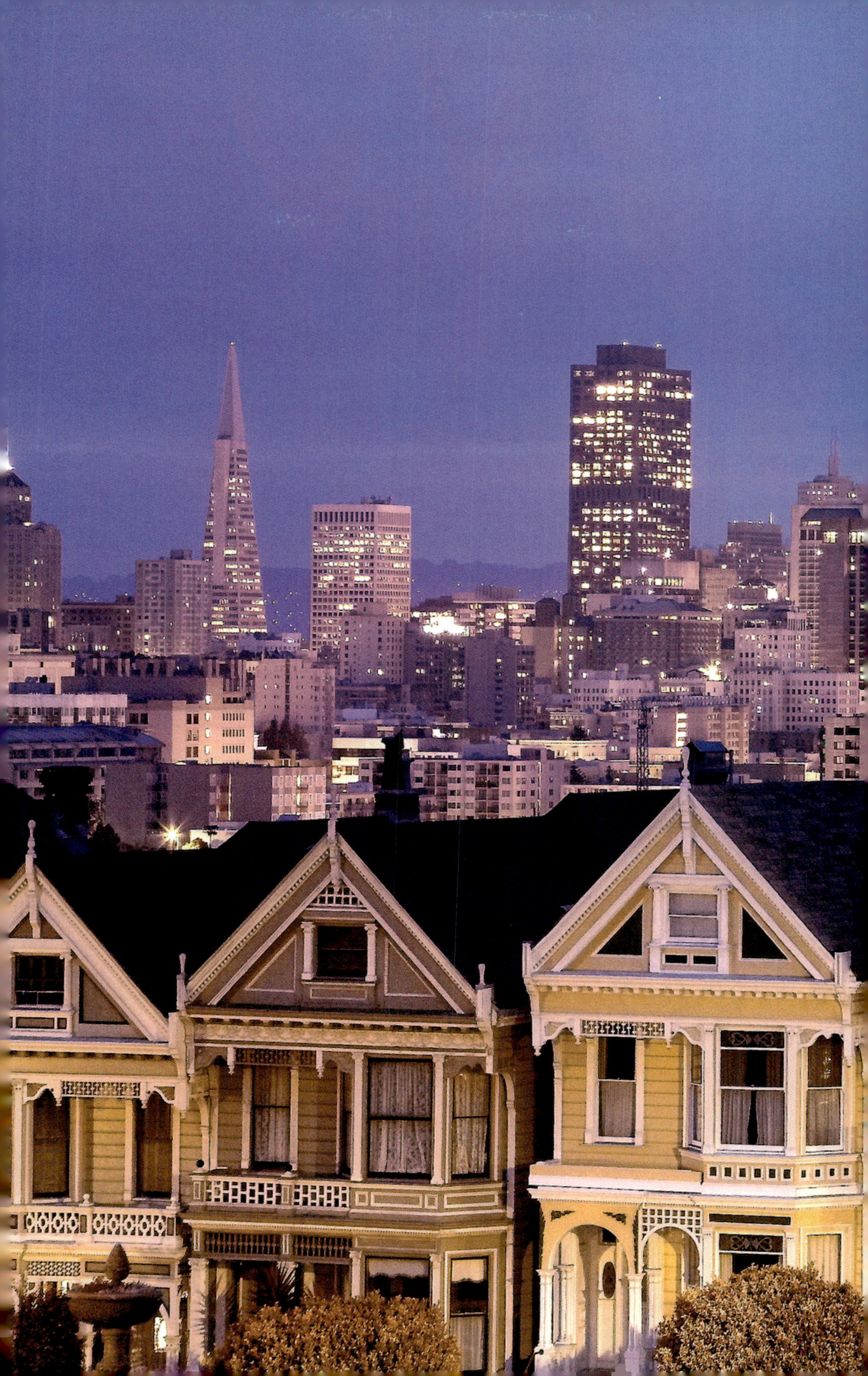

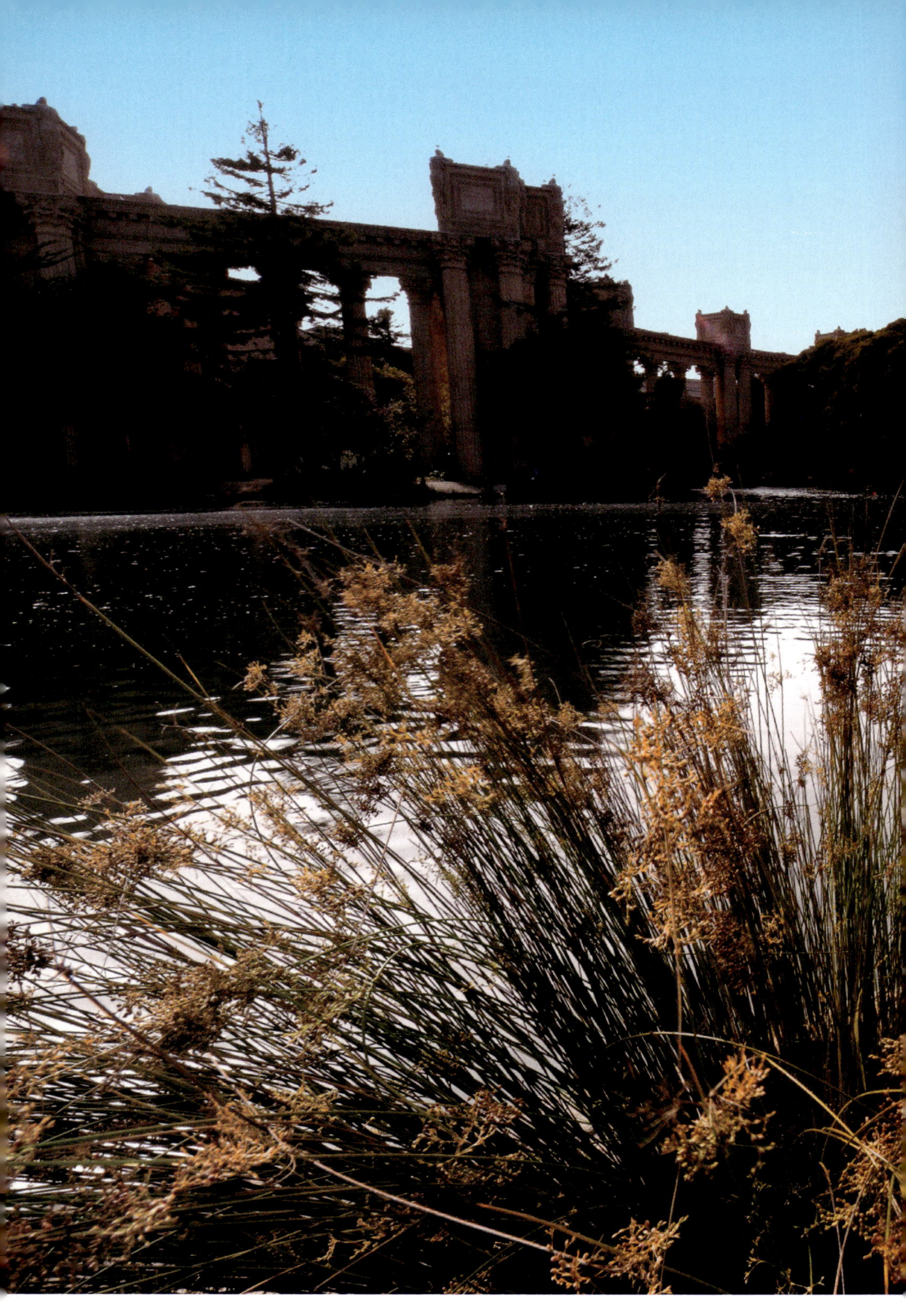

A view of the Palace of Fine Arts taken late in the day on a clear summer afternoon. Taken at ISO 200, f/22, 1/30 second with a 14-24mm lens.

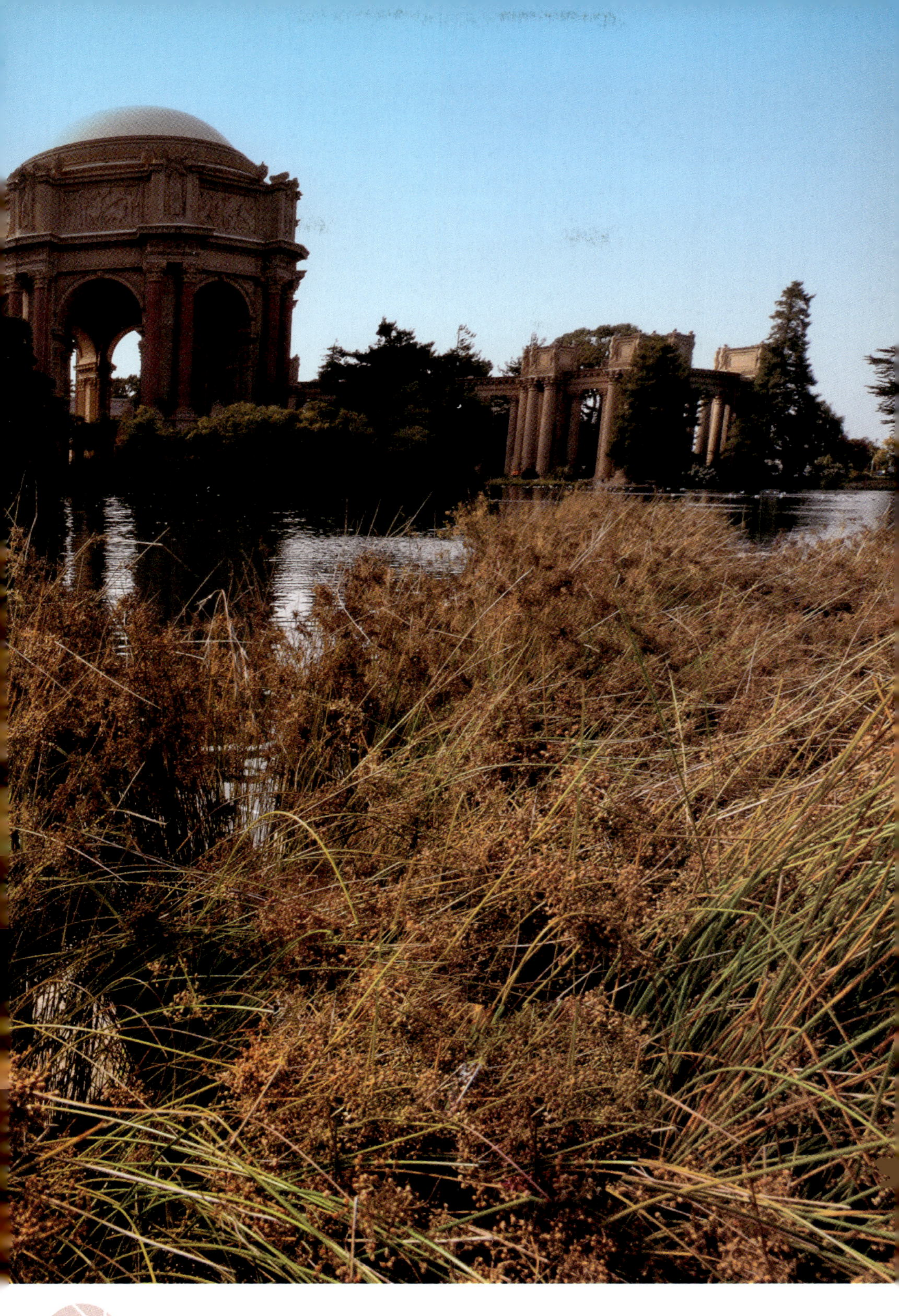

20 Palace of Fine Arts

Why It's Worth a Photograph

A remnant of San Francisco's glorious past, the Palace of Fine Arts is an exquisite arts and science complex that thrives yet feels out of place in San Francisco's Marina District. This structure was built in 1915 for the Panama-Pacific International Exposition, which celebrated the completion of the Panama Canal and the rebirth of San Francisco following the 1906 earthquake. Constructed as a temporary attraction, Bernard R. Maybeck took his inspiration from Roman and Greek architecture. What makes this worth a photograph is the contrast between the modern city and the Greco-Roman-inspired architecture that lures people to it with its unique beauty. A photo at night can give you a wonderful reflective scene of a dusky blue sky and a Roman-inspired palace. A photo after sunrise is full of the warm tones and soft light of the sun.

Where Can I Get the Best Shot?

The Palace of Fine Arts, located in the Marina District, offers the best location to photograph (see A on the map). Today, the Palace of Fine Arts remains a beautiful picturesque oasis that lures tourists in with its beauty.

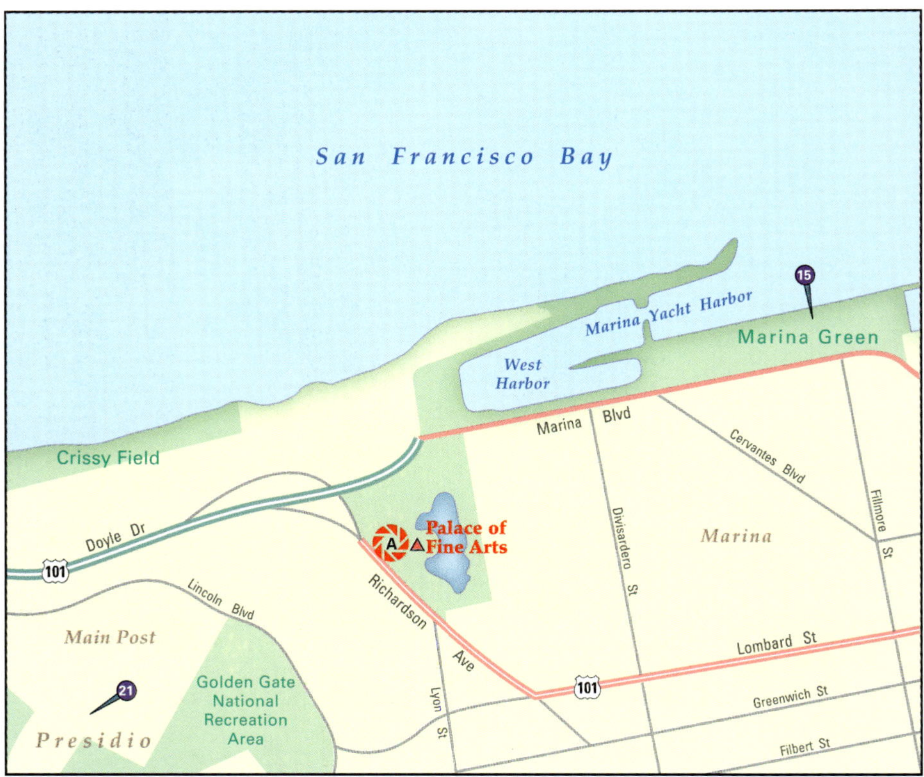

The best locations from which to photograph the Palace of Fine Arts: (A) the grounds of the Palace. Other photos ops: (15) Marina Green, (21) Presidio of San Francisco.

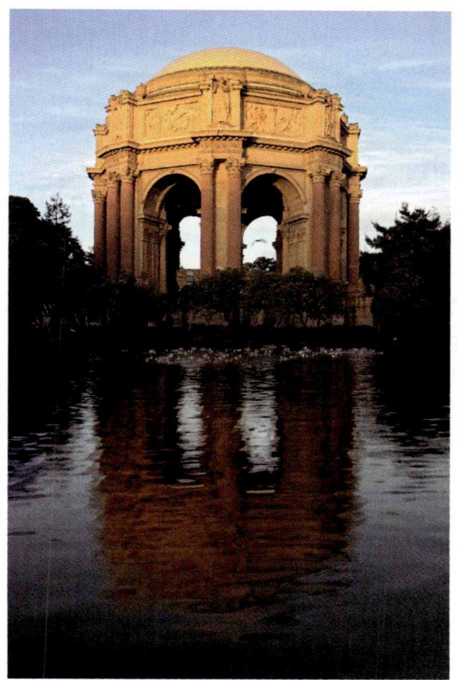

20.1 A view of the Palace of Fine Arts taken from across the pond just after sunrise on a clear winter morning (see A on the map). Taken at ISO 100, f/8, 1/15 second with a 17-35mm lens.

You can set up your gear at many great places at this location. There is a wonderful pond (see figure 20.1) that can be used as a reflective pool for a night scene. There are many trees that I like to use in my foreground to create a sense of depth. I also recommend getting up close to photograph the unique architecture from different angles with the blue sky as a background (see figure 20.2).

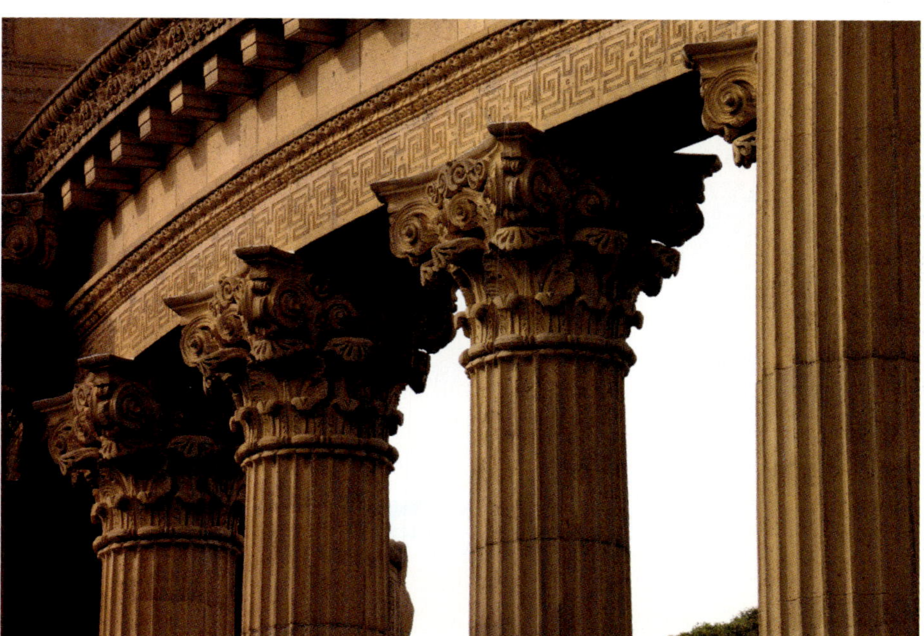

20.2 A view of the Palace of Fine Arts architecture taken just after sunrise on a clear winter morning. Taken at ISO 100, f/8, 1/160 second with a 70-200mm lens.

How Can I Get the Best Shot?

Weather plays a huge part in capturing the best photo at this location. To ensure that you get the best shot, allow yourself enough time to set up your equipment. Make sure that you arrive 30 minutes before the sun rises and plan on staying up to one hour after.

Equipment

To photograph the Palace of Fine Arts, you need to include in your bag a lens or lenses that can cover a focal length from 17-105mm. This focal length range allows you to vary your composition and creativity.

Lenses

The choice of lens always comes down to your personal preference and what you want to convey in this photo. Whether you are shooting day or night, your lens choice is instrumental for creating the ideal composition for any given subject. I recommend the following lenses to use to photograph the Palace of Fine Arts:

- **Ultrawide zoom lens in the 14-24mm range.** The ultrawide lens gives you the ability to frame the Palace of Fine Arts from one end to the other. You can be creative because more things can be included in the final photograph. When using an ultrawide lens, you must be wary about including elements on the outer edge of the frame that you may not want.
- **A standard zoom lens in the 24-100mm range.** This can give you much more versatility when traveling. A zoom lens in this range is generally considered the perfect walk-around lens for capturing anything from landscape/ cityscapes to pictures of the family.

Extras

A tripod is a must. If you don't own one, buy one. Without a tripod, night shots and low-light shooting are out of the question. I also recommend a cable release and bubble level. A cable release allows you to shoot a longer exposure without having to trigger the shutter by touching the camera, which can cause camera shake and affect the quality of your photograph. A bubble level helps you level the camera and prevent those nasty crooked shots that we all get.

Camera settings

How you set up your camera mostly depends on your shooting style or what you want to convey for that particular photo. The settings I have used for photographing the Palace of Fine Arts have been based on my composition and the depth of field needed to capture the scene. When shooting this scene with an object in the immediate foreground, you want to choose an aperture that renders sharpness from front to back. Therefore, choosing an aperture of f/22 should give you enough depth of field to render the foreground and background sharp. If I am shooting this scene where the foreground is not important, I choose an aperture of f/8 to f/11.

- **Exposure mode.** I generally shoot in Aperture Priority mode. To set my exposure, I choose the ideal aperture, which for me tends to be between f/8 and f/22. My camera then chooses the correct shutter speed. I adjust my aperture to raise or lower the shutter speed to create the desired effect. I shoot in Manual mode when there is a tricky lighting condition that is causing my meter to under- or overexpose so much that I cannot correct it with exposure compensation.
- **White balance.** White balance I never touch because I find the Auto White Balance of all modern day cameras to be pretty good.
- **ISO.** In general, to maximize your camera's image quality, I leave the ISO at 100 when shooting landscapes. The few times I increase the ISO is to increase the shutter speed or to allow me to use a smaller or larger aperture.

Exposure

For shooting the Palace of Fine Arts, I set my camera in Aperture Priority mode and let my camera choose the correct exposure. On days when the sky is overcast, I may dial in a –1/3 exposure compensation to help protect the sky from overexposing. Once again this becomes a balancing act. You need to expose what you think is most important, and sometimes this means overexposing the sky or slightly underexposing the foreground. At night allow your camera to pick the exposure; I have found that most cameras do a very good job exposing properly at night.

Ideal time to shoot

The 30 minutes just before and the hour after the sun rises are the best times to photograph the Palace of Fine Arts. The sky can be an intense dusky blue before sunrise or have a soft, warm, golden light after sunrise, which front lights the Palace and fills in all the shadows.

Working around the weather

Morning and evening fog is common during summer months in San Francisco. This is especially true for the Palace of Fine Arts because it is located next to the bay. September and October tend to be the warmest and clearest months, whereas rain can be common in late November through March. A clear morning or evening is a must to truly capture this wonderful building.

Low-light and night options

If you're going to photograph the Palace of Fine Arts and you have a choice between day or night, I recommend night. Shooting the Palace of Fine Arts at night is a must for any photographer because you can create some very dramatic lighting effects.

When shooting night shots of the Palace of Fine Arts, you must have a sturdy tripod and cable release. Put your camera in Aperture Priority mode with an ISO of 100. You can expect your shutter speed to be in the area of 5 to 30 seconds with an aperture between f/8 and f/16. These slow shutter speeds and small apertures create a wonderfully smooth, reflective surface from the pond in front of the palace. This, combined with the intense, dark blue sky and the lights illuminating the Palace, creates the perfect picture (see figure 20.3).

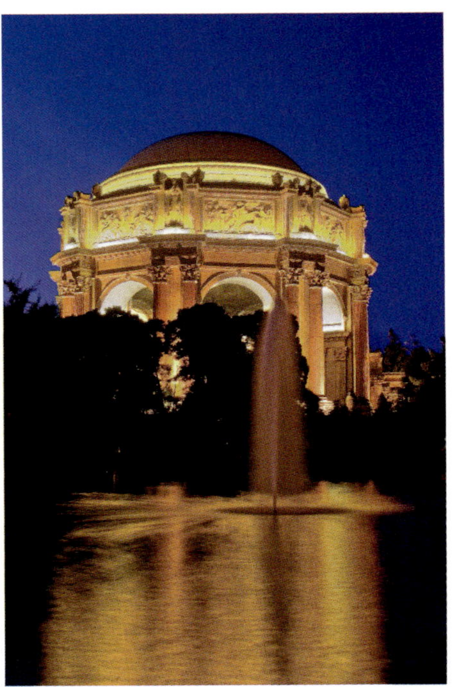

20.3 A view of the Palace of Fine Arts taken just after sunset on a clear winter evening. Taken at ISO 100, f/8, 13 seconds with a 24-70mm lens.

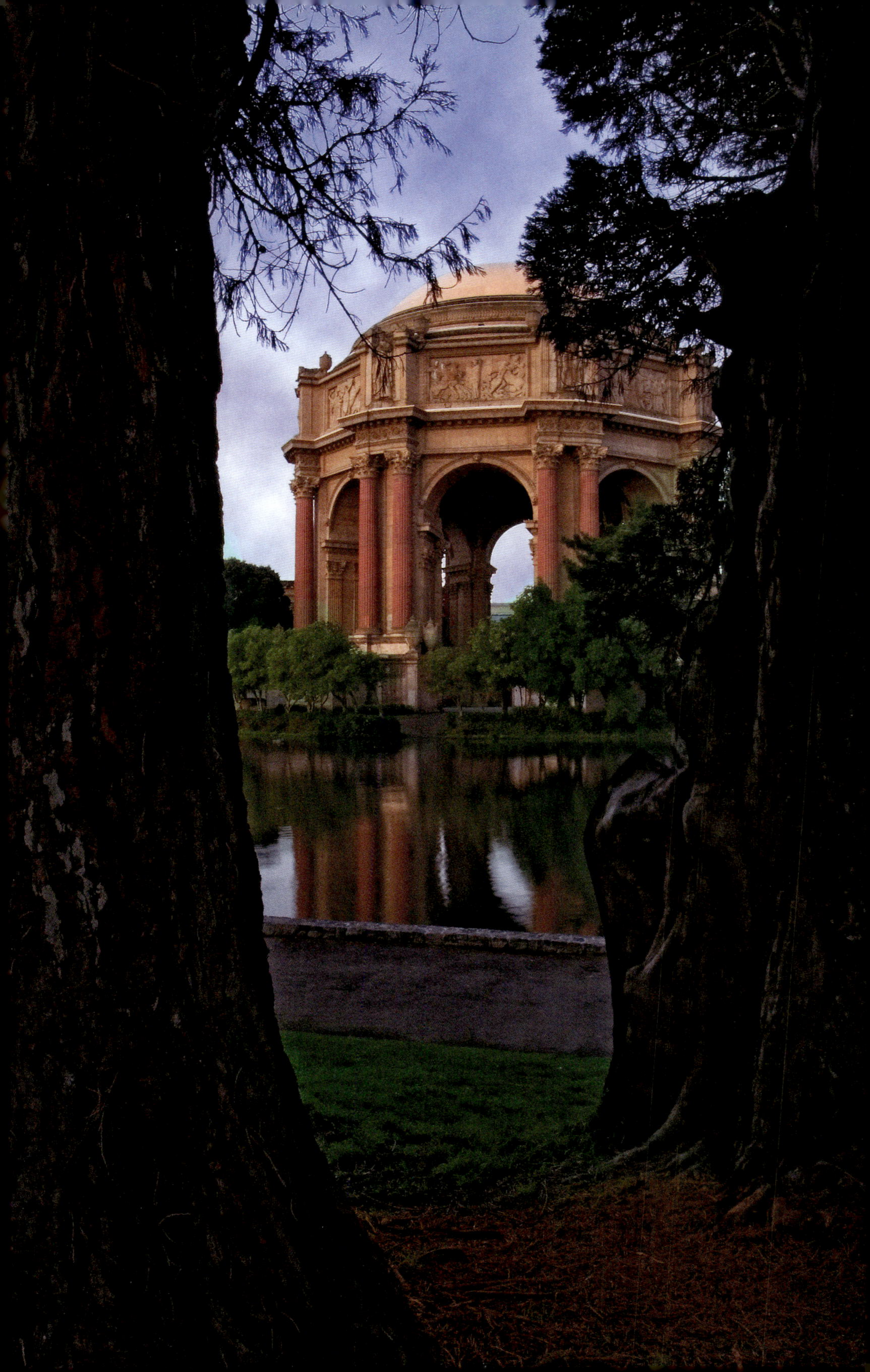

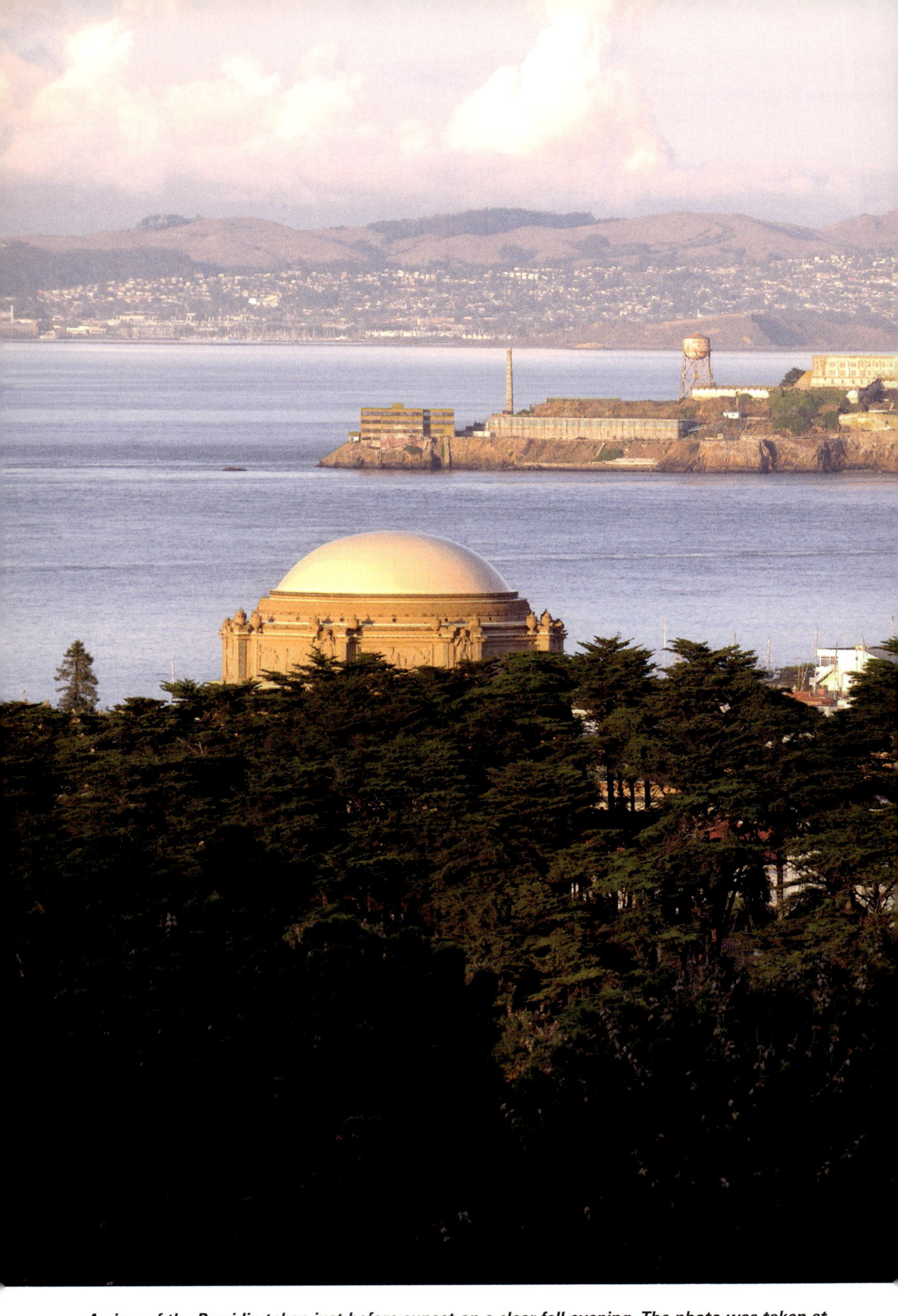

A view of the Presidio taken just before sunset on a clear fall evening. The photo was taken at ISO 100, f/8, 1/100 second, – 2/3 exposure compensation with a 70-200 mm lens.

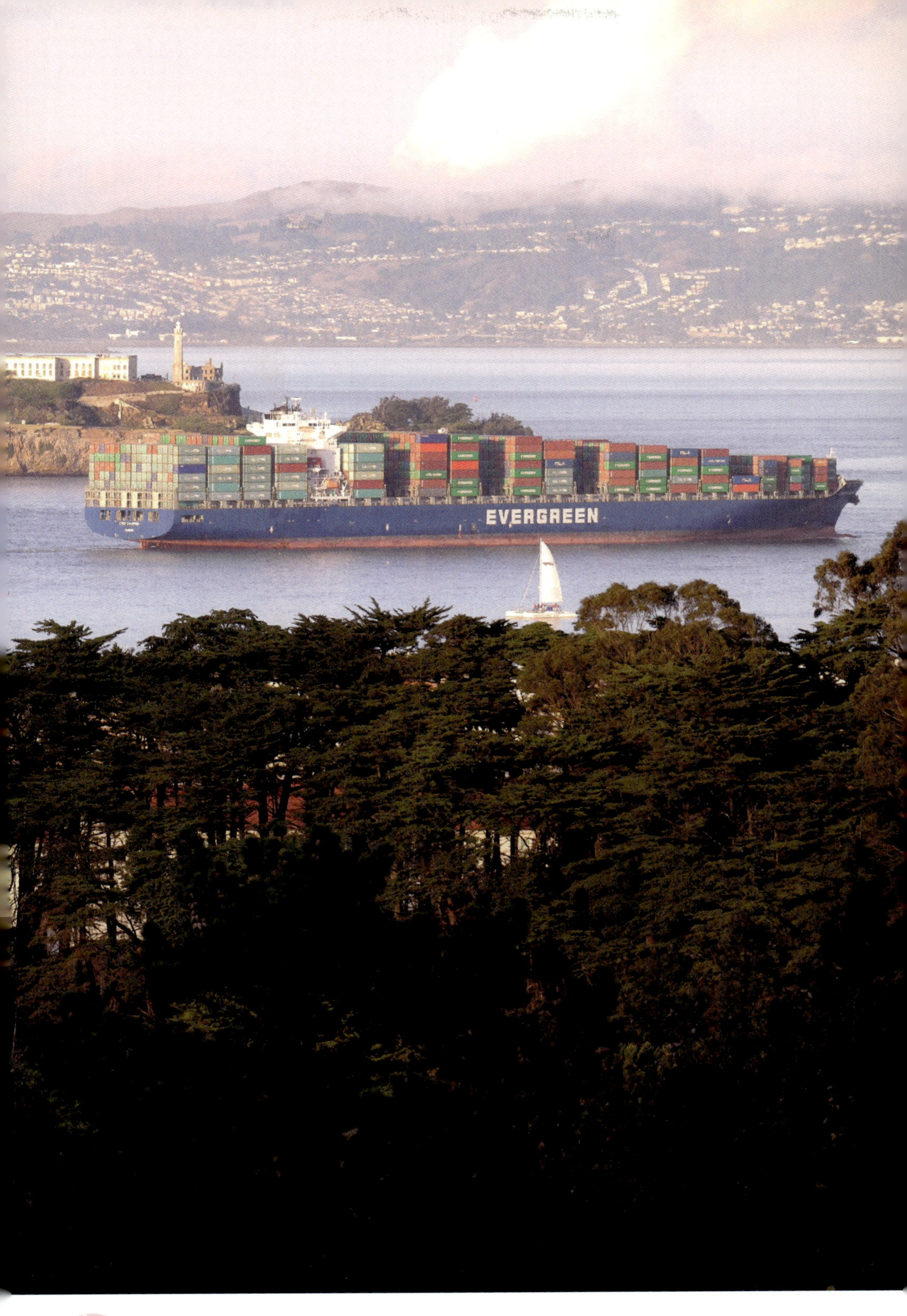

21 Presidio of San Francisco

Why It's Worth a Photograph

The Presidio of San Francisco is a 1,500-acre national park site and is part of the Golden Gate National Recreation Area. For over 200 years, the Presidio was in continuous use as a military post. Designated as a National Historic Landmark District, the Presidio has one of the largest and finest collections of any military architecture in the United States, with over 450 historic buildings. These buildings were primarily constructed by the U.S. Army from the Civil War through the end of World War II and include officers' quarters, barracks, warehouses, and hangars. Beautiful historic buildings, rich cultural landscapes, and years of cultural and natural history — from its geologic foundations millions of years ago to its current role as a refuge for endangered species — combine to make wonderful photo opportunities here.

Where Can I Get the Best Shot?

Inside the Presidio, the Presidio Victorians, Infantry Row, the eucalyptus trees, the cemetery, and Crissy Field are the best places to capture great photos of the Presidio.

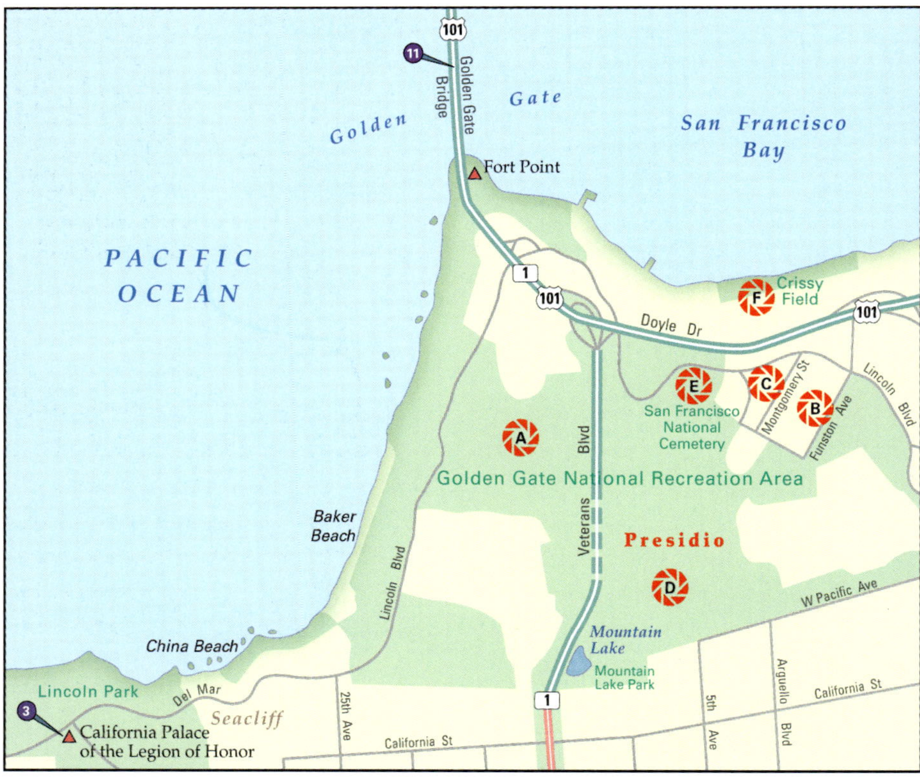

The best locations from which to photograph the Presidio: (A) Inside the Presidio, (B) Presidio Victorians, (C) Infantry Row, (D) Eucalyptus trees, (E) San Francisco National Cemetery, (F) Crissy Field. Other photo ops: (3) California Palace of the Legion of Honor, (11) Golden Gate Bridge.

Inside the Presidio

The Presidio offers so many opportunities to capture wonderful images of military artillery, barracks, and warehouses, and it also offers some of the most amazing views of the city and bay (see A on the map). Here you can capture a wonderful image looking back toward the city with a medium telephoto lens (see figure 21.1).

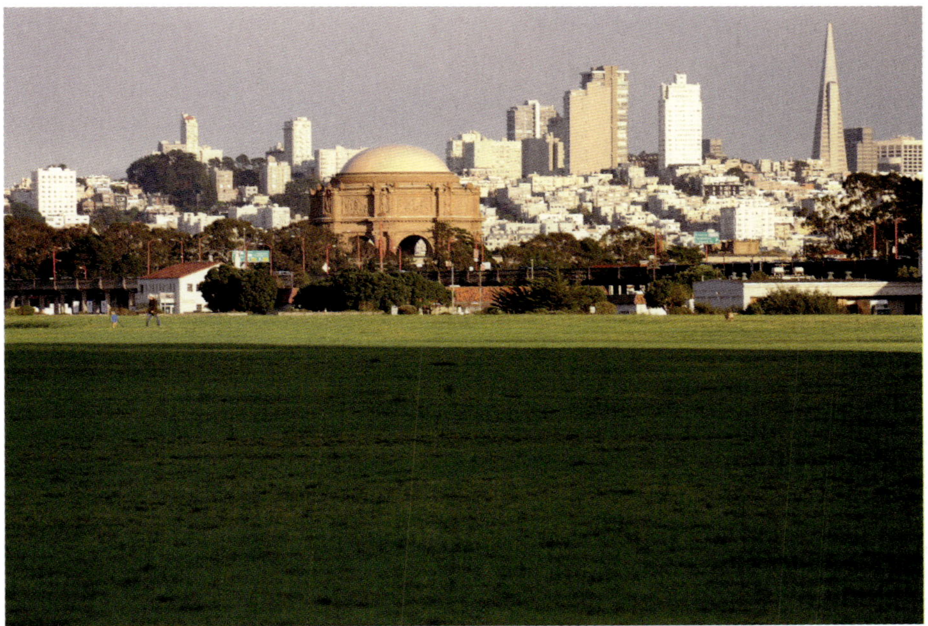

21.1 A view of the San Francisco Marina district, Russian Hill, and Pacific Heights taken from inside the Presidio (see A on the map) on a clear fall evening. Taken at ISO 100, f/8, 1/125 second with a 70-200mm lens.

Presidio Victorians

On Funston Avenue, Officers' Row in the Presidio, you can find the oldest intact Victorian streetscape in the city (see B on the map). This distinct neighborhood within the Presidio has two dozen Victorian officers' quarters in the Greek Revival, Eastlake, and mansard styles, as well as historic landscaping and is one of San Francisco's treasures. This area is truly a pleasure to photograph because these homes have been kept up to their original grandeur (see figure 21.2). A standard to medium telephoto lens is all you need to photograph these wonderful homes left over from the Presidio's historic past.

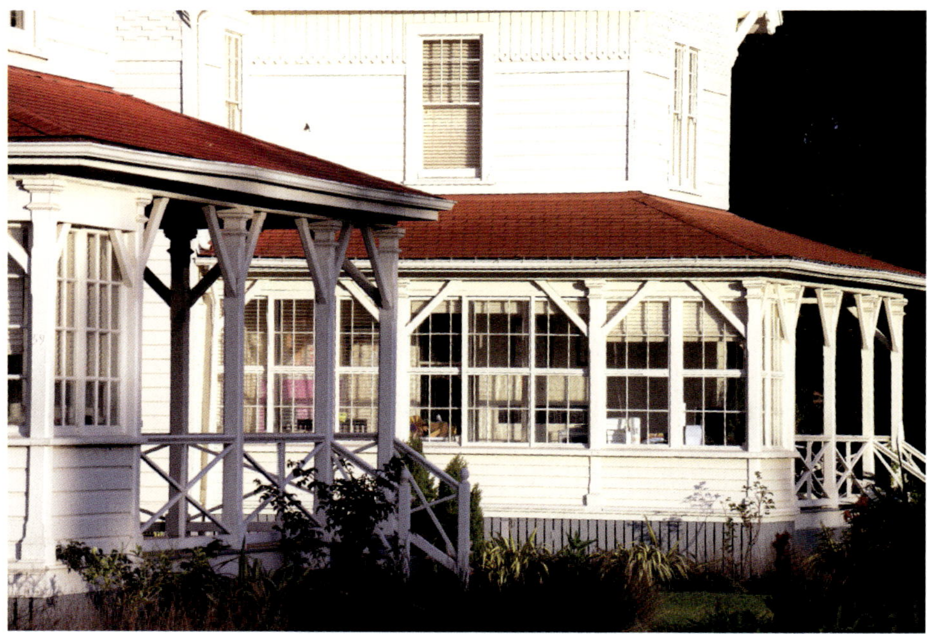

21.2 A view of the Presidio historic Victorians taken just before sunset from Funston Avenue (see B on the map). Taken at ISO 100, F8, 1/250 second, –33 exposure compensation with a 70-200mm lens.

Infantry Row

The enlisted soldiers' barracks on Montgomery Street, known as Infantry Row (see C on the map), were constructed to accommodate the troops at the Presidio during the 1890s, when many frontier forts were closed. Built in the Colonial Revival style, these were among the first brick barracks constructed in the western United States. Each could house a company of 110 soldiers and were built identically to the same floor plan. With a crisp, blue sky and long lens, you can create a wonderful composition with color and line leading your viewer's eye straight down the row and to the bay (see figure 21.3).

Eucalyptus trees

The Presidio's landscape is made up of eucalyptus, Monterey cypress, and Monterey pine trees and is one of San Francisco's and the Presidio's scenic highlights (see D on the map). Planted over a century ago as a beautification project, they offer us solitude, a quiet undisturbed picnic in covered shade, a pleasant morning jog, or a quiet stroll through dense and secluded forest. The beauty, charm, and character of the Presidio's landscape leave lasting impressions of the historic presence. Bring a wide-angle lens and wait for low, warm light to bathe the forest in wonderful colors and warm hues. Focusing on composition and leading lines takes your viewer down a path in figure 21.4.

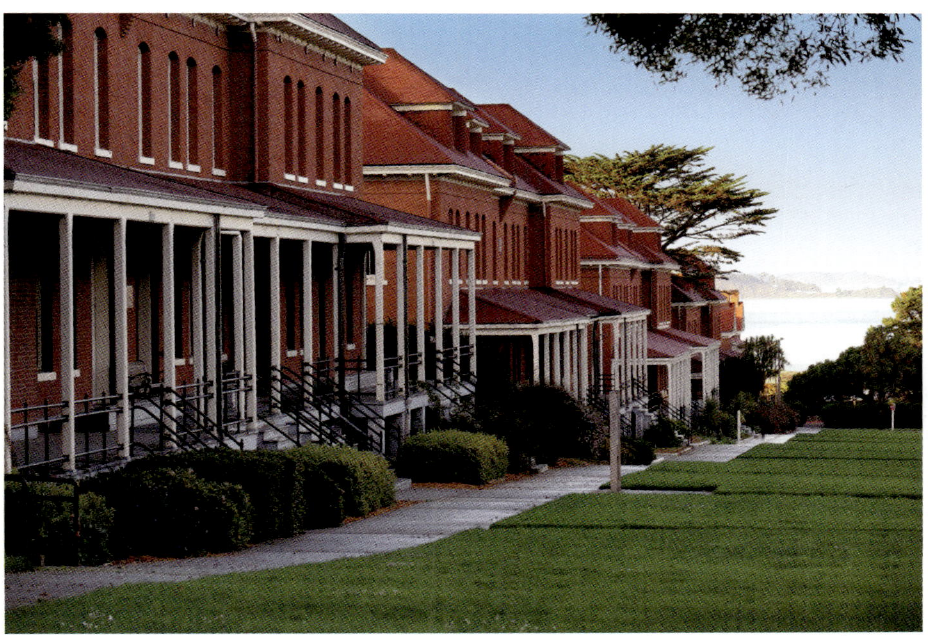

21.3 A view of Infantry Row taken on a clear fall afternoon (see C on the map). Taken at ISO 400, f/5.6, 1/200 second with a 70-200 mm lens.

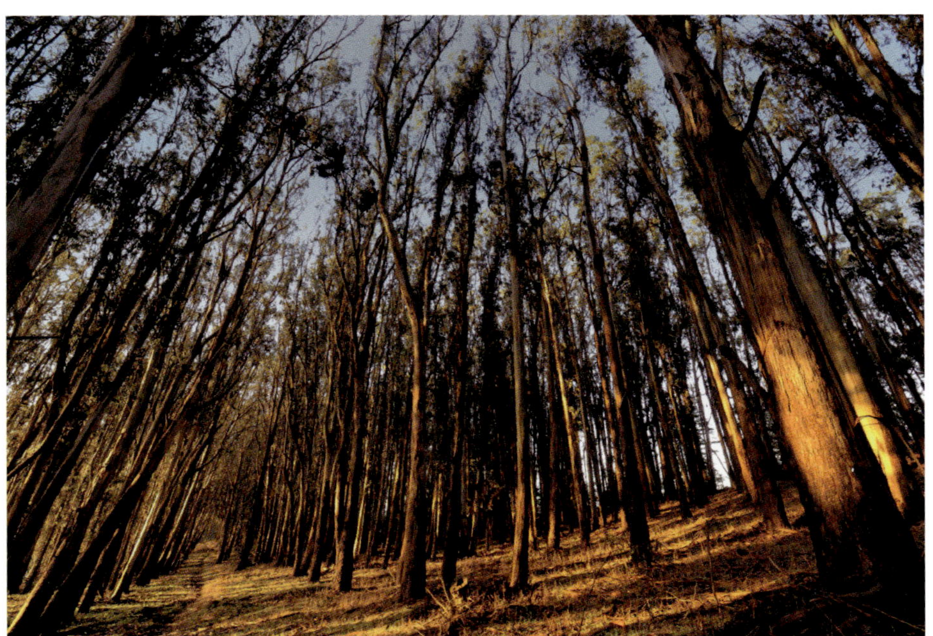

21.4 A view of a eucalyptus forest inside the Presidio taken on a warm fall evening (see D on the map). Taken handheld at ISO 400, f/8, 1/20 second with a 14-24mm lens.

San Francisco National Cemetery

Established in 1884, the 27-acre San Francisco National Cemetery (see E on the map) is a constant reminder of the Presidio as a place of service and sacrifice. The cemetery is the final resting place for over 30,000 people, including 35 Congressional Medal of Honor recipients and 450 Buffalo Soldiers, African-American regiments established by Congress in 1866 to patrol America's western frontier. A major Memorial Day commemoration takes place here each year. Mood and composition are everything when photographing a cemetery. The perfect light, some advancing fog, and an ultrawide lens can make for a stunning photo (see figure 21.5).

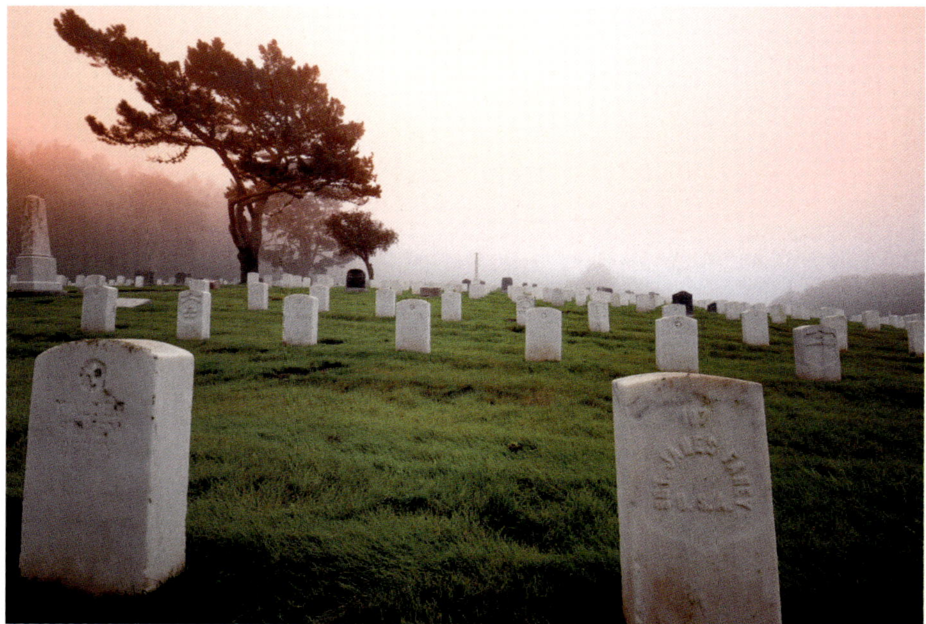

21.5 A view of the San Francisco National Cemetery taken on a cool, foggy morning as the sun was rising above the tree line (see E on the map). Taken handheld at ISO 800, f/22, 1/50 second with a 14-24mm lens.

Crissy Field

Crissy Field is linked to the early history of aviation in the United States and was the military's first Air Coast Defense Station on the Pacific coast. Crissy Field is the area along the northern shoreline of the Presidio of San Francisco (see F on the map). This area along the Presidio offers some of the most breathtaking views of San Francisco Bay. During the late fall, San Francisco can get an occasional rainstorm that can rival many of the intense tropical storms the South Pacific might encounter. These storms can generate rain and wind upwards of 50 to 80 mph. Soon after the storms subside, the city is treated to incredible cloud formations that when mixed with setting light can create some of the most magnificent sunsets (see figure 21.6).

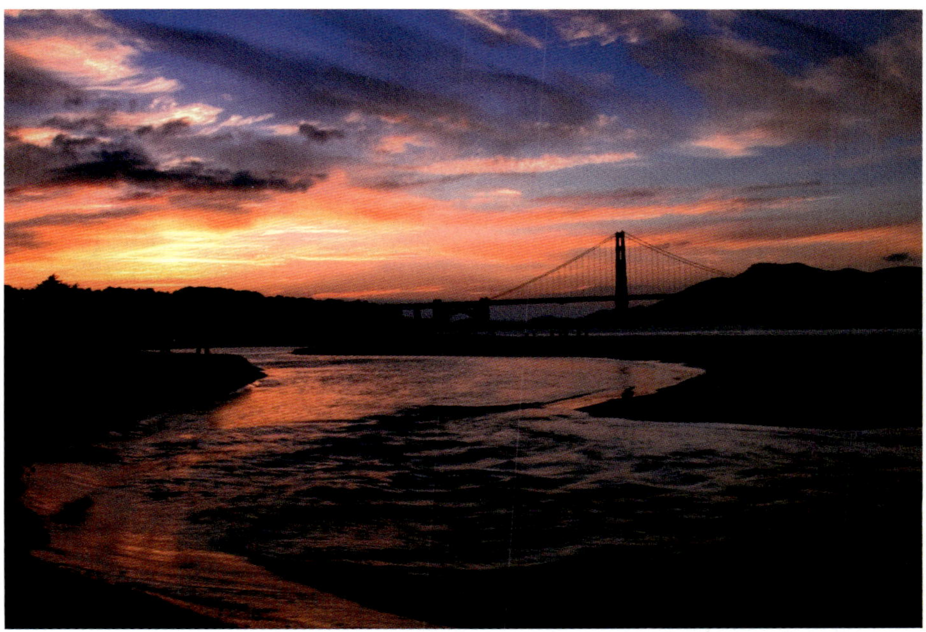

21.6 A view of the bay taken from Crissy Field during a clear fall sunset (see F on the map). Taken at ISO 100, f/22, 1/3 second with a 24-105mm lens.

How Can I Get the Best Shot?

The Presidio is a wonderful place for an early morning or afternoon walk. Make your trip when the sun is still low and the sky is clear. The city and bay views, architecture, and landscaping are truly worth photographing. Arrive early enough to allow yourself enough time to see these wonderful locations. Plan your trip accordingly; if you want to shoot the sun setting, then arrive in the afternoon. Bring the right equipment as you will need an assortment of lenses, filters, and a tripod to ensure you are able to photgraph the Presidio and all of its history.

Equipment

I bring an assortment of lenses, filters, and a sturdy tripod with me on every vacation or shoot.

Lenses

The choice of lens always comes down to what you have in your bag. The three lenses that can best serve you when visiting the Presidio are:

- **Ultrawide-angle lens in the 14-24mm range.** The ultrawide-angle lens gives you the ability to create some truly unique shots. This lens is ideal for the cemetery and eucalyptus trees in the Presidio.
- **A standard zoom lens in the 24-100mm range.** This lens can give you much more versatility when traveling. A zoom in this range is generally considered the perfect walk-around lens for capturing anything from landscape/cityscapes to pictures of the family. This lens is great for almost all areas within the Presidio. If you were to carry one lens, this should be it.
- **A medium telephoto lens somewhere in the 70-300mm range.** This lens allows you the ability to isolate a particular subject such as a tower, or gives you the extra reach when shooting subjects that are too far off for a standard zoom lens. This focal range is my favorite because it gives me the ability to isolate a subject from a distance.

Filters

There are two primary filters I recommend when photographing the Presidio. These filters are a circular polarizing filter and a neutral density filter.

- **Circular polarizing filter.** A circular polarizing filter is a filter that every photographer should have in her bag. The polarizing filter's main purpose is to cut down or eliminate glare on water, glass, and metal. It can also be used to enhance color and contrast in your photos. I use it primarily to bring out the blue sky in my photos. The maximum effect of polarization can be seen when used at a 90-degree angle from the sun. A polarizer is best used on a lens that is not wider than 24mm because it can cause the sky to be unevenly polarized.
- **Neutral density filter.** A neutral density filter allows you to shoot at a larger aperture when the sun is at its brightest, but also allows you to slow your shutter speed 2 or more stops. I have two neutral density filters: One is a 3-stop and the other is a 10-stop. This filter is great for sunset shots when the sun is setting directly in front.

Extras

A sturdy tripod is a must. Without a tripod, low-light shooting is out of the question. I also recommend a cable release. The advantage of using a cable release is that it allows you to shoot longer exposure and not have to trigger the shutter by touching the camera, which can cause camera shake and affect the quality of your photograph.

Camera settings

You can choose from many camera settings. How you set up your camera mostly depends on you and your shooting style or what you want to convey in a particular photo. For the Presidio I shot mainly in Aperture Priority mode with an aperture of f/8. For the photos where I needed a bit more depth of field, as for the cemetery or the sunset shots, I set my aperture at f/22.

- **Exposure mode.** I generally shoot in Aperture Priority mode. To set my exposure, I choose the ideal aperture, which for me tends to be between f/8 and f/16. My camera then chooses the correct shutter speed. I adjust my aperture to raise or lower the shutter speed to create the desired effect. I shoot in Manual mode when a tricky lighting condition is causing my meter to under- or overexpose.
- **Exposure compensation.** I use exposure compensation frequently as it is the easiest way to adjust exposure on the fly. I usually am more worried about blown highlights as these are nearly impossible to recover. I dial in a –1.3 to –2.3 when shooting subjects where overexposure will be a problem.
- **White balance.** I use the Auto White Balance (AWB) setting to create a more neutral color tone or Cloudy for a little more warmth. Most of the time I will leave it at AWB and adjust it in post-processing when needed. My suggestion is to stick with AWB as it gives a more neutral and true representation of the actual color.
- **ISO.** When shooting in the Presidio and using a tripod, I keep my ISO as low as possible. For those shots, when I am handholding, I increase my ISO so that I can reach a fast enough shutter speed to hand hold.

Exposure

When shooting outdoors, exposure is rarely a problem for most modern day cameras. When your camera is in Aperture Priority mode, you may have to adjust exposure compensation to protect against blown highlights or dark shadows. In Manual mode, the exposure choice is up to you. Pick the exposure based on what you want to convey. The perfect exposure creates the mood you want.

Ideal time to shoot

The ideal times to shoot are just before and just after the sun rises or sets. The early morning and late afternoon typically offer better light. The lighting is softer (more diffuse) and warmer in hue and shadows are longer. The lower sun helps make your pictures really pop. The warm, soft light and long, soft shadows really set a mood, unlike the harsh light provided during the middle of the day.

Working around the weather

The climate is Mediterranean, with wet winters and dry summers that tend to be windy and cool throughout much of the park. Summers are foggy, with the best weather in spring and fall. Dress in layers. Hiking boots are appropriate in some areas. Comfortable shoes are recommended, because you will be walking on asphalt or on sidewalks.

Getting creative

Figure 21.7 is a fun shot that can be done anywhere, but in order for you to capture this you need puddles of water and a creative imagination. A long lens, perfect light, and something to shoot were in my favor when I saw this reflection of a historical building on a pathway to the bay. This was shot as if it were any other photo. I took care to make sure the grass, water, and concrete were broken into thirds and on a diagonal. Using the Rule of Thirds and setting these thirds on a diagonal makes for a more pleasing photo.

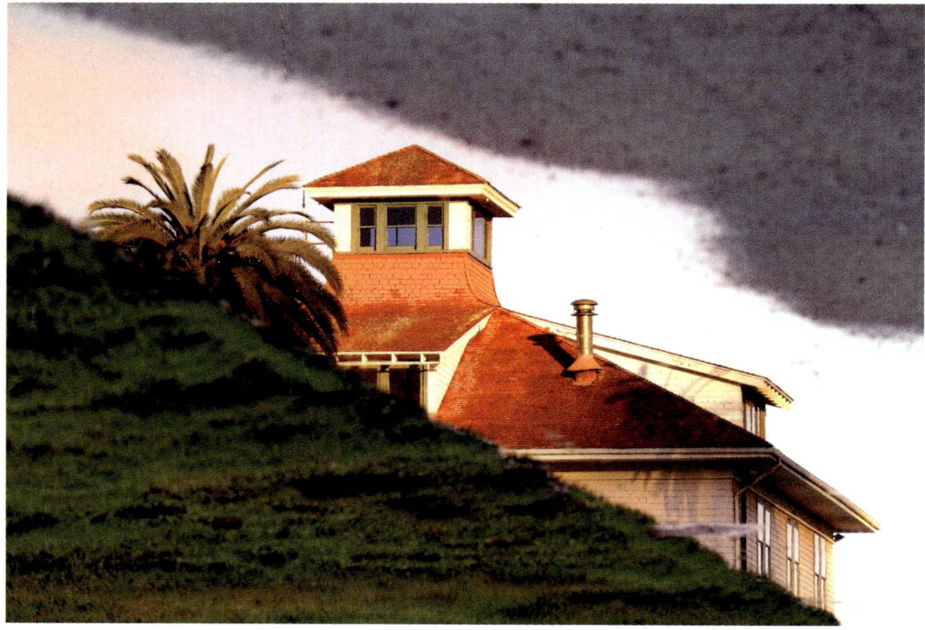

21.7 A reflection of an historical building on Crissy Field taken on a clear fall evening (see F on the map). Taken at ISO 100, f/8, 1/60 second with a 70-200mm lens.

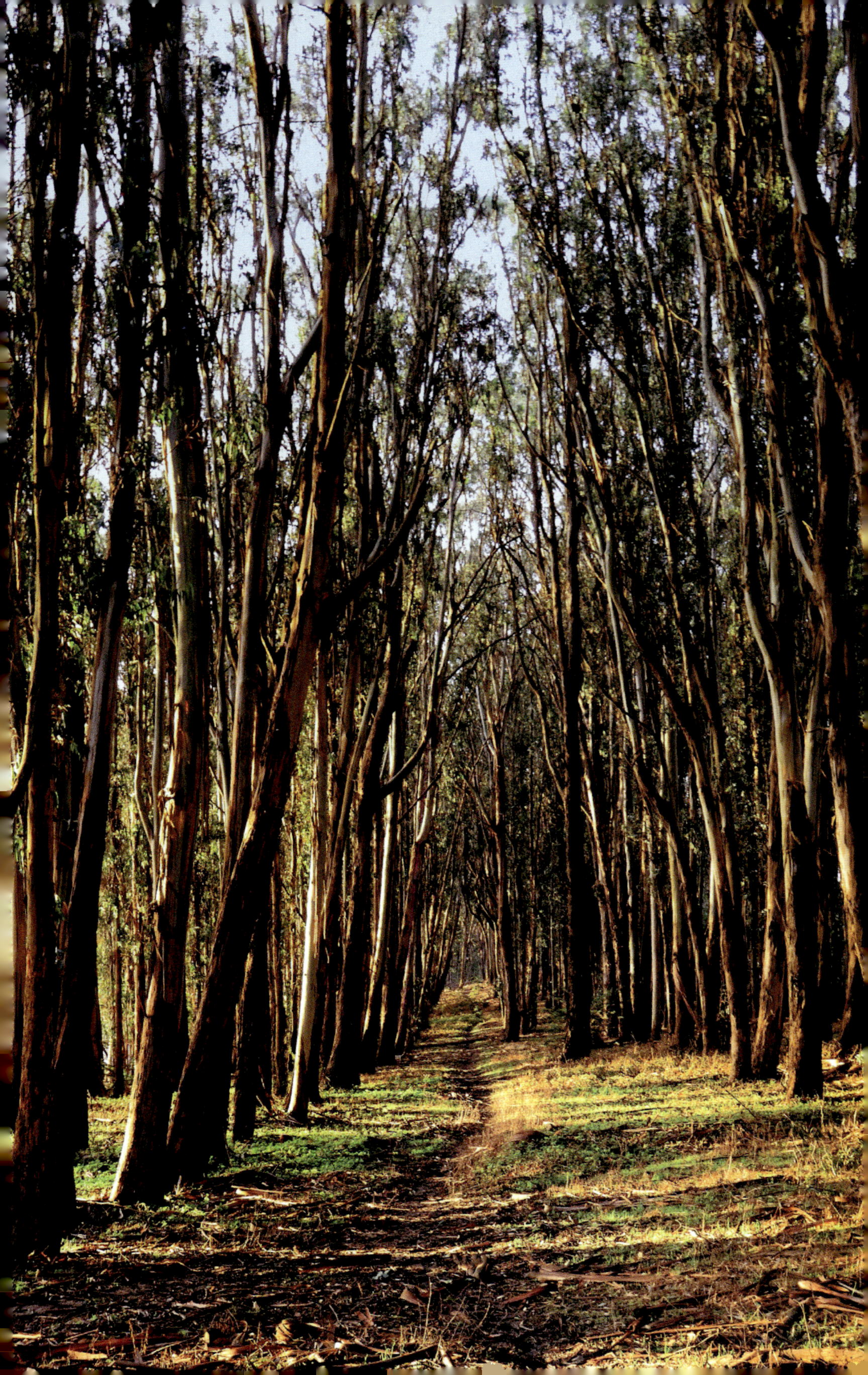

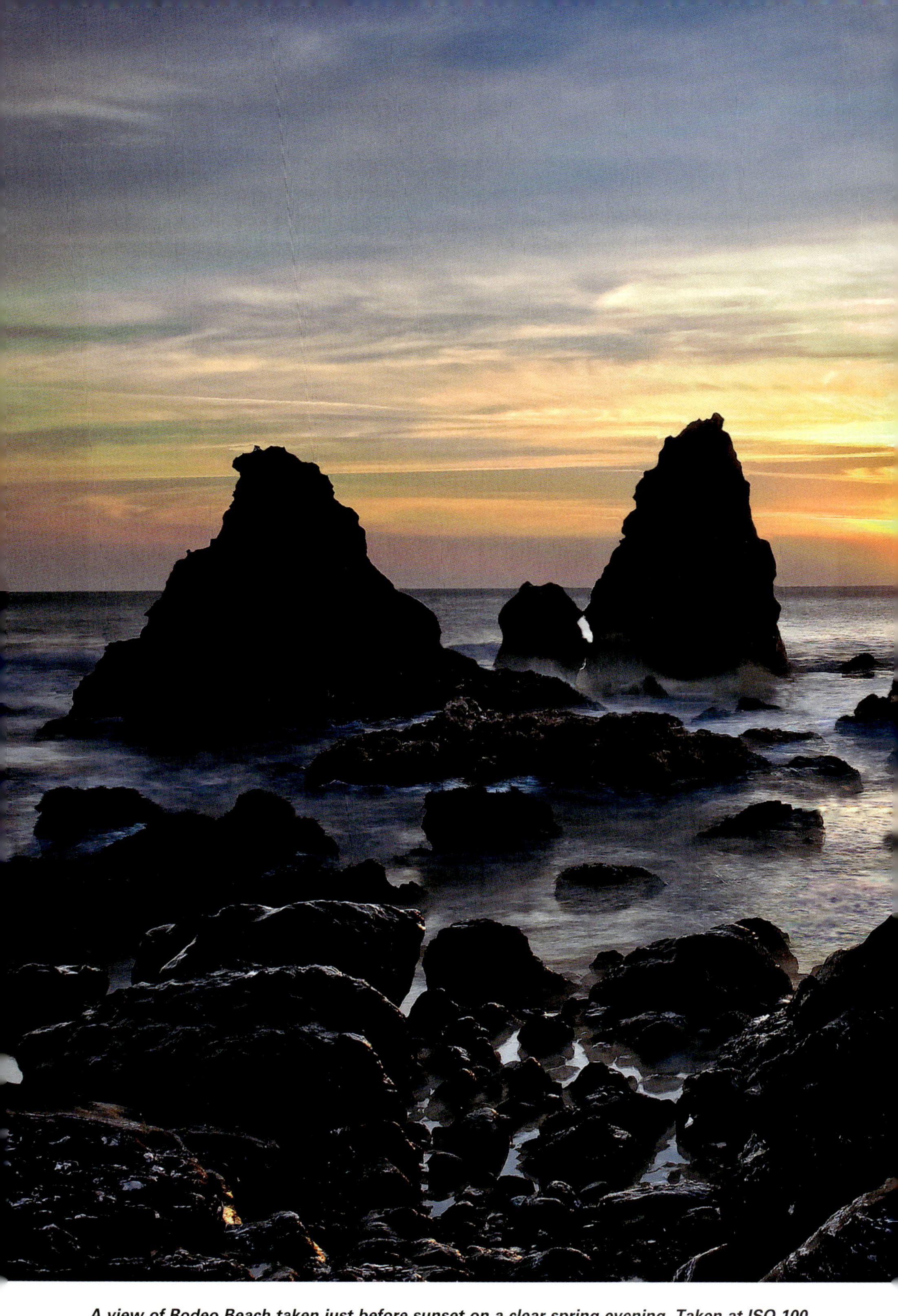

A view of Rodeo Beach taken just before sunset on a clear spring evening. Taken at ISO 100, f/11, 4 seconds with a 17-35mm lens.

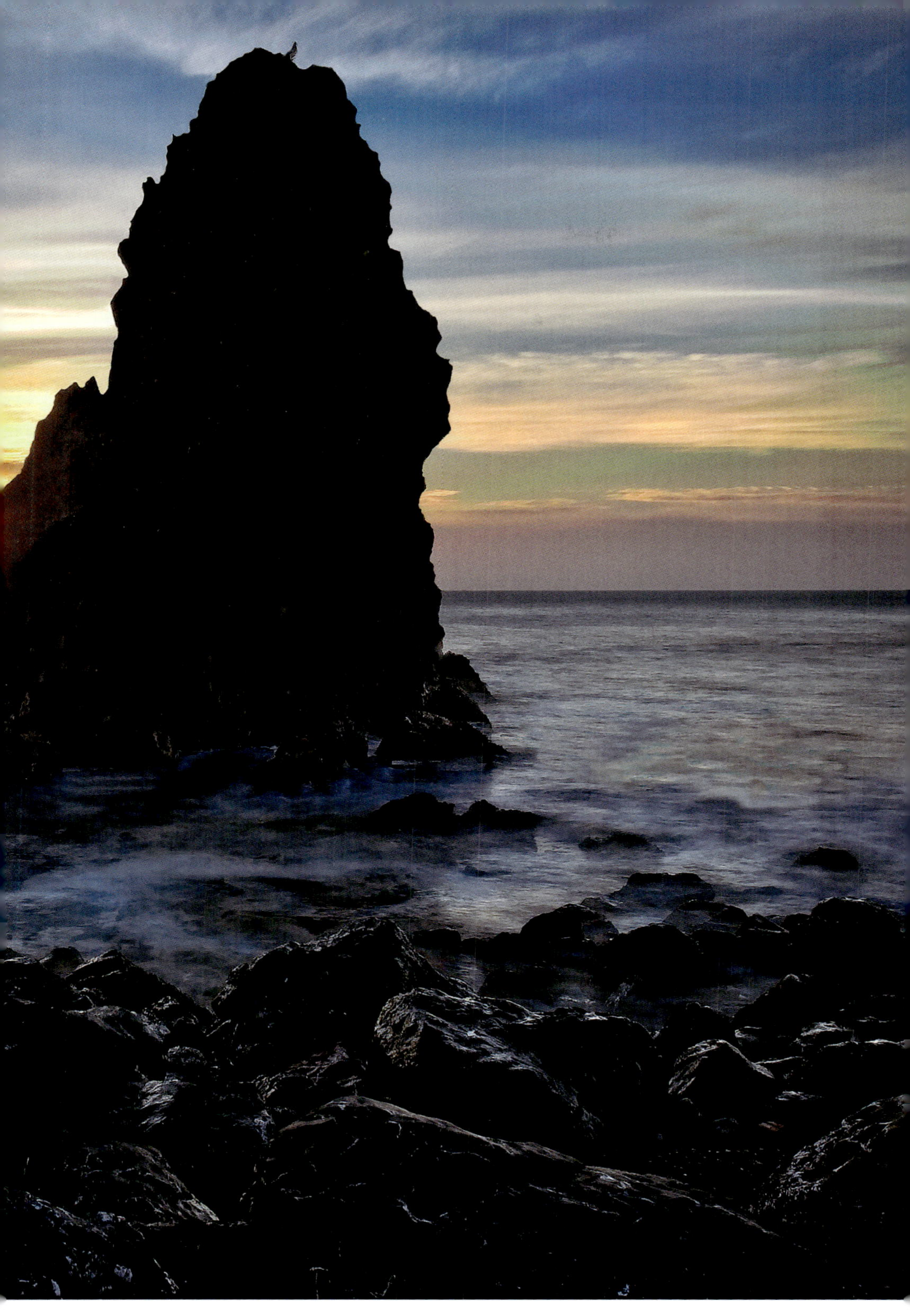

22 Rodeo Beach/Marin Headlands

Why It's Worth a Photograph

The Marin Headlands are made up of ridges and valleys, each offering its own distinct character. Many charming beaches and vistas are scattered throughout. Spring is when you can see an explosion of golden poppies and pastel accents of yellow, white, and lavender wildflowers blanketing the hillsides that offer wonderful scents. The Marin Headlands is a photographer's dream, offering unparalleled views of the Pacific Coast from an untamed Rodeo Beach, to the incredible man-made bunkers left over from the 1960s and the 150-year-old lighthouse that protects ships from the high cliffs, rough seas, and dense fog.

Where Can I Get the Best Shot?

Three wonderful locations are tucked amongst the rolling hills, valleys, and beaches that make up the Marin Headlands. The locations are Rodeo Beach, the Bunkers, and Point Bonita Lighthouse, all of which offer you the opportunity to photograph entirely different qualities of the Marin Headlands (see A, B, and C on the map).

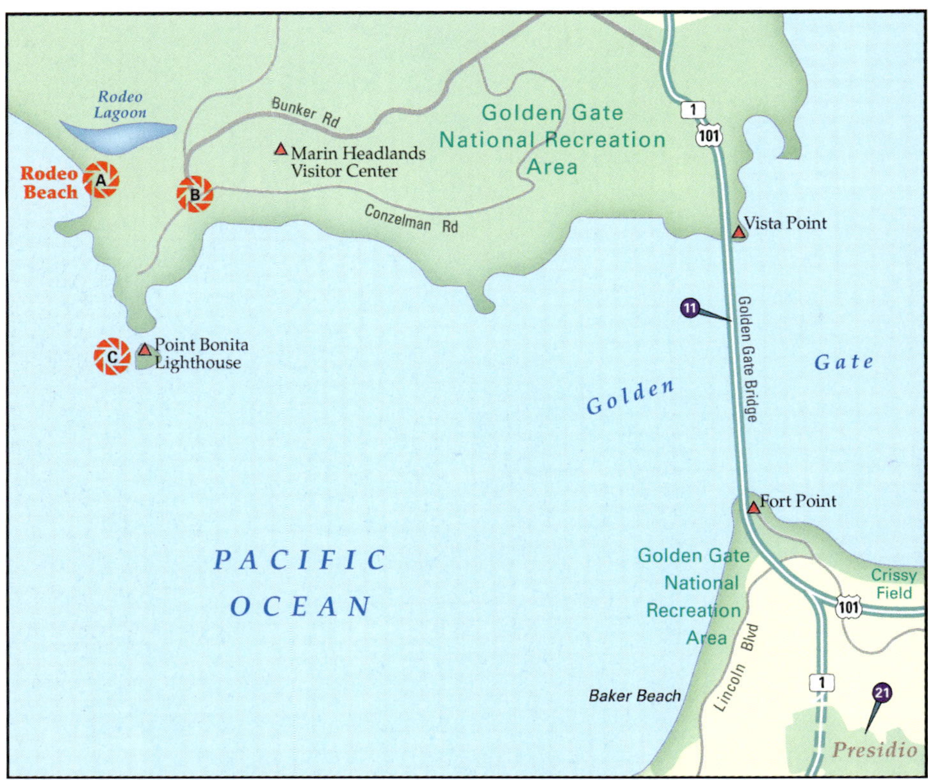

The best locations from which to photograph the Rodeo Beach/Marin Headlands: (A) Rodeo Beach, (B) Bunkers, (C) Point Bonita Lighthouse. Other photo ops: (11) Golden Gate Bridge, (21) Presidio of San Francisco.

Rodeo Beach

Rodeo Beach is by far my favorite beach to photograph in the Bay Area. The beach is open, windy, and the surf is rough, which is why Rodeo is popular with surfers. On a calm day, you may see the occasional dog venture into the cold water but for the most part the water is too daunting for anyone other than a surfer. You can walk hiking trails to different areas of the Marin Headlands, including several old military observation posts on the surrounding bluffs. One of the most famous is the former Nike missile site that has been preserved and is open as a museum. On the south side of the beach or directly left when you walk onto the beach from the parking lot, you can see rock formations just off the shore. From here, you have the opportunity to photograph a stunningly beautiful sunset. The key to photographing from this vantage point is to allow some if not all of the sun to get blocked out by the rocks. Blocking out the sun helps with your exposure and creates a wonderful ring of light around the rocks, as shown in figure 22.1. If you arrive to this location and the sky is gray and there is no sun setting, take advantage of this time to create a photo that conveys that cold dreary evening. The photo in figure 22.2 was processed from the color version to create this tinted black and white. Needless to say, to capture this picture, I got very wet!

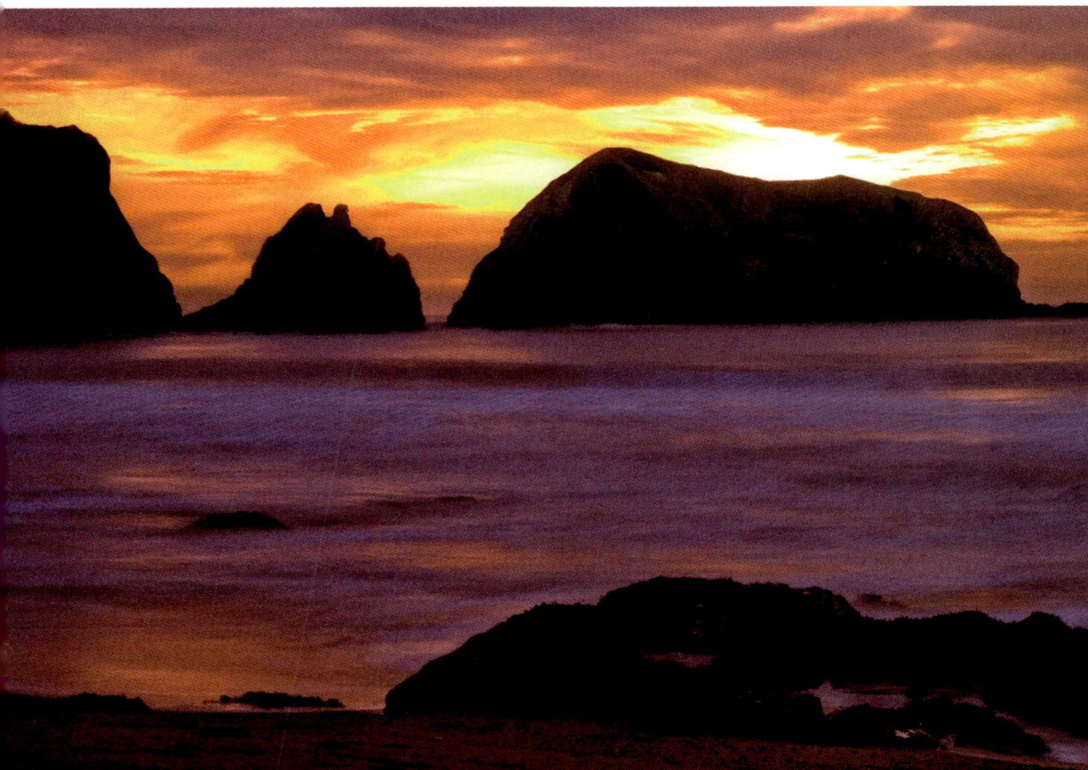

22.1 A view of Rodeo Beach taken just before sunset (see A on the map) on a clear winter evening. Taken at ISO 100, f/22, 6 seconds with a 17-35mm lens.

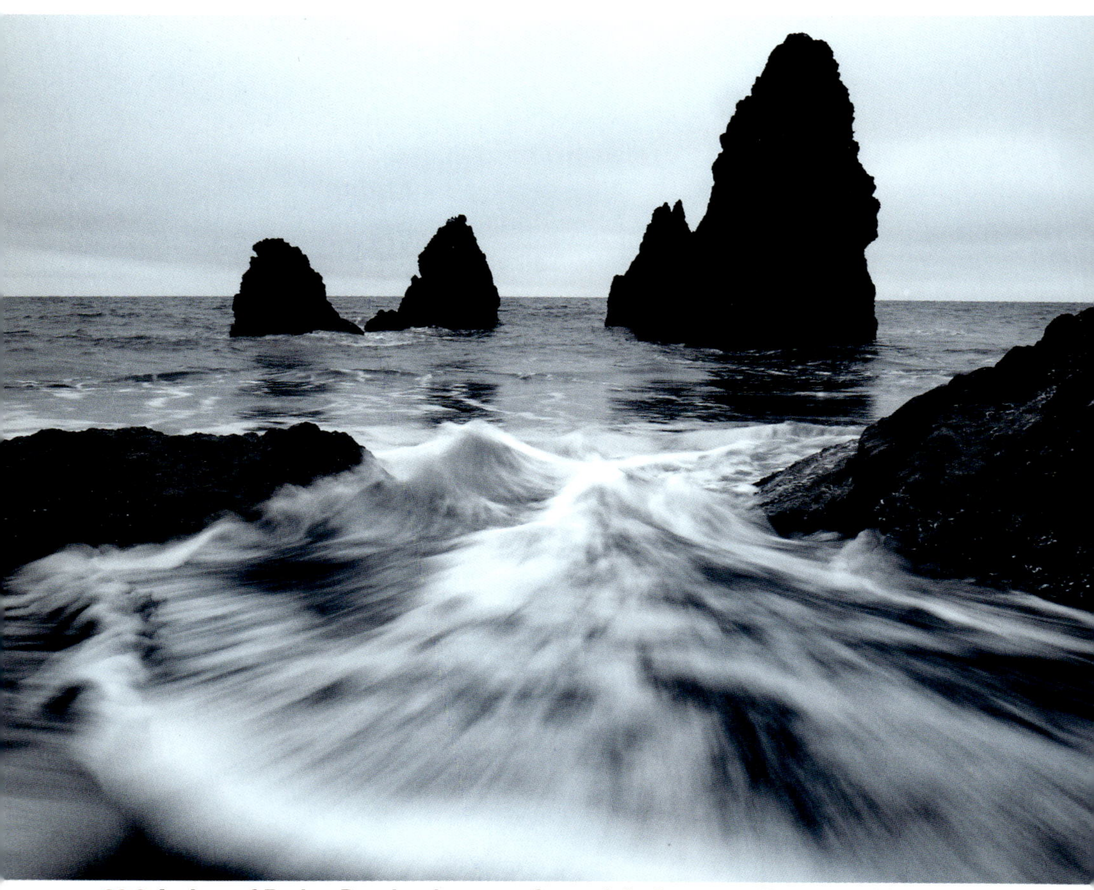

22.2 A view of Rodeo Beach taken on a foggy fall afternoon. Taken at ISO 100, f/22, 1/6 second with 17-35mm lens.

Bunkers

Marin Headlands was a military base until the late 1960s. It was the counterpart to the Presidio, designed to protect San Francisco Bay from invasion. The military constructed five installations among the rolling hills. These bunkers, tunnels, and installations offer a fun and exciting opportunity to test out your creativity. Shooting through the tunnels to densely wooded forest with sun and fog is a dramatic scene that I could shoot over and over. The cold, dark tunnels help frame the wonderfully dense and colorful forest that greets you on the other side. My recommendation is to set up inside these tunnels with a medium to wide lens and shoot outside, capturing a wonderful contrast between man and nature (see figure 22.3).

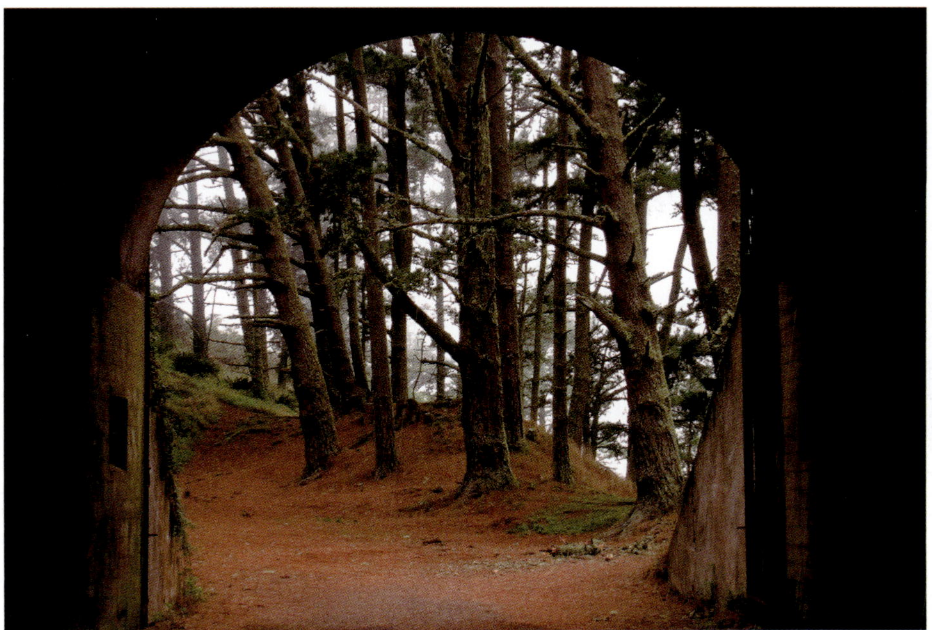

22.3 A view through the bunkers taken just after sunrise (see B on the map) on a clear fall morning. Taken at ISO 100, f/11, 1/6 second with a 24-70mm lens.

Point Bonita Lighthouse

Point Bonita Lighthouse today is part of the largest urban national park in the United States, the Golden Gate National Recreation Area. A secret treasure in the Bay Area, Point Bonita is still an active lighthouse. The U.S. Coast Guard maintains the lighthouse, and the National Park Service provides access to visitors. Point Bonita Lighthouse can only be reached by a half-mile trail that is steep in parts. Point Bonita offers a wonderful photo at sunset. The lighthouse itself sits high above the ocean on a small cliff that is only accessible by a small suspension bridge (see figures 22.4 and 22.5). From this vantage point, you can capture a breathtaking photo of the lighthouse and sun setting below the horizon. Photography is not just about sunsets and landscapes but also the nature that surrounds you, such as the California flower, the golden poppy. The roads and paths can be lined with these wonderful golden flowers (see figure 22.6). Take note: The lighthouse is only open Saturday through Monday from 12:30 p.m. to 3:30 p.m.

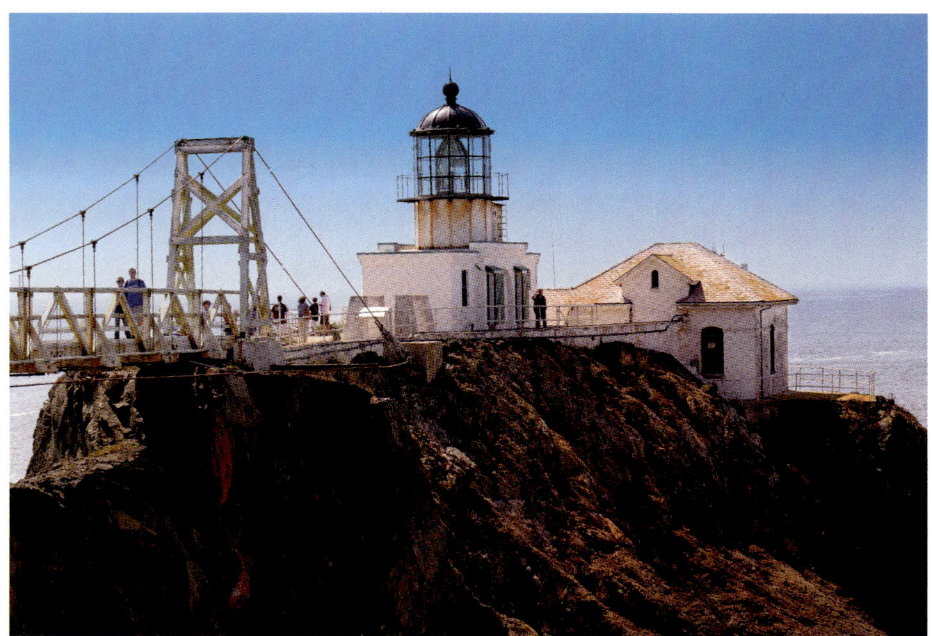

22.4 A view of the Point Bonita Lighthouse taken in the early afternoon (see C on the map) on a clear summer day. Taken at ISO 100, f/8, 1/100 second with a 70-200mm lens.

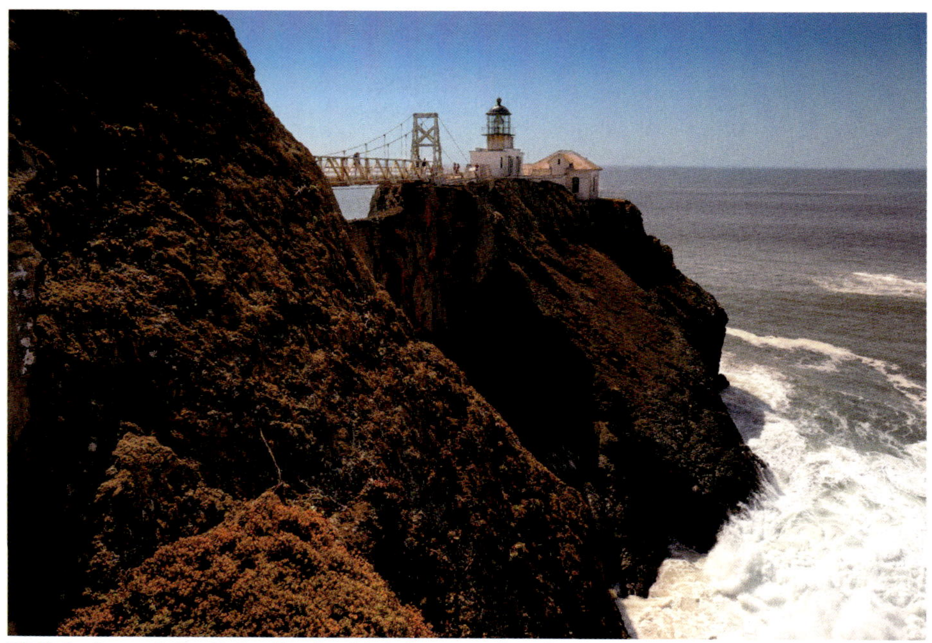

22.5 A view of the Point Bonita Lighthouse taken in the late afternoon on a clear summer day. Taken at ISO 100, f/16, 1/100 second with a 14-24mm lens.

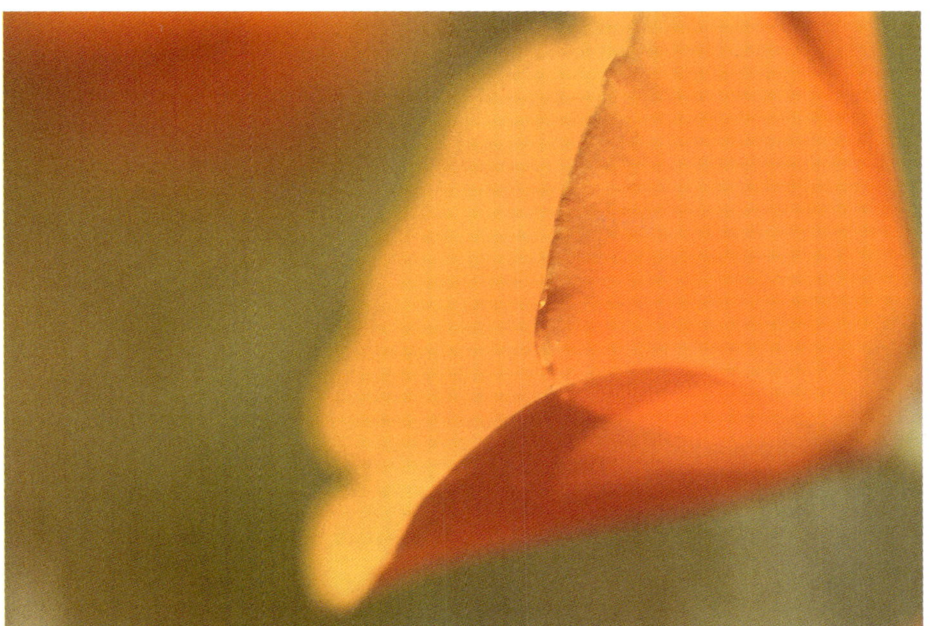

22.6 A photo of a golden poppy taken in the Marin Headlands late in the day (see B on the map) on a clear spring afternoon. Taken at ISO 100, f/4, 1/1600 second with a 100mm lens.

How Can I Get the Best Shot?

Weather plays a huge part in capturing the best photo from these locations. To get Rodeo Beach and Point Bonita Lighthouse, you have a 15-minute hike from the parking lot to get to the best shooting location. The bunkers are located at the end of Conzelman Road and are easy to get to. There is no best time of day, so plan this shoot around Point Bonita Lighthouse and Rodeo Beach. Ensure that you bring a tripod, because this piece of equipment is critical if you want to photograph Rodeo Beach at sunset and the dark bunkers during the day.

Equipment

To photograph these three locations in the Marin Headlands, you need to include in your bag a lens or lenses that can cover a focal length from 14-300mm. This focal length range allows you to vary your composition and creativity.

Lenses

The choice of lens always comes down to your personal preference and what you want to convey in your photo. Whether you are shooting day or night, your lens choice is instrumental for creating the ideal composition for any given subject. If I were to recommend a lens or set of lenses to use to photograph Rodeo Beach, the bunkers, and Point Bonita Lighthouse, they would include the following:

- **Ultrawide zoom lens in the 14-24mm range.** The ultrawide lens gives you the ability to create an ultrawide composition that can look almost 3-D-like when you include moving clouds using a slow shutter speed. The key to this lens is to have something of interest in the foreground.
- **A standard zoom lens in the 24-100mm range.** This lens can give you much more versatility when traveling. A zoom in this range is generally considered the perfect walk-around lens for capturing anything from landscape/cityscapes to pictures of the family. This is the perfect lens for Rodeo Beach, Point Bonita Lighthouse, and the bunkers. If I only had one lens, this would be the range.
- **A super-telephoto lens somewhere in the 70-300mm range.** This allows you the ability to isolate a particular subject, such as a tower, or gives you extra reach when shooting subjects that are too far off for a standard zoom lens. This focal range comes in handy when shooting the lighthouse.

Filters

There are two primary filters I use when photographing in the Marin Headlands: a circular polarizing filter and a neutral density filter.

- **Circular polarizing filter.** A circular polarizing filter is a filter I suggest you have in your bag because its main purpose is to cut down or eliminate glare on water, glass, and metal. It can also be used to enhance color and contrast in your photos. I use it primarily to bring out the blue sky in my photos. The maximum effect of polarization can be seen when used at a 90-degree angle from the sun. A polarizer is best used on a lens that is not wider than 24mm, because it can cause the sky to be unevenly polarized. I used a polarizer for Point Bonita Lighthouse because it was sidelit and I wanted to enhance the colors and contrast of the water and foliage.
- **Neutral density filter.** A neutral density (ND) filter allows you to shoot at a larger aperture when the sun is at its brightest, but also allows you to slow your shutter speed 2 or more stops. I have two ND filters: One is a 3-stop while the other is a 10-stop. I use the ND filter exclusively when shooting at Rodeo Beach to get the water to turn into a frothy, cotton candy-like surface.

Extras

A tripod is a must. If you don't own one, buy one. Without a tripod, night shots and low-light shooting are out of the question. I also recommend a cable release and bubble level. The advantage of using a cable release is it allows you to shoot longer exposures without having to trigger the shutter by touching the camera, which can cause camera shake and affect the quality of your photograph. A bubble level helps you level the camera and prevent those nasty crooked shots that we all get.

Camera settings

How you set up your camera mostly depends on you and your shooting style or what you want to convey for that particular photo. The settings I used for photographing Rodeo Beach are ISO 100 at f/11 to f/16, which gives you plenty of depth of field, a slow shutter speed, and the best image quality. For the bunkers and Point Bonita Lighthouse where depth of field and shutter speed are not important, I chose an ISO of 100 and aperture of f/8 to maximize my image quality.

- **Exposure mode.** I generally shoot in Aperture Priority mode. To set my exposure, I choose the ideal aperture, which for me tends to be between f/8 and f/22. My camera then chooses the correct shutter speed. I adjust my aperture to raise or lower the shutter speed to create the desired effect. I shoot in Manual mode when there is a tricky lighting condition that is causing my meter to underexpose or overexpose so much that I cannot correct it with exposure compensation.
- **White balance.** White balance I never touch because I find the Auto White Balance of all modern day cameras to be pretty good.
- **ISO.** In general, to maximize your camera's image quality, I leave the ISO at 100 when shooting landscapes. The few times I may increase the ISO is to increase the shutter speed or to use a smaller or larger aperture.

Exposure

If you underexpose your photo, you can introduce unwanted noise and artifacts when trying to recover the photo in post-processing. Overexposing can add blown highlights that are areas of unrecoverable data. To ensure you expose each of these scenes properly, pay close attention to the histogram on the back of your camera. If the histogram is too far to the right, you have overexposed your photo; too far to the left and you have underexposed it. Try to balance your exposure so that you capture the best exposure for any given scene. You may have to sacrifice a bit of sky or land to get the best overall exposure.

Ideal time to shoot

The ideal time to photograph Rodeo Beach is just before the sun sets. The sun will be directly in front of you, creating a dynamic light against the jagged rock formations and crashing waves. The bunkers can be shot any time of the day, although I tend to shoot them in the morning or late afternoon because I combine this shoot with my Rodeo Beach and Point Bonita Lighthouse shoots. Point Bonita Lighthouse, shown in figure 22.7, can only be shot between 12:30 p.m. and 3:30 p.m.

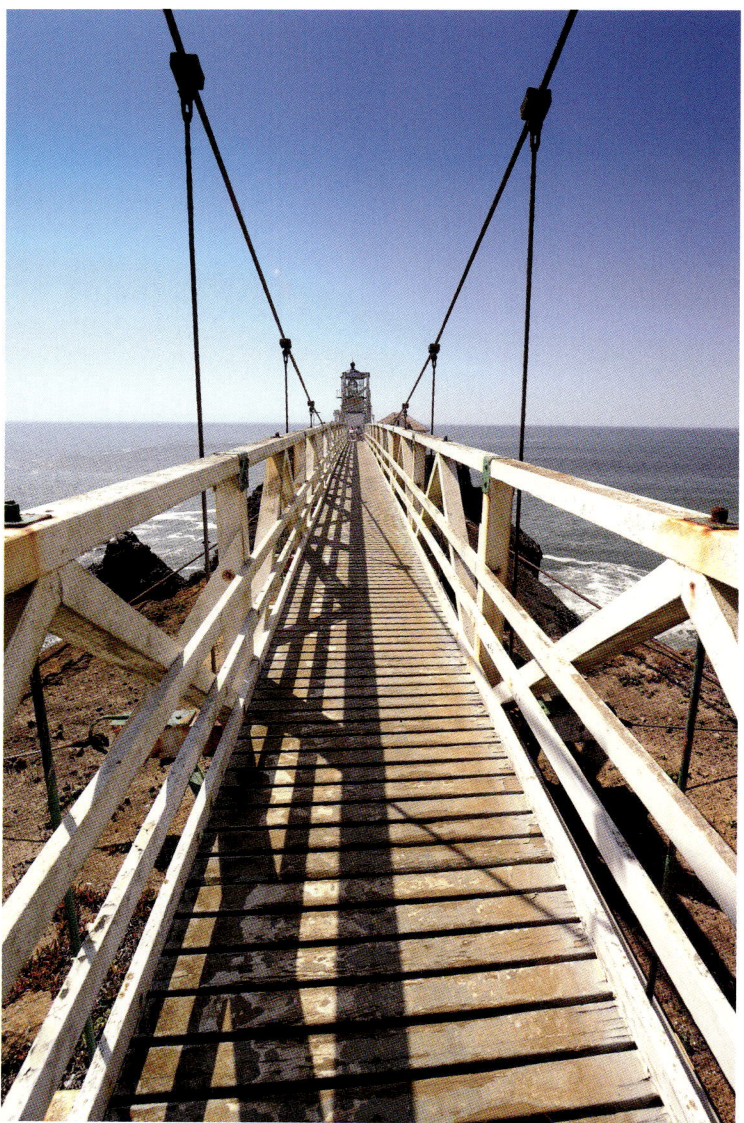

22.7 A view of the Point Bonita Lighthouse in the late afternoon (see C on the map) on a summer day. Taken at ISO 100, f/16, 1/100 second with a 14-24mm lens.

Working around the weather

Weather in the Marin Headlands can be windy, foggy, and cold. November through February in the Marin Headlands is dominated by periodic rainstorms that blow in from the Pacific Ocean. These dark, dreary, and wet days often are interspersed with cool but extremely clear days. As winter turns to spring, the weather is dominated by high winds and clear skies. The summers in the Marin Headlands alternate between stretches of several clear and warm days, giving way to several foggy and cool days. July through October provides the highest average temperatures of the year and the longest stretch of clear skies. My recommendation is to make this trip on a clear day. Although the fog can create some dramatic images, nothing beats a clear blue sky and low, warm, soft sunlight. If you do choose to shoot in the fog, be prepared to dial in a plus exposure compensation of at least +2/3 to help compensate for the camera's inability to expose properly in foggy conditions.

A view of the Saints Peter and Paul Church taken on a clear fall day. Taken at ISO 200, f/8, 1/500 second with a 70-200mm lens.

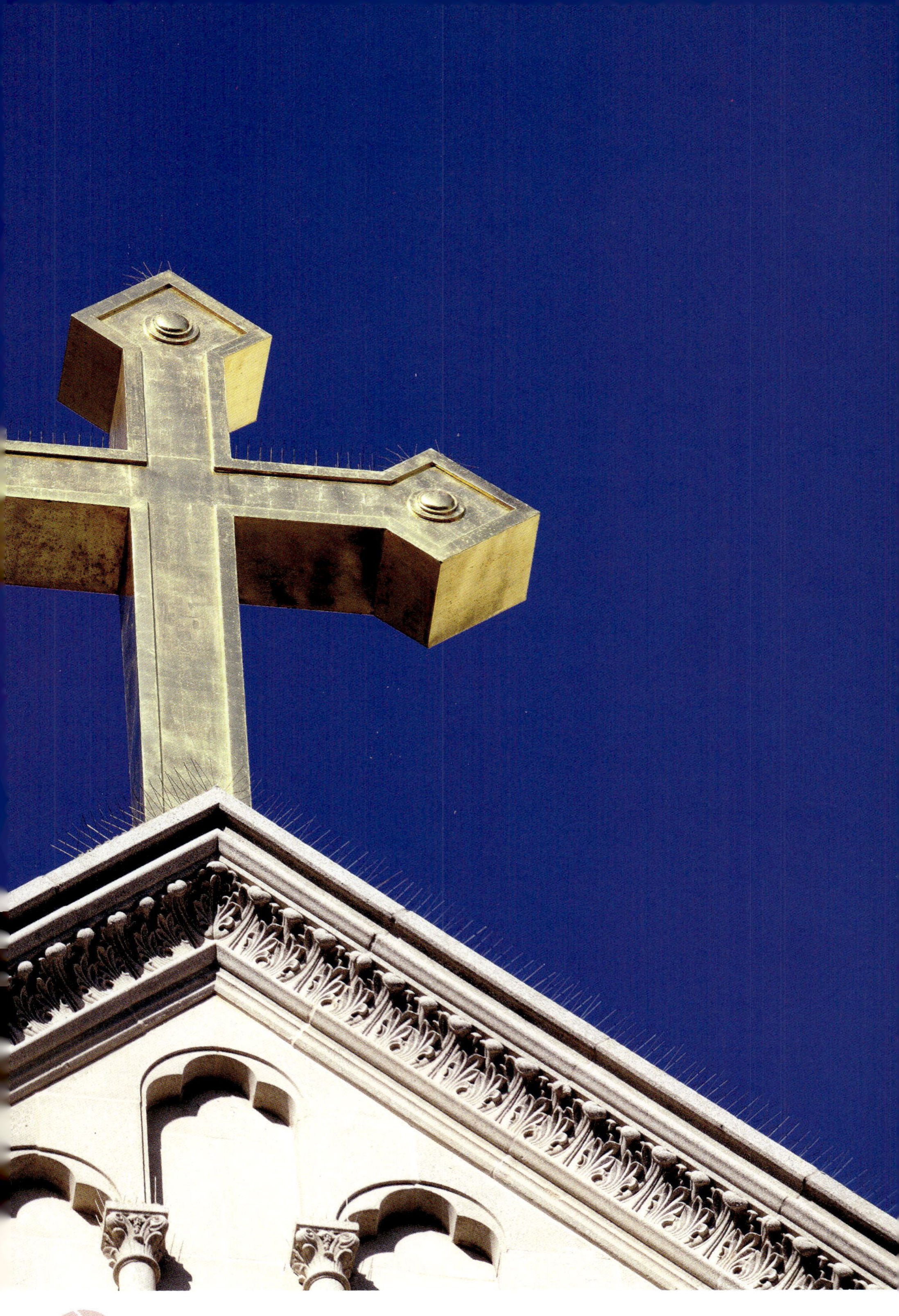

23 Saints Peter and Paul Church

Why It's Worth a Photograph

Saints Peter and Paul Church is a Roman Catholic Church in San Francisco's North Beach neighborhood, located (somewhat ironically) at 666 Filbert Street. Known as the "Italian Cathedral of the West," this building is very unusual in that the parish school is situated atop the church around its clerestory level and is accessible from stairways under each of its twin towers. The church, with its twin spires that soar almost 200 feet into the sky, was completed in 1924. For over a century, the church of Saints Peter and Paul has served parishioners and tourists who visit it daily, and it is an icon to the members of the North Beach community. The church's beautiful Italian-inspired architecture stands tall in a section of San Francisco known for its culture and people, and it makes a monumental photo for any enthusiast.

Where Can I Get the Best Shot?

The best place to photograph Saints Peter and Paul Church is from the park directly across the street, called Washington Square (see A on the map).

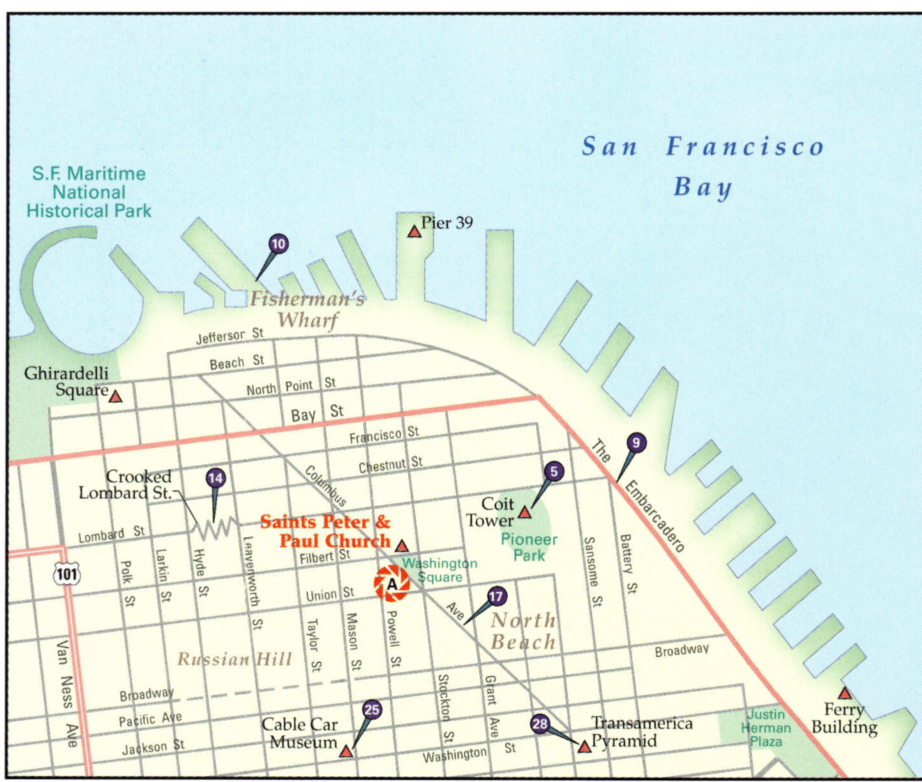

The best locations from which to photograph Saints Peter and Paul Church: (A) Washington Square. Other photo ops: (5) Coit Tower, (9) Embarcadero, (10) Fisherman's Wharf, (14) Lombard Street, (17) North Beach, (25) San Francisco cable cars, (28) Transamerica Pyramid.

Washington Square

Washington Square is a wonderful location that provides many different angles to photograph this beautiful church from. Come early or late in the day because the low sun can help to enhance the white stone façade. The best time is when the sky is a vibrant blue. The stark contrast between the blue sky and white stone church is truly breathtaking and worth a photo (see figure 23.1). Bring a combination of a longer zoom and ultrawide lens so you can capture different angles and perspectives. If you can go inside the church, bring an ultrawide lens and be prepared to bump up your ISO because a tripod may be difficult to use in the limited space.

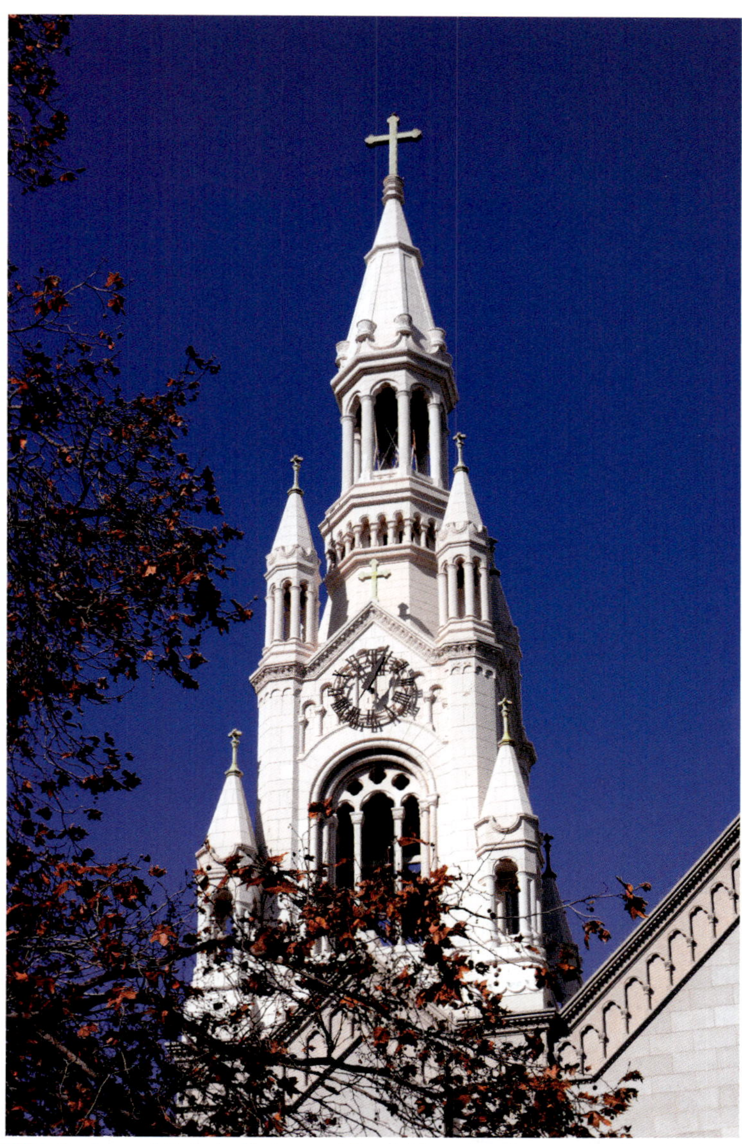

23.1 A view of Saints Peter and Paul Church taken on a clear fall day (see A on the map). Taken at ISO 100, f/22, 1/100 second with a 70-200 mm lens.

How Can I Get the Best Shot?

Early morning light can really enhance the detail in the stone. This time of day is easy to shoot and produces some nice images. A clear blue sky is a must, so the white stone does not blend into the gray sky. On a clear evening, you can take a stunning photo that glows with warm, colorful hues. This time of day can be tricky to shoot because the church tends to cause the camera to underexpose against the bright sunset. Shooting inside the church, an ultrawide lens is a must to capture the enormous space. A slightly overcast day is a benefit when you shoot inside because the stained-glass windows allow light in from the outside, making it difficult to expose the entire space without blown highlights (see figure 23.2).

Equipment

A good tripod, an ultrawide lens, and a medium telephoto lens are the three pieces of equipment that are critical for capturing sharp images of Saints Peter and Paul Church.

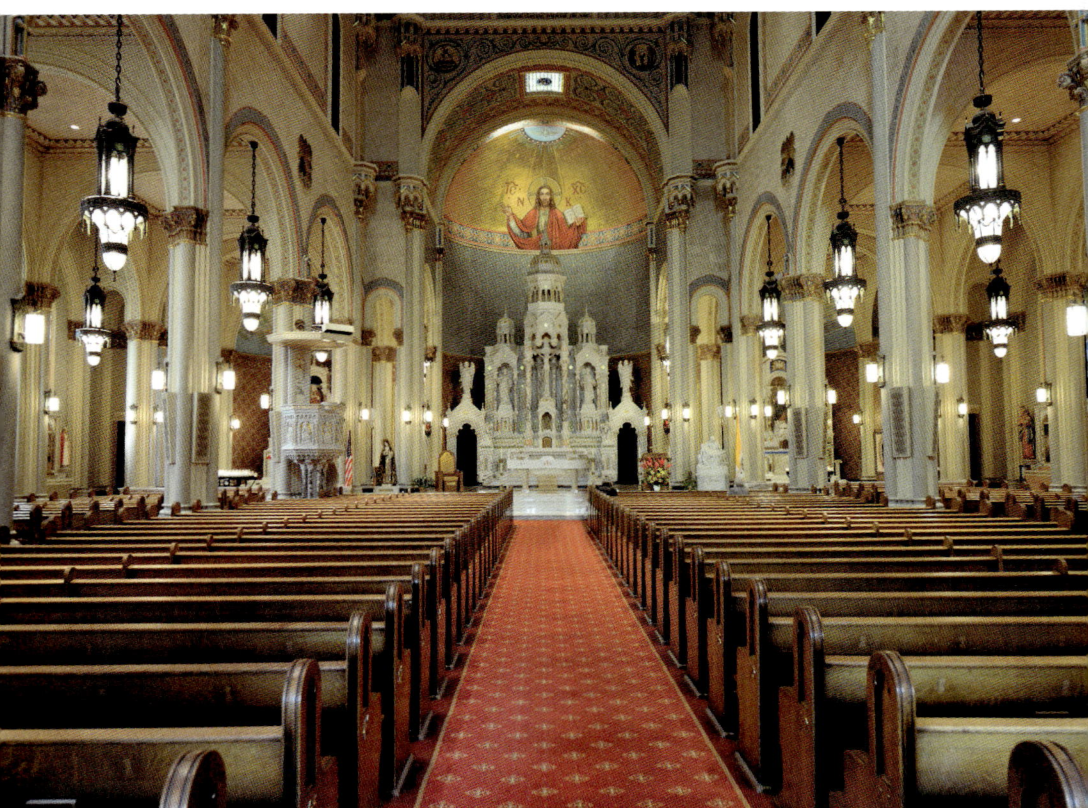

23.2 A view of the interior of Saints Peter and Paul Church. Taken at ISO 1600, f/5.6, 1/5 second with a 14-24mm lens.

Lenses

Ultrawide-angle and medium telephoto lenses are the two lenses that are essential for capturing the perfect images of Saints Peter and Paul Church.

- **Ultrawide zoom lens in the 14-24mm range.** The ultrawide lens gives you the ability to create a unique perspective. By including something in the immediate foreground, you can create a sense of depth that can lead the person's eyes to the church. It also allows you the ability to capture the interior of the church.
- **A zoom lens somewhere in the 70-200mm range.** This focal range allows you the ability to isolate the church's towers against the blue sky.

Extras

A sturdy tripod is essential for getting sharp images.

Camera settings

Setting up your camera to shoot Saints Peter and Paul Church can vary upon the time of day and whether you're shooting outside or inside. For shooting outside early in the day, use an ultrawide lens or long telephoto and set your aperture from f/8 to f/11 to maximize image quality. When shooting inside the church, use a tripod or increase your ISO to get your shutter speed fast enough for you to hand hold the camera.

- **Exposure mode.** I set my camera in Aperture Priority mode and let my camera choose the shutter speed. I dialed in a minus exposure compensation to help protect the highlights from the windows inside the church from blowing out.
- **White balance.** White balance I never touch because I find the Auto White Balance setting of all modern day cameras to be pretty good.
- **ISO.** ISO should stay as low as possible unless you are handholding your camera. Adjust your ISO to get a shutter speed that is fast enough for you to hand hold a long lens. I did not have a tripod, so I bumped up the ISO to 1600 and shot at f/2.8 to give me a 1/20 second. This was fast enough for me to hand hold.

Exposure

I allow my camera's metering system to make most of the tough decisions for me. On occasion, I have to dial in exposure compensation or shoot in Manual mode to create the desired effect. Use the histogram on the back of your camera to help judge whether or not the exposure fits what you see and what you want to convey.

Ideal time to shoot

The ideal time to shoot is in the late to early morning when the sun is still low, and the church is bathed with soft, warm light that accentuates the details.

Working around the weather

The winter months between late November and early March can have unpredictable rainstorms. Plan your mornings when it is clear and the sun is out. A blue sky is the best because it really makes the white church stand out.

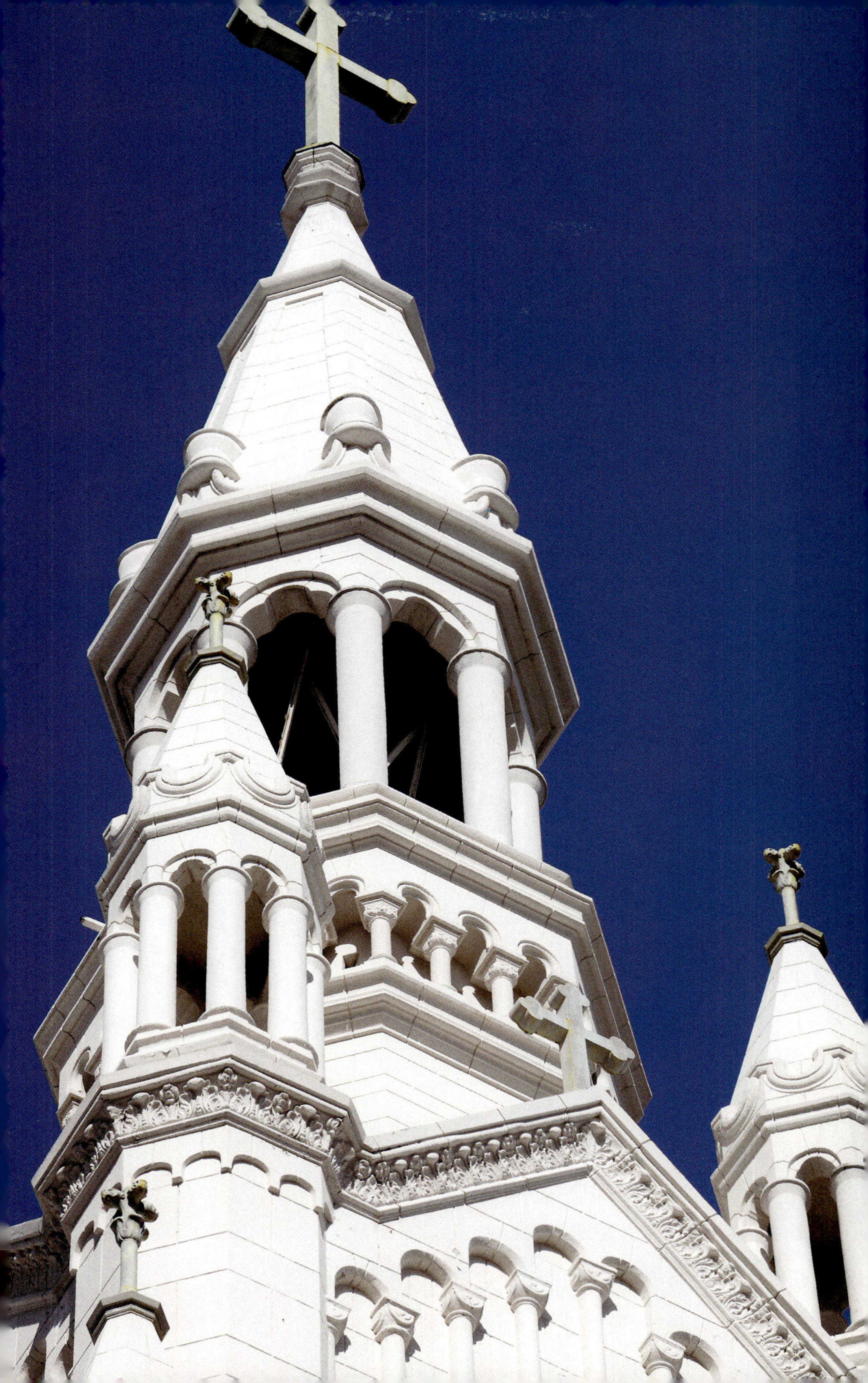

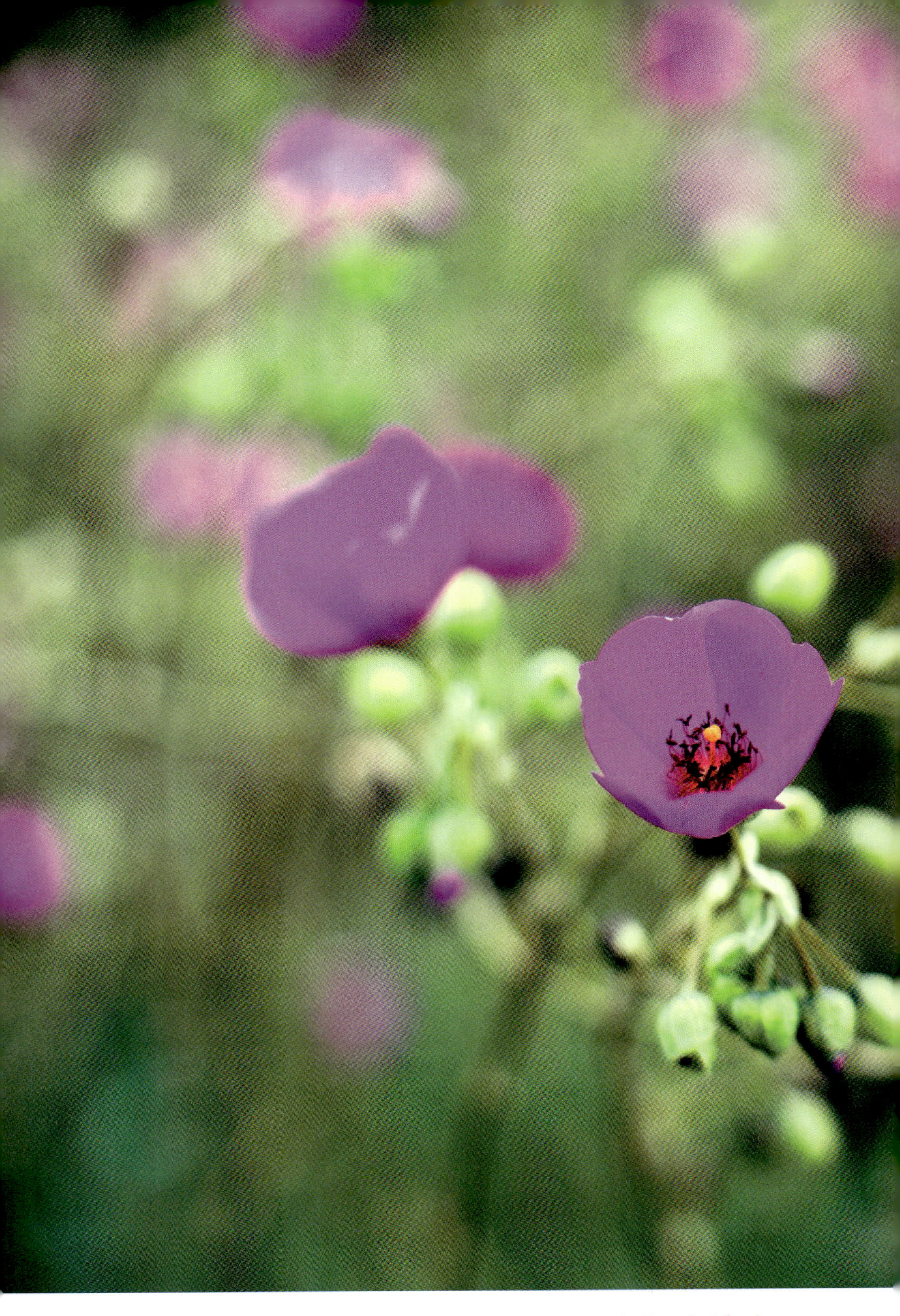

A photo taken of pink flowers on an overcast autumn afternoon at the Botanical Gardens. Taken at ISO 200, f/2, 1/100 second, –2/3 exposure compensation with a 50mm lens.

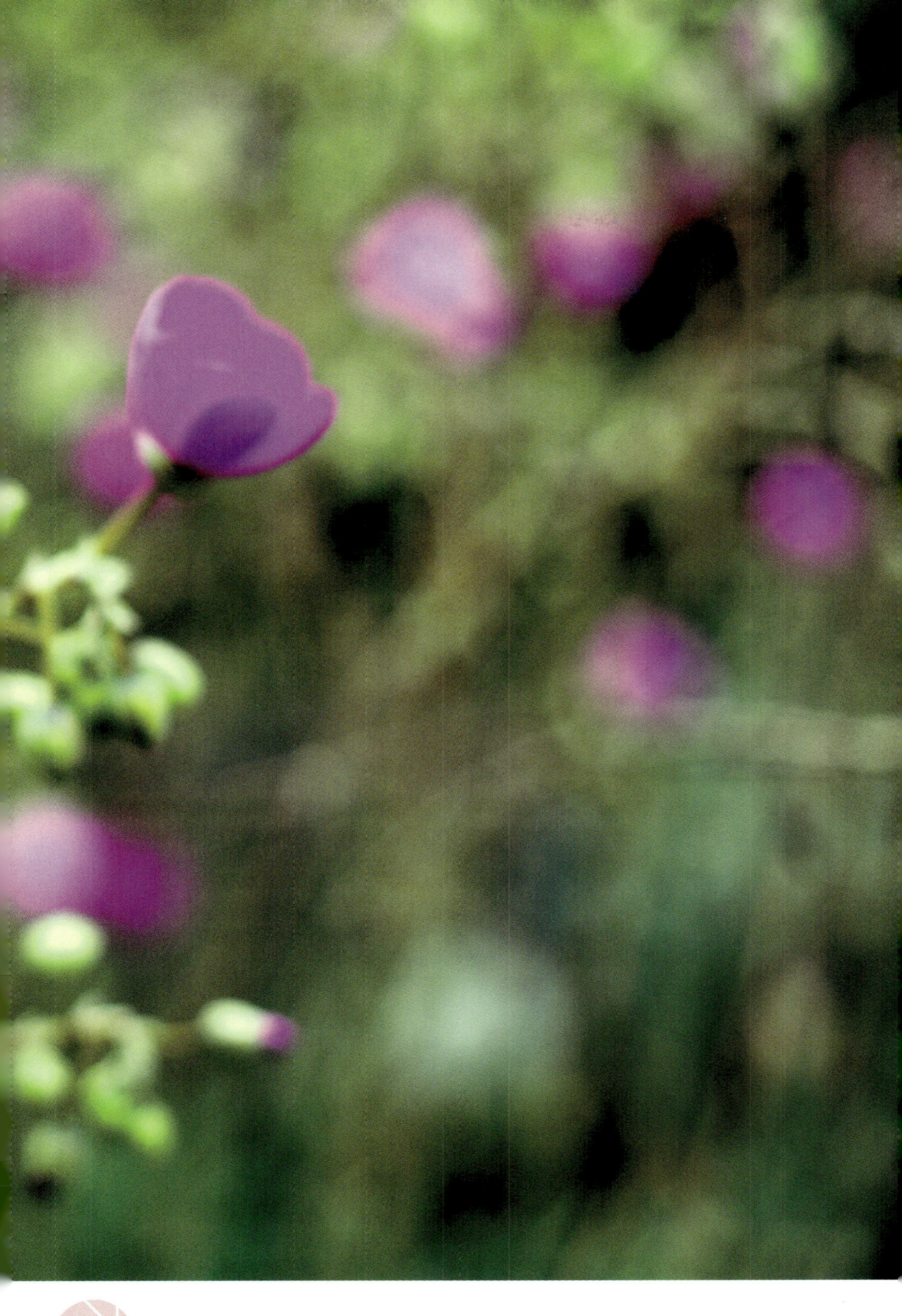

24 San Francisco Botanical Garden

Why It's Worth a Photograph

The San Francisco Botanical Garden is located one block due south of the Conservatory of Flowers on Martin Luther King Drive. San Francisco's mild Mediterranean-like climate provides the Botanical Garden the right conditions to grow and conserve plants from all over the world, including plants that are no longer found in their native habitats. There are over 50 acres of landscaped gardens and open spaces, and over 7,000 varieties of plants from around the world, offering endless subjects for a photographer.

Where Can I Get the Best Shot?

The San Francisco Botanical Garden (see A on the map) is a nature photographer's dream, with wonderfully wild exhibits, and varieties of plants and flowers from all over the world. Pick a day when the weather is slightly overcast because the soft, diffused light makes photographing colorful plants and flowers much easier, and there are no harsh shadows to compete with (see figures 24.1 and 24.2).

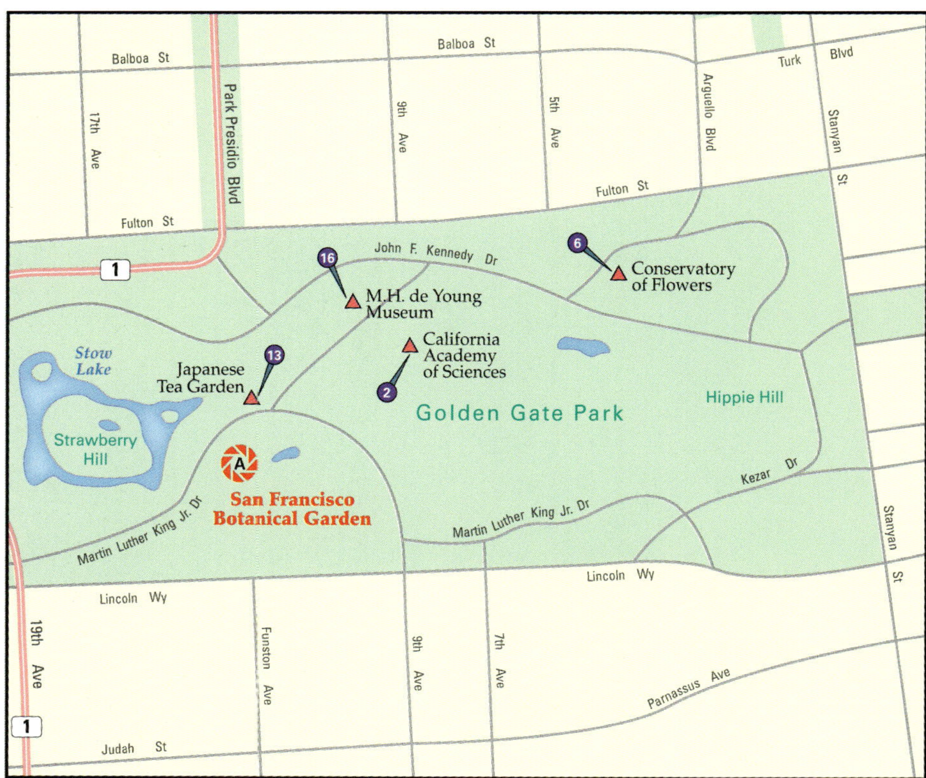

The best location from which to photograph the San Francisco Botanical Garden: (A) the grounds of the garden. Other photo ops: (2) California Academy of Sciences, (6) Conservatory of Flowers, (13) Japanese Tea Garden, (16) M.H. de Young Museum.

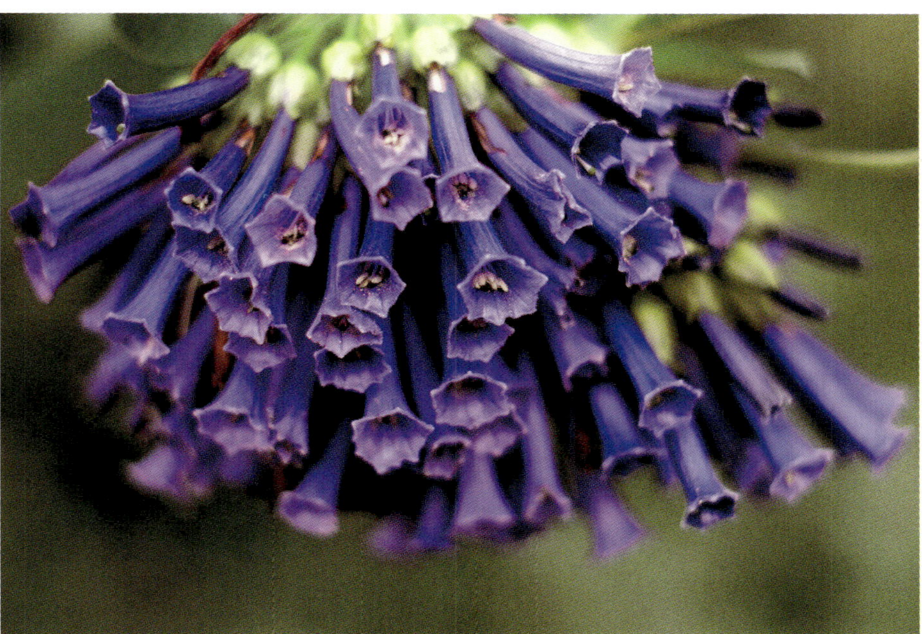

24.1 A photo taken of an Iochroma cyaneum flower on an overcast autumn afternoon at the Botanical Garden (see A on the map). Taken at ISO 200, f/1.8, 1/160 second, –2/3 exposure compensation with a 50mm lens.

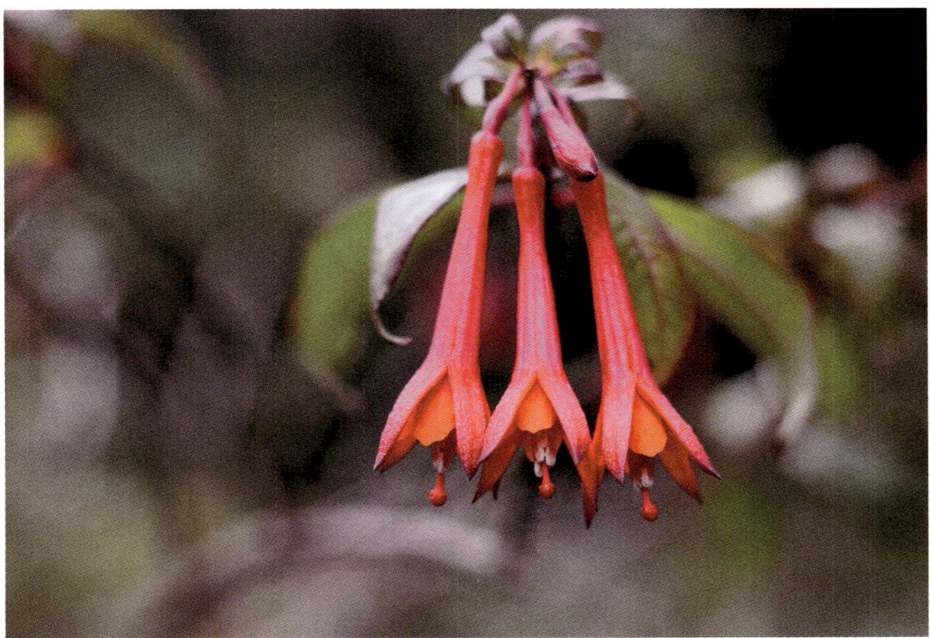

24.2 A photo taken of fuchsia flowers on an overcast autumn afternoon at the Botanical Garden. Taken at ISO 200, f/2, 1/160 second, –2/3 exposure compensation with a 50mm lens.

How Can I Get the Best Shot?

Unlike many of the other locations in this book, time of day is less important than the weather. Plan your trip to these gardens when the sky is slightly overcast or foggy. The overcast sky helps create an even, diffused light void of any harsh shadows. Bring a macro lens to get in close or a lens with a fast aperture of f/1.2 to f/1.8 to create truly wonderful photos. When shooting with a macro lens, use a tripod because you will likely be shooting with a smaller aperture. Your aperture could range from f/8 to f/22 depending on the depth of field you wish to achieve. For most macro shots, you want to create a larger depth of field having more of the subject in focus. When shooting with a fast lens at, say, f/1.4, your goal is to create a very narrow depth of field where only a small part is in perfect focus.

Equipment

A macro lens, a fast prime lens or standard zoom lens, and a tripod are the pieces of equipment you want to bring.

Lenses

A macro, standard zoom, and prime lens are the three lenses that can help you make your trip to these gardens worthwhile.

- **A macro lens.** This lens is specifically designed for close photography. A macro lens enables you to get extremely close to your subject, creating a 1:1 life-size image on your sensor. These lenses are extremely sharp and capture an enormous amount of detail.
- **A standard zoom lens in the 24-100mm range.** This lens can give you much more versatility when traveling. Most of these lenses come with some form of image stabilization and allow for a close working distance, which can be important when photographing flowers.
- **A fast prime/fixed focal length lens.** A fast prime/fixed focal length lens does not zoom. These lenses come in many focal lengths, and the most common lengths are 24, 35, 50, and 85. These lenses offer apertures much larger and come in a smaller package than most zooms. The benefit of these lenses is they allow you to shoot in much dimmer light due to the lens's light-gathering capability. These lenses tend to be very sharp and smaller than your average zooms.

Extras

A tripod is a must for macro shots as you will be very close to the subject and the slightest movement will blur the photo. A flash can also be useful to create just enough extra light to fill in the shadows. This is especially important when shooting outside as you can get varying degrees of shadows caused by trees, clouds, and your angle to the subject.

Camera settings

Setting up your camera for shooting flowers comes down to what you want to achieve. I love the artsy look of a shallow depth of field and incredibly blurred background created by using a wide open aperture on a large aperture prime lens. If using a macro lens, you may want to create more depth of field by opening up the aperture from f/11 to f/22. This allows you to capture a greater in-focus area.

- **Exposure mode.** I set my camera in Aperture Priority mode and let my camera choose the shutter speed. I may dial in a plus or minus exposure compensation depending on the overall scene. When shooting in the garden, I dialed in a –1/3 to –2/3 exposure compensation to help protect the highlighted areas.
- **White balance.** White balance I never touch as I find the Auto White Balance of all modern day cameras to be pretty good.
- **ISO.** ISO should stay as low as possible unless you are handholding your camera. Adjust your ISO to get a shutter speed that is fast enough for you to hand hold a long lens.

Exposure

Light is the key to capturing the perfect exposure. When shooting flowers outdoors, overcast skies are the ideal time to shoot. The overcast sky creates wonderful soft, diffused light that prevents harsh shadows and blown highlights.

Ideal time to shoot

The Botanical Garden is open from 8 a.m. to 4 p.m. Monday–Friday and 10 a.m. to 5 p.m. on weekends, so getting up in the wee morning hours or arriving late evening doesn't make sense. It's not as much about the time of day as it is about the light. Plan your trip around a slightly overcast day.

Working around the weather

Plan your trip to the Botanical Garden during the spring or fall when the flowers are in bloom or the fall colors have set in. The spring and fall colors are the most vibrant, and they add that extra pop to your photo. Coincidentally, these are the best months as far as the weather is concerned. You can expect little if any rain and warmer temperatures.

Getting creative

If you want to try something a little more creative, find some grass with early morning dew and get in low and tight with your macro lens. Be sure to use a tripod and set your aperture from f/2.8 to f/5.6 to really isolate the subject. Take your time setting up the shot so that you create a diagonal line through the viewfinder. Doing this creates a much more appealing composition than to place the grass in the dead center. What makes this photo so fun is the ability for the macro lens to isolate the green grass with small, red hairs and soft, round, bubbly water droplets from the rest of the grass (see figure 24.3).

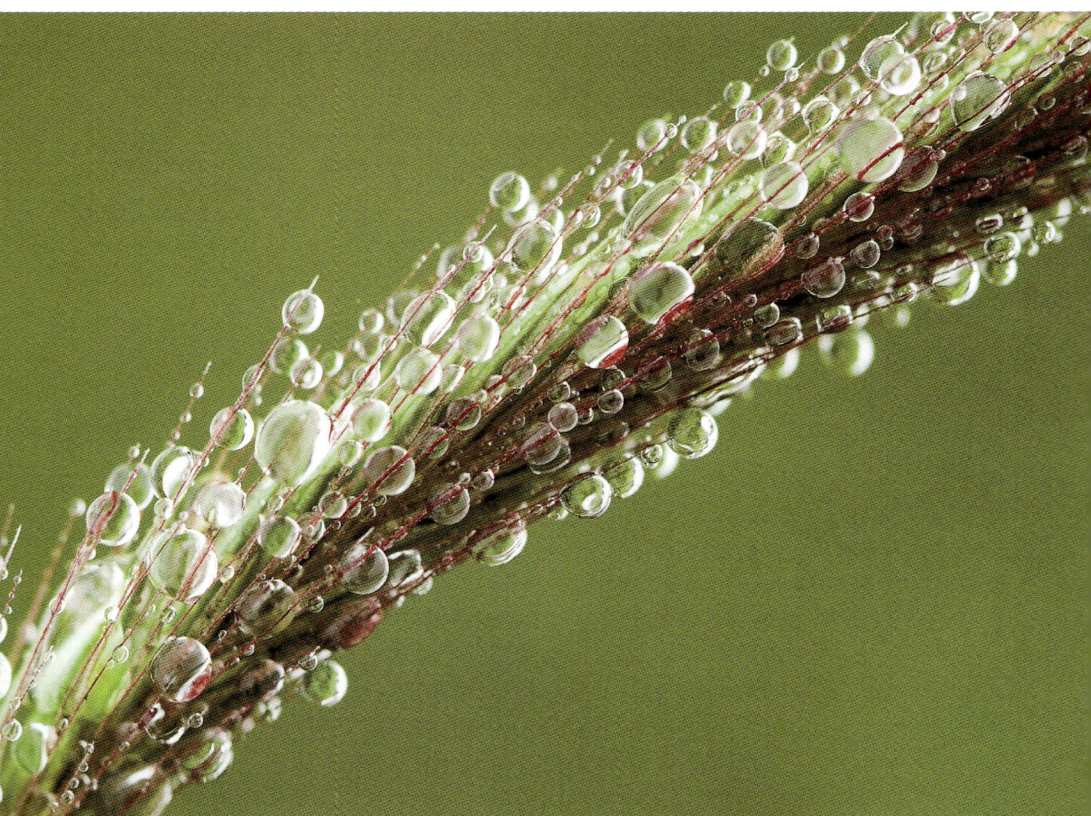

24.3 A photo taken of a dewy grass blade taken on an overcast spring morning at the Botanical Garden. Taken at ISO 400, f/4, 1/160 second with a macro lens.

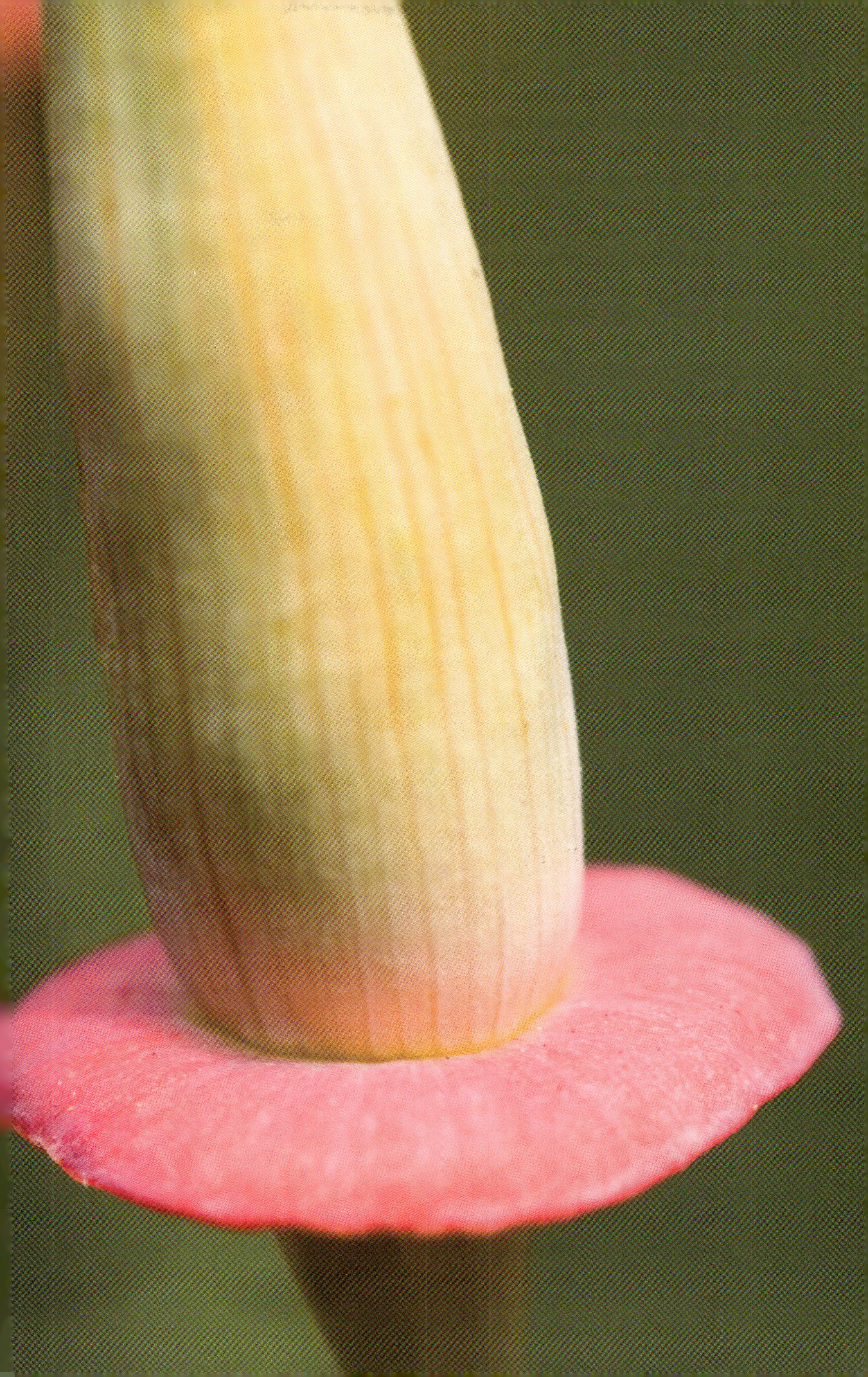

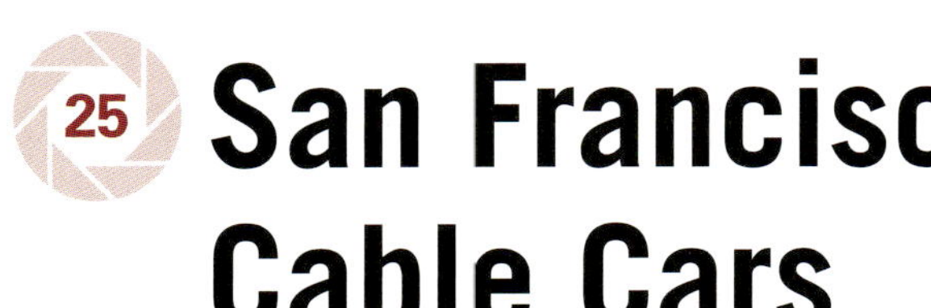

25 San Francisco Cable Cars

A view of a San Francisco cable car on California Street taken on a clear summer morning. Taken at ISO 800, f/4, 1/1000 second with a 70-200mm lens.

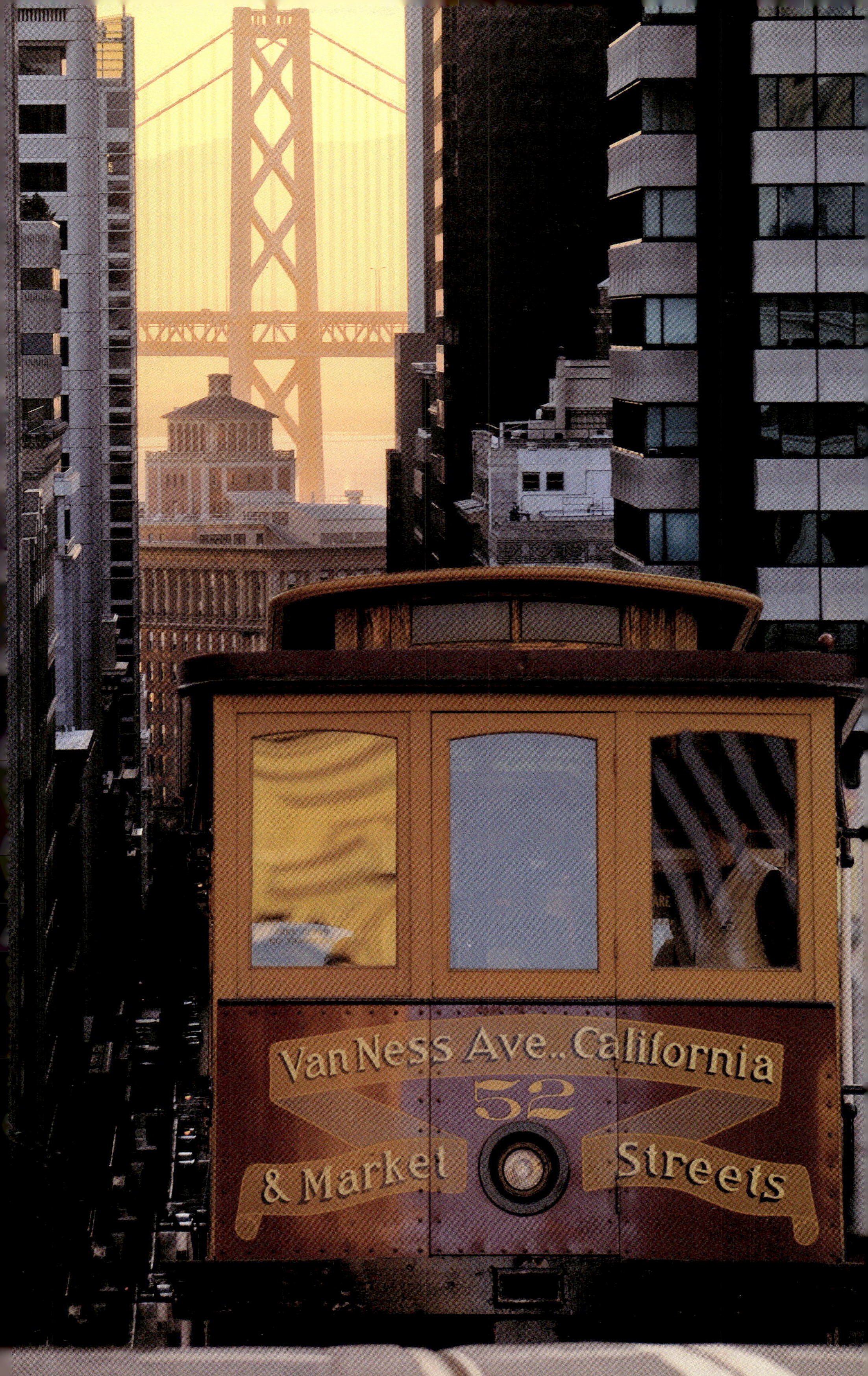
Van Ness Ave.. California
52
& Market
Streets

Why It's Worth a Photograph

The San Francisco cable car system is the last functioning manually operated cable car system in the world. Operated by the San Francisco Municipal Railway, the cars are housed and maintained at the car barn located directly above the Cable Car Museum. The cable car is an icon of San Francisco and a form of transportation from cities past. And it was a San Franciscan, Andrew Smith Hallidie, who patented the first cable car and ultimately spared many horses the excruciating work of moving people over some of the steepest hills in the country. A cable car ride beats any other form of transportation I have ever taken. You are in the open air with the wind blowing on your face, and the movements are all authentic — bumpy and rickety. Aside from being a great transportation experience, the combination of the old-style cable cars, steep hills, and modern buildings make the cable car a wonderfully unique photo opportunity.

Where Can I Get the Best Shot?

There are just a few places around San Francisco you can photograph a cable car. The two most popular and my favorites are located on a strip of Hyde Street between Chestnut Street and Francisco Street, and California Street between Mason Street and Powell Street (see A and B on the map).

Hyde Street between Chestnut Street and Francisco Street

The Powell-Hyde line runs from Union Square to Ghirardelli Square. The ride along this route is filled with twists and turns and some of the steepest hills in San Francisco. The steepest part of this ride is a section of Hyde Street between Chestnut and Francisco Streets. This stretch of road offers a vantage point that enables you to capture a cable car coming over the crest of the hill with Alcatraz and the San Francisco Bay as a backdrop (see figure 25.1).

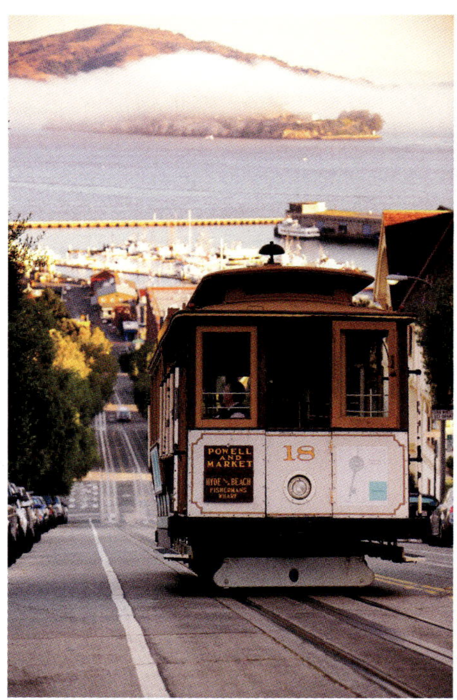

25.1 A view of a San Francisco cable car on Hyde Street taken on a clear summer morning (see A on the map). Taken at ISO 200, f/4, 1/200 second with a 70-200mm lens.

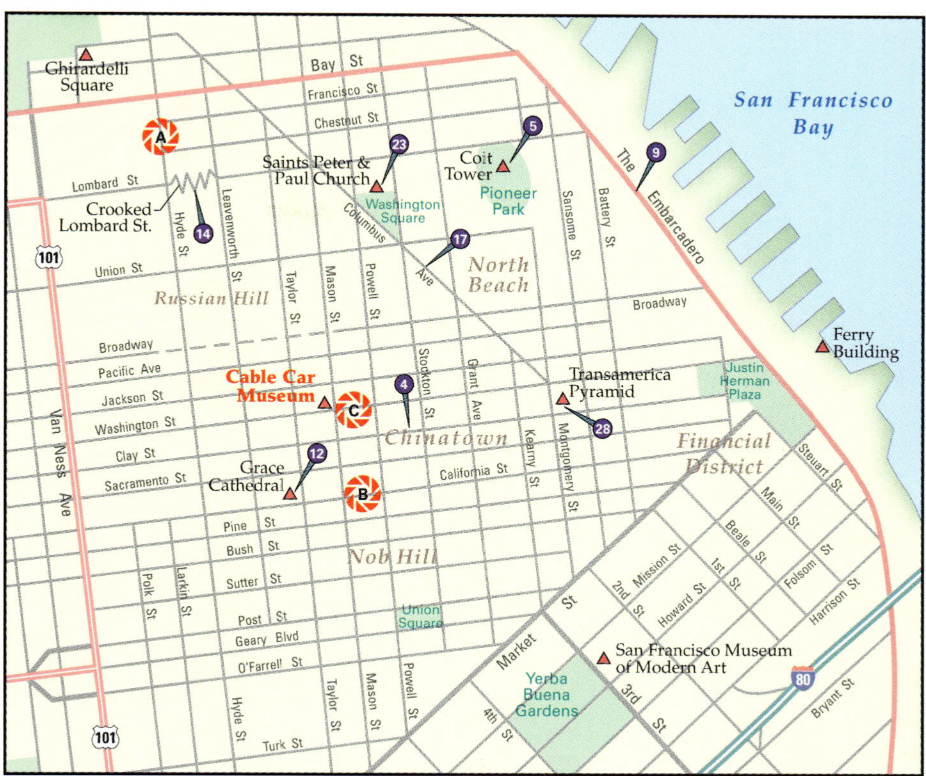

The best locations from which to photograph a cable car: (A) Hyde Street between Chestnut Street and Francisco Street, (B) California Street between Mason Street and Powell Street, (C) Cable Car Museum. Other photo ops: (4) Chinatown, (5) Coit Tower, (9) Embarcadero, (12) Grace Cathedral, (14) Lombard Street between Hyde and Leavenworth Streets, (17) North Beach, (23) Saints Peter and Paul Church, (28) Transamerica Pyramid.

California Street between Mason Street and Powell Street

The California Street line runs due west from the waterfront Embarcadero to Van Ness Avenue on California Street between Mason Street and Powell Street. There are a couple different angles to shoot from. Each angle can offer you a different scene. The two primary angles capture a cable car coming over a crest with either the financial district or the Transamerica Pyramid as a backdrop (see figure 25.2).

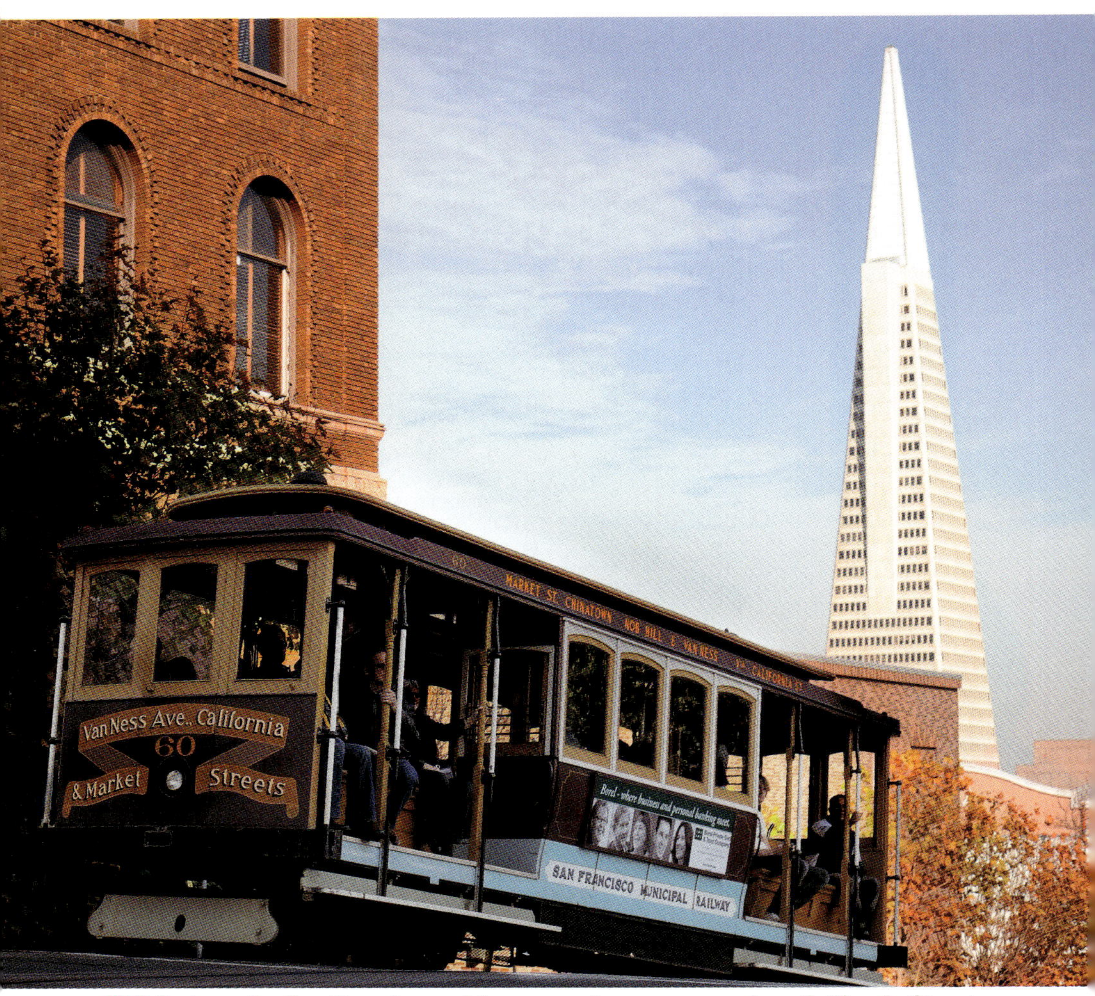

25.2 A view of a San Francisco cable car coming over a crest on California Street taken on a clear summer day (see B on the map). Taken at ISO 100, f/4, 1/800 second with a 50mm lens.

Cable Car Museum

The Cable Car Museum was established in 1974. Located in the historic Washington/Mason cable car barn and powerhouse, the Cable Car Museum offers numerous opportunities to photograph various aspects of a cable car, from the grips, track, cable, and brake mechanisms to antique cable cars from the 1870s, Sutter Street Railway No. 46 grip car, No. 54 trailer, and the only surviving car from the first cable car company. The museum deck overlooks the huge engines and winding wheels that pull the cables, and downstairs is a viewing area of the large sheaves and cable line entering the building through the channel under the street. This museum is a great place to visit if you are interested in the history and the inner workings of a cable car and how it operates (see figure 25.3).

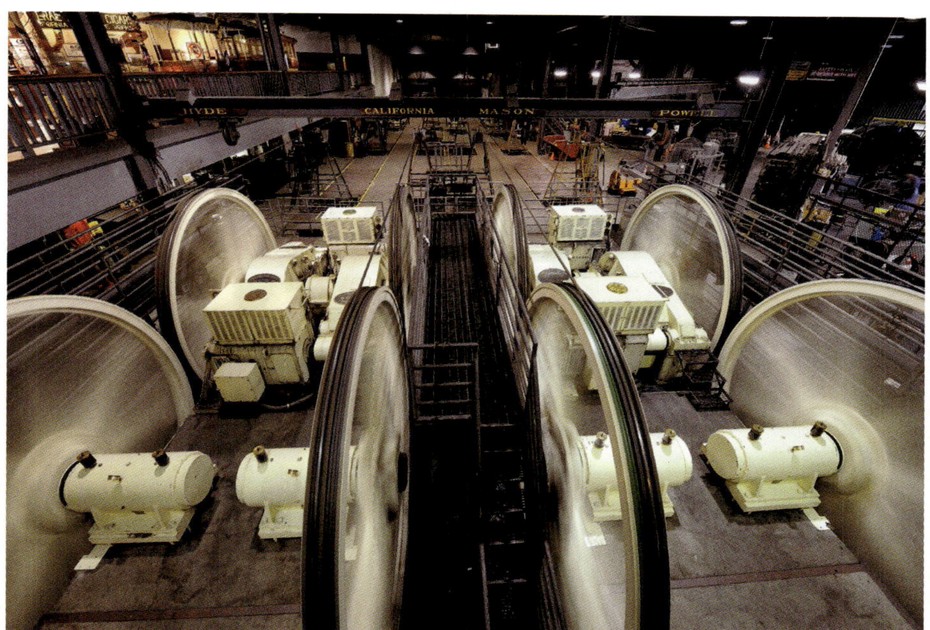

25.3 The inner workings of a cable car taken at the Cable Car Museum (see C on the map). Taken at ISO 800, f/2, 1/800 second with a 50mm lens.

How Can I Get the Best Shot?

Shutter speed, shutter speed, shutter speed. This is the key to capturing a tack-sharp image of a moving cable car. To ensure that you freeze the cable car, try to shoot with a shutter speed of at least 1/250 second.

Equipment

The choice of lens always comes down to your personal preference and what you want to convey in this photo. Whether you are shooting day or night, your lens choice is instrumental for creating the ideal composition for any given subject. The lens or set of lenses I recommend that you use to photograph a cable car are the following:

- **A standard zoom lens in the 24-100mm range.** This lens can give you much more versatility when traveling. This lens is the jack-of-all-trades and is best used for street shooting and inside buildings. This lens is also great for panning shots of a cable car speeding by.
- **A zoom lens somewhere in the 70-300mm range.** This focal range gives you the ability to isolate a cable car without having to get too close to your subject. This is extremely helpful and allows you to shoot a cable car coming directly at you without putting you in harm's way.

Camera settings

How you set up your camera comes down to time of day and amount of available light. Remember that I said to have at least a shutter speed of 1/250 of a second; to achieve this speed you may need to move your ISO up to 400 or even 800. It's best to shoot in Aperture Priority mode. I suggest an aperture between f/2.8 to f/5.6, and a focal length of at least 100mm. This focal length and aperture combination allows a fast enough shutter speed with a fair amount of background blur to help the cable car stand out from its background.

- **Exposure mode.** I set my camera in Aperture Priority mode and let my camera choose the shutter speed. I may dial in a plus exposure compensation if the sky is so bright that the cable car is underexposing. I will always sacrifice a bit of sky to expose my subject properly.
- **White balance.** White balance I never touch because I find the Auto White Balance of all modern day cameras to be pretty good.
- **ISO.** Shutter speed is critical when shooting a moving subject. Adjust your ISO to achieve a fast enough shutter speed to freeze motion. At least 1/120 second for a slow-moving cable car should be fast enough. In general 1/500 second is the minimum shutter speed to freeze moving subjects. Don't be afraid to shoot at ISO 800 or higher.

Exposure

When shooting a cable car downtown with a brightly lit sky, exposing the cable car correctly can be tough. Set your camera in Aperture Priority mode and dial in a +1/3 to +2/3 of a stop of exposure compensation to ensure you expose the cable car correctly. This may not always be the case, so use your histogram or LCD on the back of your camera to judge a test shot. Once you have a well-balanced exposure, wait for a cable car and then fire away.

Ideal time to shoot

The ideal time to shoot is in the early morning or late in the day because you want the sun low but not so low that there is not enough light to reach a shutter speed of 1/250 second. When the sun is low, it will also provide a warm, soft light, which always makes photos more pleasing.

Working around the weather

Weather is important for one reason, and that is you don't want to be out in a rainstorm with your gear waiting for a cable car to come by. My recommendation is anytime, but the winter is an ideal time to shoot. That said, the winter months between late November and early March can have unpredictable rainstorms. Plan your days when it is clear, so you can take advantage of the wonderful backdrops both of these locations offer.

Getting creative

Learning to pan is a great way to take your photography skills to the next level. Photographic pan is a technique that is used for objects that are traveling in a straight line. The camera moves from left to right or right to left as it follows the subject, which is moving at the same speed. Panning produces a very interesting effect that causes the subject to stay in focus while the background is blurred, creating a sense of motion that really makes a photo stand out. Your camera will need to be in Continuous Focus (Nikon) or AI servo (Canon) mode — this is a focus setting that all dSLR cameras have. This setting allows you to track a moving subject. Your lens adjusts and keeps your subject in focus as long as you have the Shutter button half pressed. To focus on a moving object and use the panning technique, you must use a very slow shutter speed. For example, a good shutter speed for a cable car is 1/20 second. Adjust the shutter speed as necessary for objects that are moving faster or slower (see figure 25.4).

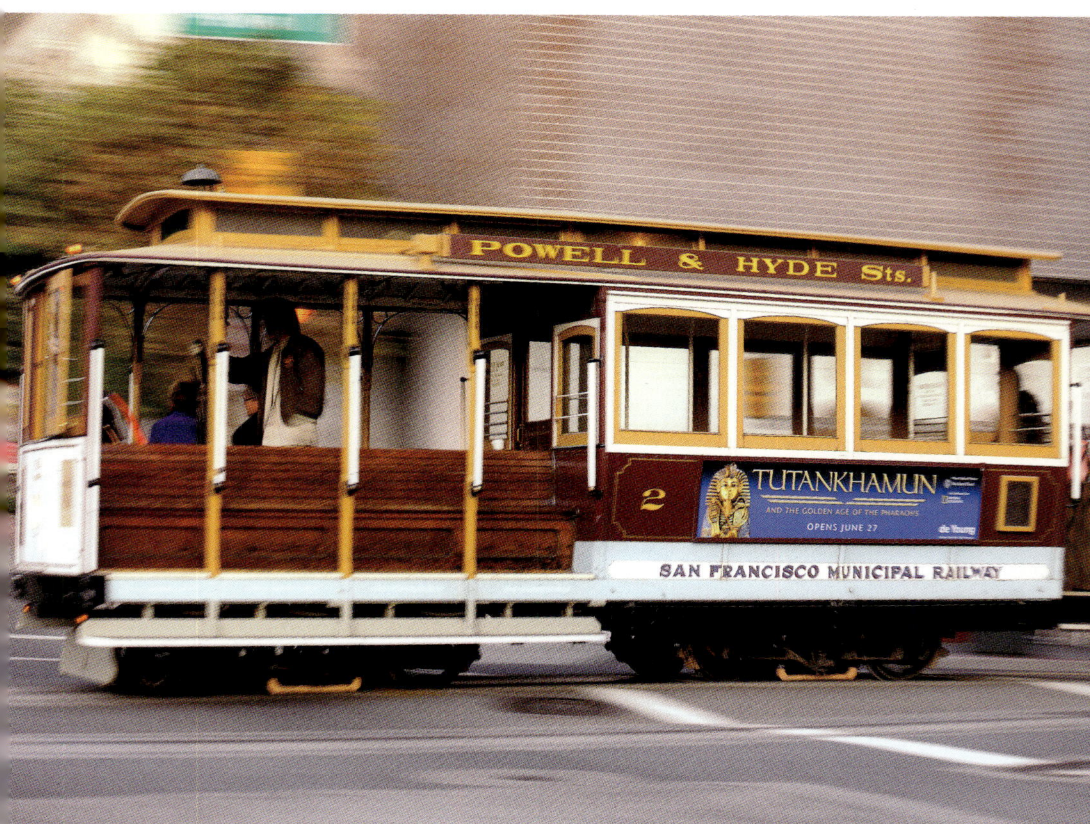

25.4 A panning shot of a cable car taken on a clear summer morning (see B on the map). Taken at ISO 100, f/8, 1/8 second with a 70-200mm lens.

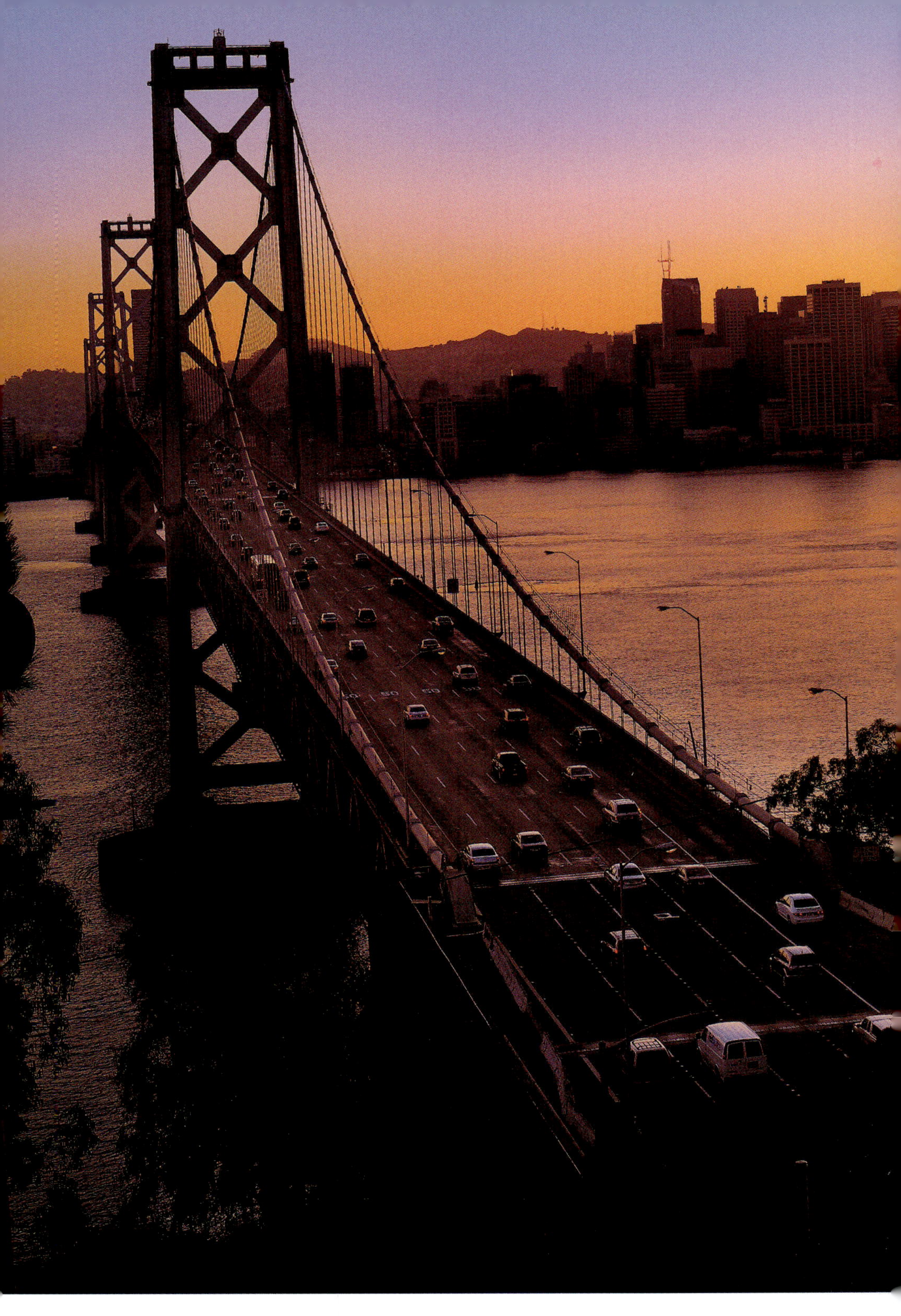

A view of the Bay Bridge taken just before sunset from Treasure Island Vista on a clear winter evening. Taken at ISO 100, f/8, 1/100 second with a 50mm lens.

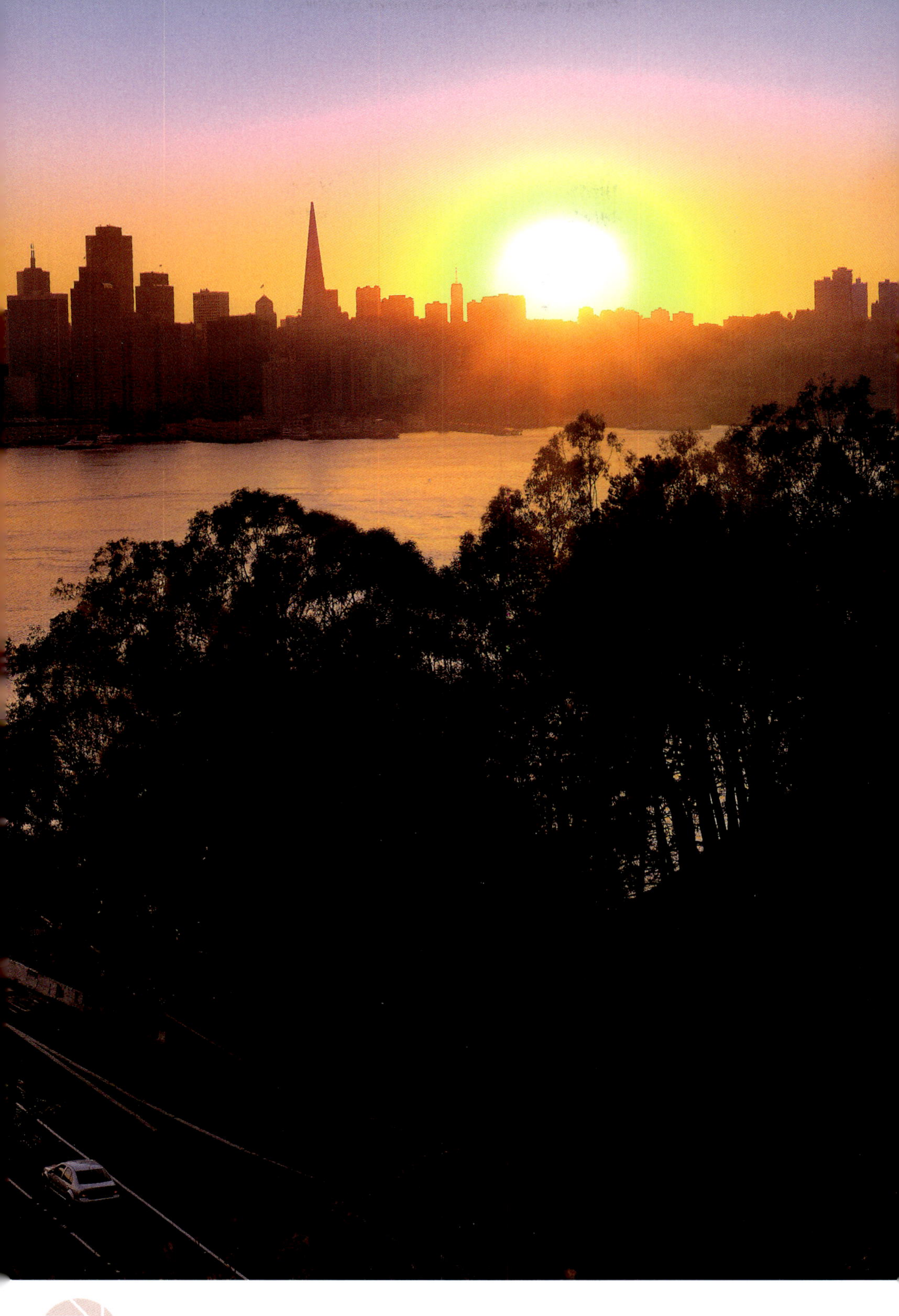

26 San Francisco-Oakland Bay Bridge

Why It's Worth a Photograph

The San Francisco-Oakland Bay Bridge, known locally as the Bay Bridge, is a bridge that is overshadowed and overlooked as a major site to visit and photograph in San Francisco. The largest and most expensive bridge of its time, the Bay Bridge faced many natural obstacles, deep water, mud flats, and high winds. The result was a unique bridge that combined the best elements of several different designs. The Yerba Buena Tunnel connecting the two halves of the bridge is the largest diameter transportation bore tunnel in the world. Today, not only is the bridge an architectural wonder, having one of the longest spans in the world, but it also carries approximately 300,000 vehicles per day on its two decks. A bridge is a bridge, but a big bridge is really something to see. The sheer size of this bridge and the architectural feats needed to construct this bridge make this a superb opportunity to capture a photo comprised of land, sea, air, and hard, cold steel basked in magnificent early morning or late evening light.

Where Can I Get the Best Shot?

There are many places around San Francisco you can photograph the Bay Bridge. A few of these places reside just across the bay allowing you to create beautiful photographs of the Bay Bridge and the San Francisco skyline. Some are scattered throughout the downtown area, creating a completely different perspective. You can find many other great vantage points when you are exploring this wonderful city.

The vantage points I detail in this chapter are my favorites for a number of reasons including accessibility, relation to the sun, and the ability to create a creative composition. My favorite locations to capture dramatic photos of the Bay Bridge are the Embarcadero, Treasure Island, Yerba Buena Island, under the Bay Bridge, and Union Street and Montgomery Street (see A–E on the map).

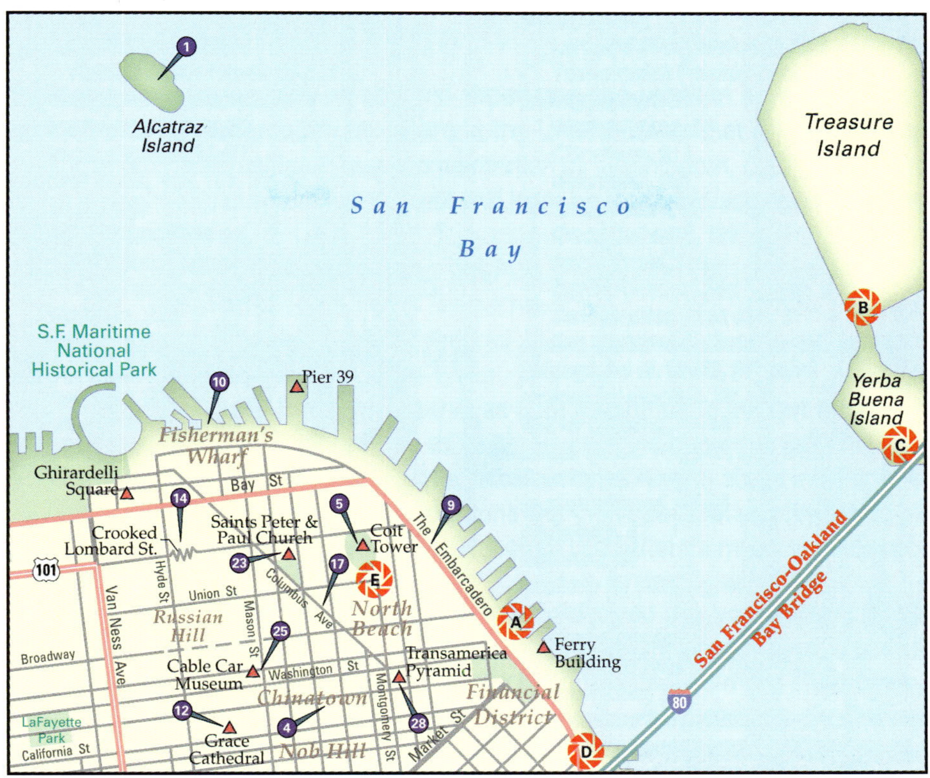

The best locations from which to photograph the Bay Bridge: (A) Embarcadero, (B) Treasure Island, (C) Yerba Buena Island, (D) under the Bay Bridge, (E) Union Street and Montgomery Street. Other photo ops: (1) Alcatraz, (4) Chinatown, (5) Coit Tower, (9) Embarcadero, (10) Fisherman's Wharf, (12) Grace Cathedral, (14) Lombard Street, (17) North Beach, (23) Saints Peter and Paul Church, (25) San Francisco cable cars, (28) Transamerica Pyramid.

Embarcadero

One of the most popular places from which to photograph the Bay Bridge is the Embarcadero. Along this two-mile stretch of waterfront, you can stop on one of the many piers and enjoy the wonderful views of the San Francisco Bay. Pier 2, one of the longest piers that is accessible for pedestrian traffic, is a great vantage point from which to photograph the bridge. In the early morning hours just before the sun comes up, you can capture a wonderful image of the bridge as a silhouette against the dusky morning sky and advancing sunrise coming up behind the horizon (see figure 26.1).

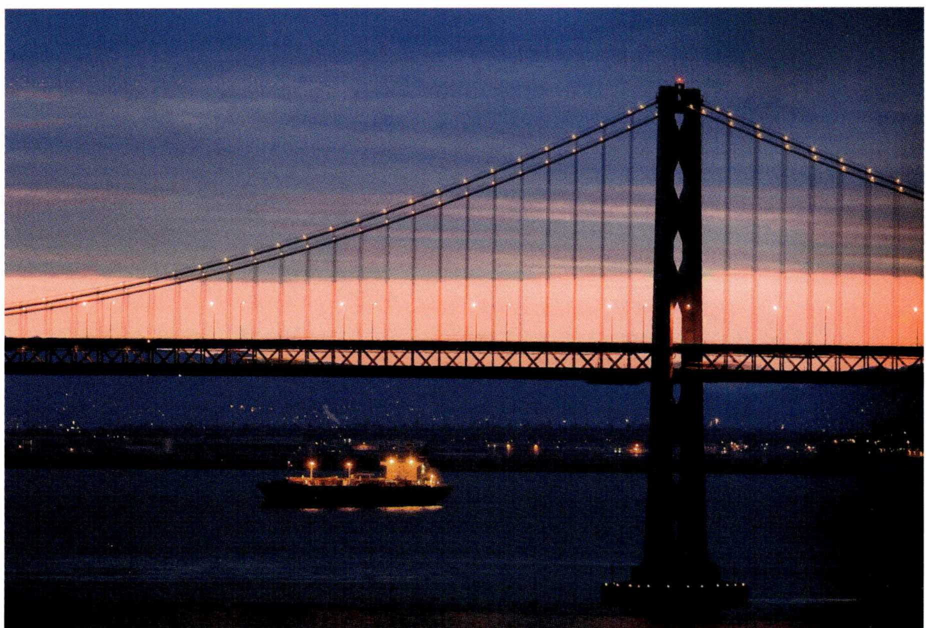

26.1 A view of the Bay Bridge taken from the Embarcadero on a clear fall morning (see A on the map). Taken at ISO 100, f/8, 1/8 second with a 70-200 mm lens.

Treasure Island

Treasure Island offers a great location to photograph the Bay Bridge and the city of San Francisco. This location is one of the premiere places because it is easily accessible and offers breathtaking views. Located at the entrance to the base on the water's edge, the best time to photograph from this location is just prior or just after sunset as the sun setting behind the city can create dramatic skies that outline the city in wonderful, colorful hues of orange, reds, and pinks. The shot in figure 26.2 was taken with an ultrawide lens just after the sun went down. You can see the wonderful combination of the intense, dusky blue sky and the soft pink hues that are left over just after the sun sets. This photo was further enhanced when I set my white balance to Tungsten to help compensate for the streetlight shining on the rocks. By setting my white balance to Tungsten, the rocks are rendered in a neutral tone rather than orange. This setting also enhanced the dusky sky by creating a vibrant blue that I love. This location is also great to photograph the much less popular eastern span. The ideal time is at sunrise as the sun comes up from behind the hills and bathes the bridge and marina sailboats in a warm, soft light (see figure 26.3)

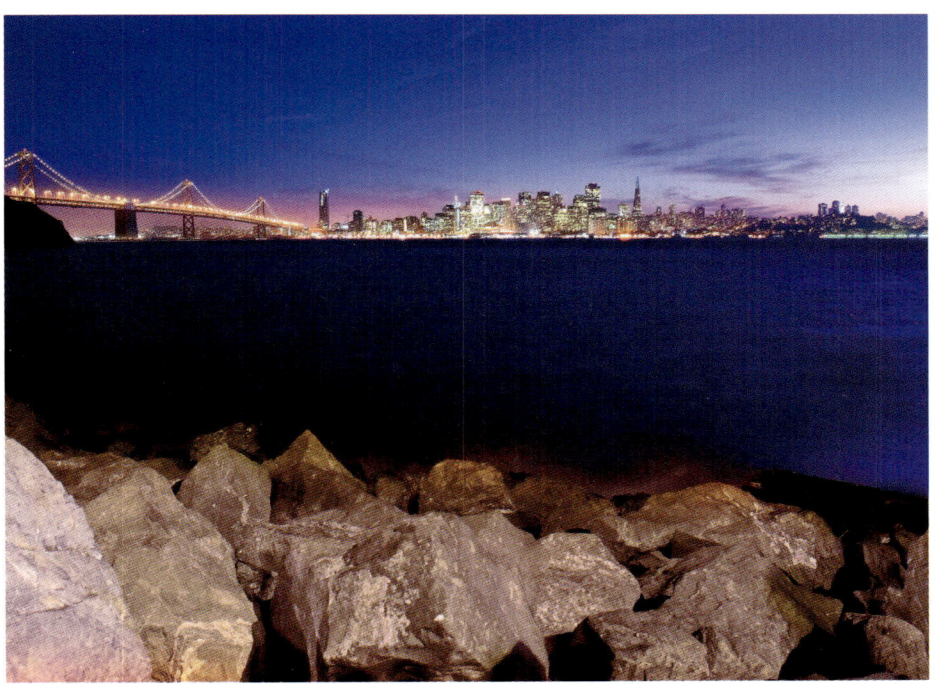

26.2 **A view of the Bay Bridge and skyline taken just after sunset on a clear fall evening (see B on the map). Taken at ISO 100, f/9, 15 seconds with a 17-40mm lens.**

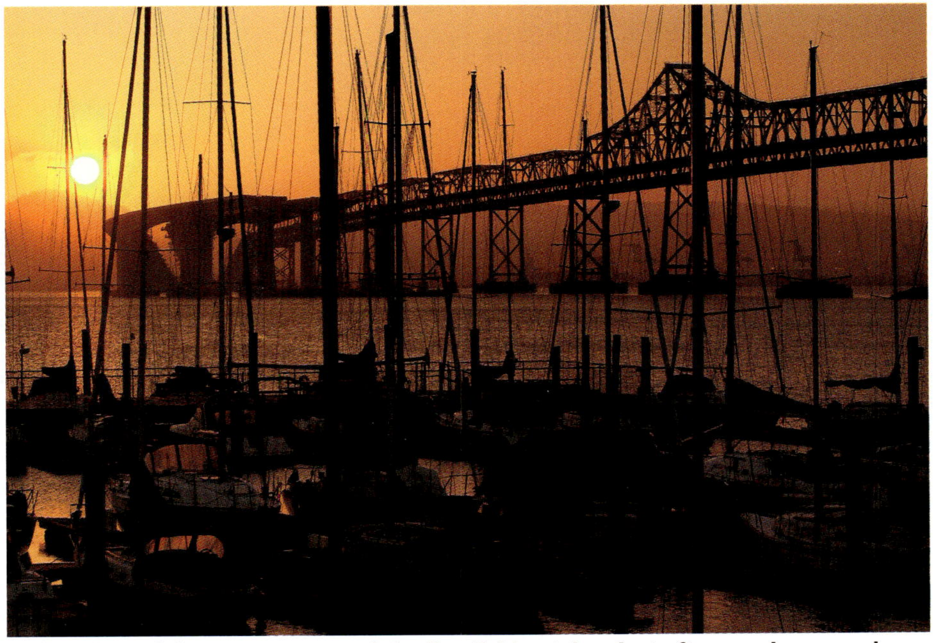

26.3 **A view of the eastern span of the Bay Bridge taken just after sunrise on a clear spring morning. Taken at ISO 100, f/9, 1/320 second with a 70-200mm lens.**

Yerba Buena Island

Yerba Buena Island offers the most dramatic place in San Francisco to capture the Bay Bridge. Although the most dramatic, this location is also the most difficult to get to. Located at the highest point of the island, this vantage point can offer you the best location to capture the bridge and its full beauty, intense sunsets, and a gorgeous city skyline at dusk. To get to this location, follow the road that takes you off the bridge around and up until you get to the top of the island. After you park, walk down to a small clearing located just above the bridge. Bring a lens or lenses that can cover a focal length between 35-and 200mm. The perfect time to arrive is 30 minutes prior to sunset and plan to stay at least one hour after the sun goes down (see figure 26.4).

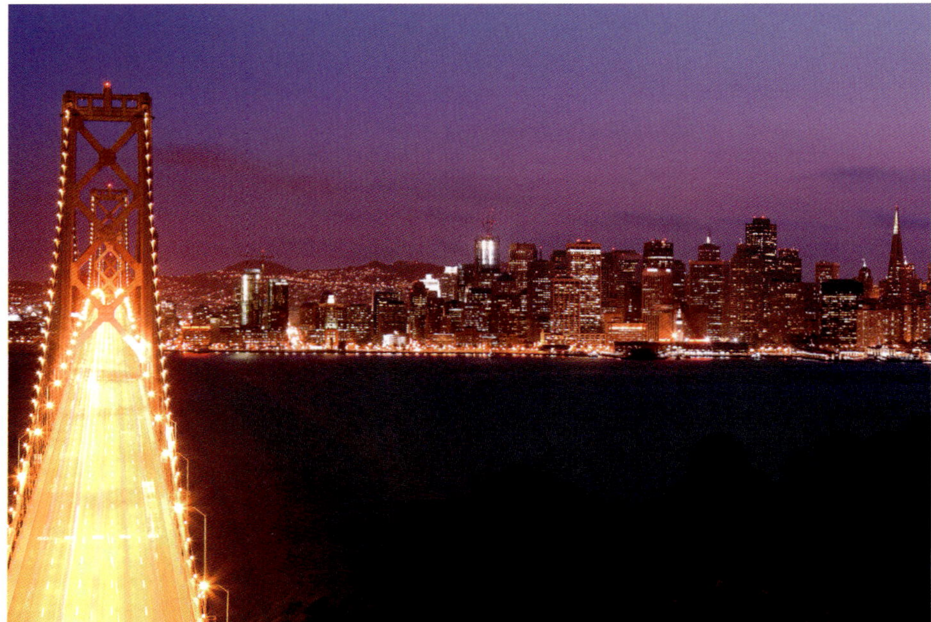

26.4 A view of the Bay Bridge and skyline taken on a clear spring night (see C on the map). Taken at ISO 100, f/8, 20 seconds with a 24-70mm lens.

Under the Bay Bridge

This location on Embarcadero at Harrison Street is right next to the bridge. The perfect place to set up is next to Fire Boat House. This location combined with a wide lens and clear sunrise can offer you a wonderful opportunity to capture the bridge and the rising sun. On a clear, calm morning with the light creeping over the horizon, a slow shutter speed's effect on the water, combined with the starburst effect created by using a smaller aperture, can be stunning (see figure 26.5).

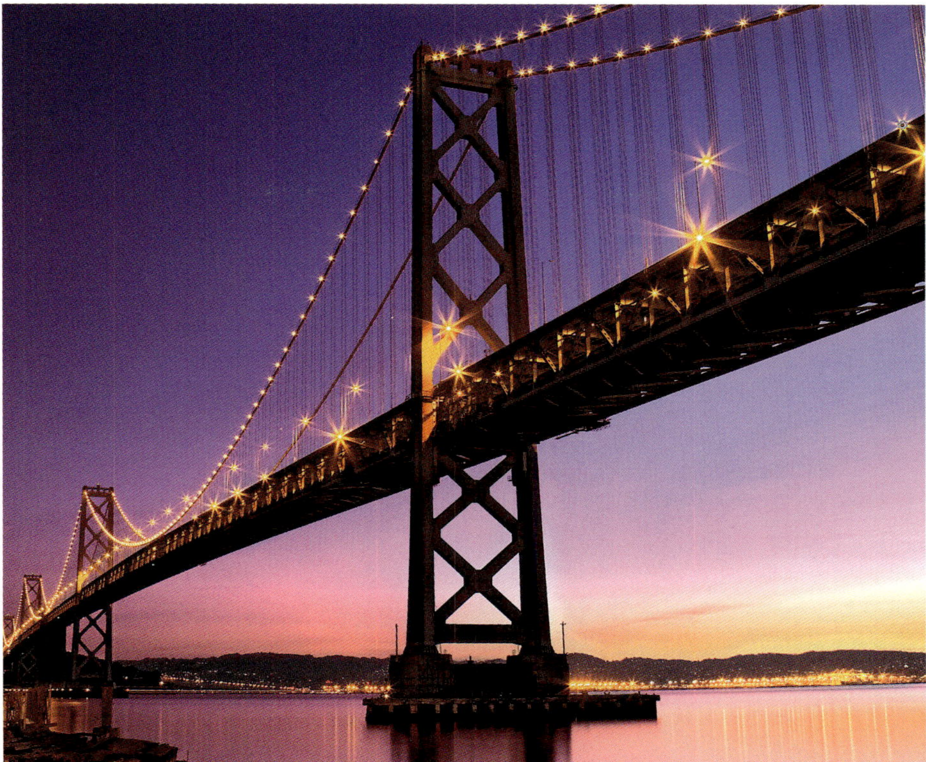

26.5 A view of the Bay Bridge at sunrise on a clear winter morning (see D on the map). Taken at ISO 100, f/11, 30 seconds with a 24-70mm lens.

Union Street and Montgomery Street

One of the least known locations to photograph the bridge is Union Street at Montgomery Street. This vantage point, high above the Embarcadero, offers a perspective you cannot capture from any other location. This hidden gem of a location and a standard zoom lens enable you to capture the bridge spanning across the bay with the Embarcadero piers below. This is a must-shoot location at sunrise because the sun rising just below the horizon basks the upper third of your photo in an intense orange light. The upper half of the suspension towers and the cables are a silhouette outline against the vibrant orange sky, while the lower half of the bridge will still be cast in darkness (see figure 26.6).

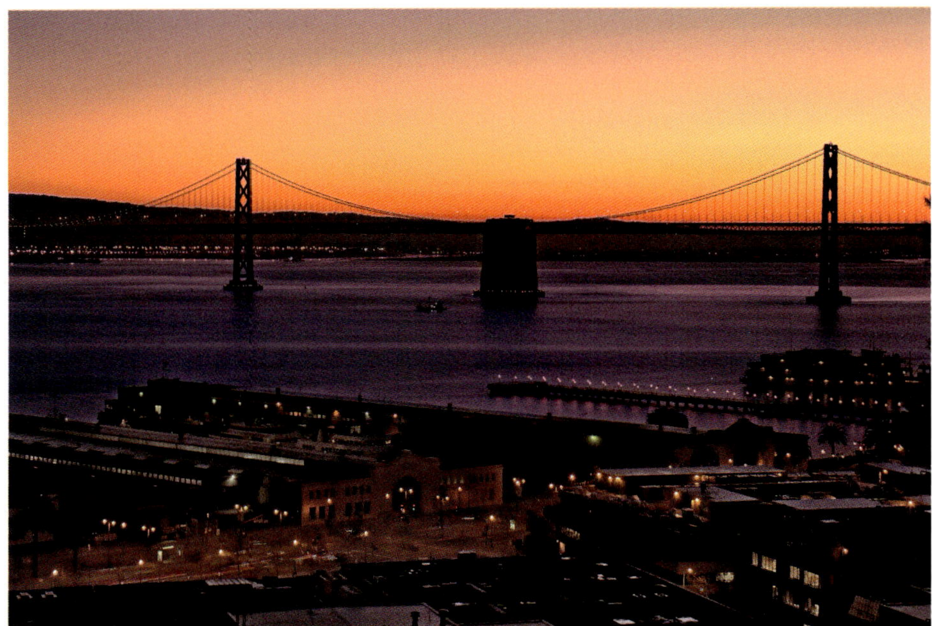

26.6 **A view of the Bay Bridge immersed in a wonderful orange sunrise on a clear winter morning (see E on the map). Taken at ISO 100, f/8, 1/100 second with a 70-200mm lens.**

How Can I Get the Best Shot?

Shooting the Bay Bridge is best done on a clear, early morning at sunrise or late afternoon at sunset when the sun is low, soft, and warm. This light creates wonderfully colorful and dramatic skies when shooting the bridge from any of the locations. When shooting the bridge at night, clear skies are a must for all but the Yerba Buena Island location because the fog can create dramatic images of the bridge, light, and cars. An assortment of lenses and a tripod are musts to be successful in capturing the Bay Bridge from each vantage point.

Equipment

An assortment of lenses ranging from an ultrawide lens to a medium telephoto lens should be in your bag along with a tripod and cable release.

Lenses

Having a nice assortment of lenses or one lens that covers a large focal length are musts, if you want to capture compelling images of the Bay Bridge.

- **Ultrawide zoom lens in the 14-24mm range.** The ultrawide lens gives you the ability to create an ultrawide angle perspective of the bridge.

- **A standard zoom lens in the 24-100mm range.** This lens should be your most used lens for photographing the Bay Bridge. Most of the locations use focal lengths within this range.
- **A super-telephoto lens somewhere in the 70-300mm range.** Like the ultrawide lens, this lens has its place in your bag. When photographing the bridge from a distance or isolating a subject, this lens is your best choice.

Extras

A tripod is a must for night shots and low-light shooting. I also recommend a cable release.

Camera settings

Shooting sunsets, sunrises, and night scenes can best be achieved in Manual mode. Set your aperture and then dial in the correct shutter speed. You may need to tweak the shutter speed to get your desired exposure. Remember, exposure is not just about balancing the correct amount of light; it is also about creating a mood. When shooting low-light and night scenes, you have to take special care to balance the shadows and the highlights.

- **Exposure mode.** Shoot in Manual mode when there are tricky lighting conditions that cause your meter to underexpose or overexpose. For most of the Bay Bridge photos, set your camera to Manual and dial in the aperture and shutter speed that gives you the creative exposure you want. Check the histogram on the back of your camera until you achieve correct exposure.
- **White balance.** Automatic White Balance is the best setting choice for shooting landscapes because it tends to give you the best output.
- **ISO.** Keep your ISO as low as possible to maximize image quality.

Exposure

When the sun gets low, metering becomes trickier. The light from the sky, dark shadows on the ground and bridge, and building and auto lights can all affect your exposure. In situations such as these, it is easier to shoot in Manual mode by setting your aperture to the desired f-stop and then adjusting the shutter speed until you create the desired effect and proper exposure. In these tricky lighting conditions, Aperture Priority and exposure compensation may not be the best choices. I use the histogram and LCD on the back of my camera all the time to check to see if I have the ideal balance between shadows and highlights. This balance is what makes the difference between a poorly exposed photo and one you want to show your friends. Remember, in many cases you may have to sacrifice a bit of highlights or shadows. You need to decide what the best creative exposure is for any given photo.

Ideal time to shoot

The ideal times to shoot are early morning, late afternoon, or when the sun is down. The hour just after the sun rises and just before the sun sets is known as the golden hour of light. Typically, lighting is softer and warmer in hue, and shadows are longer. The half hour before the sun rises and after the sun sets is known as the blue hour. This period has neither full daylight nor complete darkness. When shooting the Bay Bridge at these times, you can create some truly compelling images.

Working around the weather

Morning and evening fog is common during summer months for San Francisco, but it rarely remains throughout the day. September and October tend to be the warmest and clearest months, whereas rain can be common in late November through March. San Francisco weather literally varies from neighborhood to neighborhood; it may be sunny and pleasant in one area and foggy and cool in another. No season in San Francisco is really out of the question for photographing the Bay Bridge.

Don't let the fog scare you away. Shooting the Bay Bridge on a foggy evening can create a mystical photo of the bridge disappearing into a thick blanket of fog. The lights and fog create a wonderful soft, warm glow that expands out from the bridge into the blackness of night (see figure 26.7).

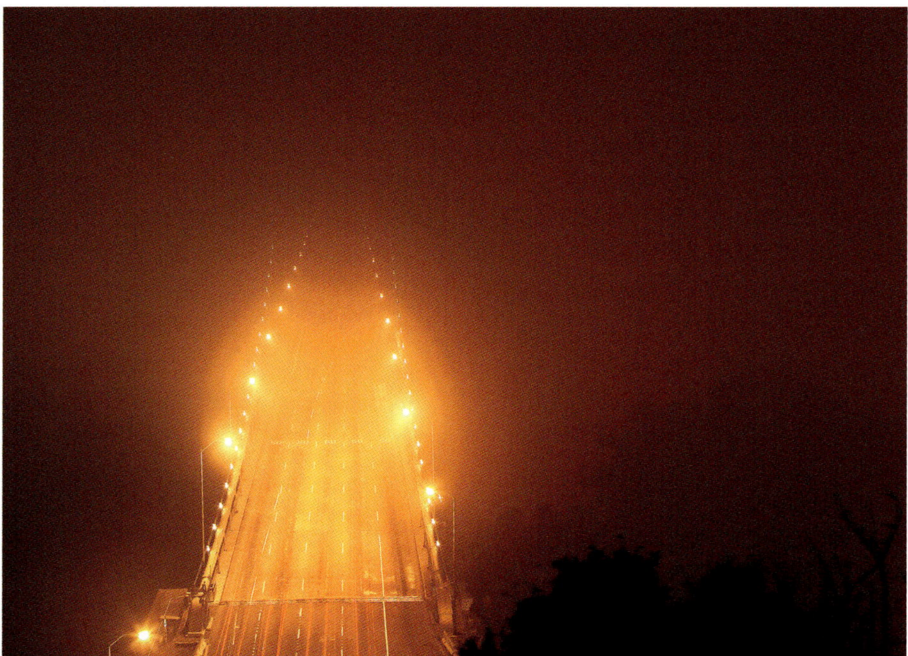

26.7 A view of the Bay Bridge covered in a glowing fog taken from Yerba Buena Island on a foggy summer evening (see B on the map). Taken at ISO 100, f/8, 10 seconds with a 24-70mm lens.

Low-light and night options

Yerba Buena Island is the best place to photograph the Bay Bridge at night. A medium lens is a must because you want to be able to frame the bridge and still see the detail of the city at night. What makes this a great low-light location is the effect that shutter speed has on the cars commuting across the bridge. Introducing motion or the perception of motion in a cityscape shot only adds to the dynamics of the photo (see figure 26.8).

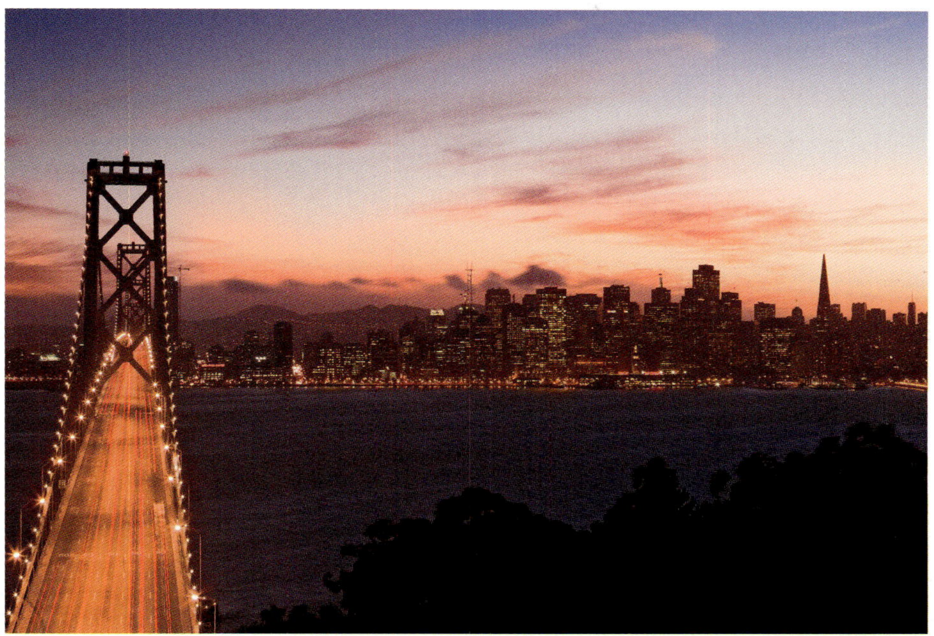

26.8 A view of cars speeding across the Bay Bridge taken from Yerba Buena Island on a clear fall evening (see B on the map). Taken at ISO 100, f/8, 13 seconds with a 70-200mm lens.

Getting creative

If you want to try something fun and creative, get out your medium telephoto lens when shooting from Yerba Buena Island. This lens can create an isolation of the traffic racing across the bridge. The slow shutter speed gives the impression that the cars are traveling much faster than the posted speed limit on the bridge's roadway (see figure 26.9).

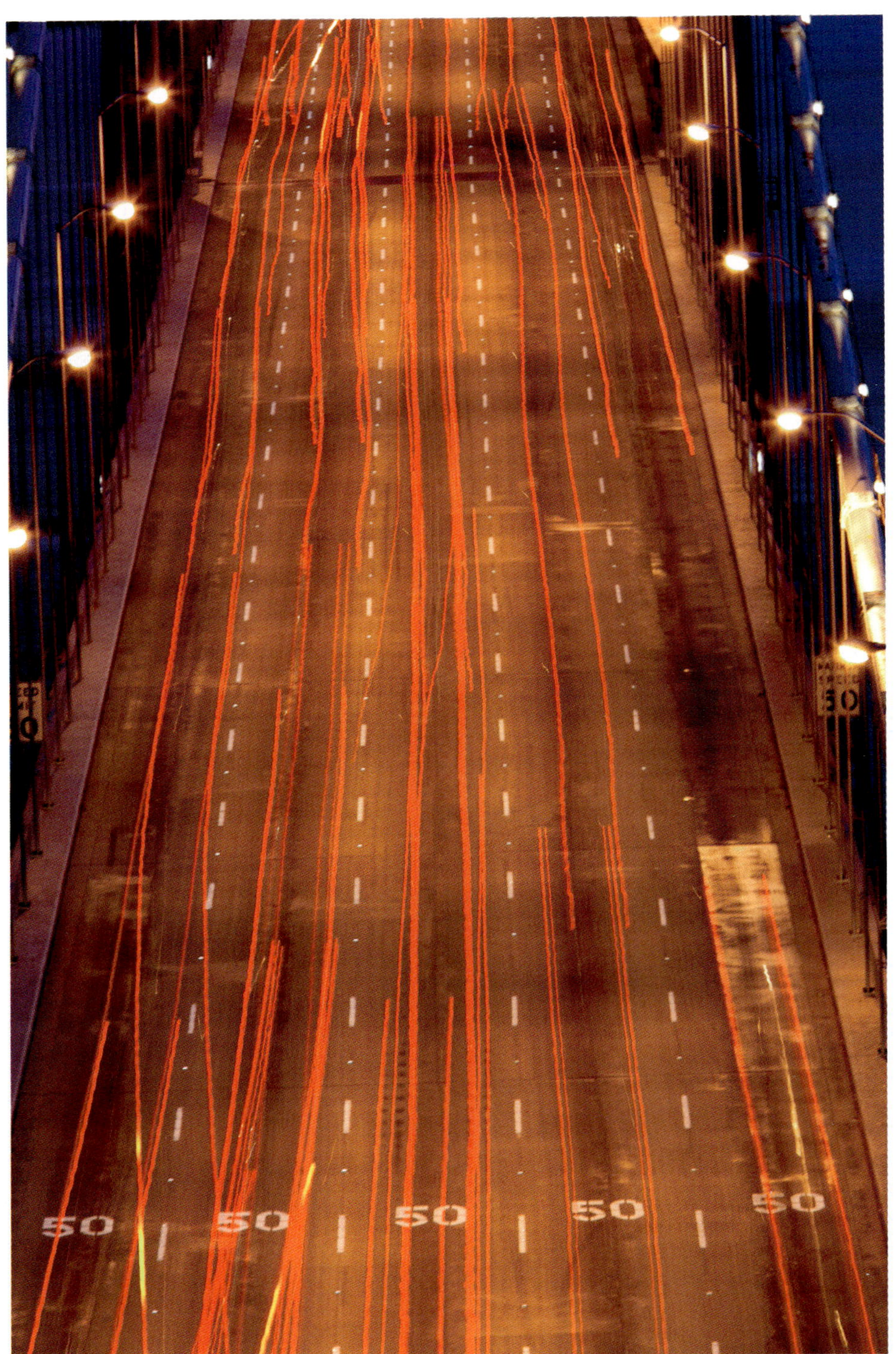

26.9 **Light trails of traffic racing across the Bay Bridge. The photo was taken at ISO 100, f/8, 8 seconds with a 70-200 mm lens.**

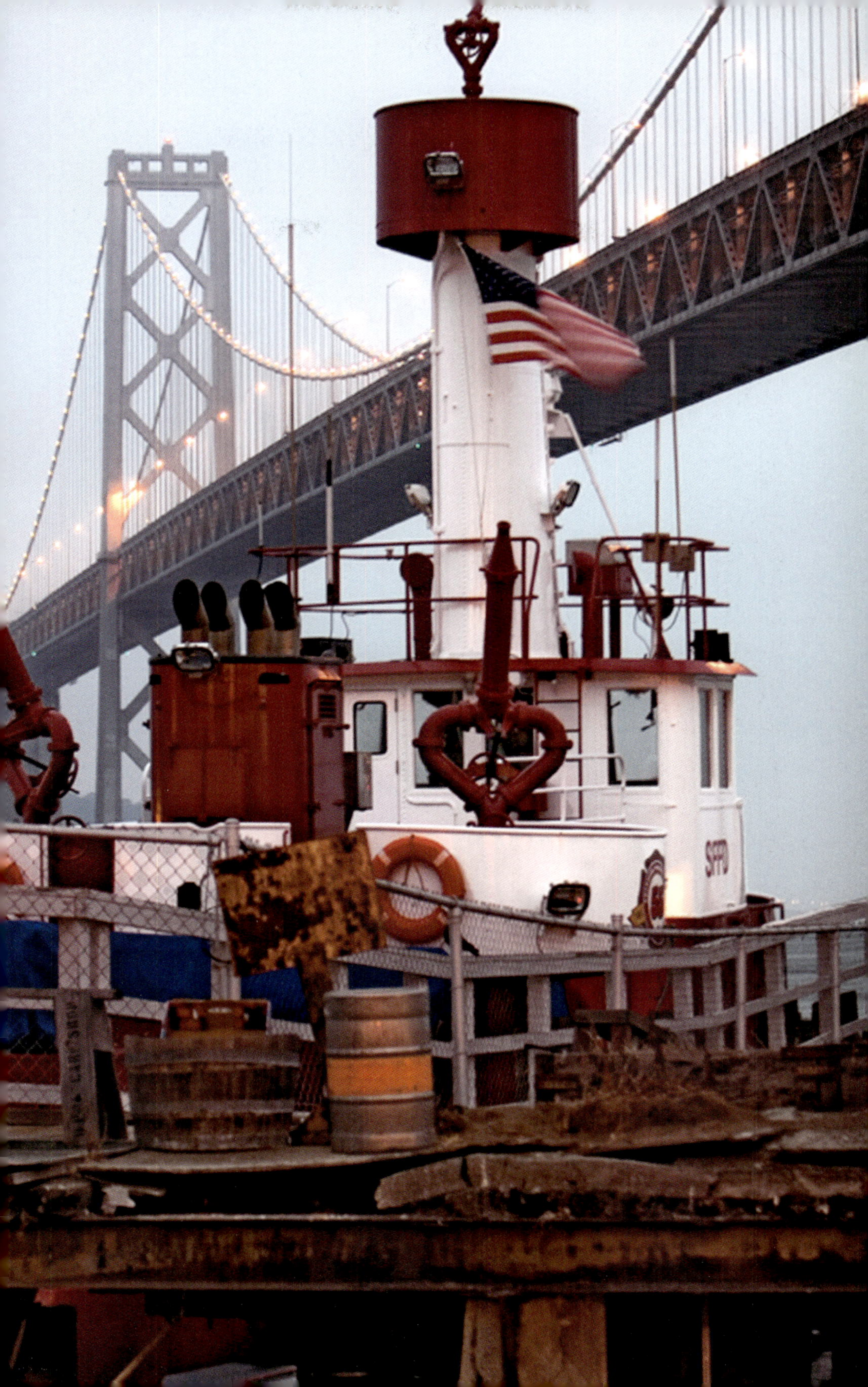
SFFD

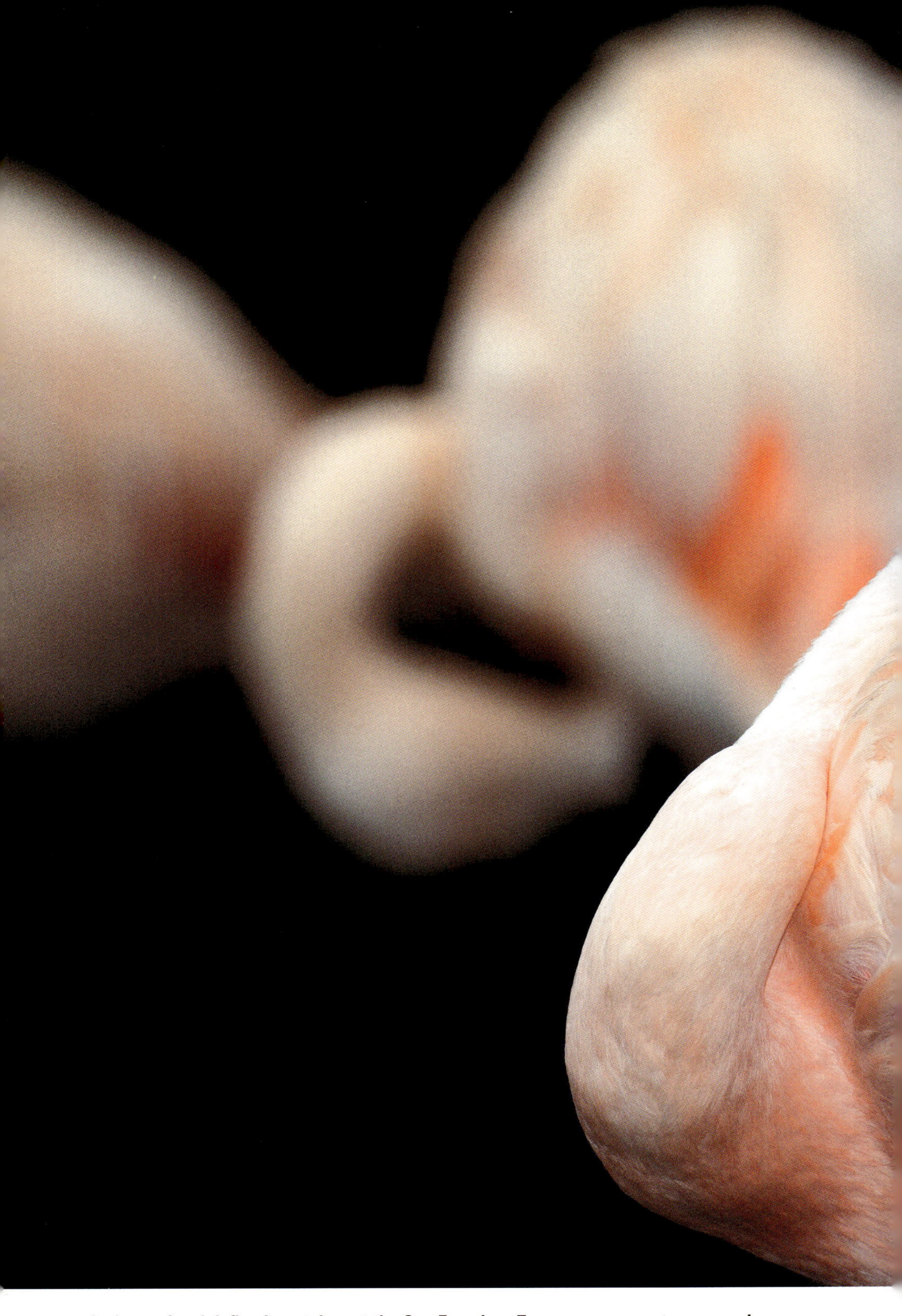

A photo of a pink flamingo taken at the San Francisco Zoo on an overcast summer day. Taken at ISO 400, f/5.6, 1/2000 second with a 400mm lens.

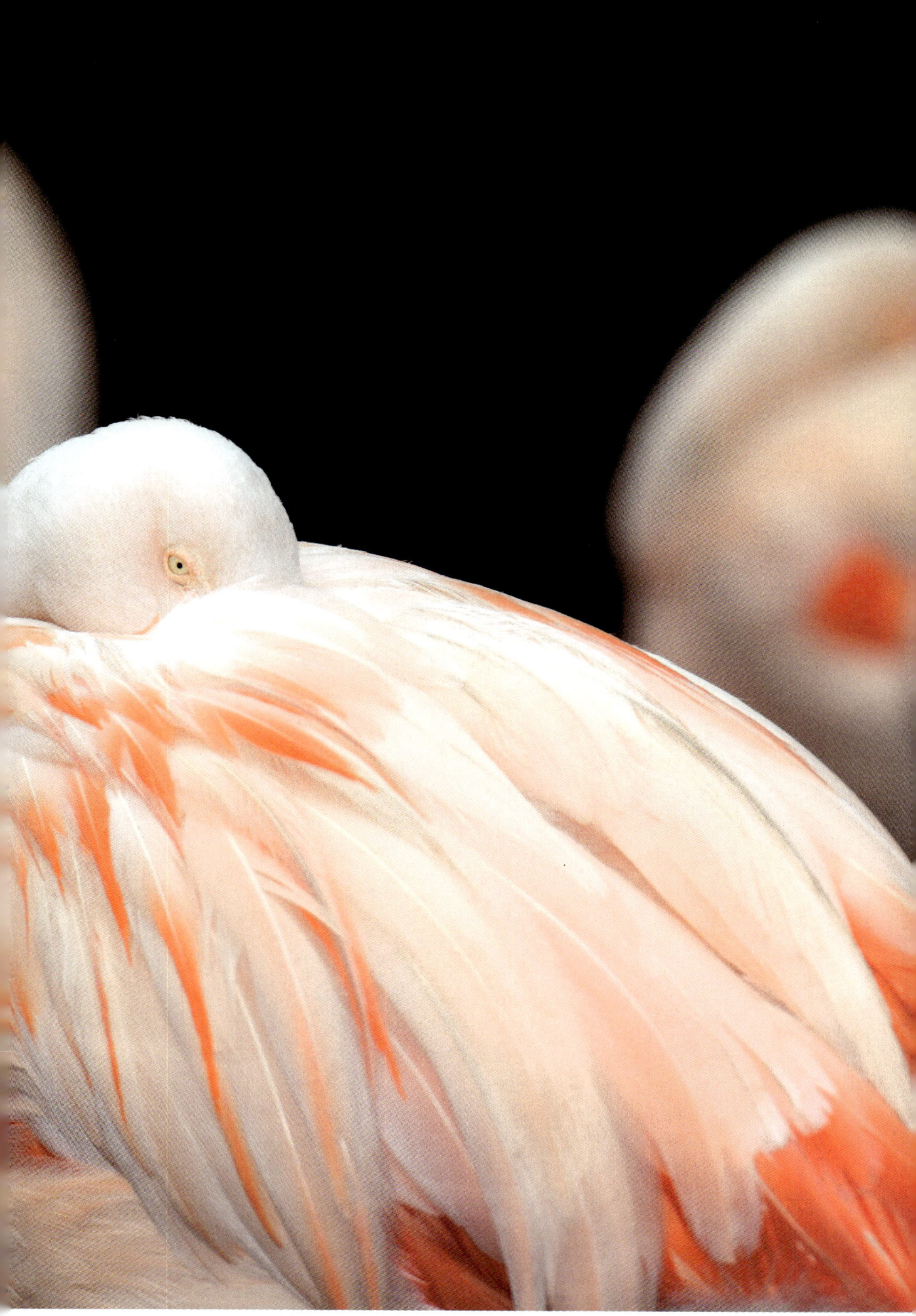

San Francisco Zoo

Why It's Worth a Photograph

There's a lot to see in this urban oasis nestled against the Pacific Ocean. The San Francisco Zoo is home to a stunning botanical collection as well as more than 250 species of animals, many of which are highly endangered. From the smallest insects to the tallest giraffe, you're sure to find a story that touches your heart and inspires you. When you look at great photographs of animals, you automatically imagine a photographer and the exotic and distant places he must have traveled to capture such wonderful photos. Although a lot of the animal photographs you see are taken in the wild, many wonderful animal pictures are taken at the zoo! Zoo animals make wonderful subjects because they live a more sheltered life than their brothers in the wild. The animals you find in the zoo tend to be in good shape without cuts, scratches, and nicks that cover the faces of those still in the wild. Why is it worth a photograph? The zoo gives you a chance to photograph a wild animal in a protective environment and still capture the essence of that animal.

Where Can I Get the Best Shot?

There are many wonderful animals at the San Francisco Zoo (see A on the map). My recommendation is to get the zoo map and decide which of the animals you would like to photograph. My favorite areas are the African Savanna, Jones Family Gorilla Preserve, and the Lion and Tiger House. Each of these locations, as well as many others, offers plenty of room to photograph the animals. My recommendation is to find an area on either side of the exhibits where you can create an angle that will allow you to photograph the animal without any distracting backgrounds (see figure 27.1).

How Can I Get the Best Shot?

Get to the zoo as early as possible to avoid the large crowds. Most animals are more active in the morning. An active animal is always more interesting. Fill the frame whenever you can. The larger you can make the animal appear, the more dramatic the picture will be. Use a monopod or tripod to help stabilize the camera and prevent camera shake. Avoid clutter by moving your feet or changing your angle. You are trying to create an illusion of being in the wild, so the last thing you want to see is a steel door directly behind your subject. Shooting with the largest aperture your lens allows creates a narrow depth of field and helps to eliminate unwanted background clutter.

Use a flash to add a bit of fill light on your subject. This makes the animal stand out from the background and can add a bit of catch light in the eyes. Wait for the right expression or movement — an animal jumping, walking, or growling is much more interesting than an animal sleeping (see figure 27.2).

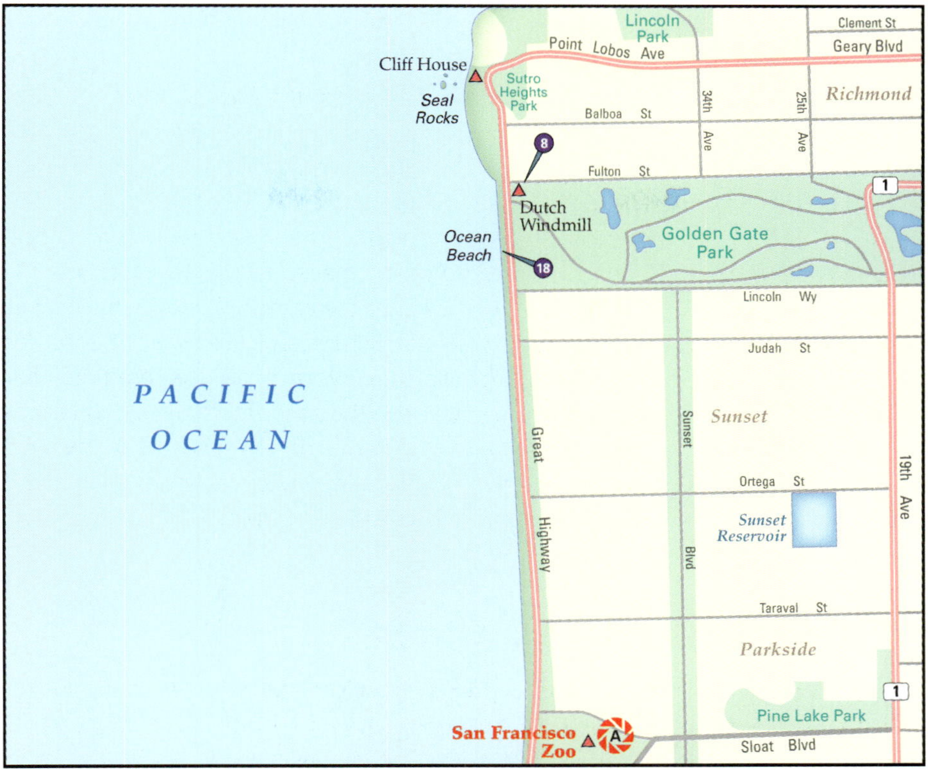

The best locations from which to photograph the San Francisco Zoo: (A) the grounds of the zoo. Other photo ops: (8) Dutch Windmill, (18) Ocean Beach.

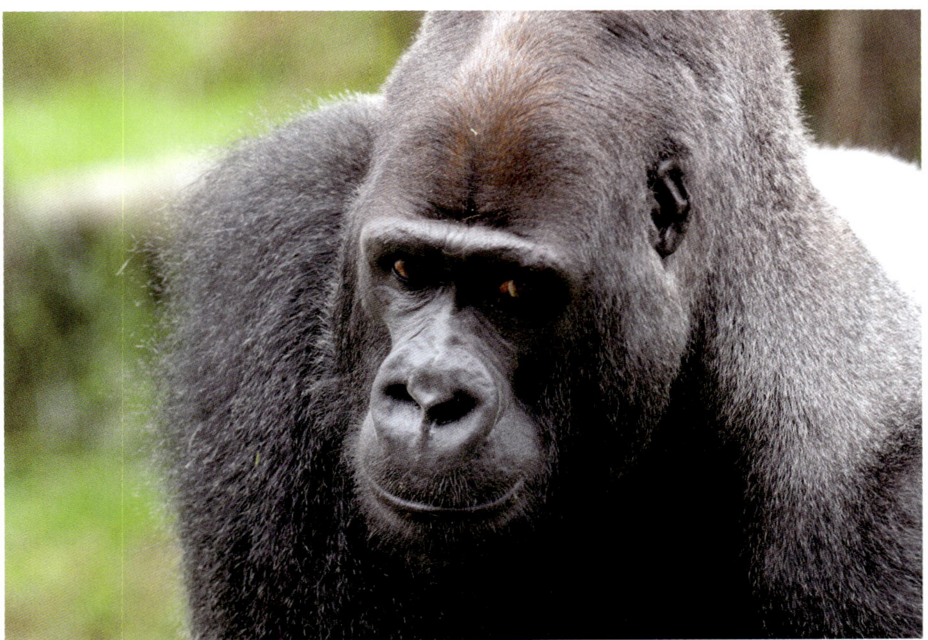

27.1 A photo of a male gorilla taken at the San Francisco Zoo on an overcast summer day. The photo was taken at ISO 400, f/6.3, for 1/50 second with a 400mm lens.

Equipment

A trip to the zoo is a chance to bring a minimal amount of gear. One or two lenses and a tripod or monopod are all you will need.

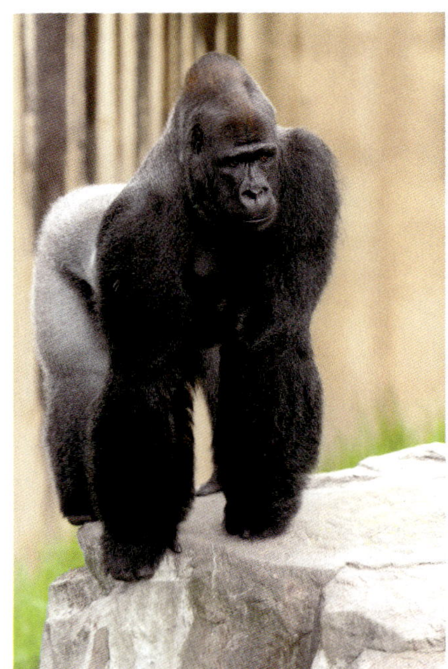

27.2 **A photo of a male gorilla watching over his territory taken at the San Francisco Zoo on overcast summer day. Taken at ISO 400, f/5.6, 1/125 second with a 400mm lens.**

Lenses

If I could bring only one lens, it would be the 300mm telephoto lens. Why such a long lens? A lens of this length allows you to fill the frame and separate the animal from its surroundings.

- **A standard zoom lens in the 24-100mm range.** This lens can give you much more versatility when traveling. A zoom in this range is generally considered the perfect walk-around lens, and for the zoo, this can be a great lens for shooting some of the animals that are closer.
- **A telephoto lens somewhere in the 100-400mm range.** This lens allows you the ability to isolate a particular subject, such as the eagle in figure 27.3, and gives you the extra reach when shooting from far off.

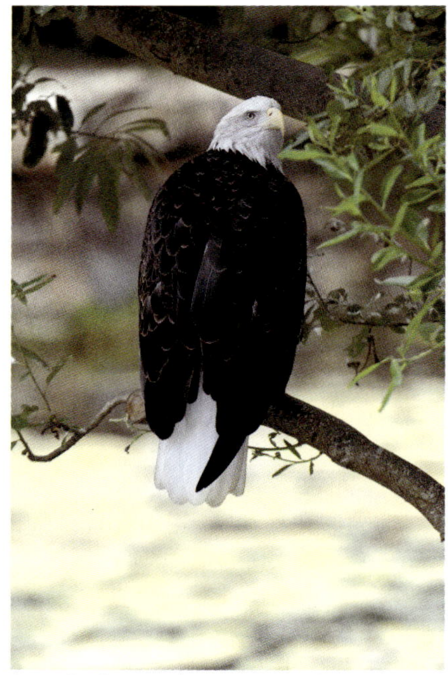

27.3 **A photo of an eagle taken at the San Francisco Zoo on overcast summer day. Taken at ISO 800, f/5.6, 1/1000 second with a 400mm lens.**

Extras

I bring a flash with me when photographing the animals. A flash is great for just adding a bit of fill light to the subject, which can really make the picture pop.

Camera settings

The settings can vary when shooting animals. I choose to shoot at an aperture of f/2.8 to f/4 with a lens greater than 200mm. I shoot at these small apertures to help separate the animals from their backgrounds. Your ISO can also vary because you want to keep a shutter speed of at least 1/500 second.

- **Exposure mode.** Set your camera in Aperture Priority mode and let the camera choose the shutter speed. I may dial in a plus exposure composition if the background is bright. A bright background will cause the entire scene to underexpose. The opposite can be said with a dark green or black background; the entire scene can overexpose. I will sacrifice the background to expose my subject properly.
- **Exposure compensation.** Exposure compensation can come in handy when photographing animals. Sometimes, you need a bit more light to expose the animals properly. In this case, you want to add more light or dial in a plus setting on your camera. Remember that your subject is more important than a few blown highlights in the background.
- **White balance.** White balance I never touch because I find the Auto White Balance of all modern day cameras to be pretty good.
- **ISO.** In general, to maximize your camera's image quality, leave the ISO at 100 when shooting landscapes. But for shooting a moving target such as an animal, you may want to bump up your ISO above 100. With a focal length of 200 to 400mm, you are going to want to keep a shutter speed of at least equal to or greater than your focal length. Keep in mind that freezing motion will take a shutter speed of at least 1/500 second.

Exposure

Photographing animals in a zoo is much like photographing people in the street; you want to capture them in their environment without their noticing. The key thing to remember is to expose for the face and not the scene. What this means is you want to adjust your exposure to expose the face properly. You do this by shooting in Aperture Priority mode and adding +1/3 to + 2/3 of exposure compensation to ensure the face is properly exposed. If you have a flash, you can use it to help add a bit of fill light to your subject. The flash helps fill in any deep shadows caused by high, harsh overhead sun.

Ideal time to shoot

The ideal time to shoot is when the zoo is open, which is daily from 10 a.m. to 5 p.m. Any time of day will suffice. I personally would choose a time when the sky is slightly overcast or foggy. This can help diffuse the harsh sun and create a softbox effect on the animals.

Working around the weather

The San Francisco Zoo is located at the far southwest corner of San Francisco, adjacent to the Pacific Ocean. This area is one of the coldest, windiest, and foggiest places in San Francisco. November through February at the zoo is dominated by periodic rainstorms that blow in from the Pacific Ocean. As winter turns to spring, the weather can be much milder and quite pleasant. The summer months tend to have a combination of several clear and warm days, giving way to several foggy and cool days. July through October brings the highest average temperatures of the year and the longest stretch of clear skies. Plan your trip to the zoo accordingly. Shooting in foggy, overcast weather is the best time to photograph the animals (see figure 27.4).

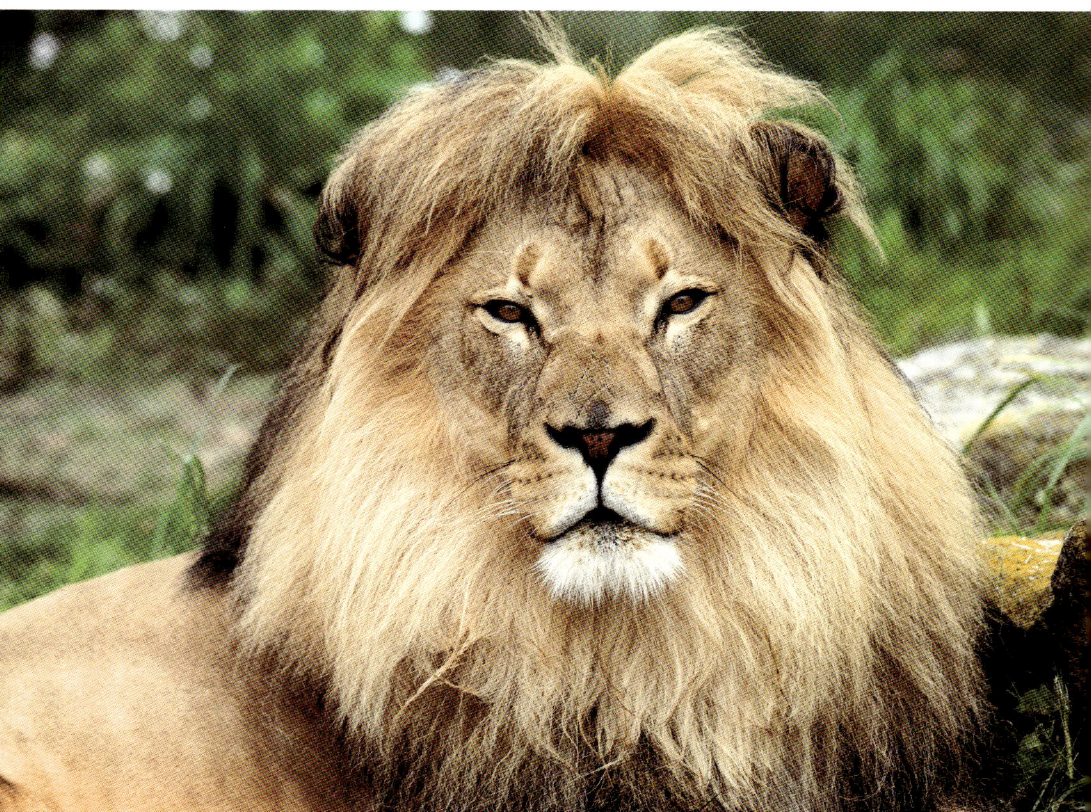

27.4 A photo of a male lion taken at the San Francisco Zoo on an overcast summer day. Taken at ISO 400, f/5.6, 1/800 second with a 400mm lens.

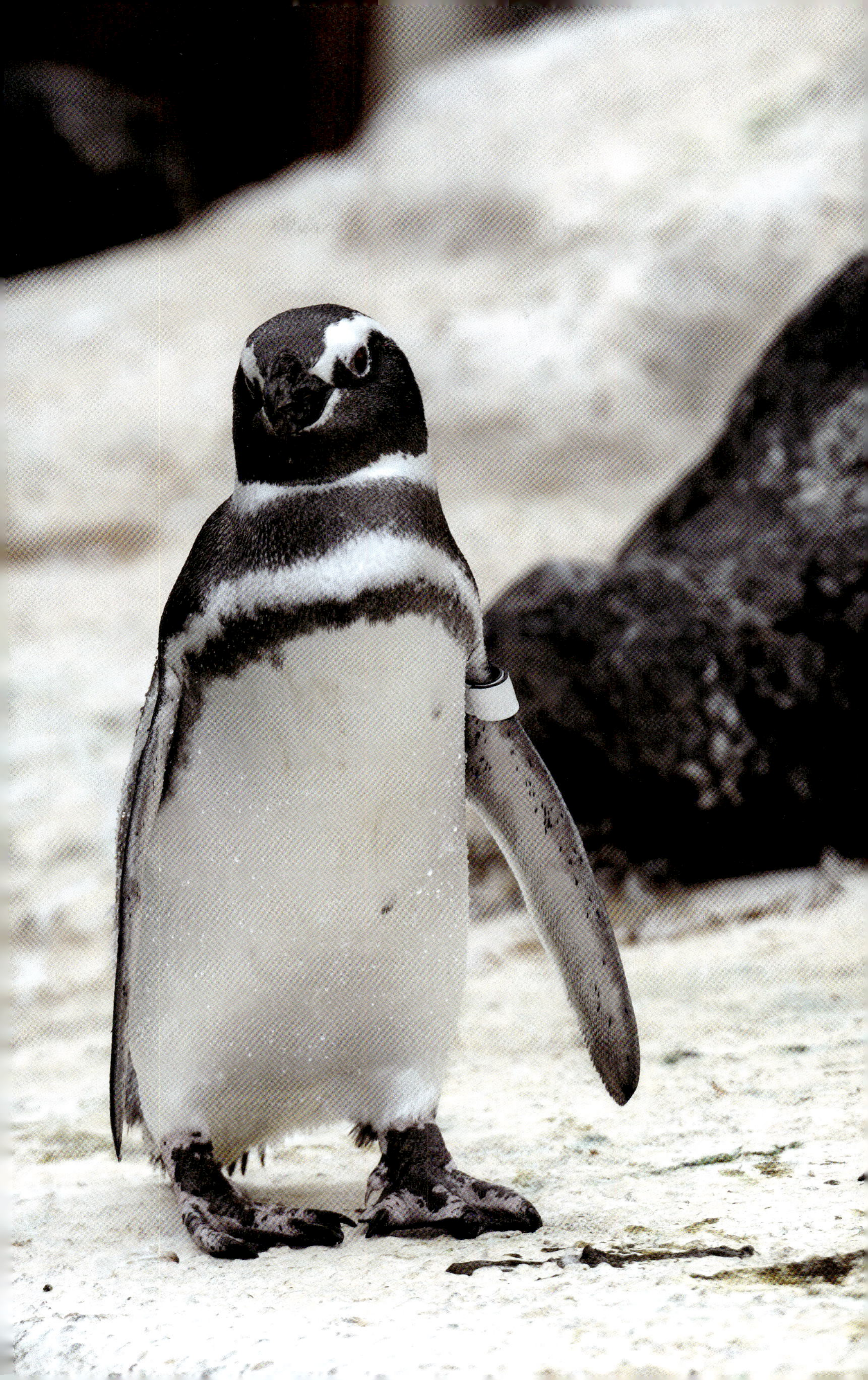

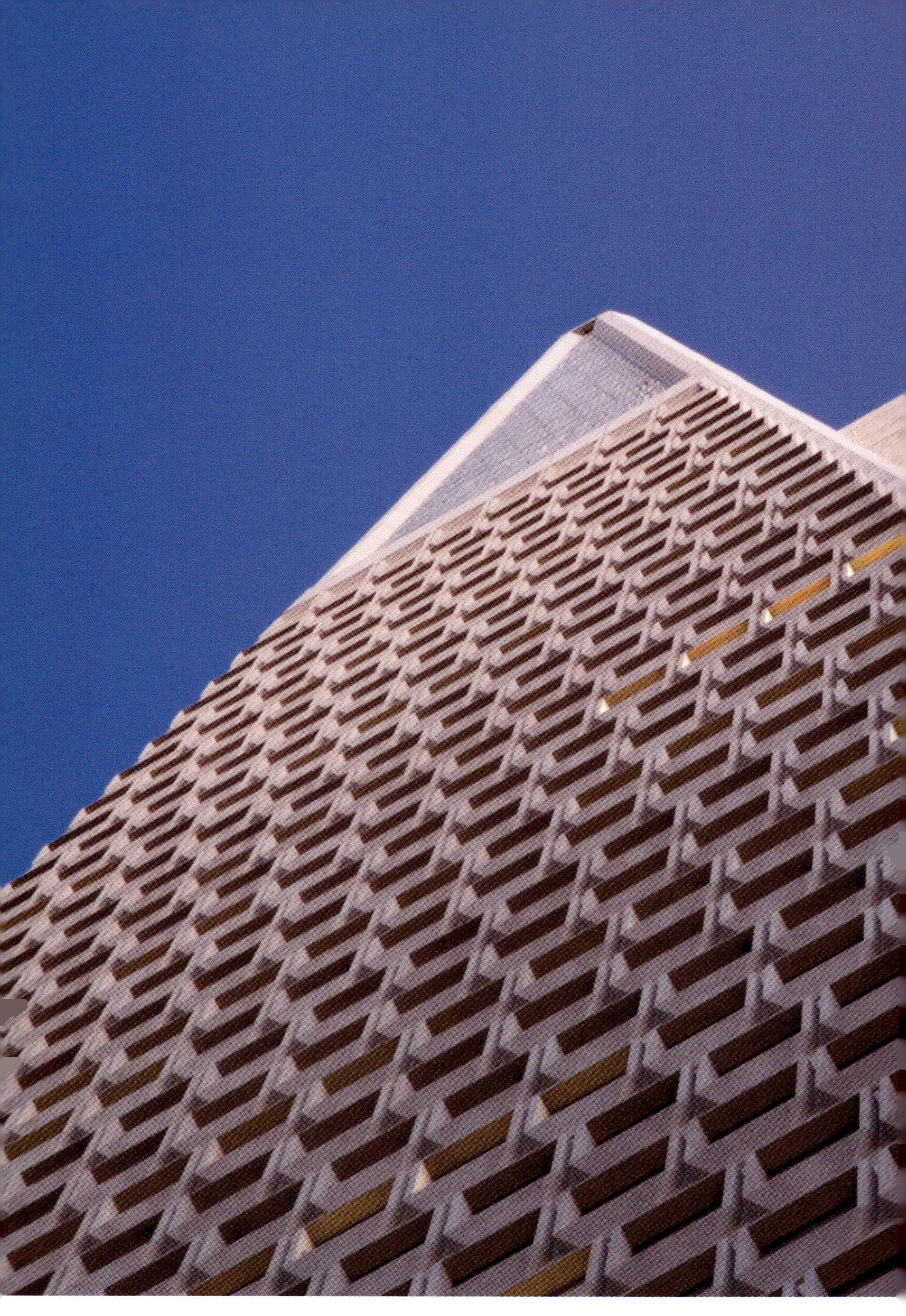

A view of the Transamerica Pyramid taken just before sunrise from Montgomery Street on a clear winter morning. Taken at ISO 100, f/18, 30 seconds with a 70-200mm lens.

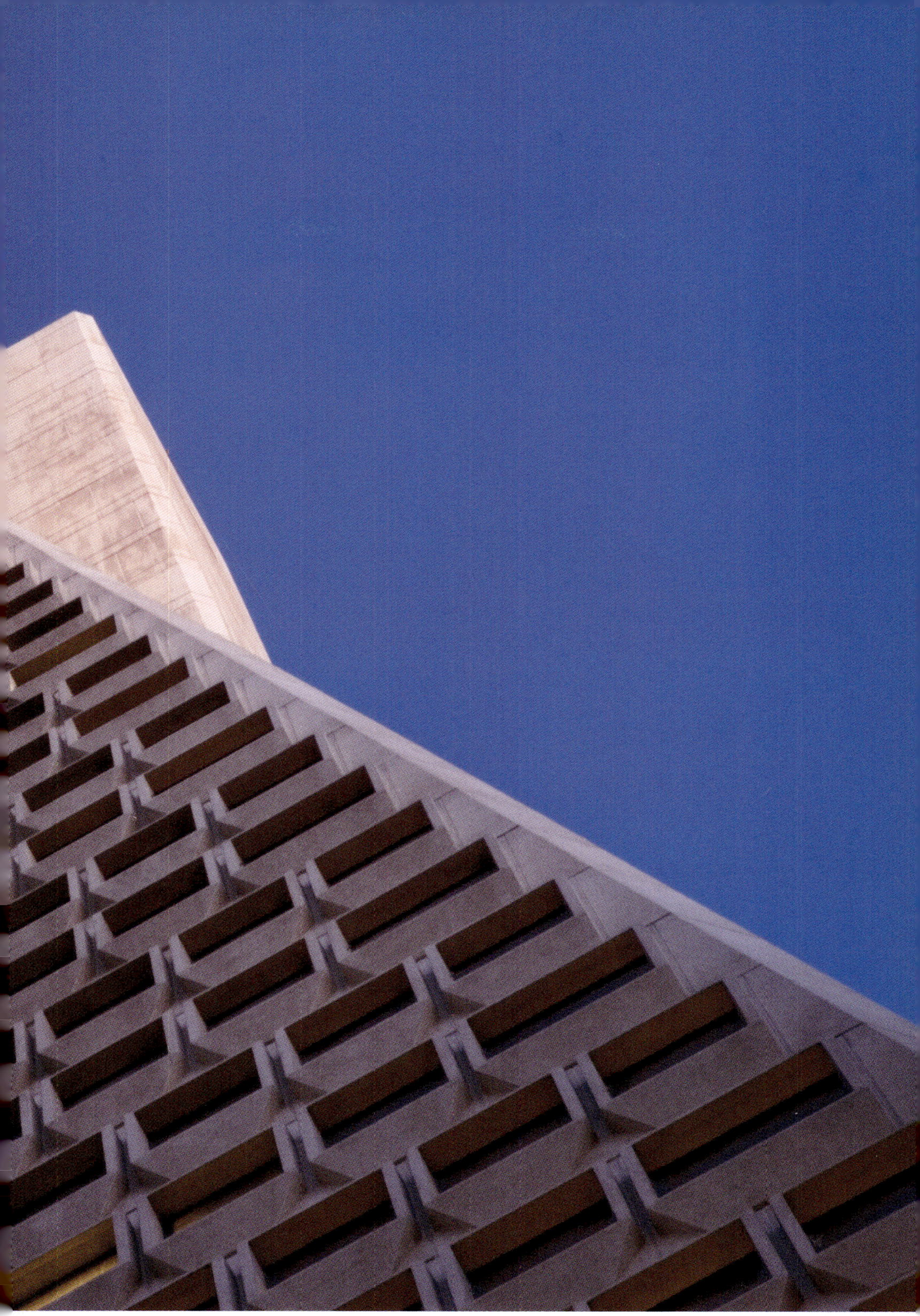

28 Transamerica Pyramid

Why It's Worth a Photograph

The Transamerica Pyramid is the most recognizable skyscraper in the San Francisco skyline. Although the building no longer is the headquarters of the Transamerica Corporation, it is still strongly associated with the company. Built on the historic Montgomery Block, it has a structural height of 853 feet and was the tallest skyscraper west of the Mississippi from 1972 to 1974. It is currently ranked as being tied for the 106th tallest building in the world. No longer the tallest building in San Francisco — that honor now belongs to the Sutro Tower at 977 feet — the Pyramid's unique structure is what draws people to it. There is no other skyscraper in the U.S. that can compare to the architectural creativity that the Transamerica Pyramid displays. The building is a tall, four-sided pyramid with two wings on opposite sides of the building. The top 212 feet of the building is the spire. Four cameras are pointed in the four cardinal directions at the top of this spire, forming a virtual observation deck. Four monitors in the lobby, whose direction and zoom can be controlled by visitors, display the cameras' views 24 hours a day. An observation deck on the 27th floor was closed after the September 11, 2001, terrorist attacks in New York City and replaced by the virtual observation deck. During the holiday season of Thanksgiving, Christmas, and the 4th of July, a bright, white light is seen on top of the pyramid. Even if it isn't the tallest building in San Francisco, the Transamerica Pyramid is still a striking presence on the skyline. Its unusual design drew both praise and ridicule as it rose between the city's Financial District and the cafes of North Beach nearly 40 years ago. Today, the sleek tower rivals the Golden Gate Bridge, Alcatraz, and the cable car as the symbol of San Francisco.

Where Can I Get the Best Shot?

You can find many places around San Francisco to photograph the Transamerica Pyramid. These places are scattered throughout downtown, Embarcadero, and North Beach. Each of these locations offers you an entirely different perspective. My favorite locations to capture dramatic photos of the Transamerica Pyramid are Pier 7, Columbus Street at Broadway Street, Montgomery Street at Green Street, Montgomery Street between Clay Street and Washington Street, and Coit Tower (see A–E on the map).

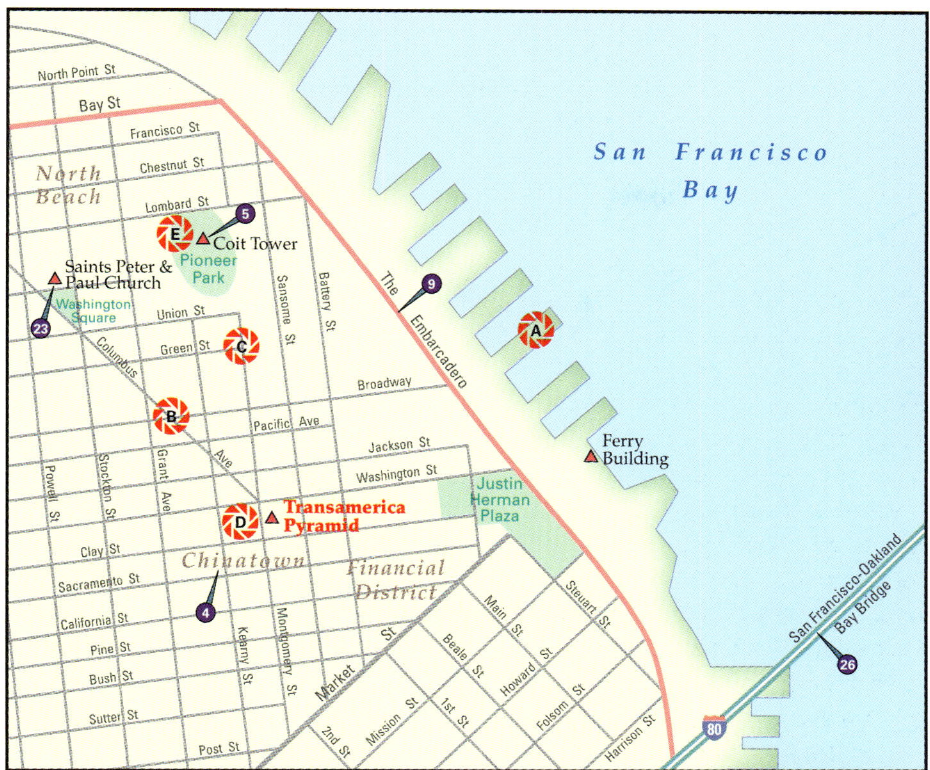

The best locations from which to photograph the Transamerica Pyramid: (A) Pier 7 Embarcadero, (B) Columbus Street at Broadway Street, (C) Montgomery Street at Green Street, (D) Montgomery Street between Clay Street and Washington Street, (E) Coit Tower. Other photo ops: (4) Chinatown, (5) Coit Tower, (9) Embarcadero, (23) Saints Peter and Paul Church, (26) San Francisco-Oakland Bay Bridge.

Pier 7 Embarcadero

One of my favorite places to photograph the Transamerica Pyramid is from the Embarcadero. Along this two-mile stretch of waterfront are many piers to stop and enjoy the wonderful views of San Francisco and the bay. Pier 7, one of the longest pedestrian-only piers, is the perfect vantage point to photograph the pyramid. In the wee, early morning hours just before the sun comes up or just after the sun goes down, you can capture a wonderful image of the pyramid against a dusky sky with the boardwalk and lamppost leading the eye straight to the building. This shot is such a great image with many different elements; the vibrant colors, leading line, and powerful subject all make for a dramatic photo (see figure 28.1).

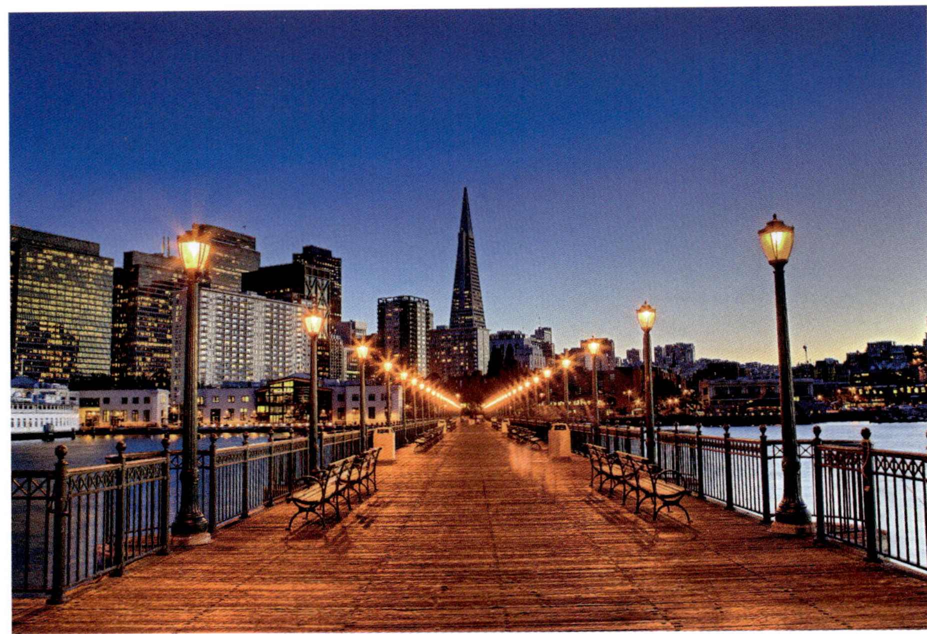

28.1 A view of the Transamerica Pyramid taken from Pier 7 on a clear summer evening (see A on the map). Taken at ISO 100, f/8, 10 seconds with a 24-70mm lens.

Columbus Street at Broadway Street

My favorite location is at Columbus at Broadway streets. This location, on the outskirts of North Beach, offers you a wonderful opportunity to shoot the pyramid from the street to the sky. It is the only view where the building is not obstructed by other buildings. If you shoot this in the evening during rush hour, you can expect to capture, as I did, the streaming lights of cars passing by. You need a tripod and an ultrawide lens to capture this shot (see figure 28.2)

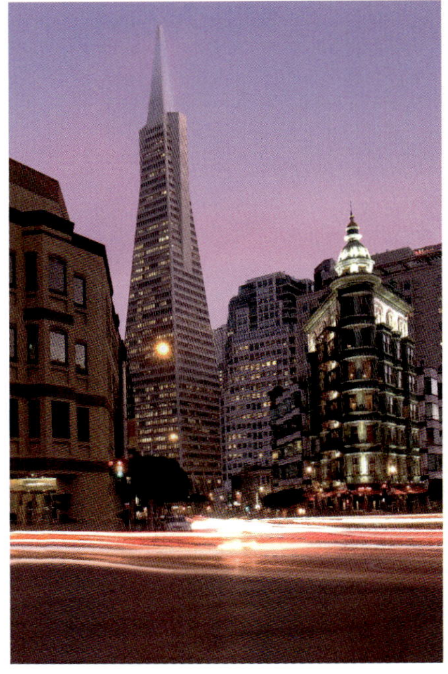

28.2 A view of the Transamerica Pyramid taken just after sunset on a clear winter evening (see B on the map). Taken at ISO 100, f/11, 8 seconds with a 17-40mm lens.

Montgomery Street at Green Street

Montgomery Street at Green Street is one of the least-known locations from which to photograph the Transamerica Pyramid. This vantage point located on a stairway that takes you up and over a hill is the perfect place to capture the pyramid and the entire downtown. On a clear night, this raised vantage point gives you a clear view of all of downtown. On this night, as you can see in figure 28.3, the city was blanketed in a thin, wet layer of fog. The fog adds a certain element to the photo, creating this eerie, dark winter mood that you might not otherwise be able to convey without it. Armed with a standard zoom lens and a Tungsten white balance setting helped create this wonderfully moody photo.

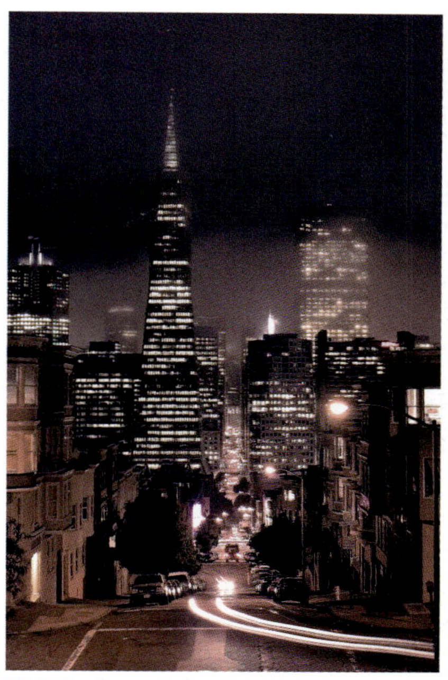

28.3 A view of the Transamerica Pyramid taken on a cold, foggy night (see C on the map). Taken at ISO 100, f/4, 8 seconds with a 17-40mm lens.

Montgomery Street between Clay Street and Washington Street

What you might think is the premiere location to photograph the Transamerica Pyramid from is also inaccessible. Since September 11, 2001, the Montgomery Street block directly under the building is off limits to all tripod-toting photographers. I found this out the hard way one morning when I was escorted off the premises and instructed that I could set up across the street. So this is what I recommend. This location is great for capturing abstract images of the pyramid with a long lens. The unique architecture of the building and a long lens can help you create some really cool abstract photos that will have your friends guessing what they are. When I first showed my wife, Jennifer, the photo in figure 28.4, she immediately thought I had taken a picture of a cheese grater. I'd call that abstract.

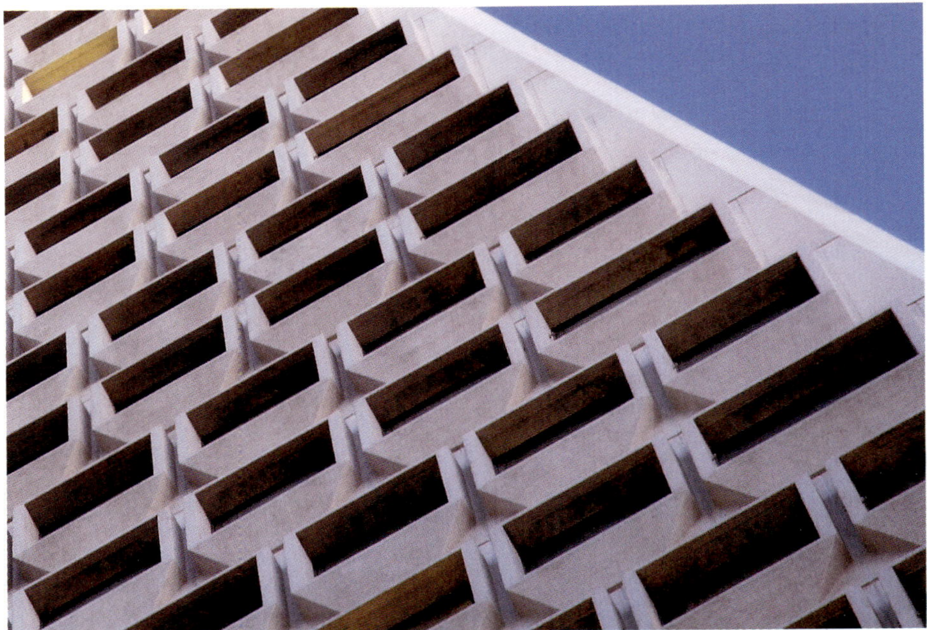

28.4 An abstract view of the Transamerica Pyramid and a hint of sky at sunrise on a clear winter morning (see D on the map). Taken at ISO 100, f/16, 30 seconds with a 70-200mm lens.

Coit Tower

The final vantage point I recommend for taking a picture of the Transamerica Pyramid is from Coit Tower. This location offers wonderful panoramic views of the city and the bay. On the downtown side of the Coit Tower parking lot is a series of fences, trees, and bushes — a location I think is a perfect opportunity to frame the pyramid with the leaves from a tree in full fall color (see figure 28.5).

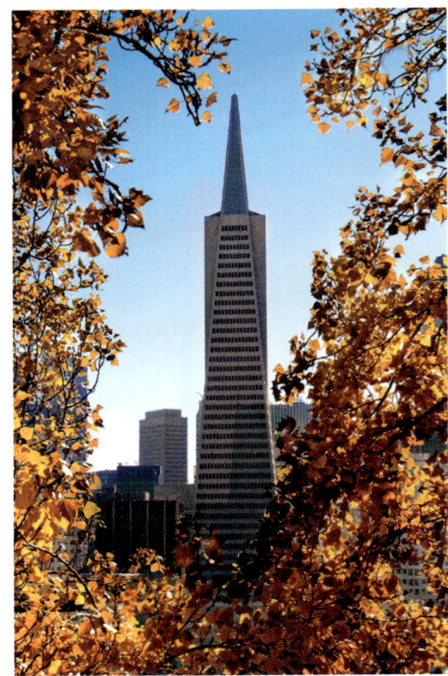

28.5 A view of Transamerica Pyramid framed by wonderful fall colors on a clear winter morning (see E on the map). Taken at ISO 100, f/11, 1/250 second with a 24-70mm lens.

How Can I Get the Best Shot?

Shooting the pyramid is best done on a clear morning, late afternoon, or at blue hour when there is neither full daylight nor complete darkness. The light during these times creates brilliant blue skies that really help separate the white stone facade of the pyramid from the sky, making the building "pop" in your photo. An assortment of lenses and a sturdy tripod are a must to successfully photograph the pyramid from each of these locations.

Equipment

An assortment of lenses ranging from an ultrawide to a medium telephoto should be in your bag along with a tripod and cable release.

Lenses

Having an assortment of lenses, or one lens, that cover a large focal length are a must it you want to capture the Transamerica Pyramid in a multitude of ways. These focal ranges allow you to capture a series of photos from different perspectives.

- **Ultrawide zoom lens in the 14-24mm range.** The ultrawide lens gives you the ability to capture the pyramid from an unusually close angle. This lens gives you the ability to include a wider perspective when photographing from a distance.
- **A standard zoom lens in the 24-100mm range.** This lens should be your most used lens for capturing nearly 80 percent of your images of the Transamerica Pyramid.
- **A super-telephoto lens somewhere in the 70-300mm range.** Like the ultrawide lens, this lens has its place. When photographing the pyramid, you can isolate the building from a distance.

Extras

A tripod is a must for all night shots and low-light shooting. I also recommend a cable release.

Camera settings

Shooting sunsets, sunrises, and night scenes can best be achieved in Aperture Priority mode. Set your aperture and then dial in the correct shutter speed. You may need to tweak your exposure compensation to get your desired exposure.

- **Exposure mode.** Shoot in Aperture Priority mode for most of the pyramid photos. I shot most of these at f/8 to f/11 to maximize image quality.
- **White balance.** Auto White Balance is the best choice for shooting downtown because using it tends to give you the best output.
- **ISO.** Keep your ISO as low as possible to maximize image quality.

Exposure

When the sun gets low, metering becomes trickier. The light from the sky, dark shadows on the ground, and streetlights can all affect your exposure. In situations like these, it can be easier to shoot in Manual mode and adjust the aperture and shutter speed to create the desired effect. I use the histogram on the back of the camera all the time to check to see if I have the ideal balance between shadows and highlights. Remember, in many cases you may have to sacrifice a bit of highlights or shadows. You need to decide what the best creative exposure is for any given photo.

Ideal time to shoot

The ideal time to shoot is early morning, late afternoon, or when the sun is down. My favorite time of day to shoot is once the sun has gone down. As you can see from many of the photos in this chapter, integrating a sense of motion in a cityscape creates a photo that is far more appealing then one of just a building. When shooting the pyramid at this time, you can create some truly compelling images.

Working around the weather

During the summer months, morning and evening fog is common for San Francisco, but it rarely remains throughout the day. September and October tend to be the warmest and clearest months, whereas rain can be common late November through March. San Francisco weather literally varies from neighborhood to neighborhood; it may be sunny and pleasant in one area and foggy and cool in another. Most of the time, you want to be out photographing the Transamerica Pyramid on clear days or nights. On occasions when the fog is not too thick, a nighttime picture can have a very compelling mood that your typical fair weather photo won't have.

Low-light and night options

There are many great low-light locations from which you can photograph the Transamerica Pyramid. Pier 7 and Columbus Street at Broadway Street are the two best locations. You can shoot from these locations either before the sun comes up or after the sun goes down. Remember, you want the sky to be a dusky blue, so set up your gear prior to the sun going down, sit back, and be patient.

Getting creative

If you want to try something fun and creative and a bit crazy (maybe dangerous is more like it), this is the location for you. Located in the intersection of Columbus Street and Broadway is a pedestrian crosswalk with an island just big enough for one person and a tripod. Shoot this image during the blue hour, which falls during rush hour in the winter months. A wide-angle lens and slow shutter speed give you a compelling image complete with leading lines, vibrant colors, and *danger*. This is a must-frame, must-brag-about photo. Just ignore the constant car horns and explicit foul comments you may hear while you stand in the middle of the intersection (see figure 28.6).

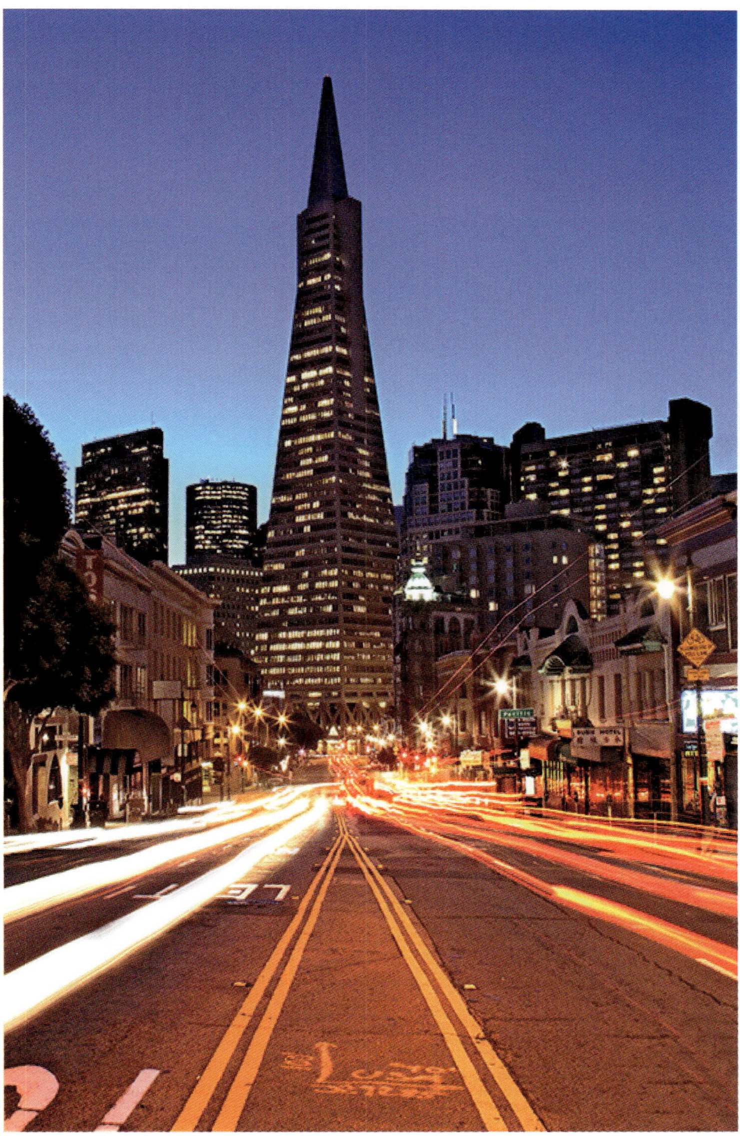

28.6 A compelling image of the Transamerica Pyramid taken on a clear winter morning as rush hour traffic speeds by (see B on the map). Taken at ISO 100, f/11, 30 seconds with a 24-70mm lens.

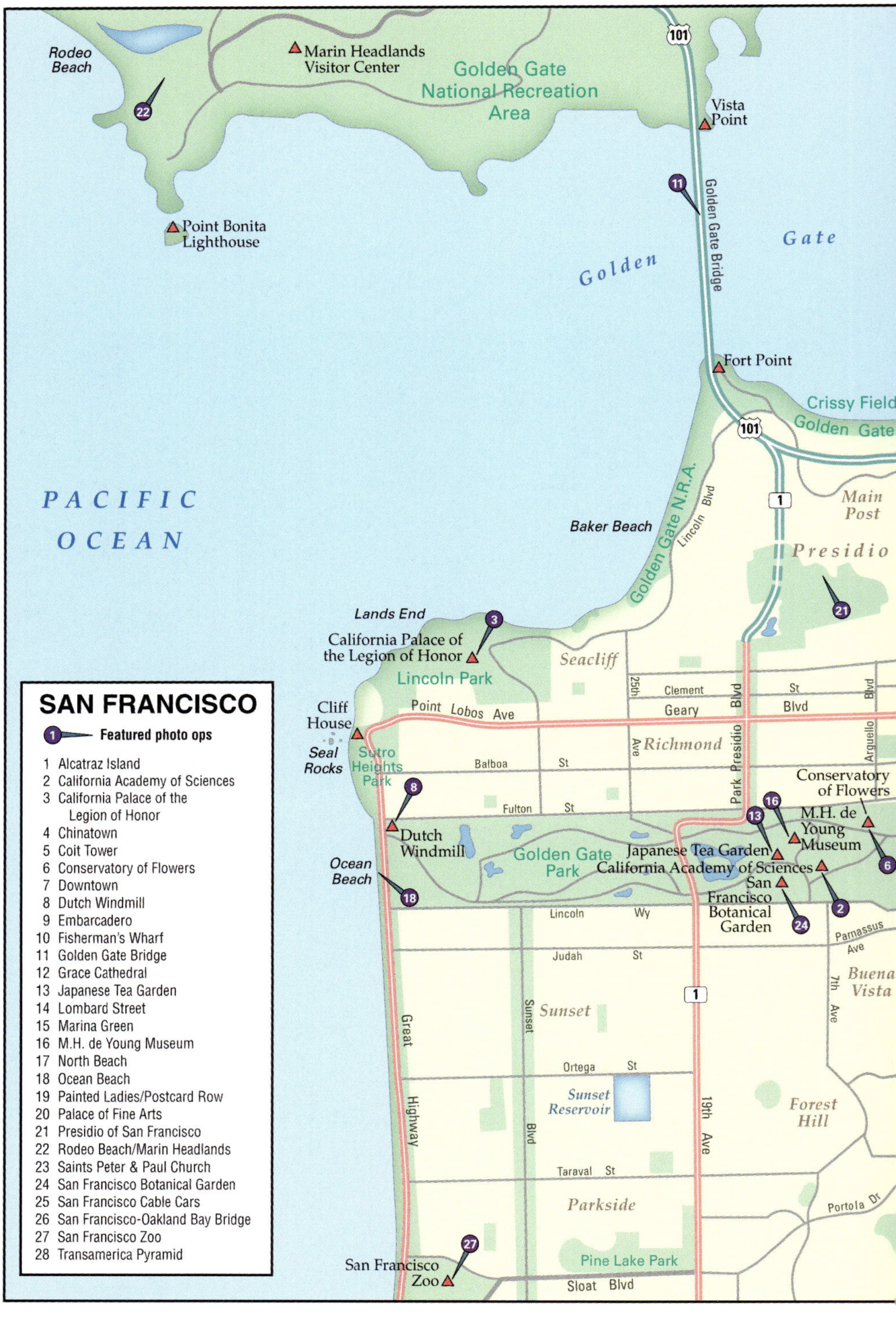
SAN FRANCISCO
Featured photo ops
1 Alcatraz Island
2 California Academy of Sciences
3 California Palace of the Legion of Honor
4 Chinatown
5 Coit Tower
6 Conservatory of Flowers
7 Downtown
8 Dutch Windmill
9 Embarcadero
10 Fisherman's Wharf
11 Golden Gate Bridge
12 Grace Cathedral
13 Japanese Tea Garden
14 Lombard Street
15 Marina Green
16 M.H. de Young Museum
17 North Beach
18 Ocean Beach
19 Painted Ladies/Postcard Row
20 Palace of Fine Arts
21 Presidio of San Francisco
22 Rodeo Beach/Marin Headlands
23 Saints Peter & Paul Church
24 San Francisco Botanical Garden
25 San Francisco Cable Cars
26 San Francisco-Oakland Bay Bridge
27 San Francisco Zoo
28 Transamerica Pyramid
Rodeo Beach
Marin Headlands Visitor Center
Golden Gate National Recreation Area
101
Vista Point
Point Bonita Lighthouse
Golden Gate Bridge
Golden
Gate
Fort Point
Crissy Field
Golden Gate
PACIFIC OCEAN
Main Post
Presidio
Baker Beach
Golden Gate N.R.A.
Lincoln Blvd
1
Lands End
California Palace of the Legion of Honor
Seacliff
Lincoln Park
Cliff House
Seal Rocks
Sutro Heights Park
Point Lobos Ave
Clement
St
25th Ave
Geary
Blvd
Richmond
Park Presidio Blvd
Arguello Blvd
Balboa
St
Fulton
St
Conservatory of Flowers
M.H. de Young Museum
Dutch Windmill
Golden Gate Park
Japanese Tea Garden
California Academy of Sciences
Ocean Beach
San Francisco Botanical Garden
Lincoln
Wy
Parnassus Ave
Judah
St
Buena Vista
7th Ave
Great Highway
Sunset Blvd
Sunset
Ortega
St
Sunset Reservoir
19th Ave
Forest Hill
Taraval
St
Parkside
Portola Dr
Pine Lake Park
San Francisco Zoo
Sloat
Blvd

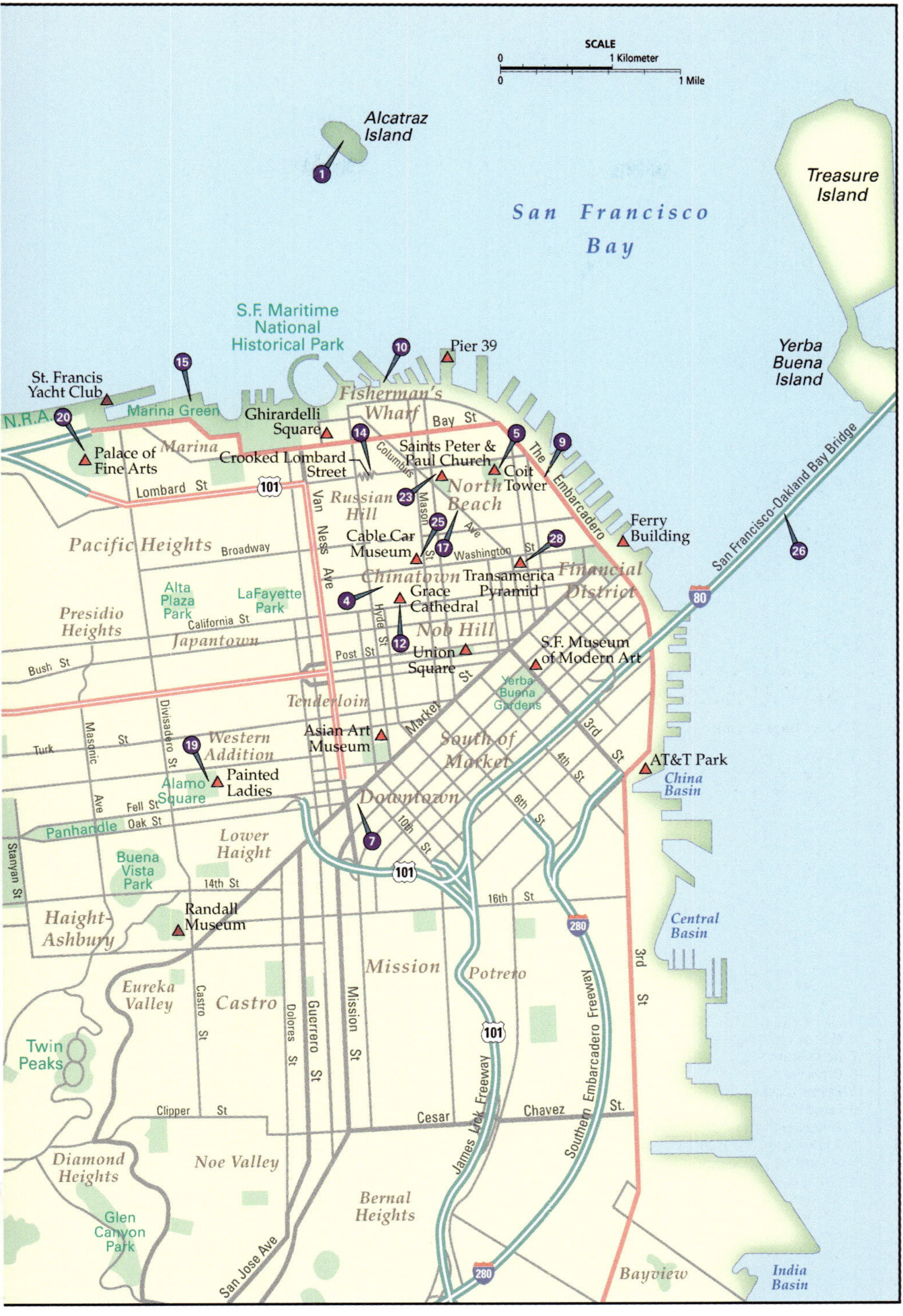
SCALE
1 Kilometer
1 Mile
Alcatraz Island
Treasure Island
San Francisco Bay
Yerba Buena Island
S.F. Maritime National Historical Park
Pier 39
St. Francis Yacht Club
Marina Green
Fisherman's Wharf
Ghirardelli Square
Bay St
N.R.A.
Palace of Fine Arts
Marina
Crooked Lombard Street
Columbus
Saints Peter & Paul Church
Coit Tower
The Embarcadero
San Francisco-Oakland Bay Bridge
Lombard St
Russian Hill
North Beach
Mason
Ferry Building
Pacific Heights
Broadway
Van Ness Ave
Cable Car Museum
Washington St
Chinatown
Transamerica Pyramid
Financial District
Alta Plaza Park
LaFayette Park
Grace Cathedral
Presidio Heights
California St
Hyde St
Nob Hill
Japantown
S.F. Museum of Modern Art
Bush St
Post St
Union Square
Yerba Buena Gardens
Tenderloin
Market St
3rd St
Divisadero St
Masonic Ave
Turk St
Western Addition
Asian Art Museum
South of Market
4th St
AT&T Park
China Basin
Alamo Square
Painted Ladies
Downtown
6th St
Fell St
Oak St
10th St
Panhandle
Lower Haight
Stanyan St
Buena Vista Park
14th St
16th St
Haight-Ashbury
Randall Museum
Central Basin
Mission
Potrero
Eureka Valley
Castro
Castro St
Dolores St
Guerrero St
Mission St
Southern Embarcadero Freeway
Twin Peaks
James Lick Freeway
Clipper St
Cesar Chavez St.
Diamond Heights
Noe Valley
Bernal Heights
Glen Canyon Park
San Jose Ave
Bayview
India Basin

Index

D

E

F

G

H

M

N

O

T